SAVAGE GRANDEUR AND NOBLEST THOUGHTS

Discovering the Lake District 1750–1820

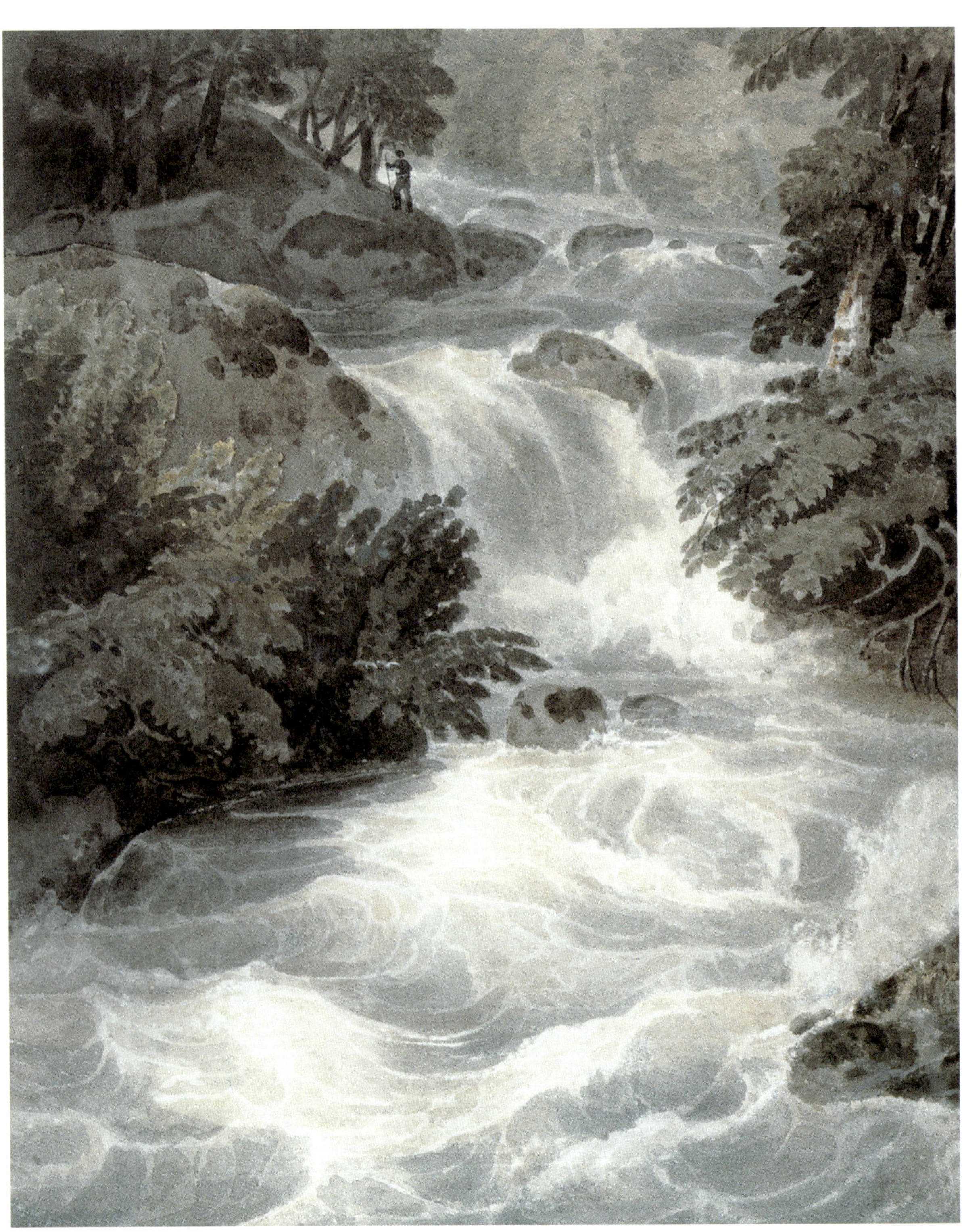

Savage Grandeur and Noblest Thoughts

Discovering the Lake District 1750–1820

Cecilia Powell
Stephen Hebron

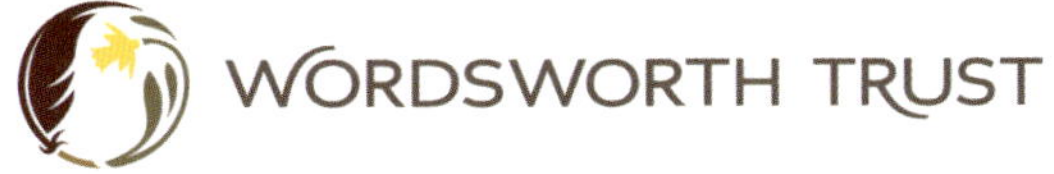

Published by the Wordsworth Trust
Dove Cottage, Grasmere, Cumbria LA22 9SH

ISBN 978-1-905256-42-6

Designed by Stephen Hebron
Picture research by Jane Connolly
Set in Monotype Dante
Printed by Titus Wilson, Kendal

Frontispiece:
William Havell, *The Beck at Ambleside after Much Rain* (cat. 60)

Supported by
The W.W. Spooner Charitable Trust
The Northern Rock Foundation
The Sir John Fisher Charitable Foundation
The Westmorland Arts Trust
James Cropper plc

CONTENTS

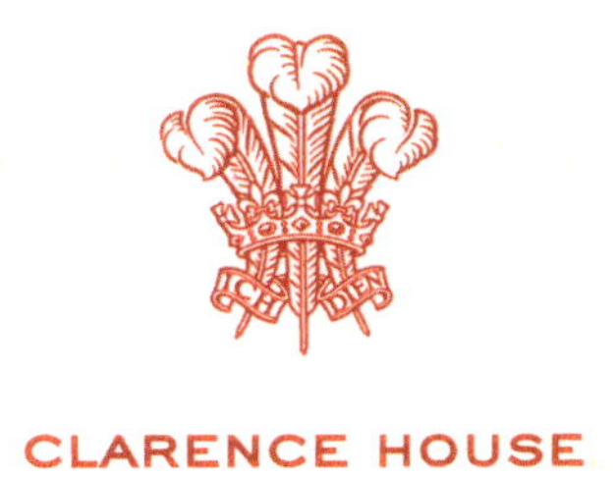

CLARENCE HOUSE

As Patron of the Wordsworth Trust, it gives me great pleasure to have been asked to contribute this foreword. Whilst many are aware of the Trust's vast literary library, it is perhaps less well-known that the Trust also houses a remarkable collection of paintings, prints and drawings of the Lake District – from the period 1750 – 1820.

It was during that period that some of our greatest artists – Gainsborough, Turner, Constable – along with a number of talented amateurs – were first inspired by the Lake District's combination of "beauty, horror and immensity." This superb exhibition will be of interest not just to lovers of fine art, but to anyone who takes pleasure, as I do, in the sublime landscape of the Lake District. The collection allows us to glimpse some of this country's most magnificent scenery, such as we see "on those heavenly days that cannot die."

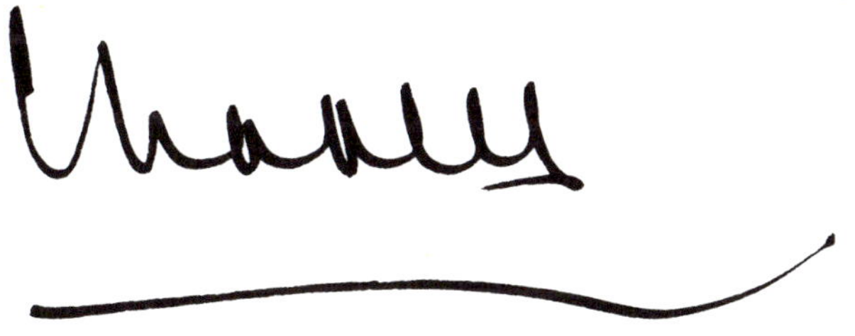

PREFACE

The Wordsworth Trust now enters its fourth decade of presenting and curating innovatory and scholarly exhibitions in the hamlet of Town End, Grasmere. The first major exhibition at the Grasmere and Wordsworth Museum opened on 20 May 1982. *The Discovery of the Lake District 1750–1810* provided the context for understanding how Wordsworth in 1810 made his completely original proposition, that the Lake District was a 'sort of national property, in which every man has a right and interest who has an eye to perceive and a heart to enjoy'. The following year, in a continuation exhibition, *The Lake District Discovered 1810–1850*, the roles of the artists, the tourists and Wordsworth were examined. The notes and commentary to both catalogues were written by Peter Bicknell and Robert Woof, their first major co-operation. Peter Bicknell became a Trustee of the Wordsworth Trust, and his seminal bibliographical study, *The Picturesque Scenery of the Lake District 1752–1855*, remains the accepted standard work of reference.

The W.W. Spooner Charitable Trust first became supporters of the Wordsworth Trust in 1996, when we assisted in the purchase of various drawings and sketch books. In April 2000 Spooner made a long term commitment to finance acquisitions to extend and enhance the Wordsworth Trust's collection of early English watercolours. The first acquisition comprised two important works in bodycolour attributed to John Laporte (1761–1839): *North View on the Road leading from Keswick to Ambleside. Taken from the Six mile-stone* and *Derwentwater, and the Vale of Keswick from Ashness; Bassenthwaite Lake in the Distance*. Ashness was referred to by Wordsworth in his *Guide to the Lakes* as affording 'a fine bird's eye view'.

Our best focused intentions were soon happily distracted by Robert who wrote on 14 February 2000:

> £100,000 is required for the major manuscript of *Ecclesiastical Sketches* which has just appeared in London, brought over from America. As you know, 90% of Wordsworth's papers are already with us, so to have this new 46-page manuscript, full of Wordsworth's compositions, is an important discovery, and one which the Trustees are duty-bound to try to acquire.

On 25 May, with a generous grant of £89,000 from the Heritage Lottery Fund, a major donation from the Spooner Trust, and additional help from Trinity College and St John's College, Cambridge, the Wordsworth Trust acquired the autograph manuscript.

I soon discovered that Robert always had a very comprehensive 'wish list', and frequently a 'must have' would claim our immediate attention! An early case in point was introduced by Robert:

> A picture of 'The Leech Gatherer' by Robert Fowler of Liverpool, *c.*1890, is a wonderful large watercolour done by an artist who is now receiving fresh recognition. It is one of the largest 19th century pictures to be dedicated to a Wordsworth theme. In truth, Wordsworth did not attract many visual artists, a negligible response compared to Byron, Scott and Tennyson. But this very absence of response makes this painting all the more interesting and significant. It has quite a Chinese flavour in its presentation; and it certainly is the kind of picture that the Trust has a duty to try to purchase. As you will understand, most of our collections belong to the 18th and early 19th centuries, and this is exceptional as being one of the major late responses.

On 26 September 1800 Dorothy and William Wordsworth met a leech gatherer on his way to Carlisle. Dorothy's journal entry of 3 October, and the eventual transformation of setting and subject in Wordsworth's 'Resolution and Independence', written from May to July 1802, provide the inspiration for Fowler's impressive drawing, albeit he favoured his own, more familiar, landscape of North Wales as the setting. In early October Fowler's dramatic *Leech Gatherer* came home to Grasmere. In the last decade some 100 drawings have followed at a less frenetic pace!

In September 2005, Robert, Stephen Hebron and I discussed the possibility of selective Spooner Trust support for the Wordsworth Trust's future exhibition programme. *The Spooner Collection of British Watercolours* was shown in Grasmere in 2005. Stephen, as ever the consummate planner, had in place a detailed profile of the potential subjects Robert wished to follow: *The Solitude of Mountains – Constable and the Lake District* in 2006, *Dante Rediscovered* in 2007, and *Edward Lear the Landscape Artist: Tours of Ireland and the English Lakes, 1835 and 1836* in 2008. We had already agreed in principle that the Spooner Trust would support, in 2008, *Paths to Fame – Turner Watercolours from the Courtauld Gallery*. The idea for the current exhibition then emerged. Stephen offered inspiration by reviewing possible anniversaries, and bi-centennial celebrations. In 1810 William Wordsworth provided, anonymously, the introduction to the Rev. Joseph Wilkinson's *Select Views in Cumberland, Westmoreland and Lancashire*. Robert immediately proposed we revisit the discovery of the lakes. He enjoyed reminding us of Thomas Gray's 1769 description of the Vale of Grasmere: 'Not a single red tile, no flaring Gentleman's house or garden-walls break in upon the repose of this little unsuspected paradise; but all is peace, rusticity & happy poverty, in its neatest and most becoming attire'. With mischievous delight he would tell us that, in Gray's description of Grasmere as a 'little unsuspected paradise' where 'all is peace, rusticity & happy poverty', the word 'happy' was added as an afterthought in the original journal. The proposed exhibition for 2010 was in place. In August 2008 I was delighted when Cecilia Powell was able to accept our invitation to act as Guest Curator.

It was a lifetime challenge for Robert to acquire a Turner drawing of the Lake District, and in autumn 2005 this became a reality with the purchase of Turner's *Ullswater, Cumberland*, with generosity and unprecedented support from the

National Heritage Memorial Fund, the Wolfson Foundation, the Art Fund, the MLA / V&A Purchase Grant Fund, the Golden Charitable Trust and an anonymous donor. John Ruskin described Turner's *Picturesque Views in England and Wales* as 'the great central work of Turner's life' and *Ullswater* as 'one of three [drawings] that are in the most perfect peace'. Towards the middle of October 2005 Robert and Pamela enjoyed the Turner in Sykeside for two days, basking in its ethereal glow: 'Imagined mountains now gleam transubstantially in the setting sunlight, which casts long purple shadows over the lake'. These were moments of shared joy and happiness in being so close to Turner's genius, for Robert deep satisfaction and gratitude. This was to be Robert's last major acquisition.

We offer our deepest appreciation to Cecilia Powell who has curated the exhibition with great flair and boundless enthusiasm. Cecilia as Guest Curator has provided invaluable guidance upon the collections and the Wordsworth Trust has benefited greatly from her relaxed and informative suggestions. It is imperative that the Trust's collections continue to benefit from the highest standards of independent research and scholarship. This catalogue is truly erudite, and will long be treasured by those interested in the discovery of the lakes. We thank Stephen Hebron, who has co-ordinated the project with his usual kind good humour. His scholarly essay offers a fascinating study of the literary discovery of the Lakes, and he has provided another catalogue design of rare distinction.

We would like to thank Jeff Cowton for his own resourceful response to many challenges, and also for encouraging the youthful talents of the Trust's staff and interns who have gained invaluable experience. We thank Amy Concannon, Jane Connolly and Charlotte Booth for their assured dedication and energetic support. We thank Michael McGregor for his kind and thoughtful contribution to all our deliberations and for providing constructive support at all times.

I would like to acknowledge and express deep personal gratitude to my co-Trustees, James Hill, Tom Ramsden, Julia McKiddie, Jonathan Wright and John Priestley, who have always been generously supportive of our partnership with the Wordsworth Trust, by way of active encouragement and always being prepared to go that elusive extra mile with imaginative funding.

I owe a great debt to Pamela Woof for her enlightened interpretation of Wordsworth's works and for her joyous recollection of four decades which have transformed the affairs and standing of the Wordsworth Trust.

To Robert Woof belongs the inspiration and the dedication, but his legacy is secure in the hands of his 'young people', now outstanding professionals in their own right, resolutely steeped in the history and traditions of this great institution and centre of British Romanticism.

Michael Broughton
Chairman, The W.W. Spooner Charitable Trust

ACKNOWLEDGEMENTS

This exhibition and catalogue would not have been possible without the generous support of our sponsors. We are especially grateful to Michael Broughton, Chairman of the W.W. Spooner Charitable Trust, for his enthusiastic backing throughout the period since the inception of the project.

At the Wordsworth Trust we have enjoyed the constant friendly help of Michael McGregor and his staff, in particular Charlotte Booth, Lucy Clarke, Amy Concannon, Jane Connolly, Carrie Taylor and Rebecca Turner as well as the Trust's President, Pamela Woof. Jeff Cowton wonderfully combines incomparable knowledge of the Trust's collections with a quiet good-humoured ability to cope with incessant demands and we are truly grateful to him.

We would also like to acknowledge the support and assistance of many others: Philip Athill, Gordon Baddeley, Bruno Beer, Hugh Belsey, Mary Burkett, Tom Edwards, Trevor Fawcett, Paul Goldman, Venetia Harlow, Lynette Harris, Hannah Hawksworth, David Hill, Chris Hogg, Sierra Kaag, Samantha Lackey, Kate and Mike Metcalfe, Rachel Moss, Charles Nugent, Sheila O'Connell, Constance Parrish, Jan Piggott, Nick Powell, Lynda Pratt, Nick Rogers, Kim Sloan, Susan Sloman, Peter Urquhart, Emma Wright.

Cecilia Powell
Stephen Hebron

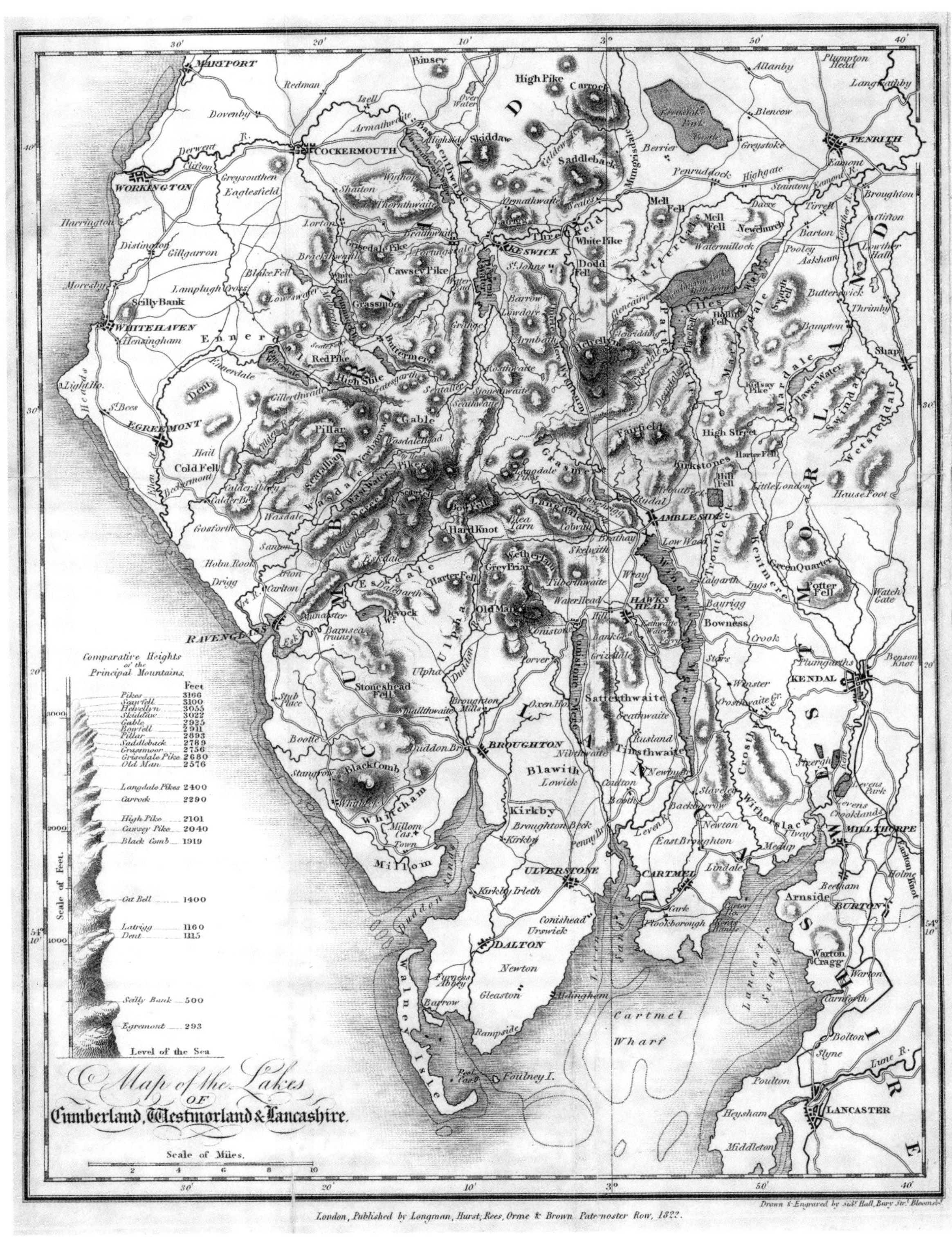

'Map of the Lakes of Cumberland, Westmorland & Lancashire' published in William Wordsworth, *A Description of the Scenery of the Lakes* (1822).

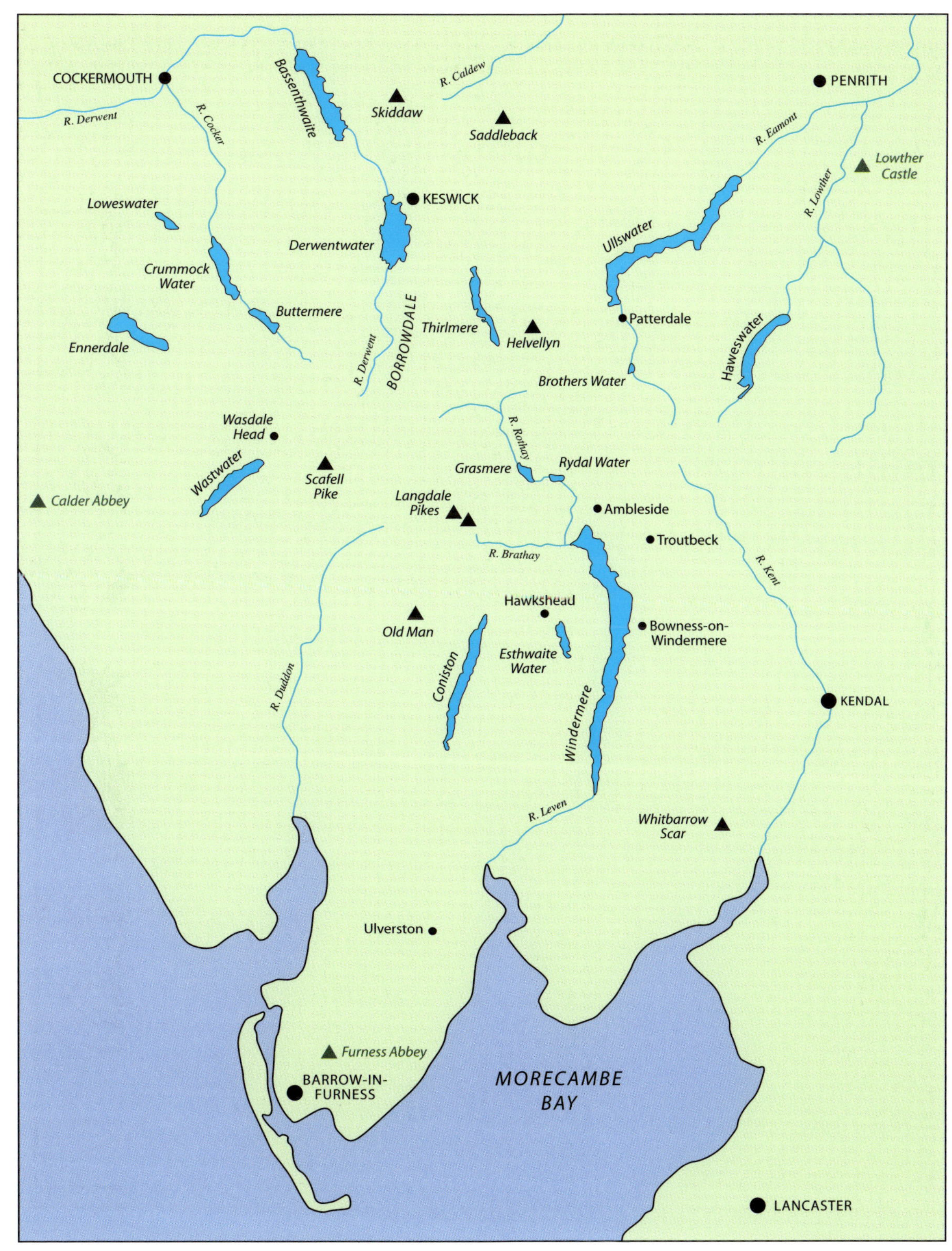

THE LAKE DISTRICT

LAMPS AFTER AN ILLUMINATION

Cecilia Powell

'We thought we had got into Fairy Land', wrote the essayist and poet Charles Lamb after returning to London from a visit to his friend Samuel Taylor Coleridge in Keswick. 'Such an impression I never received from objects of sight before, nor do I suppose that I can ever again. Glorious creatures, fine old fellows, Skiddaw &c. I never shall forget thee.... I have satisfied myself, that there is such a thing as that, which tourists call *romantic*, which I very much suspected before: they make such a spluttering about it, and toss their splendid epithets around them, till they give as dim a light, as four oClock next morning the Lamps do after an illumination.... But I am returned ... & you cannot conceive the degradation I felt at first, from being accustommed to wander free as air among mountains, & bathe in rivers without being controuled by any one, to come home and *work*: I felt very *little*. I had been dreaming I was a very great man.'[1] When Lamb writes of his elation at seeing the Lake District for the first time, and the near-impossibility of doing it justice in words, he speaks for countless visitors in his own day and ours: however rich the language employed, it cannot convey the actual experience. As a man who appreciated art, he might also have commented on the challenge of depicting the area adequately on paper or canvas. Like the writer, the artist can only provide a partial and imperfect rendering of the reality. Undeterred by such difficulties, however, writers and artists have been discovering the Lake District and, through their work, enabling others to discover it for nearly three centuries. As will be seen in this exhibition and catalogue, there is no single, unified 'discovery' of the area; the process was, is and will continue to be one that is intangible, complex and open-ended: both personal to every visitor and infinite in scope. A commentator can only offer a few signposts along the way.

Savage grandeur and noblest thoughts

The phrases 'savage grandeur' and 'noblest thoughts' in our title come from Dr John Dalton's *Descriptive Poem addressed to Two Ladies, at their return from viewing the mines near Whitehaven*, first printed in 1755 (cat. 5), where they follow an encomium of the 'rough rocks of dread Lodore' with its 'boist'rous sweep' of foaming waters:

> Horrors like these at first alarm,
> But soon with savage grandeur charm,
> And raise to noblest thoughts the mind.

1. Letter of 24 September 1802 to Thomas Manning, quoted from *The Letters of Charles and Mary Lamb*, ed. Edwin J. Marrs, Jr, vol. II, 1976, pp. 68–70.

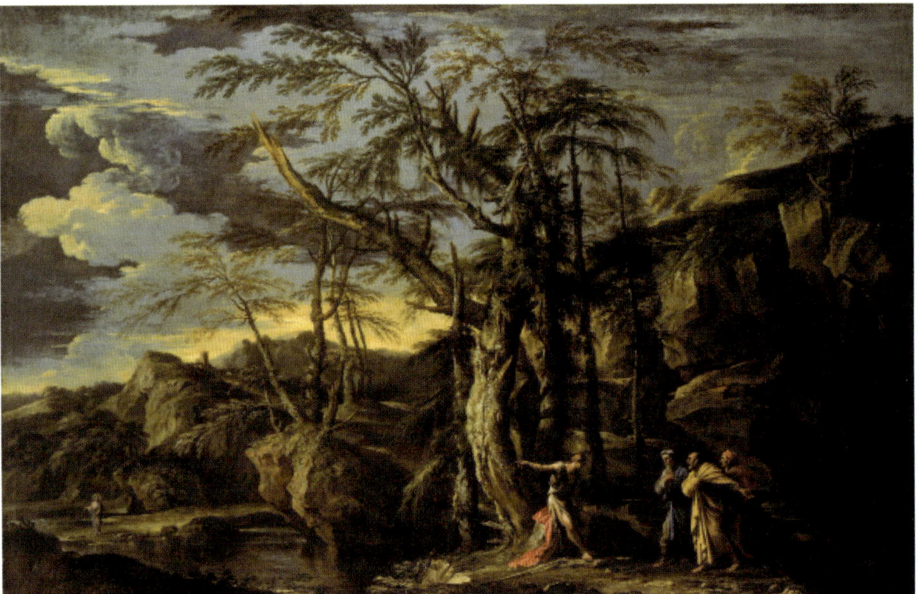

Fig. 1 Salvator Rosa, *Landscape with St John the Baptist pointing out Christ*, oil on canvas, late 1650s (Kelvingrove Art Gallery, Glasgow).

Modern readers can take these concepts in their stride quite easily but they were unusual for their time. 'Savage' signified a landscape that was hostile, barren, desolate, unproductive and infertile, a landscape that was unappealing to travellers and, as yet, of only limited interest to artists, while 'noble thoughts' – let alone 'noblest' – were customarily aroused by the deeds of men, not by scenery. Artists and art-lovers were aware of the depictions of such scenery by the Neapolitan painter Salvator Rosa (1615–73) which led Horace Walpole to evoke his crossing of the Alps with the poet Thomas Gray in 1739 as 'Precipices, mountains, torrents, wolves, rumblings, Salvator Rosa' and earned the painter the sobriquet 'savage Rosa' from another poet, James Thomson, in 1748.[2] They would also have been aware that these rocky landscapes, dominated by blasted trees and fearsome foliage and filled with tension or foreboding, served as backgrounds to the true subject-matter. The landscapes – usually based on Rosa's familiarity with the Apennines in central Italy – clarified and enhanced the human drama depicted in the foreground: a hermit retreating from the world, an assault by bandits in a remote region, the temptation of a saint in the desert or a biblical subject such as that in fig. 1: St John the Baptist, the archetypal wilderness-figure, pointing out the minute and vulnerable figure of Christ to his earliest disciples.[3]

Until shortly before Dalton's poem wild and barren scenery in Britain had not been generally regarded as a fit subject for artists and early representations of it were prompted by particular needs and circumstances. Four large bird's-

2. *The Letters of Horace Walpole, Earl of Orford…*, 1846, vol. I, p. 21; Thomson, 'The Castle of Indolence', I.xxxviii.9.

3. The subject is taken from John 1:35–7.

eye views of Coniston Water and Piel Castle dating from 1732–3 are perhaps the work of a map-maker or a surveyor,[4] while the primitive Rosa-esque outline of Skiddaw that appeared in the *Gentleman's Magazine* in the same year that Thomson referred to 'savage Rosa' was a by-product of a recent survey of the Cumberland coast (fig. 6 on p. 13 and see cat. 1–2). The Alps, too, held few attractions for British artists until later in the century, the earliest depictions by a professional artist being those made by William Pars in 1770. Not surprisingly, Pars was one of the first artists to show a Lakes subject at the Royal Academy, displaying a watercolour of Derwentwater together with one of a lake in Ireland, at its fourth annual exhibition in 1772.[5] However, there had been, for some years, a growing appreciation of mountain scenery both in art and in the experience of landscape itself. The emotions aroused by the vastness and obscurity of mountains, together with their life-threatening associations of pain and danger, were analysed by the statesman Edmund Burke in his highly influential treatise, *A Philosophical Enquiry into the Origin of our Ideas of the Sublime and Beautiful,* first published in 1757 and reissued, much revised, in 1759. At the heart of the new enjoyment of 'the Sublime' in landscape lay the idea that, if we are not actually in physical danger, we may positively delight in menacing scenery, dark and gloomy mountains, 'splendid confusion', the noise of vast cataracts and raging storms; if our lives are not at risk, our natural terror is transformed into pleasurable astonishment.[6] Although Burke said little about landscape painting as such, few artists after 1760 would have been unaware of his ideas; John Constable owned a copy of the *Enquiry* and knowledge of it is implicit in many of the works of J.M.W. Turner.

Throughout the period covered by this exhibition the artistic exploration and celebration of the Lake District went hand-in-hand with identical activities in other upland parts of Britain and comparisons were frequently drawn between the respective merits of the different areas: the same artists who made tours of the Lakes also visited the Peak District in Derbyshire, the Yorkshire dales, the mountainous parts of Wales, the highlands of Scotland and the lakes in Ireland and portrayed them in very similar ways. All became agreeable destinations for those with the means and leisure to travel. In Jane Austen's *Pride and Prejudice* 'all the celebrated beauties of Matlock, Chatsworth, Dovedale, or the Peak' are proposed by the Gardiners as an exciting alternative to the tour of the Lakes that Elizabeth Bennet had set her heart on,[7] and many southerners with less than a month at their disposal

4. These pen and ink studies by the otherwise unknown Stephen Penn, with named and numbered features, appeared on the art market in 1941; one, now in the Victoria & Albert Museum, was reproduced in Bicknell and Woof, 1982, p. 10; one is in the Whitworth Art Gallery, University of Manchester (Nugent, 2003, p. 212); one in the Huntington Art Gallery, San Marino, California; and one was illustrated in Iolo Williams, *Early English Watercolours*, 1952, fig. 30.

5. RA 1772, nos 180–1, *Part of the lake of Sligo, in Ireland* and *Part of the lake of Keswick, in Cumberland, stained drawings.*

6. *The Works of the Right Honourable Edmund Burke*, 1826, vol. 1, pp. 150–201.

7. Begun 1796, revised and published 1813, chapter 42.

for a 'northern tour' must, like the Gardiners, have been happy to settle for Derbyshire. When visitors to the RA were confronted with pairs like that of Pars in 1772 or, a little later, that of John Rathbone (*Summer's evening, a view near Matlock, Derbyshire* and *Misty morning, a view near Winder Meer Lake, Cumberland*)[8] what could such a change of plan possibly matter?

As these examples illustrate, artists would often show several works in the same exhibition depicting different parts of the country, thus casting their nets as wide as possible in the search for potential purchasers and future commissions. The first large engravings of rugged and dramatic British scenery were those by Thomas Smith depicting his native Derbyshire, which began appearing in 1743, followed within a decade by ones of Yorkshire,[9] while the early catalogues of the Royal Academy show that Wales exerted a powerful appeal, usually far beyond that of any other area. For about a decade around 1782–91, when Joseph Farington, Philip James de Loutherbourg, John Laporte and Thomas Walmsley were among the exhibitors, the Lake District challenged the supremacy of Wales, making an especially dominant appearance in the Great Room at Somerset House in 1784 when De Loutherbourg's colossal depiction of *Brather Bridge, which divides Westmoreland from Cumberland* was hung immediately below an equally massive portrait of the Prince of Wales by the Academy's first president, Sir Joshua Reynolds.[10] The same regions were well represented in the early exhibitions of the Society of Painters in Water Colours, founded in 1804, though interest in Derbyshire had ebbed away, being replaced by a fascination with Scotland (now a much more accessible destination). Here the Lakes were consistently prominent, thanks to a stream of exhibits from John Glover, Joshua Cristall, William Havell, Paul Sandby Munn, Ramsay Richard Reinagle and others.

It is quite hard to estimate the number of Lake District scenes shown in the early exhibitions of the Royal Academy since many paintings bore the simple title *Landscape* and gave no hint of their subject or the inspiration behind them (just as countless portraits preserved the anonymity of the sitter through such generic titles as *Portrait of a Lady*). Thomas Gainsborough almost invariably exhibited his landscapes thus, with the result that the titles by which they are known today are the invention of later cataloguers; among his numerous untitled private drawings there may well be Lake District motifs

8. RA 1789, nos 378–9.

9. E.g. *A Prospect in the upper part of Dove-Dale*, advertised as one 'eight of the most extraordinary Natural Prospects in the Mountainous Part of Derbyshire and Staffordshire, commonly called the Peak' (see Clayton, 1997, pp. 157–8 and ill. 173).

10. See the contemporary watercolours of the Great Room by E.F. Burney, reproduced in Solkin (ed.), 2001, figs 17–19. The composition of *Brather Bridge* (no. 71) was almost identical to that used by Farington in his *Brathay Bridge, near Ambleside* engraved in 1787; Burney shows that it was flanked by two much smaller works by De Loutherbourg, *A cottage in Patterdale* and *Skiddaw* (nos 63 and 78; see cat. 25). The present catalogue follows the titles as printed in the original RA catalogues, which contain erratic capitalisation and are notorious for their mis-spellings.

that await identification.[11] What we do know from the named early exhibits at the RA is that Derwentwater and Windermere were the most popular subjects; that Farington was the first to show a painting of the waterfall at Rydal (in 1780); and that Lakes exhibits became more numerous in the 1780s, almost certainly as a result of the publication in 1778 of West's *Guide to the Lakes* in which the author stressed its value to artists.[12] It is also clear that some artists were using high viewpoints as early as the 1770s, rather than staying close to the highway or hugging the lakeshore; one of the earliest artists to do so was John Feary, whose *Grasmere* (from a modestly elevated field) was to serve as the frontispiece to numerous revised editions of West's *Guide* from 1780 onwards.[13]

By contrast to those artists who were content to exhibit unidentified landscapes, others gave their works very specific titles, sometimes even stressing their own alertness to the subtleties of weather, atmosphere and light in a way that is usually associated with Turner and Constable around the turn of the century and later – the 'varying or accidental' beauties of the Lakes as writers called them, as opposed to the permanent features of lake and fell. In 1770 the Dublin-born painter George Barret showed the very first named Lakes painting to appear at the RA, *A study from Nature on the lake at Ullswater, in Cumberland*, the very title of which proclaims that he had studied his subject attentively. (At the end of that decade he was responsible for a decorative cycle of paintings adorning an entire room at Norbury Park in Surrey, recently designed by Thomas Sandby for the collector William Lock (1732–1810) whose circle included many artists and writers. The scenes (fig. 2) were loosely based on motifs from the Lake District and filled with transitory effects – shifting clouds, running water, rustling leaves – that provided an all-embracing illusion of a Cumbrian landscape; even the ceiling of the room was painted with clouds.[14]) In 1781 Barret exhibited *View of Winandermere lake in Westmoreland, – the effect the sun beginning to appear in the morning, with the mists breaking and dispersing* – a title that looks forward to those of Turner in years to come, as does that of William Thompson in 1782: *Glenridding in*

11. See cat. 23.

12. The numbers were still very small within the exhibition as a whole: in the first decade of the RA, when the annual exhibits rose from 136 to over 400, there were never more than three named Lakes scenes a year; in 1785, when there were fourteen named depictions of the Lakes (the highest number in the 1780s) the total number of exhibits was 641; by 1800 there were regularly over 1,100 exhibits but named Lakes scenes had still never exceeded eighteen a year.

13. John Feary, *A view of Windermere lake, Westmoreland, taken on Furness Fell, Lancashire*, RA 1776, no. 371, which predates by a year Thomas Hearne's well-known view of Derwentwater from the slopes of Skiddaw (Yale Center for British Art, New Haven). Feary's work appears in the RA catalogue, with others, in a postscript entitled 'Omitted'; this merely signifies that the printers had failed to include it in the appropriate place earlier in the catalogue which was then organised alphabetically by artist.

14. In 1793 a room at Drakelow Hall, Derbyshire, was decorated by Paul Sandby in comparable fashion; one wall is preserved in the Victoria & Albert Museum (see Bonehill and Daniels (ed.), 2009–10, p. 20).

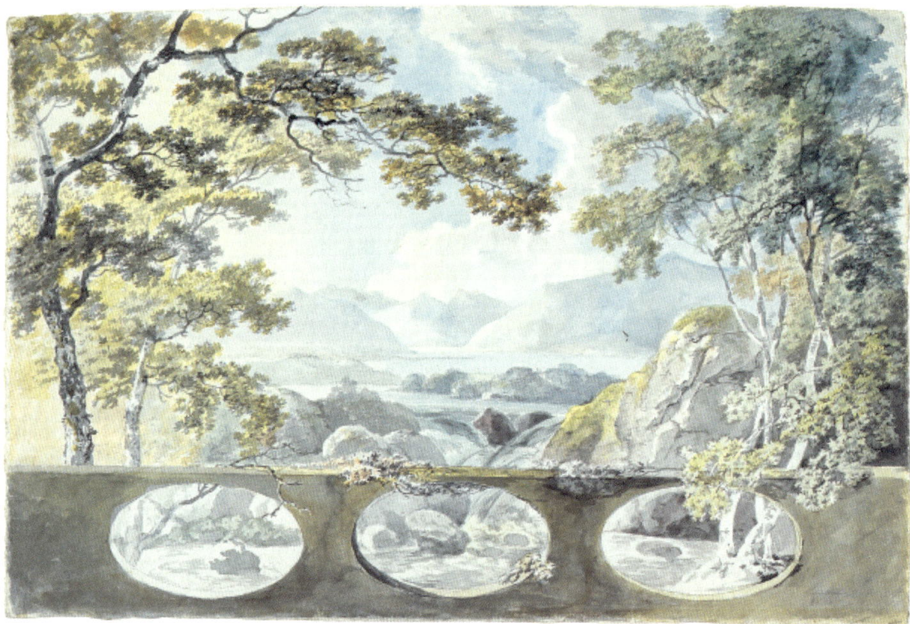

Fig. 2 George Barret, *Decorative Landscape: Study for a Room at Norbury Park*, pencil and watercolour, *c.*1780 (Courtauld Gallery, London).

Westmoreland, with the effect of the rainbow after rain. It was not until 1798 that Turner exhibited his first depictions of the Lakes: *Morning amongst the Coniston Fells, Cumberland* (accompanied by four lines from Book V of *Paradise Lost*) and *Buttermere Lake, with part of Cromackwater, Cumberland, a shower* (with lines derived from one of the earliest English poems to show a genuine love of nature, Thomson's *Seasons*).[15]

Such introductions of atmospheric details relating to calm and storm, or morning and evening, and the integration of appropriate literary or historical dimensions served to elevate the status of landscape painting in the hierarchy of art in Britain, where it had long been scorned, like a poor relation. In 1719 the portrait-painter Jonathan Richardson had made a strong case for the importance of painting as a liberal art rather than a mechanical trade or a mere pastime: 'We PAINTERS are upon the level with Writers, as being Poets, Historians, Philosophers and Divines, we Entertain, and Instruct equally with Them.' But not all painters were equal in eighteenth-century England. At the Royal Academy there was a professor of anatomy and a professor of perspective but there was no professor of landscape painting. The aristocracy and gentry furnished their houses with landscapes painted by the Old Masters of Italy, France and the Low Countries but would rarely do more to encourage native landscape painting than commission a 'house portrait' or a view of their estate. The results, in the hands of a specialist in this work such as the Irish artist Thomas Sautelle Roberts, could often include an extremely

15. Both in Tate Britain and reproduced in Turner On-line at www.tate.org.uk. The Coniston Fells did not, of course, lie in Cumberland but in Lancashire. Turner's five lines accompanying *Buttermere Lake* conflated lines 189–205 from Thomson's 'Spring'.

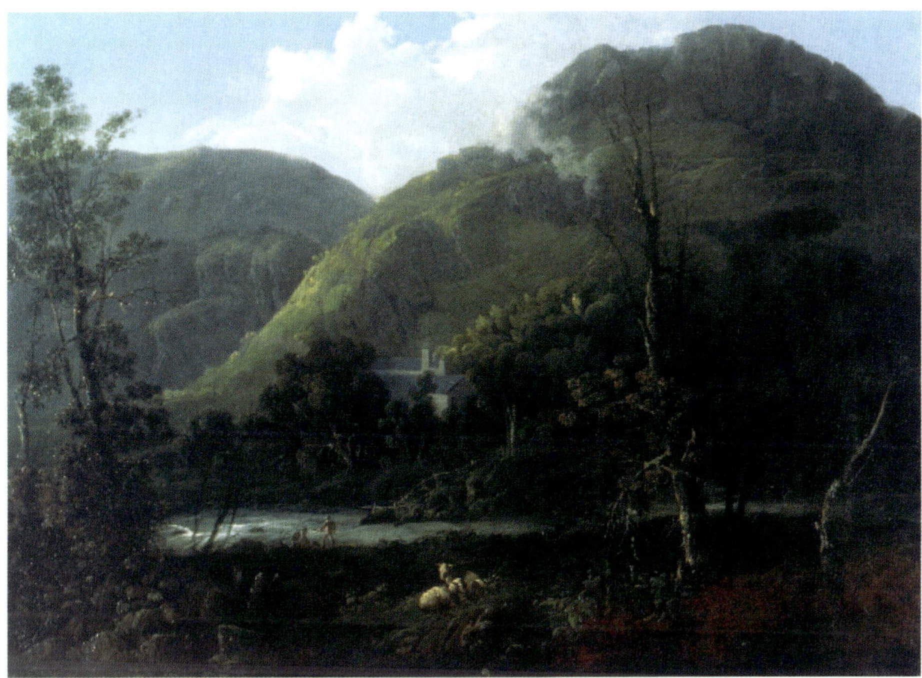

Fig. 3 Thomas Sautelle Roberts, *Rydal Hall*, oil on canvas, *c.*1790 (The Wordsworth Trust).

pleasing landscape setting (fig. 3) but writers on the Lakes such as Dr John Brown in the 1750s (cat. 9) longed for the abilities of seventeenth-century foreign landscape artists with which to do justice to the wider and grander beauties of the area; there were simply no comparable British names to invoke, in the way that there are today. Gainsborough, despite his deep love of landscape, relied for his livelihood on 'face-painting'; Reynolds enriched his own portraits with historical references and nuances. As Richardson had put it, 'A History is preferable to a Landscape, Sea-piece, Animals, Fruit, Flowers, or any other Still-Life, pieces of Drollery, *&c.*; the reason is, the latter Kinds may Please, and in proportion as they do so they are Estimable, and that is according to every one's Taste, but they cannot Improve the Mind, they excite no Noble Sentiments.'[16] The history of landscape painting in Britain over the following century – and beyond – is, in part at least, the history of artists who passionately believed exactly the opposite.

An alternative vision: 'calm, beautiful and serene'

Besides Rosa, the Old Masters who influenced British taste at this period included the seventeenth-century painters of the Low Countries, such as Jacob van Ruisdael, with their naturalistic approach to more domesticated types of landscape and their wealth of rural motifs – in scenes that bore little physical similarity to those of Cumbria. Nevertheless these artists played an important part in the depiction of the Lakes, most especially in the work of Gainsborough. However, the artist most strongly associated with the softer

16. Jonathan Richardson, *Two Discourses…*, 1719, pp. 42–4.

and gentler, cultivated and inhabited, parts of the region – Windermere and Grasmere, say, rather than Derwentwater and Borrowdale – was Claude Lorrain (1604/5–82). A native of Lorraine who spent almost his entire career in Rome and was inspired, above all, by the countryside around that city, 'his work penetrated British culture at every point, from nature poetry to landscape gardening and even architecture'.[17] Paintings by Claude were in British collections in his own lifetime and by 1820 over half his entire oeuvre of almost 300 paintings was in Britain. Although these were owned by wealthy private individuals, several major collectors were only too pleased to display them to fellow-enthusiasts and encouraged young artists to study or copy them (as Sir George Beaumont did with Constable) while the works reached an even wider audience in the form of prints. Several Claudes were engraved in England as early as the 1740s, followed by others around 1760; in 1777 the engraver Richard Earlom published two large volumes reproducing the 200 drawings that Claude had made after his own paintings, his *Liber Veritatis.*[18] Claude had been a decisive influence on Richard Wilson (*c.*1713–82), the first major British artist to dedicate himself to landscape (whose life ended in near-paupery) and he was later to be a lifelong inspiration to Turner who in 1811 praised his art in a lecture at the Royal Academy beginning with the words, 'Pure as Italian air, calm, beautiful and serene'.[19]

The landscapes depicted in Claude's paintings are imaginary and generalised, distillations of his intensive studies in the Roman Campagna. Like those of Rosa they set the scene for narrative subjects but their ingredients and moods are very different. *Landscape with the Marriage of Isaac and Rebekah* (fig. 4, often called simply *The Mill*) shows the smiling face of nature, its beauty, richness and fertility complementing the celebratory music and dance and bright colours in the foreground.[20] This is the epitome of Claude's 'delicate sunshine' strewn over cultivated vales, groves and lake referred to by Dr John Brown and was one of 'Mr. Angerstein's pictures' that John Harden took Thomas Jameson to study in Angerstein's own house at 100 Pall Mall in 1809.[21] ('*Mon dieu! – such Claudes!* … perfectly miraculous', Lamb had exclaimed to William Hazlitt earlier.[22]) In 1824 it formed part of the newly founded National Gallery to which Turner bequeathed two of his own paint-

17. Michael Kitson, 'Claude Lorrain' in Joll, Butlin and Herrmann (ed.), 2001, p. 48.

18. At that time in the collection of the Duke of Devonshire at Chatsworth, the *Liber Veritatis* drawings are now in the British Museum. A third volume, reproducing further Claude drawings, was published in 1819, bringing the total to 300.

19. See Jerrold Ziff, '"Backgrounds: Introduction of Architecture and Landscape". A Lecture by J.M.W. Turner', *Journal of the Warburg and Courtauld Institutes*, 26 (1963), pp. 124–7.

20. Painted for a nephew of Pope Innocent X. Genesis 24 has a long and moving account of the finding of Isaac's beautiful young bride. The marriage itself is described in the briefest way possible but has long been regarded by Catholics as symbolic of Christ's union with the Church.

21. Farington, *Diary*, 17 May 1809: IX.3457.

22. Letter of 15 March 1806, quoted from Marrs, ed. cit., p. 223.

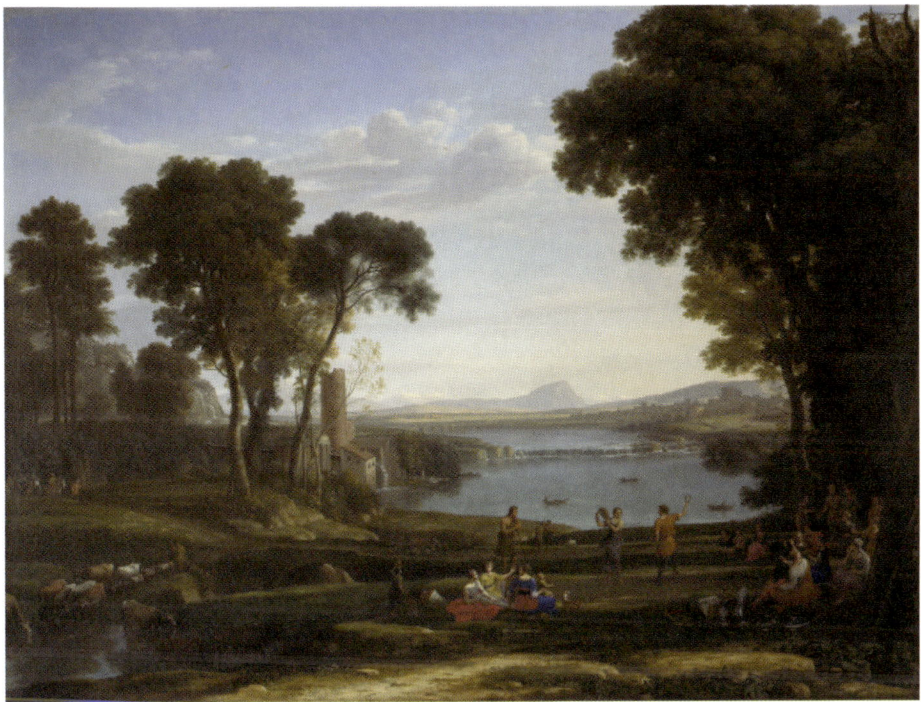

Fig. 4 Claude Lorrain, *Landscape with the Marriage of Isaac and Rebekah ('The Mill')*, oil on canvas, 1648 (National Gallery, London).

ings on condition that they be hung next to *The Mill* and a Claude seaport. Claude's influence – whether direct or at second or even third hand – lies behind many of the works in this exhibition.

Networks in north and south

By 1819 Wordsworth was telling his friend Francis Wrangham that 'all the world comes to the Lakes'[23] – a development for which his own work was at least partly responsible. But all movements, whether artistic, literary or otherwise, gain momentum through networks of individuals. An intricate series of relationships underpins the activities of the writers and artists in this exhibition. Many of the artists were based in London, sharing membership of a constantly shifting array of institutions including the Society of Artists (which organised the first free exhibition in England of the work of living artists in 1760), the Royal Academy of Arts, founded in 1768, and the Society of Painters in Water Colours, formed in 1804 by a small band of artists who felt their works were overshadowed by the oil paintings with which they shared wall-space at the Academy. Several of the artists were linked by relationships such as that of teacher and pupil (Edward Dayes and Thomas Girtin; Francis Towne and John White Abbott) or patron and protégé (Beaumont and both Girtin and Constable) or by long-term friendship (Farington, Hearne and

23. *The Letters of William and Dorothy Wordsworth. II. The Middle Years*, part 1, ed. Ernest de Selincourt, rev. Mary Moorman, 1969, p. 842.

Beaumont) or family ties (William Daniell and William Westall). As can be seen from 'The Artists and the Lakes' (pp. 141–72), some were born into families of professional artists (Daniell, Anthony Devis, William Havell, Paul Sandby Munn, Ramsay Richard Reinagle).

An equally important network linked professionals and amateurs in Liverpool, by now England's principal port for the Atlantic trade and a highly prosperous town. Thomas Chubbard, Daniel Daulby and Peter Holland were all active in the attempts to found an art academy there from 1769 onwards (a period when Joseph Wright of Derby was a temporary resident); these efforts resulted in the first provincial art exhibition in England in 1774 and eventually led to the founding of the Liverpool Academy in 1810, the Liverpool Royal Institution in 1814, and joint exhibitions of these two bodies from 1822 onwards. Liverpool was also one of the earliest places in Britain to enjoy a flourishing trade in prints, an important dimension for both Holland and Daulby.[24] Many other artists also had strong northern connections: Anthony Devis, Farington and William Green all hailed from Lancashire, Francis Nicholson and Julius Caesar Ibbetson from Yorkshire, while John 'Warwick' Smith was closely associated with the Gilpin family at Scaleby Castle near Carlisle from an early age. In north and south alike there existed what amounted to a commercial network of activities and practices. The majority of the artists represented in the present exhibition gave drawing lessons and many also published drawing manuals; the same clientele bought paintings and prints and paid for such private tuition; by exhibiting or advertising one commodity, an artist would almost certainly attract interest in another.

Within the Lake District itself, Brathay Hall near Ambleside became a magnet for visiting artists from north and south after it became the home of the gifted amateur painter from Ireland, John Harden, and his Scottish wife Jessy, who had studied painting in Edinburgh and was acquainted with the leading artists there: from 1804 onwards the household at Brathay provided good company and musical entertainments as well as intelligent conversation on art and literature. Alongside these connections with clear implications for the discovery and depiction of the Lake District there exist others whose importance is tangential but worth noting. Ten years after Constable's 1806 visit to the Lakes – and to the Hardens – his closest friend, the Rev. John Fisher of Weymouth, married the eldest daughter of Wordsworth's uncle, the Rev. William Cookson, who had supplied the letterpress to Farington's *Views of the Lakes* in the 1780s.[25] Later still, after the latter's death, the Constable family moved into his house in Upper Charlotte Street, the scene of so many

24. See Hopkinson, 2007.

25. Equally close networks existed among engravers and publishers, with many enterprises being family concerns (e.g. the engraving and publishing business of William Byrne; see cat. 17, 27–8). William Woollett (whose work included celebrated landscape engravings after Farington's teacher Richard Wilson) numbered the meticulous watercolourist Thomas Hearne (cat. 15–17) among his pupils as well as such engravers as Thomas Morris (cat. 25) and Benjamin Pouncy (fig. 39 on p. 134).

discussions about the art world in general and Farington's beloved Lakes in particular.

Among all these connections – some well known, others only recently surfacing – few are more fascinating than those of the lady amateurs. Lady Mary Lowther (cat. 7) was the wife of Sir James Lowther (later Lord Lonsdale) who famously failed to pay his family's debts to the Wordsworth children after the death of their father, his agent, in 1783. She survived some fifteen years of unhappiness in the retirement of Lowther Hall, largely through the 'learned Education' advocated by her maternal grandmother, Lady Mary Wortley Montagu, as a desirable preparation for just such circumstances. 'I know by Experience', wrote the latter to the young Lady Mary's mother, 'it is in the power of Study not only to make solitude tolerable but agreeable. … I can assure you I have never had halfe [*sic*] an hour heavy on my Hands for want of something to do. … At the same time I recommend Books, I neither exclude Work [i.e. needlework] nor drawing.' There was, however, a *caveat*: a girl should always 'conceal whatever Learning she attains, with as much solicitude as she would hide crookedness or lameness'.[26]

Drawing was also an important occupation for Elizabeth Wharton of Durham (cat. 66), whose family had long enjoyed the friendship of the Lowthers. More importantly, she was the daughter of Dr Thomas Wharton who attempted to visit the Lakes in the company of his Cambridge friend Thomas Gray and turned back, afflicted with asthma, leaving Gray to explore the area alone in 1769. Thomas Wharton's visit to the Lakes was the most important visit 'that never was' – a real-life precedent for that of Elizabeth Bennet in literature (also with major repercussions) and one of which Jane Austen herself would surely have been aware. Gray's letters to Wharton, describing all his experiences and reactions to Lake scenery in poetical and evocative language, were published in 1775, the year of Austen's birth, but it is very likely that the young Elizabeth Wharton would have heard them read aloud by her father on their arrival.

The image multiplied

The earliest and the latest works of art in this exhibition are prints, the first being one of several illustrations contributed by the north-country polymath George Smith of Wigton to the *Gentleman's Magazine* (cat. 1),[27] the last forming part of a series on the vale of Keswick by William Westall, in which he was assisted by his friend Robert Southey (cat. 77). Whereas Westall was responsible for his own engraved plates, ensuring that the product that reached the public corresponded as perfectly as possible to his own vision and was of breath-taking beauty (fig. 5), many of the other prints in the exhibition are 'reproductive' engravings. The artist's work was passed to a professional

26. Letters of 28 January and 6 March 1753, quoted from *The Complete Letters of Lady Mary Wortley Montagu*, ed. Robert Halsband, 1967, vol. III, pp. 20–7.

27. On Smith see de Montluzin, 2004.

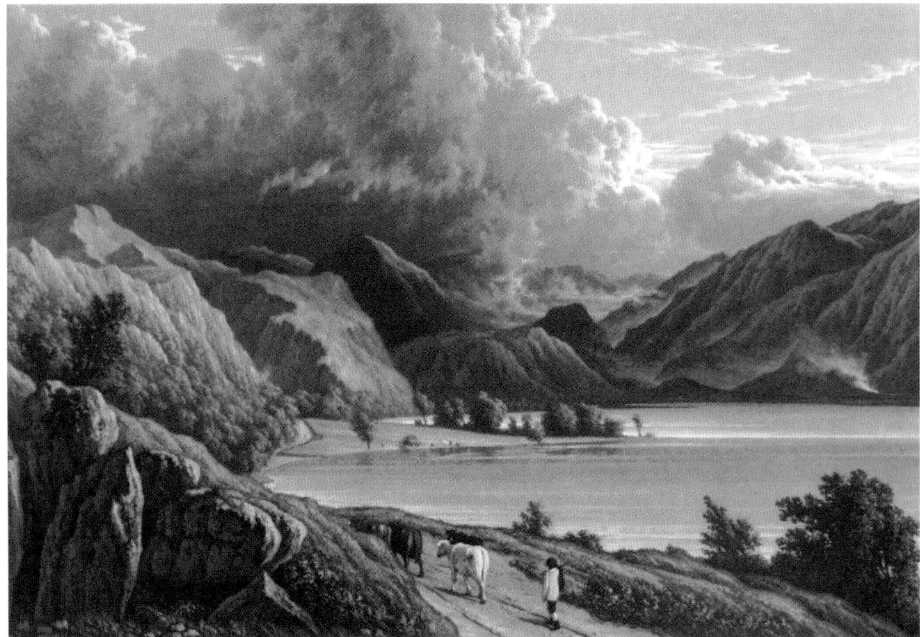

Fig. 5 William Westall, *Keswick Lake from Barrow Common*, aquatint 1820 (The Wordsworth Trust).

engraver for copying in another medium – or 'translating' as it was sometimes called – and, while some artists (including Farington and, later, Turner) would have supervised the engraver's work closely, others would have been unable to exercise such tight control. Notable among those who orchestrated their own print-making and print-publishing in the mid eighteenth century were Thomas Smith of Derby (cat. 6, 8) and the Londoner William Bellers (cat. 3–4). Following the example of William Hogarth (1697–1764), who had dispensed with engravers and printsellers and personally handled the publication and sale of the six scenes of *A Harlot's Progress* in 1732, Smith and Bellers became painter print-publishers, controlling and protecting every aspect of their work, as artists still seek to do today.

Prints of the Lake District reached a wide audience, being disseminated in many different ways. Large engravings were frequently published by subscription, sought in advance through the press, and they appeared singly or in series (often over a period of years), with or without accompanying texts, at this time known as 'letterpress' (cat. 17, 28). Such prints were destined for gentlemen's libraries and were much in demand not only in Britain where, by the mid 1780s, 'almost every man of taste is in some degree a collector of prints',[28] but also, increasingly, abroad; the letterpress was therefore printed in both English and French as a matter of course (see cat. 25). In the spring of 1787 it was reported: 'The trade at home is chiefly in low-priced prints. … Of the more costly productions the French exceed by three to one the buyers in England. In Paris alone [the subscriptions to one print] exceeded ours as

28. Joseph Strutt, *Biographical Dictionary of Engravers*, 1785–6, preface, quoted in Fawcett, 1974, p. 97 n.148.

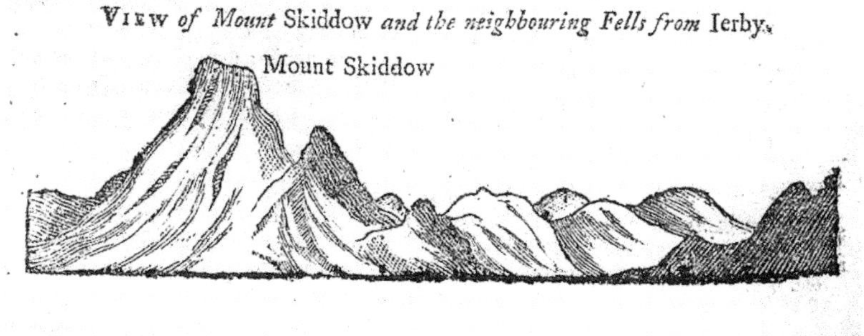

Fig. 6 After George Smith, *View of Mount Skiddow and the neighbouring Fells from Ierby*, woodcut from the *Gentleman's Magazine*, July 1748.

seventeen to three. … Spain is also beginning to deal largely in this commodity. A late order from Madrid … exceeded 1,500 pounds sterling.'[29] The economic importance of British print exports as a whole (dominated, naturally, by figure subjects) was widely recognised and played its part in the rise of the printseller John Boydell to become Lord Mayor of London in 1790. But the success-story could not be maintained. The French Revolution and invasion of neighbouring territories, followed by the outbreak of war between Britain and France in 1793 and the closure of French ports to British goods, all had a disastrous impact on the print export trade as well as on that of trade in general and it was years before it recovered (see cat. 74). Meanwhile, smaller prints of the Lakes by leading engravers appeared as book illustrations in the narratives of tours such as those by Thomas Newte, published in 1788, and Joseph Mawman, dating from 1805 (cat. 26 and 51), which enjoyed a more popular readership. The simple ones in the *Gentleman's Magazine*, founded in 1731, reached a huge monthly audience: 10,000 within its first decade, if the magazine itself was to be believed, but more like 5,000–6,000 by the time of cat. 1-2, according to modern estimates.[30] George Smith claimed that his map of the northern lakes, published in 1751 (cat. 2), was the first of its kind, 'the only one that was ever drawn'; his equally detailed map of *The Caudebec Fells* with the northernmost part of the Lake District marked '*DESOLATE AND MOUNTANOUS*' (cat. 1) and his very simple outline of Skiddaw (fig. 6) were published even earlier.

The dissemination of images through prints meant that they could reach thousands, comparable to the readership of influential works in prose and poetry, whereas an oil painting or watercolour would typically be enjoyed simply by an individual and his circle of friends. Moreover, prints – whether in the long-established media of etching and line-engraving or in the very recently invented one of aquatint – were of especial importance in an age

29. Quoted in Whitley, 1928, vol. 2, p. 72. See also Clayton, 1997, chapter 8.

30. John Cannon, '*Gentleman's Magazine*', *The Oxford Companion to British History,* 2002, Encyclopaedia.com 14 April 2010; E.A. Reitan, 'Expanding Horizons: Maps in the *Gentleman's Magazine*, 1731–1754', *Imago Mundi*, vol. 39, 1985, p. 54.

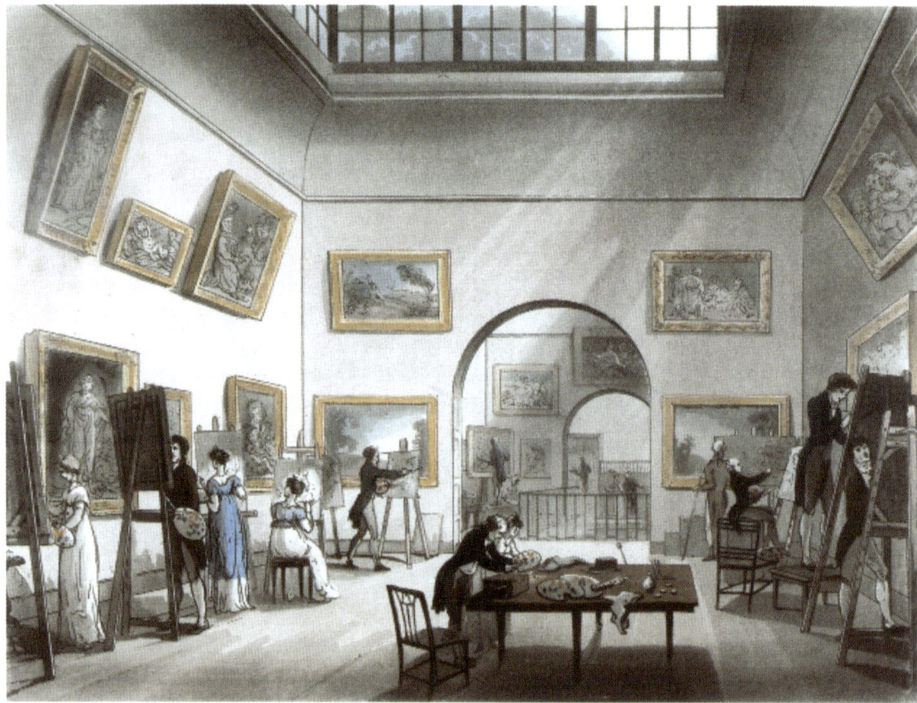

Fig. 7 J. Bluck after Thomas Rowlandson, *British Institution, Pall Mall*, aquatint, 1808, from Ackermann's *Microcosm of London* (The Wordsworth Trust).

when art education was conducted largely through the activity of copying. Students at the Royal Academy Schools learned to draw the human figure by copying plaster casts of the most famous sculptures of classical antiquity; they became proficient in composing historical scenes by copying engravings or painted copies after Raphael and other Old Masters. Amateurs would copy any watercolours and engravings they could lay their hands on, or that were provided by their tutors. In the mid 1790s Turner, Girtin and other young artists in London spent many invaluable evenings copying watercolours by the most outstanding living artists in the collection of the physician Thomas Monro. This informal arrangement has become colloquially known as the 'Monro Academy' although there was never any tuition involved; close scrutiny, discussion and competition were the spurs to progress, not to mention the small fee Monro provided and the supper of oysters.[31] After the British Institution was founded in 1805 by a group of wealthy collectors, including Sir George Beaumont, to provide alternative opportunities to those of the RA, it held two exhibitions a year: a summer selling exhibition for contemporary artists and a winter one consisting of loans from private sources in order to showcase the art of the past. Study and copying were actively encouraged here (fig. 7), as it was by Beaumont in his own home for the artists he favoured, such as Constable. The present exhibition includes several fascinating examples of copies, made for many purposes and in diverse circumstances, including a tiny private memorandum of part of a lost painting by

31. Farington, *Diary*, 12 November 1798: III.1090.

Wright of Derby (cat. 41); one of Chubbard's small copies of engravings for a unique personal album of Lake scenery (cat. 44); an engraving after Glover from a drawing manual, one of the early nineteenth century's numerous equivalents of a 'Teach Yourself How to Paint' book (cat. 68); and two large coloured scenes after Farington prints that, if exhibited, would have attracted accusations of plagiarism (cat. 29–30). All such copies played their part in the ongoing process of discovering and understanding the Lakes.

Poetical painting and picturesque beauty

In 1805, the same year that saw the first exhibition of the Society of Painters in Water Colours and the birth of the British Institution, Henry Fuseli, professor of painting at the Royal Academy, delivered his lecture entitled 'Invention' in which he roundly dismissed, 'as the last branch of uninteresting subjects, that kind of landscape which is entirely occupied with the tame delineation of a given spot: an enumeration of hill and dale, clumps of trees, shrubs, water, meadows, cottages, and houses; what is commonly called views. These, if not assisted by nature, dictated by taste, or chosen for character, may delight the owner of the acres they enclose, the inhabitants of the spot, perhaps the antiquary or the traveller, but to every other eye they are little more than topography.'[32] Later in the same passage he describes how the work of the greatest painters (ranging from Titian to Wilson) 'spurns all relation with this kind of map-work. To them nature disclosed her bosom in the varied light of rising, meridian, setting suns; in twilight, night, and dawn. Height, depth, solitude, strike, terrify, absorb, bewilder, in their scenery.' Topography – the accurate depiction of a real place – had no appeal for the Swiss-born Fuseli who specialised in imaginative subjects from history and literature and made no bones about stating that '*Poetical* Painting' was alien to the English whose taste and feelings were all for realities rather than the ideal.[33] Despite such strictures, topography continued to flourish in Britain and elsewhere, providing employment for artists, engravers and publishers and furnishing tourists and armchair travellers with fine scenes. A solid topographical training provided one of the cornerstones in the development of Turner's imaginative genius. Whatever Fuseli might say, topography served many purposes beyond the purely local (and in his eyes trivial), not least of which was the creation of pride and patriotism during a prolonged period of war. In any case, we are today more conscious of the pitfalls of drawing too firm a distinction between the 'merely topographical' and 'art'.[34]

If the war with France – and the impossibility of travel in continental Europe – was a major factor in the growth of English interest in the country's own natural splendours and architectural heritage, an even more important

32. *Lectures on Painting, by the Royal Academicians. Barry, Opie, and Fuseli*, ed. Ralph N. Wornum, 1848, p. 449.

33. Farington, *Diary*, 24 July 1805: VII.2594.

34. See Felicity Myrone, '"The Monarch of the Plain": Paul Sandby and Topography', in Bonehill and Daniels (ed.), 2009–10, pp. 57–71.

catalyst had been the idea of 'picturesque beauty'.[35] At its simplest level this phrase referred to the beauty found in the pictures of the Old Masters: not only those of Claude and Rosa but also the work of Nicolas Poussin, his brother-in-law Gaspard Dughet (also, confusingly, referred to as 'Poussin' in this period), Titian, Rubens and many others whose work was in British collections or known through engravings. Discussion of the concept spread slowly and then like wildfire, fuelled especially by the many publications of the schoolmaster-parson William Gilpin (see cat. 13). Originally circulated amongst his friends in manuscript, Gilpin's writings stimulated intense debate as to exactly which visual ingredients could properly be included within the term 'picturesque' and whether 'the picturesque' and 'the beautiful' could rightly be regarded as a single concept. The search for 'picturesque beauty' within Britain itself, assessing actual views against artistic prototypes, created a positive industry in 'picturesque tourism' with excursions being made by Gilpin's readers all over the country and appropriate viewpoints being endlessly searched out, praised or criticised. A vogue arose for portable 'knick-knacks' and optical devices such as the 'landscape glass' or 'Claude glass', a small convex mirror of tinted glass that provided the user with a tonally unified, partial view of the landscape – and necessarily involved turning one's back on the real thing with its open horizons and variety of colouring. In many circumstances, however, the use of the glass was so astonishing that the reversal in the scenery was irrelevant; this was certainly so when the young William Wilberforce took a boat on Derwentwater with Farington and William Cookson in 1779. He wrote in his journal: 'It was perfectly calm & the Mountains, Rocks & Trees etc. were reflected so perfectly on the Water that one could have discern'd in the Reflection the smallest object & in the Glass (which answer'd delightfully) it was difficult to say which was the Shadow and which the Reality.'[36]

Gilpin achieved lasting personal fame as 'Dr Syntax', a comic character invented soon after his death (cat. 58–9), while his ideas have passed into common currency. The word 'picturesque' was soon attached to a whole host of nouns, from 'views' and 'scenery' (much favoured for book titles) to 'imagination' and 'travel' – and even to the fictional 'picturesque gentleman' Captain Fitzchrome who, armed with portfolio and camp stool, passed many days 'drawing old trees and mounds of grass' and sitting on rocks, making sketches of waterfalls and mountain pools.[37] It was not long before the cult of the picturesque provoked not merely satire and ridicule but serious recognition of its limitations. Lamb's remarks on the 'splutterings' of tourists had their parallels in Wordsworth's footnote, nine years earlier, to his *Descriptive Sketches taken during a Pedestrian Tour among the Alps*, 1793: 'I had once given to

35. For detailed and wide-ranging coverage of this theme see Andrews, 1989, and Andrews (ed.), 1994, which follows the debate through to 1860.

36. Wilberforce, ed. Wrangham, 1983, p. 59.

37. 'Picturesque travel' formed the subject of one of Gilpin's *Three Essays* on aspects of the picturesque published in 1792 and dedicated to William Lock of Norbury Park (reprinted in Andrews (ed.), 1994, vol. II, pp. 20–5); Thomas Love Peacock, *Crotchet Castle*, 1831, chapters III and XII.

these sketches the title of Picturesque; but the Alps are insulted in applying to them that term. Whoever, in attempting to describe their sublime features, should confine himself to the cold rules of painting would give his reader but a very imperfect idea of those emotions which they have the irresistible power of communicating to the most impassive imaginations.'

Elevating the mind

When Wilberforce spent three weeks in the Lakes in September 1779 he was an undergraduate at Cambridge and, although he had been influenced by Methodism in his boyhood, he had not yet acquired the deep religious faith that underpinned his later life and inspired his campaigns against the slave trade and slavery itself. As a result his journal is entirely secular: he analyses the scenery in aesthetic, classical and poetical terms; he chronicles his experiences with local guides as well as his meetings with friends and acquaintances; he records the condition of the roads and his frustration over poor maps and he mentions the shortcomings of West's *Guide*. Wilberforce even discusses the ruins of Calder Abbey in purely architectural terms.[38] Later in life this would not have been so: 'Mountains, views and waterfalls would be described not only as sublime and majestic, but also as evidence of God's goodness', as reminders of 'the dispensations of Divine Providence'.[39] Mountain areas have given rise to religious feelings since at least the time of the Psalmist. In the period covered by this exhibition landscape artists in many countries had this experience, a prime example being Caspar David Friedrich, the German contemporary of Girtin, Turner and Constable, who filled his paintings with religious symbolism and overtones. This reaction did not, by and large, occur in British depictions of the Lake District, although some works seem to bear an aura of Christian teaching. Turner's *Morning amongst the Coniston Fells* exemplifies the paradisal character that many contemporaries associated with the Lakes while Westall's *Keswick Lake from Saddleback* (fig. 8, overleaf) bears an uncanny resemblance to the work of the Pre-Raphaelite William Holman Hunt some thirty years later, where pastoral painting and Christian symbolism are totally at one.[40]

If a religious dimension is missing from the majority of Lake District views in this period, so also are the historical associations that visitors found, and enjoyed, on visits to Wales and Scotland with their abundance of ruined castles and ancient legends. A comparable absence of romantic links with the past existed in the West Country where in 1799 Southey found it hard to believe that no historical event or even legends of 'giants & devils & magicians' were attached to the Valley of the Rocks near Lynmouth: 'I could find

38. Wilberforce, ed. Wrangham, 1983. West had died on the very day Wilberforce left Cambridge for the first leg of his tour, 10 July 1779, and revisions for the second edition were already under way.

39. Ibid., foreword by the Earl of Birkenhead, pp. 11–12.

40. *Our English Coasts, 1852*, shown at the RA in 1853 with the inscription 'The Lost Sheep', and later exhibited by Hunt as *Strayed Sheep* (Tate Britain).

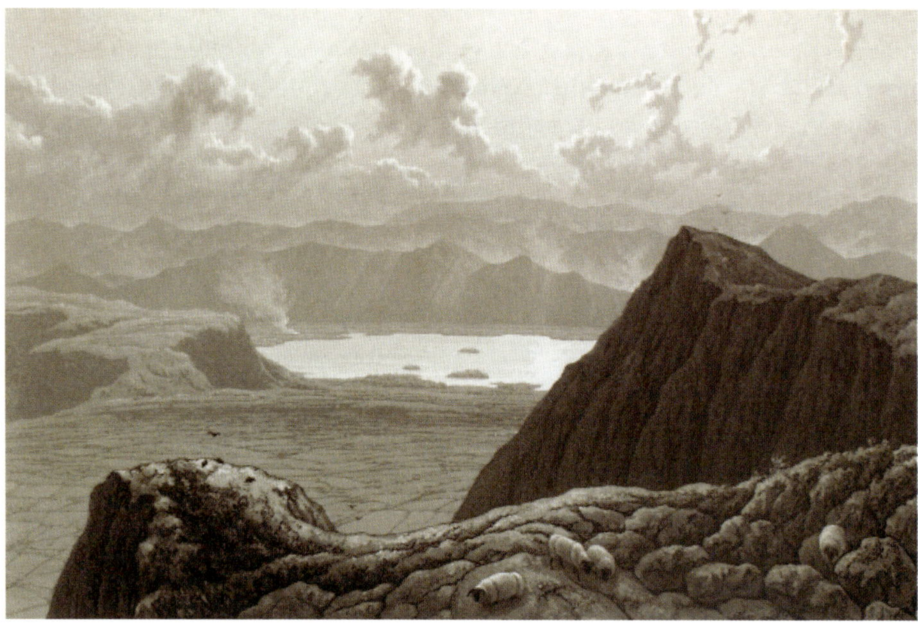

Fig. 8 William Westall, *Keswick Lake from Saddleback*, aquatint, 1820 (The Wordsworth Trust).

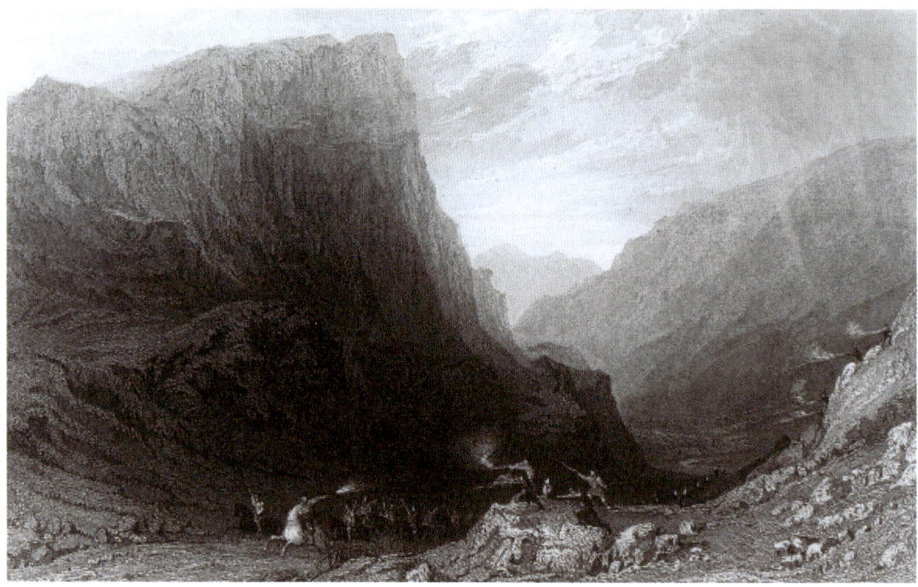

Fig. 9 William Floyd after Thomas Allom, *Honister Crag*, engraving, 1833 (The Wordsworth Trust).

none – not even a lie preserved'.[41] As Wordsworth wrote of the Lake District a decade later, 'these lakes and inner vallies are unadorned by any of the remains of ancient grandeur, castles, or monastic edifices, which are only found upon the skirts of this country, as Furness Abbey, Calder Abbey, the Priory of Lannercost, Gleaston Castle, – the original residence of the Flemings, – and the numerous ancient castles of the Cliffords and the Dacres.'[42] Novelists had to invent such fantasies as 'Grasmere Abbey' and Wordsworth himself was not above fabricating a few local legends where none was available.[43] Artists in the Lakes were left in the position of having to decide between alternatives: to confine the figures in their landscapes to woodcutters and milkmaids, fishermen and ferry-users; to append poetical quotations to their scenes in order to provide an extra dimension of human interest (see p. 164); or to exercise their imagination and present near-fictitious conflicts such as that graphically shown in Thomas Allom's *Honister Crag* (fig. 9) of which the accompanying letterpress drily remarks, 'The nature of the illustration obliges us to summon forth "far-forgotten things," referring, as it does, to a desperate struggle between two rival clans of Border freebooters … over which passing centuries have thrown a darkening veil.' This struggle is nevertheless described in immense detail.[44] Each approach had its attractions and limitations, with the most successful reconciliation between actuality and ideal being reached in the transfigured reality presented in the mature work of Turner. His *Ullswater, Cumberland* (fig. 10, overleaf), painted around the time that Wordsworth's *Guide to the Lakes* reached its definitive form, builds on the topographical tradition but is infused with the sublime qualities of vastness, magnificence and astonishment; though a finished work, destined to be engraved for a volume entitled (almost inevitably) *Picturesque Views in England and Wales*, it suggests the infinity that Burke associated with unfinished sketches that entertain the imagination with 'the promise of something more'.[45]

The glorious scenery of the Lakes enthralled and entertained its numerous visitors in the age of Wordsworth and Turner but it also achieved far more. Wordsworth's concept that the love of nature leads on to the love of mankind can be seen at work even in such an early production as 'An Evening Walk, Addressed to a Young Lady'.[46] Here, after describing a visit to the lower fall at Rydal, he pays homage to nature with

41. *The Collected Letters of Robert Southey. Part 2: 1798–1803*, ed. Ian Packer and Lynda Pratt (Romantic Circles, forthcoming summer 2010), no. 432 to Humphry Davy and no. 427 to Charles Danvers.

42. *Select Views*, 1810.

43. Charlotte Smith, *Ethelinde, or The Recluse of the Lake*, 1789; David Chandler, 'Supplying a Grace: Wordsworth's Tales of Romantic Cumbria', lecture given at the Wordsworth Winter School, Grasmere, February 2010.

44. Thomas Rose, *Westmorland, Cumberland, Durham, and Northumberland, illustrated*, 3 vols, 1832–5; reprinted in various publications including *The British Switzerland*, 1856–60, which is quoted above.

45. Burke, ed. cit., p. 186.

46. First published 1793, revised 1794.

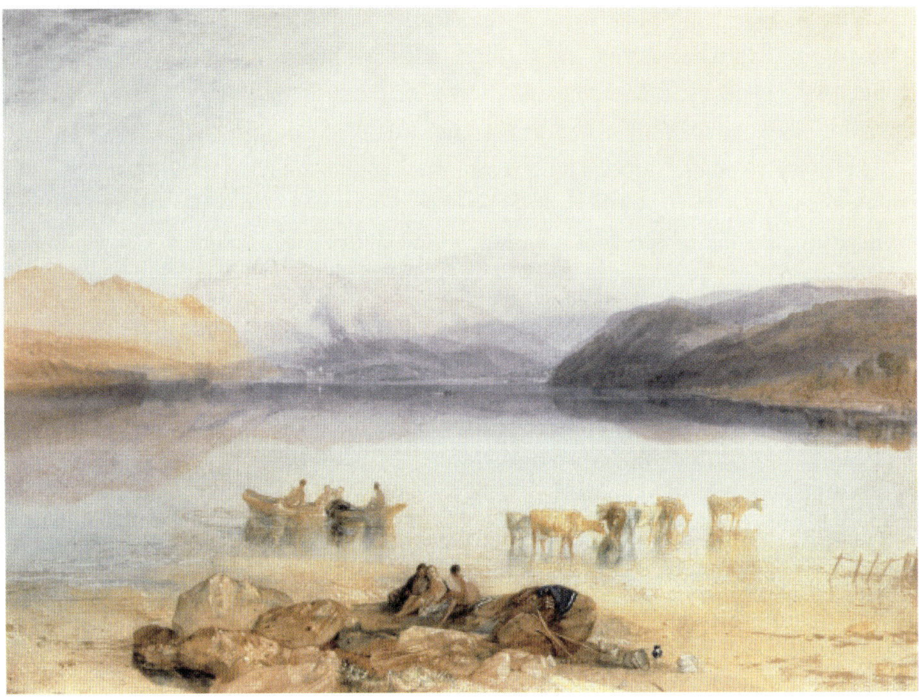

Fig. 10 J.M.W. Turner, *Ullswater, Cumberland*, watercolour, *c.*1835 (The Wordsworth Trust).

> Harmonious thoughts, a soul by truth refined,
> Entire affection for all human kind.

The societies that were founded in London and Liverpool and elsewhere for the encouragement and practice of the arts had a deeply moral purpose, seeing a liberal education as the key to a better life and a better society. Daniel Daulby may have pursued an Arcadian lifestyle when he retired to Rydal Mount in 1796, his family relishing their achievements as amateur farmers,[47] but earlier he had been active in the anti-slavery movement in Liverpool, as the dedication page of Holland's *Select Views of the Lakes* of 1792 makes clear. This essay began with a quotation from John Dalton's *Descriptive Poem addressed to Two Ladies*, a work of 1755 that has featured in books on the Lake District from West's *Guide* onwards. However, Dalton's poem extends much further than his eulogy on the vale of Keswick; he also devotes around half his poem to the mines under the sea at Whitehaven, conventionally couched in classical language and filled with overt references to Milton's Hell in *Paradise Lost* but displaying virtually no concern with the life of 'the sooty collier'.[48] Nothing could be further from this account than the equivalent published in 1816, in the letterpress to a series of topographical views by William Daniell that deliberately avoided the use of the word 'picturesque' in its title. Here the reader found an outspoken attack on the working conditions in the mines

47. Murdoch, 1984, pp. 44, 85.

48. The complete text can be found in *A Collection of Poems in Two Volumes. By Several Hands,* printed for G. Pearch, 1768, vol. 1, pp. 23–43.

and the misery and depravity of the women and children who toil there; a comparison between their plight and that of slaves in distant lands, lately relieved through British legislation, leads to an impassioned plea to the mine-owner, Lord Lonsdale, for their release from servitude (see cat. 73).

Truly the 'savage grandeur' of the district of the Lakes has inspired 'noblest thoughts' with consequences reaching far beyond what the eye can see from its highest peaks – or even from the floating cloud between Great Gable and Scafell on which Wordsworth invited the reader to join him at the beginning of his *Guide to the Lakes*.

A PRACTISED PENCIL, AND AN ELOQUENT PEN

Stephen Hebron

As part of his 1775 edition of the poems of Thomas Gray, William Mason published Gray's account of his tour of the Lake District, made in 1769. Mason thought highly of the poet's descriptive writing, praising, in a footnote, its 'judicious care', but he did not find it sufficiently informative. Only one account of the Lakes completely satisfied him, and that was because the author, William Gilpin, had accompanied his verbal descriptions with drawings; he had 'a practised pencil' as well as 'an eloquent pen'.[1]

Since the mid eighteenth century the beauties of the Lake District have provided a subject for both pencil and pen. Today's publications, be they guides, historical studies, coffee-table books or exhibition catalogues, typically integrate images with words. The most popular guidebooks for walkers of the last fifty years, by Alfred Wainwright, are painstaking and meticulous combinations of handwritten texts, maps and line drawings. But the flexibilities offered by modern lithographic, and now digital, printing were not, of course, available to the first writers on the Lake District. Copper engravings were expensive to produce, and had to be printed on a separate press from the type, and on a different kind of paper. Mason lamented that Gilpin's illustrated tour of the Lakes was still only in manuscript form, but admitted that 'the great expence of plates would make its publication almost impracticable'. More often than not, a writer's words had to stand alone, and the ability of language to communicate visual information about an unfamiliar landscape was thereby put rather critically to the test.

John Dalton published his *Descriptive Poem addressed to Two Ladies, at their return from viewing the mines near Whitehaven* (cat. 5) in a handsome quarto in 1755. The poem is essentially a rather conventional panegyric to Lord Lowther, who, unlike those noblemen who every summer rushed off to their continental villas, took a paternal interest in the prosperity of his regional property and in the well-being of its inhabitants. Thanks to him, Whitehaven had been transformed from an insignificant fishing village into a thriving port, and extensive coalmines had been sunk off the coast. Dalton begins with a description of the infernal splendours of these mines, and then gives, by way of comparison, descriptions first of the serene beauties of the River Lowther, and then of 'Sweet Keswick's vale', where one found the 'beauteous brook of Borrodale' and 'the rough rocks of dread Lodore':

1. In addition to the familiar slender stick of graphite, in the eighteenth and early nineteenth centuries 'pencil' also meant a 'paintbrush made with fine hair tapered to a point, *esp.* a small brush suitable for delicate work' (*OED*). More figuratively, a pencil signified artistic skill, while a pen was the instrument of authorship.

I view with wonder and delight,
A pleasing tho' an awful sight:
For, seen with them, the verdant Isles
Soften with more delicious smiles,
More tempting twine their opening bowers,
More lively glow the purple flowers,
More smoothly slopes the border gay,
In fairer circle bends the bay,
And last, to fix our wand'ring eyes,
Thy roofs, O Keswick, brighter rise
The lake and lofty hills between,
Where giant Skiddow shuts the scene.
  SUPREME of mountains, Skiddow, hail!
To whom all Britain sinks a vale!
Lo, his imperial brow I see
From foul usurping vapours free!
'Twere glorious now his side to climb,
Boldly to scale his top sublime ... (pp. 21–2)

Dalton here gives the earliest literary account of the scenery of the Lakes, but if separated from the place names his description could really be of any mountainous region. His audience, unless they knew Derwentwater, or the recently published engraving of the lake by William Bellers (cat. 3), would not have had a much clearer picture of what the area really looked like after reading the poem, beyond the fact that there was a vigorous cascade (Lodore), a valley of craggy cliffs (Borrowdale) and a high mountain (Skiddaw).

A Descriptive Poem had extensive notes by William Brownrigg, a resident of Whitehaven. Brownrigg aims to help the puzzled reader by elaborating upon Dalton's rather cryptic references to aspects of the mines: he explains, for instance, the noxious inflammable air, or 'damps', that made the mines so dangerous; the newly improved fire engine; and the curious sparking wheel with which the mines were lit (unlike naked flames, sparks did not ignite the damps). For the later parts of the poem he gives further information about the places Dalton is describing. Brownrigg thought this necessary: in a supplementary 'Letter to the Author', printed immediately after Dalton's lines, he expresses his admiration for the 'poetic landskips', but also his worry that the general unfamiliarity of the Lake District would prevent Dalton from successfully communicating its beauties:

> Much of the pleasure which we receive from descriptions of the country must arise from calling to mind those rural scenes that have given us delight, and from comparing them with their representations; and observing with what art and judgment those representations are copied after nature. ... it must be owned that ... you labour under some disadvantage, from the choice of your subject in a retired part; which does not fall so much under the eye of the curious as Windsor Forest and some other places, whose charms have been displayed by some of our best poets. (p. 26)

But thankfully, Brownrigg goes on, Dalton's brother, an artist, had supplied some illustrations which hopefully will 'remove the difficulty here hinted at; and the Public will have the pleasure of seeing the sister arts mutually reflecting light upon each other, and conspiring, by a friendly emulation, to set off these beautiful scenes to the best advantage' (p. 26). It is uncertain whether or not these drawings were ever engraved; at any rate, the images have not survived.

It was the wish to share a pleasure, and to provide detailed information, that inspired the next literary description of the Lake District. John Brown originally wrote his *Description of the Lake at Keswick* as part of a letter to a friend, Lord Lyttelton, who did not know the Lakes. It was first published in 1766 in the *London Chronicle* and then, posthumously, in a series of pamphlets (cat. 9). Brown describes the cultivated fields, projecting cliffs and more distant mountains that together create the permanent form and character of Derwentwater, and then, in companionable fashion, takes the reader on a journey around the lake, pointing out its '*varying* or *accidental* beauties': the perpetually changing shapes, tints and hues; the contrasts of light and shade; the different effects wrought by the weather. In conclusion, Brown writes that 'a walk by still moonlight … among these enchanting dales, opens a scene of such delicate beauty, repose, and solemnity, as exceeds all descriptions'. Brown was an amateur artist as well as a writer, but he made no attempt to complement his description of Keswick with visual images. In his text he does, however, make reference to three celebrated artists, Claude Lorrain, Salvator Rosa and Gaspard Dughet:

> the full perfection of Keswick consists of three circumstances, *beauty*, *horror*, and *immensity* united … But to give you a complete idea of these three perfections, as they are joined in Keswick, would require the united powers of Claude, Salvator, and Poussin. The first should throw his delicate sunshine over the cultivated vales, the scattered cots, the groves, the lake, and wooded islands. The second should dash out the horror of the rugged cliffs, the steeps, the hanging woods, and foaming waterfalls; while the grand pencil of Poussin should crown the whole with the majesty of the impending mountains.

The agricultural reformer and intrepid traveller Arthur Young visited the Lake District not long after Brown wrote his *Description*, as part of an extensive tour through northern England. He published a full account of this journey, as a series of letters, in his *Six Months Tour through the North of England* (3 volumes, 1770). This was principally a research trip, a survey of the relative wealth of northern England's towns and villages, and there is a certain amount of purely factual information ('Labour', 'Provisions', 'Implements', 'Building'). Interspersed with this, however, are passages of natural description, in which Young paid tribute to the 'picturesque', the 'sublime' and the 'horribly romantic'. Occasionally he felt the need for illustration. Describing his own journey by boat around Derwentwater, 'so famous all over England' (II, p. 214), he was particularly struck by the waterfalls, and printed three rather crude engravings to illustrate his descriptions. Later on he attempts to convey in words what he suspects cannot really be described, scenes 'which call for the pencil of a genius to catch graces from nature beyond the reach of the most elaborate art'. 'It would be mere vanity to attempt to describe a scene which beggars all description', he writes of a view of Windermere from Bowness, 'but that you may have some faint idea of the outlines of this wonderful picture, I will just give the particulars of which it consists.' The reality of this particular view, he maintains, is beyond the reach of writer or artist, so he calls upon his reader's imagination:

> Strain your imagination to command the idea of so noble an expanse of water thus gloriously environed; spotted with islands more beautiful than would have issued from the pencil of the happiest painter. Picture the mountains rearing their majestic heads with native sublimity; the vast rocks boldly projecting their terrible craggy points: And in the path of beauty, the variegated inclosures of the most charming verdure, hanging to the eye in every picturesque form that can grace a landscape, with the most exquisite touches of *la belle nature:* If you raise your fancy to something infinitely beyond this assemblage of rural elegancies, you may have a faint notion of the unexampled beauties of this ravishing landscape. (II, 241)

The true beauty of such a landscape, in other words, was more closely realised in one's imagination than in any literary or even artistic imitation.

In addition to the limitations of language, these three early writers – Dalton, Brown and Young – were conscious of something else: the need to be diverting as well as informative, and, as far as possible, keep things short. Dalton breaks off his description of Skiddaw and restrains his muse: 'Hills, rocks, and dales have been too long / The subject of thy rambling song'. 'So much for what I would call the *permanent* beauties of this astonishing scene' writes Brown in his letter. 'Were I not afraid of being tiresome, I could now dwell as long on its *varying* or *accidental* beauties'. Young spares his reader as lengthy a description of Windermere as he had given him of Derwentwater, 'as I have already troubled you with several recitals of these water expeditions'. Such polite concern for the reader's patience was itself a literary convention, but these writers are nevertheless aware that, not to put too fine a point on it, extended descriptions of scenery could be rather boring, the eighteenth-century equivalent of being shown someone else's holiday snaps. William Hutchinson's *An Excursion to the Lakes, in Westmoreland and Cumberland, August 1773* was first published in 1774 (anonymously), and again a year later (cat. 11). It was popular because it was an entertaining account of a summer excursion. Hutchinson included a number of detailed delineations of the scenery, particularly around Borrowdale, which were rather derivative of earlier writers, particularly Brown, but mixed them up with passages of antiquarian study and local history, with religious reflections and musings on the health-giving delights of travel. Scenic description is lightened with anecdote: boating on Ullswater to the sound of echoing guns and french horns, or being surprised by a sudden thunder-storm on the summit of Skiddaw: 'Our guide laid upon the earth terrified and amazed, in his ejaculations accusing us of presumption and impiety; – danger made us solemn indeed, we had no where to fly for safety, no place to cover our heads; to descend was to rush into the very inflammable vapour from whence our perils proceeded, to stay was equally hazardous ...' (pp. 160–1).

The first edition of Hutchinson's *Excursion* contained no illustrations, save a small vignette of Bowes Castle on the title page, but he and his companion (his younger brother Richard) nevertheless travelled with pencil in hand as well as pen, sketching not only the scenery but unsuspecting locals, like a girl they met somewhere between Thirlmere and Grasmere: 'My companion, in a rapture, snatched out his pencil, and began to imitate; but the unaffected impatiency, and sweet confusion of the maid, overcame our wishes to detain her, and we let her pass reluctantly' (p. 166). Richard Hutchinson died unexpectedly, aged twenty-three, before the publication of the second edition of the *Excursion*. Had he survived, then this edition may well have contained engravings of his landscape studies. Here William Hutchinson mourns his brother as 'my fellow traveller, my draughtsman. ... With him the unfinished draughts of those admirable views were lost' (pp. 25–6).

Thomas Gray's account of his Lake District tour was published by William Mason in the same year as the second edition of Hutchinson's *Excursion*, and just four years after Gray's death (cat. 12). When Gray made his journey in 1769 he had only Dalton's poem and Brown's letter as literary precedents. Not that he ever looked upon his Lakes journal, which took the form of a series of letters to his sick friend Dr Wharton, as something that might be published: the passages where he equates the scale and dangers of the Lakes with those of the Alps are obviously fanciful, and probably playful, and the quieter, reflective passages are affecting because of their private tone:

> In the evening I walked alone down to the lake by the side of Crow-park after sunset, and saw the solemn colouring of night draw on, the last gleam of sunshine fading away on the hill-tops, the deep serene of the waters, and the long shadows of the mountains thrown across them, till they nearly touched the hithermost shore. At a distance were heard the murmurs of many waterfalls, not audible in the day-time; I wished for the moon, but she was *dark to me and silent,*
>
> *Hid in her vacant interlunar cave.* (p. 359)

In the preface to the second edition of *Lyrical Ballads* (1800), Wordsworth distanced himself from Gray's 'curiously elaborate' poetic diction. By contrast, he admired Gray's Lakes journal for the simplicity of its descriptions. What is more, passages such as the one quoted above are quietly as expressive of the writer's personality as they are of the landscape being described. One, in fact, enhances the other. On his 1818 walking tour of northern England and Scotland, John Keats also wrote journal letters to a sick friend, in this case his younger brother Tom. '[D]escriptions are bad at all times', he told Tom in an early letter, 'I did not intend to give you any; but how can I help it? I am anxious you should taste a little of our pleasure'.[2] Writing to his brother and sister-in-law from Scotland, Keats apologised for a 'dull specimen of description': 'For myself I hate descriptions. I would not send it were it not mine.'[3]

The literary qualities of Gray's writing would seem to obviate the need for illustration, but William Mason still felt it was lacking: 'Without the pencil nothing indeed is to be described with precision', he commented in his edition of Gray's journal, 'and even then that pencil ought to be in the very hand of the writer, ready to supply with outlines every thing that his pen cannot express by words.' Mason does admit to being 'entertained by well-written descriptions', not because of their precision, but

> because they amuse when they do not inform me; and because, after I have seen the places described, they serve to recall to my memory the original scene, almost as well as the truest drawing or picture. In the meanwhile, my mind is flattered by thinking it has acquired some conception of the place, and rests contented in an innocent error, which nothing but ocular proof can detect, and which, when detected, does not diminish the pleasure I had before received, but augments it by superadding the charms of comparison and verification. (pp. 376–7)

The year after the publication of Gray's tour, 1776, Richard Cumberland published his 'Ode to the Sun', a poem written, and set, in the Lakes (cat. 14). Cumberland was conscious of his predecessors: in his poem he entreats 'Keswick's vale' to mourn Gray, who 'saw your scenes in harmony divine', and in a preface addressed to George Romney he commented on the way Gray's descriptions could 'give life to scenes which I should have conceived nothing but the pencil could convey'. In this preface Cumberland also published, for the first time, the poem with which John Brown had originally concluded his descriptive letter, 'Now sunk the sun'. But he shared Mason's doubts about the usefulness of the kind of writing that emulated the informative function of maps. Did Romney, an artist, get more from it?

> As for the minute delineations, which some travellers affect to give of scenes that come under their contemplation, they seldom convey to my apprehension any map of the place they describe. To you perhaps, whose pictures are language, language may be a picture; and as I know you can paint our very words, words may in return paint that to you, of which a less intuitive mind takes no conception; the bulk of mankind however collect little from these descriptions but the amusement of reading them; and the most they can effect is to refresh the memories of them, who have been on the spot, or to inspire those, who have not been, with a resolution of going thither. (p. 6)

2. Keats to Tom Keats, 27 June 1818; *Letters of John Keats*, ed. Hyder Edward Rollins (Cambridge, MA, 1958), I, p. 301.

3. Keats to George and Georgiana Keats, 18 September 1819 (copying for them an earlier letter); ibid., II, p. 199.

The idea that descriptions of natural scenery served, first and foremost, as an enticement for lovers of landscape to come and see the real thing, was the basis upon which Thomas West published, in 1778, the first Lake District guidebook (cat. 18). His *Guide to the Lakes* was written, as the title page stated, not just for *the Lovers of Landscape Studies* but for *all who have visited, or intend to visit the Lakes in Cumberland, Westmorland and Lancashire*. West's prose contains a generous amount of description, plentifully embellished with adjectives (beautiful, awful, grand, sublime, varied, pleasing, picturesque); he quotes Gray, Young and Mason; but these descriptions are interspersed with more practical information. Guiding his readers to optimum viewing points, or 'stations', around the lakes, he instructs them to turn this way or that, and points out particular rocks, trees, gates and buildings as navigational aids as they follow his recommended paths. Views are described as if the reader were actually before them, and indeed one can imagine tourists travelling with West's *Guide* in hand, looking up at the view, then down at the page for further information. What is more, West assures the reader that he will not spoil the 'agreeable surprise' (p. 3) by giving too much away, maintaining that the pleasure derived from accidental beauties 'is personal, and best understood when received' (p. 15). Description simply leads one to the reality:

> To describe every picturesque view, that this region of landscape presents would be endless labour; and did language furnish expression to convey ideas of the innumerable changes, in the many grand constituent objects in these magnificent scenes, the imagination would be fatigued with the detail, and description weakened by redundancy. It is more pleasing to speculative curiosity to play upon, what it wishes not to be informed of, the difference among such scenes as approach the nearest in likeness, and the agreement between such as appear most discordant; this is the sport of fancy, or the result of taste and judgment, from self-information, and has the greatest effect on the mind. The province of the Guide is to point out the station, and leave to the company the enjoyment of reflection, and pleasures of the imagination. (p. 110)

Ever mindful of practicalities, West reassures his readers that Gray's digressions on the dangers of the Lakes were 'hyperboles, the sport of fancy that he was pleased to indulge himself in.' The mountains were not as massive as the Alps: 'SKIDDAW, HELVELLYN, and CATCHIDECAM,[4] are but dwarfs when compared with mount MAUDITE above the lake of GENEVA, and the guardian mountains of the RHONE'. Nor were the roads dangerous: 'If the roads in some places are narrow and difficult, they are at least safe; no villainous banditti haunt the mountains; innocent people live in the dells. Every

4. The endlessly various spelling of place names (often presented, as here, in small capitals) is one of the pleasures of reading these early books on the Lake District. Arthur Young apologised twice for his 'many barbarous, and, probably, wrong spelt names', explaining that he never saw them in print, and so was forced to approximate spellings from what he heard from locals. So we find, for example, 'Hull's-water' (Ullswater) and 'Basnet'(Bassenthwaite) in Hutchinson, and 'Seat-sandby' (Seat Sandal) in West.

cottager is narrative of all he knows; and mountain virtue, and pastoral hospitality are found at every farm.' (pp. 139–40)

The *Guide* was immediately popular, but West died before he could complete a second edition. The task was taken over by a Lancaster schoolmaster, William Cockin, who added the early descriptions by Gray, Dalton, Brown, Cumberland and others to the book as Addenda (cat. 19). At the same time, Cockin published a poem of his own, *Ode to the Genius of the Lakes*, which celebrated the growing popularity of the region (cat. 20). For Cockin, it was the people that made the place special. In its former state it was unappreciated; now, in 'these happier days of genuine taste', visitors arrived every summer 'in gayest trim' and roved over the hills 'with raptur'd eye'. And the landscape, 'whose pleasure is to please', is grateful to them. Cockin's visitors included budding young poets who tried their hand at celebrating the landscape in verse. His own poem is such an amateur attempt, written, he writes in his preface, not from any literary ambition, but in the hope that it will fall into the hands of '*actual tourists*'. Writing, like amateur sketching, thus became part of the Lakes experience.

Meanwhile, the account by Gilpin that Mason had seen and so admired had been circulating widely in its manuscript form, including at court. Now in the Bodleian Library,[5] its eight volumes comprise 834 pages of Gilpin's handwritten text and are illustrated with maps, diagrams and plans, and over 150 landscape drawings. Each volume has its own index. Gilpin entitled the work, based upon a journey he had made in 1772, 'A tour through *England*; more particularly the mountainous parts of *Cumberland*, and *Westmorland*: with a view chiefly to illustrate the principles of picturesque beauty in landscape'. 'Picturesque' he had defined in 1768 as 'a term expressive of that peculiar kind of beauty, which is agreeable in a picture'.[6] Preferring rugged scenery to the smooth, regular lines of the conventionally beautiful, he judged the landscape according to his picturesque principles, and adapted it, if necessary, in his illustrations.

Gilpin worked towards a printed version of his manuscript tour, worrying over how best to reproduce the illustrations. *Observations, Relative Chiefly to Picturesque Beauty ... on Several Parts of England; Particularly the Mountains, and Lakes of Cumberland, and Westmoreland* was eventually published, with rather flat aquatints, in 1786. Contrary to the praise Mason had given the manuscript in 1775, the aquatint illustrations, Gilpin wrote in his preface, were not intended as exact portraits, precise delineations of particular scenes. Rather, they were intended as either illustrations of his picturesque principles (principles which indeed make up a significant portion of the printed text), or general impressions of the Lake District scenery. 'It is certainly an error in landscape-painting, to comprehend too much', he wrote, 'it turns a picture into a map' (I, p. 154). Gilpin also reflects upon the limitations of language when it came to expressing visual ideas:

5. Oxford, Bodleian Library, MS. Eng. misc. e. 488/1–8.
6. William Gilpin, *An Essay on Prints* (London, 1768), p. 2.

> Language is equally unable to convey these to the eye; as the eye is to convey the various divisions of sound to the ear.
>
> The pencil, it is true, offers a more perfect mode of description. It speaks a language more intelligible; and describes the scene in stronger, and more varied terms. The shapes, the hues of objects it delineates, and marks, with more exactness. … But … all that words can express, or even the pencil describe, are gross, insipid substitutes of the living scene. We may be pleased with the description, and the picture: but the soul can *feel* neither, unless the force of our own imagination aid the poet's, or the painter's art; exalt the idea; *and picture things unseen*. (II, pp. 10–11)

Gilpin's theories are not always clear, and sometimes he even tied himself up in knots, but he always insisted that they were no more than 'amusements', like drawing with the pencil, and writing with the pen. And he was not attempting exact delineations of the landscape: he left that to others. In the preface to the third edition of the *Observations* (1792), he wrote that he had seen what he considered to be the most accurate 'portraits' of the Lakes yet published, the views by Joseph Farington (cat. 27–8). Farington's engravings were accompanied by letterpress descriptions written by William Wordsworth's uncle, William Cookson, with parallel translations into French. Cookson very competently gave his readers what they needed: he told them what they were looking at, provided some historical information, and then concluded with a bit of lyrical description. He drew quite extensively on earlier accounts, particularly Thomas Gray's, and his texts are more like keys to the illustrations than separate descriptions to stand on their own merits. He himself thought them rather uninspired. Nevertheless, the book exemplified the amalgam of precise image and informative text that Mason had so admired in Gilpin's manuscript tour.

⋆

At the end of the eighteenth century and the beginning of the nineteenth, the various texts summarised above became increasingly read, quoted and anthologised as the Lake District grew ever more popular. Divorced from the liveliness of their original occasion and purpose, they became increasingly clichéed and static. Writers of any originality were wary of imitating them. Keats began his 1818 tour with a few natural descriptions, but turned increasingly to the people he encountered; he liked them 'better than scenery' he said. And as he told his sister on his return, he had received 'a doze of the Picturesque with which I ought to be contented for some time'.[7] 'Of the fashionable travellers, who pass through Grasmere in the summer months, I have observed no small number *asleep*,' Samuel Taylor Coleridge wrote in the *Morning Post*. 'A much greater number are *reading* descriptions of the place, or lost in admiration of the landscape in aqua-tinta. Still, however, I hope, and trust, that a majority will remain of those, who have kept their eyes open, and

7. Keats to Fanny Keats, 12 April 1819 (*Letters*, II, p. 52).

their hearts awake.'[8] He himself went out on the fells and tried to catch the most transitory impressions of light and form and movement in scintillating notebook entries: 'how shall I express the Banks waters all fused Silver, that House too its slates rainwet silver in the sun, & its shadows running down in the water like a column – the Woods on the right shadowy with Sunshine, and in front of me the sloping hollow of sunpatched Fields, sloping up into Hills so playful, the playful Hills so going away in snow-streaked savage black mountain'.[9]

Only one of the great Romantic writers sought to add to printed Lake District literature, and that, unsurprisingly, was William Wordsworth, who in 1809 consented to introduce a set of illustrations by Joseph Wilkinson (cat. 78). Published the following year, Wilkinson's prints rivalled in scale, if nothing else, the earlier series of engravings by Farington. Wordsworth's text appeared, anonymously, as an introduction to them. Ten years later he published a revised version of this text as *A Topographical Description of the Country of the Lakes, in the North of England* (cat. 79). Numerous separate editions appeared thereafter.

Wordsworth's *Description* has an authority and a confidence that, quite apart from its exceptional literary quality, puts it in a class of its own amongst Lake District literature. He begins by asking the reader to adopt the station of a cloud midway between Great Gable and Scafell. From here he describes the lakes spreading out around the observer like the spokes of a wheel. After this striking beginning he then concentrates, in the first section, 'View of the country as formed by nature', on the various physical characteristics of the landscape. He describes the MOUNTAINS, 'lifting themselves in ridges like the waves of a tumultuous sea', covered in turf 'rendered rich and green by the moisture of the climate', and in their rocky parts 'bluish, or hoary grey'; the winding VALES; the LAKES, bodies 'of still water under the influence of no current; reflecting therefore the clouds, the light, and all the imagery of the sky and surrounding hills'; the ISLANDS and TARNS; and the WOODS of oak, ash, birch, and wych-elm 'which intermingle beautifully with the fields.'[10]

Wordsworth describes the natural features of the area with the precision and focus of a miniaturist, from the fine blue gravel thrown up by waves on to the margins of the lakes, to the lichens and mosses ('their profusion, beauty, and variety, exceed those of any other country I have seen'). These details are not haphazardly scattered about, however, but intricately woven together to create a single and harmonious picture. There is an 'endlessly playing into each other of form and colour'; the changing light creates innumerable intermixtures of shapes and tints. The principal unifying element is water, which in its various forms creates effects 'like that of magic': the mists

8. Article of 20 November 1802; *Collected Works of Samuel Taylor Coleridge: Essays on his Times*, ed. David V. Erdman, 3 vols (Princeton, 1978), I, p. 406.

9. *Notebooks of Samuel Taylor Coleridge*, ed. Kathleen Coburn *et al.*, 10 vols (Princeton, 1957–2002), I, 549 5.121 ff27-25v.

10. Quoted here from the edition published separately in 1822 as *A Description of the Scenery of the Lakes in the North of England*.

and vapours rising from the lakes at dawn which 'give a visionary character to everything around them'; the 'fleecy clouds resting upon the hill-tops … how pregnant with imagination for the poet!'; the pellucid surfaces of the lakes which hold perfect reflections of the mountains and sky; the infinite number of brooks and torrents; the sudden showers flying from hill to hill, 'not less grateful to the eye than finely interwoven passages of gay and sad music are touching to the ear'.

In the second part of the *Description*, 'Aspects of the Country, as Affected by its inhabitants', Wordsworth treats those features of the Lake District that are 'indebted to the hand of man'. From the earliest times, when 'aboriginal colonies of the Celtic tribes were first driven or drawn towards it', to the recent past, Wordsworth describes the prevailing characteristics of life in the Lakes as modesty, industry, and deep seclusion. The fields, even the sides of the mountains, are intersected by stone walls which divide the land into homesteads, crofts and mountain-enclosures. The cottages 'are scattered over the vallies, and under the hill sides, and on the rocks'; they are to be found 'in the more retired dales, without any intrusion of more assuming buildings', and are linked by narrow lanes, pathways and bridges. The picture Wordsworth paints of this ideal, secluded life has a visionary quality:

> Thus has been given a faithful description, the minuteness of which the reader will pardon, of the face of this country as it was, and had been through centuries, till within the last sixty years. Towards the head of these Dales was found a perfect Republic of Shepherds and Agriculturists, among whom the plough of each man was confined to the maintenance of his own family, or to the occasional accommodation of his neighbour. Two or three cows furnished each family with milk and cheese. The chapel was the only edifice that presided over these dwellings, the supreme head of this pure Commonwealth; the members of which existed in the midst of a powerful empire, like an ideal society or an organized community, whose constitution had been imposed and regulated by the mountains which protected it. (pp. 63–4)

Such was the case, at least, until 'the last sixty years'. In the third section of the *Description*, 'Changes, and Rules of Taste for Preventing Their Bad Effects', Wordsworth turns to the recent past, and the discovery of the Lake District by those who 'wander over the island in search of sequestered spots, distinguished as they might accidentally have learned, for the sublimity or beauty of the forms of Nature there to be seen'. He writes approvingly of John Brown's letter, 'in which the attractions of the Vale of Keswick were delineated with a powerful pencil, and a feeling of a genuine enthusiast', and particularly of Thomas Gray's journal. Here, however, his writing acquires an elegiac strain: Gray died 'soon after his forlorn and melancholy pilgrimage'; his journal 'feelingly showed how the gloom of ill health and low spirits had been irradiated by objects'; and he had seen the Lake District before it had been seized on by travellers and settlers, and 'instantly defaced by the intrusion'. If the first part of Wordsworth's description is rich with intricate and interconnecting details, and the second a visionary reflection upon a way of life, then the third part is more like a polemic. Wordsworth complains of insensitive newcomers who build garish houses on the top of hills for the views they afford, 'improve' the appearance of islands, and plant out-of-place trees like the fast-growing larch. He sees such changes everywhere, and his feelings about the celebrity of the Lake District are mixed. On the one hand, he understands that the region is a source of delight for persons of good taste, who deem it 'a sort of national property, in which every man has a right and interest who has an eye to perceive and a heart to enjoy.' On the other hand, the *Description* is an elegy for an irretrievably altered place, and a vanishing way of life.

In a letter to Catherine Clarkson, Dorothy Wordsworth described Wordsworth's *Description* as 'the only regular and I may say *scientific* account of the present and past state and appearance of the country that has yet appeared.'[11] In a later letter to Lady Beaumont, Wordsworth himself explained that 'what I wished to accomplish was to give a model of the manner in which topographical descriptions ought to be executed, in order to their being either useful or intelligible, by evolving truly and distinctly one appearance from another.'[12] Despite this scientific, informative intent and the emphasis on delineation and appearance, Wordsworth never expresses any anxiety about the difficulties of verbal description. Nor, unlike earlier writers on the Lake District, does he ever feel a need for images. Indeed, for its second publication, in 1820, all references to Wilkinson's prints were removed. But despite their anxieties, those earlier writers never really needed images either. What marks each of them out is the individuality of their voice. It is this, as much as the physical and historical information imparted, which gave life to their descriptive writing, and which played so important a part in the discovery of the Lake District: the early enthusiasm of Dalton and Brown; the sensitive observations of Gray; the pleasant diversions of Hutchinson; the informative prose of West; the theoretical amusements of Gilpin. Wordsworth, above all, infuses his descriptions with a depth of attachment and an elegiac intensity that are as strong today as when they were written. The depth of his emotional and intellectual attachment to the area is apparent in every sentence, and he draws upon, and expresses, the riches of his memory and imagination as much as the physical reality of the landscape. The Lake District is always being rediscovered, and its particular beauties re-expressed by anyone with a practised pencil or an eloquent pen.

11. Dorothy Wordsworth to Catherine Clarkson, 18 November 1809; *The Letters of William and Dorothy Wordsworth. II. The Middle Years*, part 1, ed. Ernest de Selincourt, rev. Mary Moorman, 1969, p. 372.

12. Wordsworth to Lady Beaumont, 10 May 1810; ibid., p. 404.

CATALOGUE

NOTE TO THE CATALOGUE

Authors:

CFP Cecilia Powell
SH Stephen Hebron

Abbreviations:

ARA Asssociate Member of the Royal Academy
BI British Institution
RA Royal Academy *or* Royal Academician
SPWC Society of Painters in Water Colours

All works belong to the Wordsworth Trust, apart from cat. 36, 45 and 65 which are on long-term loan to the Wordsworth Trust.

All measurements are in centimetres, height before width.

For print-making terms see the note on pp. 177–8.

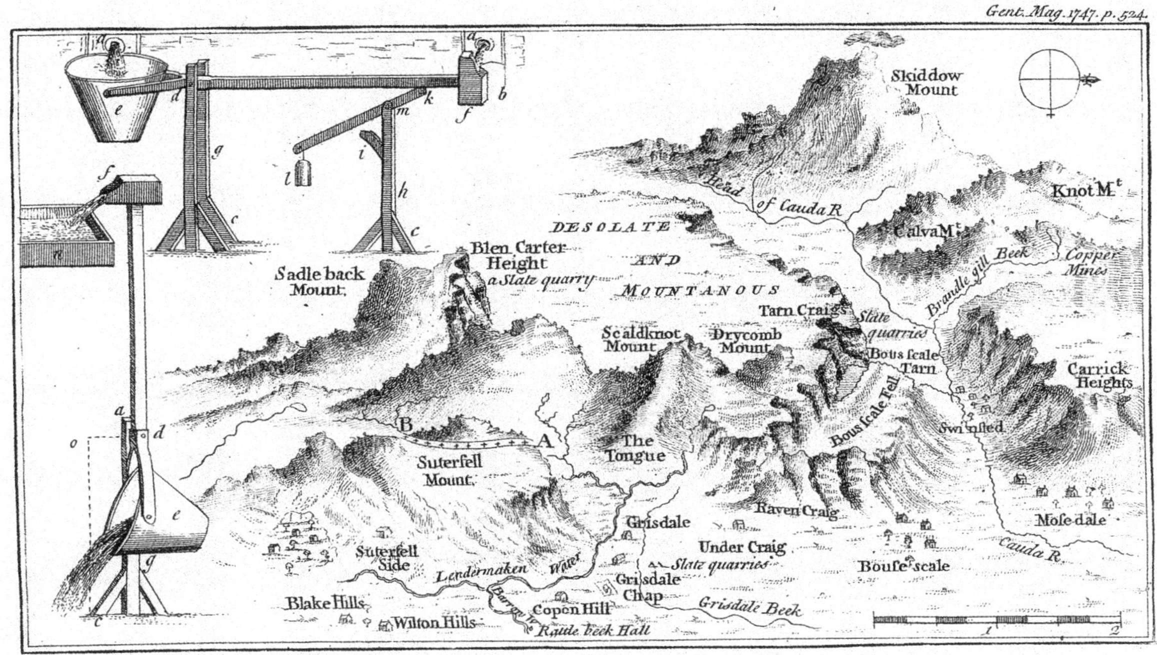

Cat. 1

I

After GEORGE SMITH (1700–73)
The Caudebec Fells
1747
Engraving, 11.4 × 19.6 cm
Engraved inscription: above right, *Gent. Mag. 1747. p. 524.*
Gift of Nick and Cecilia Powell, in memory of Bill Ruddick, 2010

A Scottish émigré living near Carlisle, the schoolmaster and polymath George Smith was a regular contributor to the *Gentleman's Magazine*, a monthly compendium of learned articles and topical discussions established in London in 1731. In November 1747 he published an article, 'A Journey to Caudebec Fells, with a Map and Description of the Same', describing the fells around the river Caldew as 'that lateral detachment of the *British Alps*, which overspreads great part of *Cumberland*, distinguished by insuperable precipices, and tow'ring peaks, and exhibiting landskapes of a quite different and more romantic air than any part of the general ridge, and of nearer affinity to the *Switzerland* Alps'. His intention had been to visit the blacklead mines, 'the peculiar product of these mountains', but the weather proved so unfavourable that he deferred that excursion (see cat. 2) and concentrated his attention on the stretch of the Caldew valley shown in the right-hand part of cat. 1. There he found villages in the deep narrow valley that for two months of the year felt no more benefit from the sun's rays than the Cimmerians of antiquity or the Laplanders in the northernmost parts of Norway and met villagers who believed they saw stars reflected in the river at midday in midwinter. In his article he identifies plants, shrubs and trees, comments on ravens, analyses rocks, and describes the course of the Caldew and its tributaries. His map makes no claim to be a work of art; it is functional, showing the territory vividly and informatively, with mines, quarries and settlements clearly marked. Contour lines were not yet in use so mountains and hills are depicted as in a bird's-eye view; the map has a scale, but is oriented with the north shown to the right. However, it undoubtedly captures the 'romantic air' of the northern fells, contrasting known and documented river valleys with an area that was marked *'DESOLATE AND MOUNTANOUS'* and which we know today as the most northerly part of the Lake District. Both the map and Smith's article are important stages in the exploration and discovery of the Lakes in the mid eighteenth century.

Smith devoted one page of his article to a mysterious phenomenon reported to him on his travels: on midsummer's eve in 1735, and again on the same

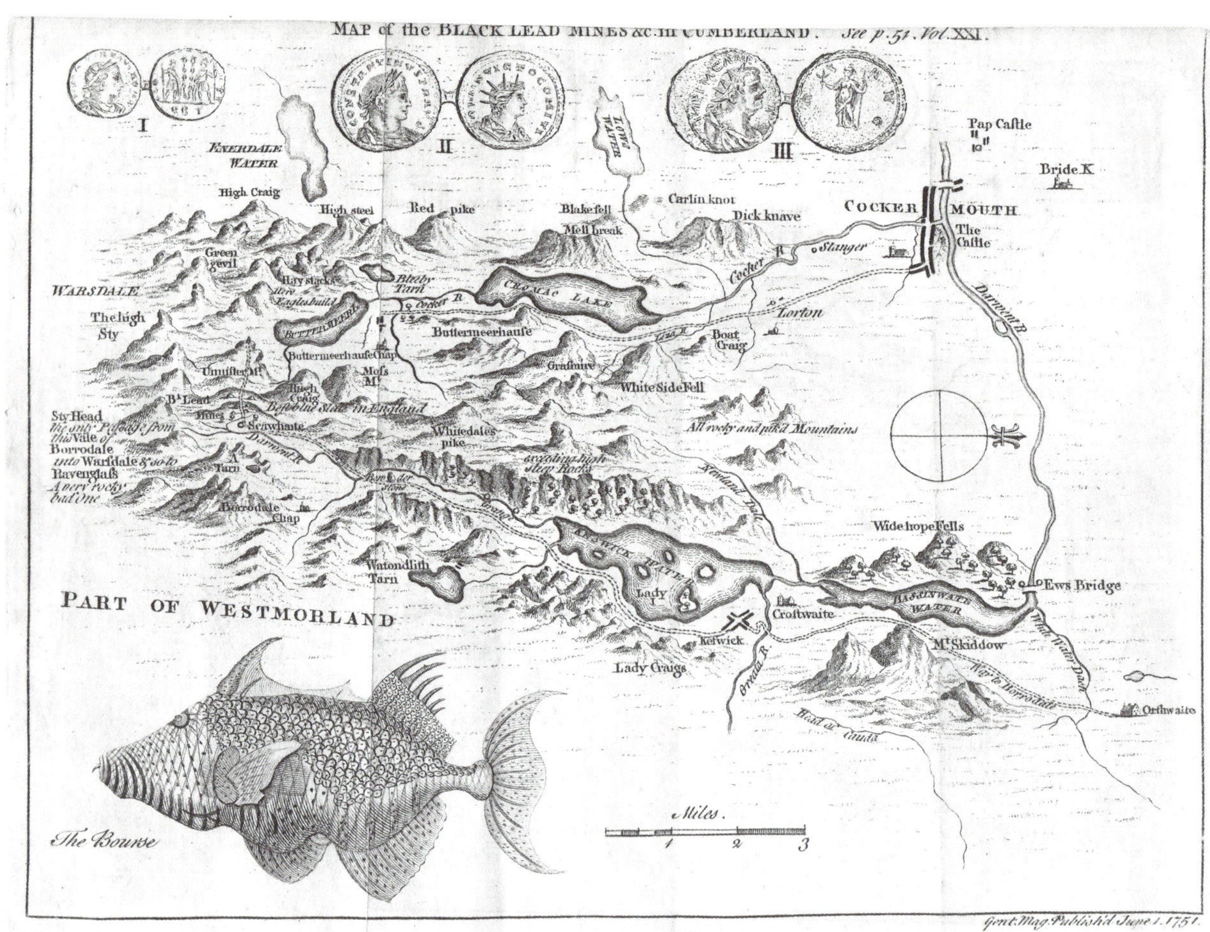

Cat. 2

day on three further occasions, an army had been witnessed on the side of Souterfell, marching from north to south for over an hour (marked A … B on the map). Although the reports had 'the air of a romance', he considered them scientifically, attributing the phenomenon to an undulating or agitated lambent meteor. The diagrams to the left of the map, showing a machine for raising water, have no connection with his account of his journey but illustrate the article that followed it. CFP

2

After GEORGE SMITH (1700–73)
Map of the Black Lead Mines &c. in Cumberland
1751
Engraving, 20.1 × 24.8 cm
Engraved inscriptions: above centre, with title and *See p. 51. Vol. XXI*; below right, *Gent. Mag. Publish'd June 1. 1751.*
Gift of Nick and Cecilia Powell, in memory of Bill Ruddick, 2010

The black mineral graphite (also known as blacklead and plumbago) was first discovered near Seathwaite in Borrowdale in the sixteenth century and soon became a highly valuable commodity, being used in the manufacture of cannon balls and round-shot. Another important use of graphite was, and remains, as a writing material – hence its name, dating from 1789. The Seathwaite deposit uniquely consisting of soft sticks, these were initially bound in wool or string for the marking of sheep and later sheathed in wood to create pencils; England thus enjoyed a monopoly of pencil production until the mid nineteenth century. The mines were one of the wonders of the Lakes, attracting the regular attention of tourists; they were also well guarded and only rarely opened but from time to time they and their guardians were attacked by thieves. When the *Gentleman's Magazine* reported, in January 1751, that a 'gang of villains' had recently made such an attempt, George Smith contributed an account of the visit he had paid to the mines in August 1749 (postponed from 1747; see cat. 1). This was immediately printed in the February issue of the *Gentleman's Magazine* with a fold-out map illustrating his route (cat. 2) appearing in the issue for May. (Its publication date, 'June 1. 1751', reflects the fact that the magazine was published retrospectively, providing, *inter alia*, a chronicle of events for the month named on its cover.) As was customary with the magazine, the page contains illustrations for several different articles; the array of ancient coins (found near Portsmouth) and the 'uncommon Fish called a Bourse' have, sadly, no connection with Smith's excursion.

While Smith's article is highly informative and scientific on the subject of blacklead, his extended descriptions of scenery often verge on the poetical with frequent allusions to classical mythology: the islands on Derwentwater (called Keswick Water on his map) were 'so many *Ortygias*, or islands of *Calypso*'; Borrowdale, entered through 'a *Herculean* streight', 'would have filled a poetical imagination with the ideas of the *Dryades*, the *Bacchum in remotis*, and other fables of antiquity'. Elsewhere his reactions to scenery, both terrible and beautiful, look forward to later, more famous, accounts of the Lake District. Of the view from Skiddaw he wrote, 'The spot upon which I stood is one intire shiver of slate, and the precipice to the westward is frightful.' While Skiddaw and its neighbours 'have the appearance of huge fragments of rock, irregularly heaped on one another', in the nearby prospects 'nature has lavished such variety of beauty as can scarce be believed upon report, or imagined by the most luxuriant fancy'; the vale of Bassenthwaite, 'watered by a fine lake', appeared 'like a paradise to the West' with 'a very pleasing and romantic appearance'. When Smith and his companion reached their final destination above the mines, they were appalled at 'the horrid projection of vast promontories; the vicinity of the clouds, the thunder of the explosions in the slate quarries, the dreadful solitude, the distance of the plain below, and the mountains heaped on mountains that were piled around us, desolate, and waste, like the ruins of a world which we only had survived, excited such ideas of horror as are not to be expressed. We turned from this fearful prospect afraid even of ourselves.' Smith's commentary had a perfect counterpart in his pictorial map with its subtly differentiated depiction of hills and crags, wooded fells and barren peaks, enlivened by such annotations as 'Here Eagles build' and 'Best blue Slate in England'. CFP

3

JEAN-BAPTISTE-CLAUDE CHATELAIN and FRANCIS RAVENET after WILLIAM BELLERS (fl. 1734–73)
A View of Derwent-Water, Towards Borrodale
1752
Etching and engraving, 41 × 50.5 cm
Engraved inscriptions: below, with title (followed by sub-title *A Lake near Keswick in Cumberland*) and names of artist (*Painted after Nature by William Bellers*) and engravers (*Chatelin*); below left, *Printed and Sold by William Bellers in Poppins Court, Fleet Street, LONDON*; below right, 'N° 1'; centre, dedication around coat of arms, 'To Edward Stephenson, Esq.ʳ of Cumberland / *This PLATE is inscrib'd by his most Obliged humble Servant Will.ᵐ Bellers / Publish'd according to Act of Parliament October the 10.ᵗʰ 1752'*
Purchased, 1986

A View of Derwent-Water, Towards Borrodale was the first of a group of engravings of the Lake District published in the 1750s by the London painter and print-dealer William Bellers and is among the earliest works of art to celebrate the scenery of the Lake District. Its view is looking southwards and the artist has deliberately compressed the scenery round the lake to enhance the drama of his image. In the distance, to the left of centre, the falls of Lodore tumble copiously in a series of cascades (they were later to be described in West's *Guide* as 'the Niagara of the lake'), while a strong contrast between a shadowy eminence and its well-lit neighbour indicates the mysterious defile beneath Castle Crag that takes the traveller through the 'Jaws of Borrowdale'. Apart from a solitary cottage on one of the islands, this would appear to be a savage and inhospitable place untouched by mankind, were it not for the presence of the figures in the extensive foreground that occupies of a third of the scene: an elegantly dressed family out walking and two men with their dog. To modern eyes the scene presents an astonishing contrast between the figures and their setting, but the contrast was probably less vivid for Bellers' contemporaries than it appears today. In the 1740s and 1750s the young Gainsborough (who trained under the French draughtsman and engraver Hubert Gravelot) also showed ladies and gentlemen in silks and satins in outdoor settings; these were both naturalistic (reflecting their estates) or artificial and imaginary (echoing the rococo settings of the French painter

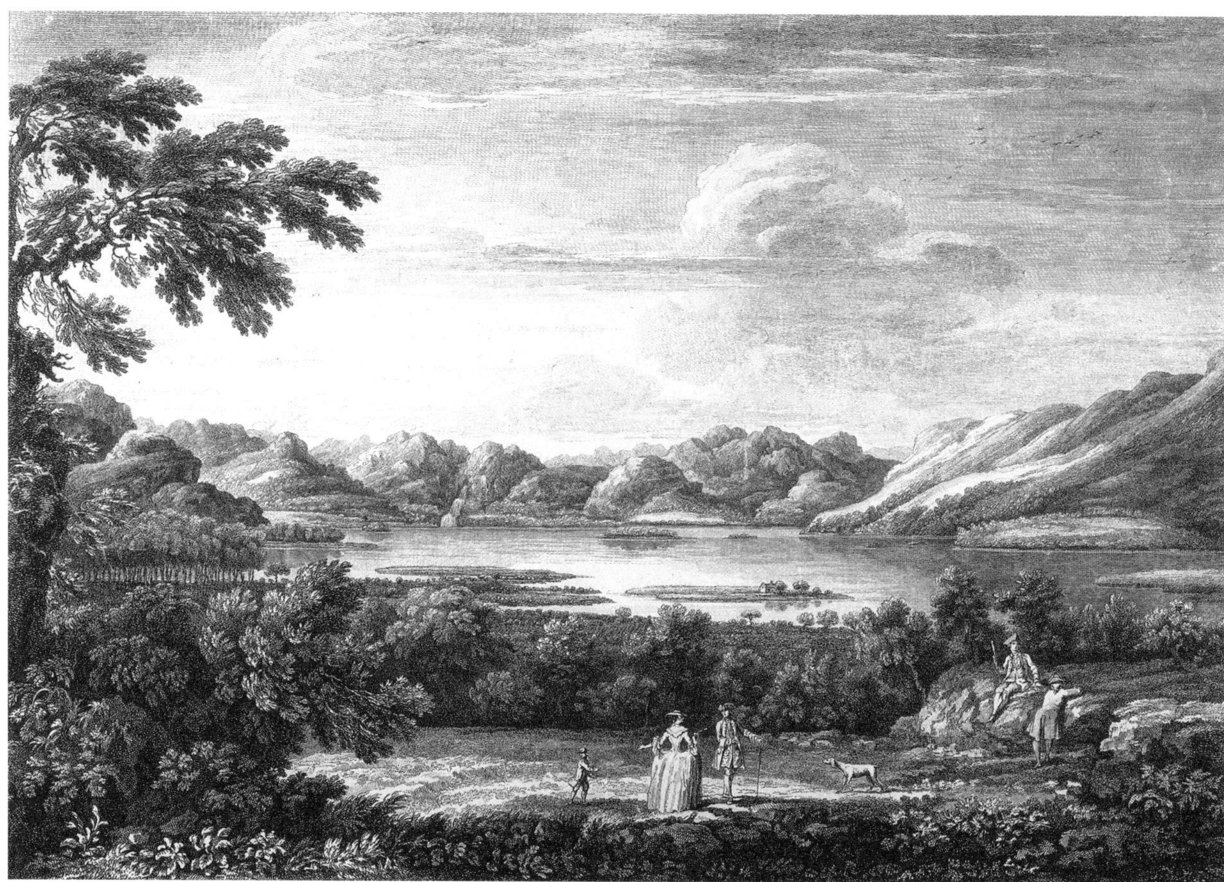

Cat. 3

François Boucher). The figures in cat. 3 come from the same tradition.

Bellers' painting of Derwentwater, like most of his work, is now untraced. He himself drew the initial etched outlines for this scene but for the main part of the work he employed engravers of French origin working in London, engraving in England at the time being largely dominated by Frenchmen. Both Jean-Baptiste-Claude Chatelain (*c.*1710–*c.*1758) and Francis (or Simon-François) Ravenet (1706–74) were distinguished engravers, Chatelain also working as a draughtsman and drawing-master while Ravenet, who had executed two of the scenes in Hogarth's *Marriage à-la-mode* in the 1740s, was elected one of the first 'Associate Engravers' of the Royal Academy in 1770. The foreground figures were contributed by Louis-Philippe Boitard, then still in his teens.

A View of Derwent-Water, Towards Borrodale was sold as one of Bellers' *Six Select Views in the North of England*. The group was advertised in the *London Evening Post* in December 1753 when prospective subscribers were advised that five of the prints could be inspected at Bellers' house in Poppins Court, Fleet Street (close to Ludgate Circus), where subscriptions were also taken in (one guinea for the set). The official launch of the entire set seems to have taken place in April 1754. The six prints were reissued, with a further three scenes, in 1757.

Bellers dedicated each of his prints of Cumberland and Westmorland to an appropriate landowner in the area depicted: the two of Derwentwater (1752, 1753) bore inscriptions naming Edward Stephenson and the Marquess of Rockingham; that of Windermere (1753) was dedicated to Sir William Fleming of Rydal; that of Haweswater (1753) to Sir James Lowther; and those of Ullswater (1753, 1754) to Charles Howard, Esq., of Greystoke. The dedicatee of *A View of Derwent-Water,* Edward Stephenson (1691–1768), spent his working life in the service of the East India Company, holding the post of Governor of Bengal in 1728 (though, remarkably, for

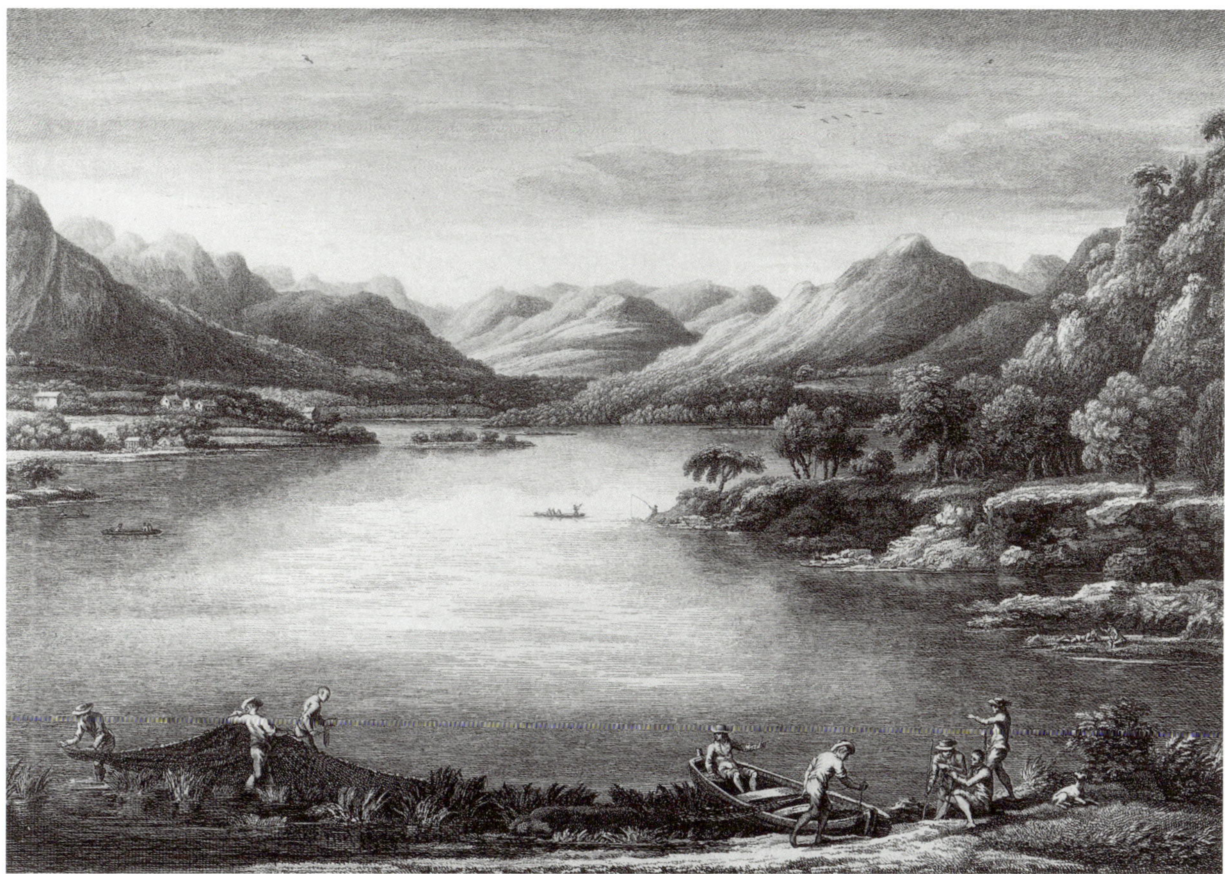

Cat. 4

just one day) and returning to Britain with a considerable fortune in 1730. Amongst other properties he bought the manor of Scaleby from the Gilpin family in 1741. CFP

4

JEAN-BAPTISTE-CLAUDE CHATELAIN and JAMES MASON after WILLIAM BELLERS (fl. 1734–73)
A View of the Head of Ulswater toward Patterdale
1754, as reissued in 1774
Etching and engraving, 40.4 × 52.4 cm
Engraved inscriptions: below, with title and names of artist (*Painted after Nature by W.m Bellers*) and engravers (*Chatelin*); below left, *Published Jan. 17th 1774 by John Boydell Engraver in Cheapside & Robt Sayer Map and Printseller in Fleet-Street*; centre, dedication around coat of arms, *'To* Charles Howard *Esq.r of* Greystock, *in Cumberland / This Plate is inscrib'd by his most Obliged humble Servant Will.m Bellers'*; below right, '7'

Having published his Lakes prints in the 1750s (see cat. 3), William Bellers seems to have concentrated on painting and between 1761 and 1773 he exhibited no fewer than sixty-five paintings or drawings with the Free Society of Artists; of these a high proportion were subjects in Cumberland and Westmorland. His name thus became familiar to many with an interest in the north of England at this time and he is mentioned by the poet Gray in his account of his own visit to Gordale Scar, Yorkshire, in the course of his tour to the Lakes in 1769.

A View of the Head of Ulswater toward Patterdale, engraved by Jean-Baptiste-Claude Chatelain and James Mason, was first published – by Bellers himself – in April 1754 but the version exhibited here dates from twenty years later. In 1774 it was reissued, together with others in the series, by John Boydell, the most important London print-seller of his age with a superb stock of engravings and a shop in Cheapside. Boydell dealt in works by the Old

Masters and by living or recently deceased British artists; he instigated new print-publishing projects (most famously the 'Boydell Shakespeare' series, initiated in 1786); and he regularly enlarged his stock by buying up desirable second-hand plates when they became available. In 1767 Bellers' plates (together with their copyright) were jointly acquired by Boydell and another print-dealer, Robert Sayer, who proceeded to republish them in the early 1770s. As can be seen by comparing cat. 3 and 4, the original date of publication continues to appear below the scene but the wording of the publication date line has been altered, the final central line being replaced by a new line at lower left.

In cat. 4 Bellers provides a huge enclosed view, as if in a colossal amphitheatre: looking south to the dense array of peaks at the head of Ullswater and downwards at the point on the shore where Aira Beck enters the lake between Gowbarrow Park and Glencoyne Park. He shows Norfolk Island near the centre, at the narrowest part of the lake, and his viewpoint must have been in Gowbarrow Park, long owned by the Howard family of Greystoke Castle near Penrith. It was here that, around 1780, Charles Howard of Greystoke, later Duke of Norfolk, the son of the dedicatee of the engraving, built Lyulph's Tower as a hunting-lodge in mock Gothic style on the site of the remains of an earlier tower.

The fishermen in the foreground play an important role in animating Bellers' scene and have their origin in the works of the Old Masters rather than in observation of the present day. However, they are not inappropriate. Early accounts of Ullswater mention that it abounded in many varieties of fish including char and trout; West's *Guide* reported that trout weighing over thirty pounds were reputedly caught here. CFP

5

JOHN DALTON (1709–63)
A Descriptive Poem addressed to Two Ladies, at their return from viewing the mines near Whitehaven. To which are added, some thoughts on building and planting
London: 1755
Gift of Peter Bicknell, 1982

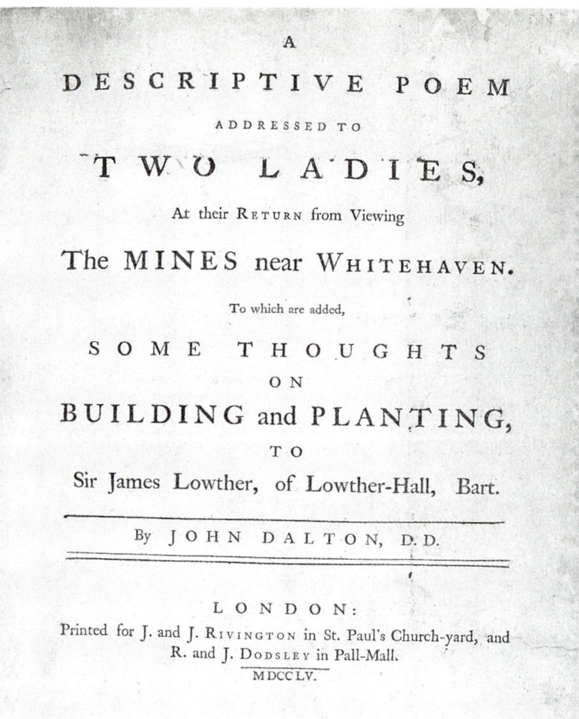
A
DESCRIPTIVE POEM
ADDRESSED TO
TWO LADIES,
At their RETURN from Viewing
The MINES near WHITEHAVEN.
To which are added,
SOME THOUGHTS
ON
BUILDING and PLANTING,
TO
Sir James Lowther, of Lowther-Hall, Bart.

By JOHN DALTON, D.D.

LONDON:
Printed for J. and J. RIVINGTON in St. Paul's Church-yard, and R. and J. DODSLEY in Pall-Mall.
MDCCLV.

Cat. 5

John Dalton was baptised in Dean, Cumberland, and educated at Lowther, and then at Queen's College, Oxford, where he was eventually elected a fellow. He worked first as a tutor to Lord Beauchamp, the only son of the Earl of Hertford, and then as a practising Church of England clergyman (while still enjoying the patronage of the Duke of Somerset). Dalton had a literary turn of mind: he adapted John Milton's *Comus* for the stage (with music by Thomas Arne), and published a number of sermons and moral epistles. His *Descriptive Poem* describes the beauties of his native landscape. It was written, he wrote in a preface, as no more than a private amusement, but his friends had persuaded him to publish it: 'It was owing to the strong inclination, by which he was prompted to express the pleasure he had received, in a visit paid to his native country after a long absence, from the view of the several uncommon, grand, or beautiful scenes of nature and of art, which he here attempts to describe.' In the first part of the poem Dalton accompanies the two ladies of the title on their journey through the awful depths of the coal mines that Sir James Lowther (1673–1755) had sunk off the coast of Whitehaven; in the second half he follows the course of the river Lowther through 'Sweet Keswick's vale' to Derwentwater and 'SUPREME of mountains, Skiddaw'. In his preface Dalton laments the felling of the ancient oaks in Crow Park (depicted in Smith's engraving, cat. 6). He warns potential visitors that they will not find the sylvan beauties

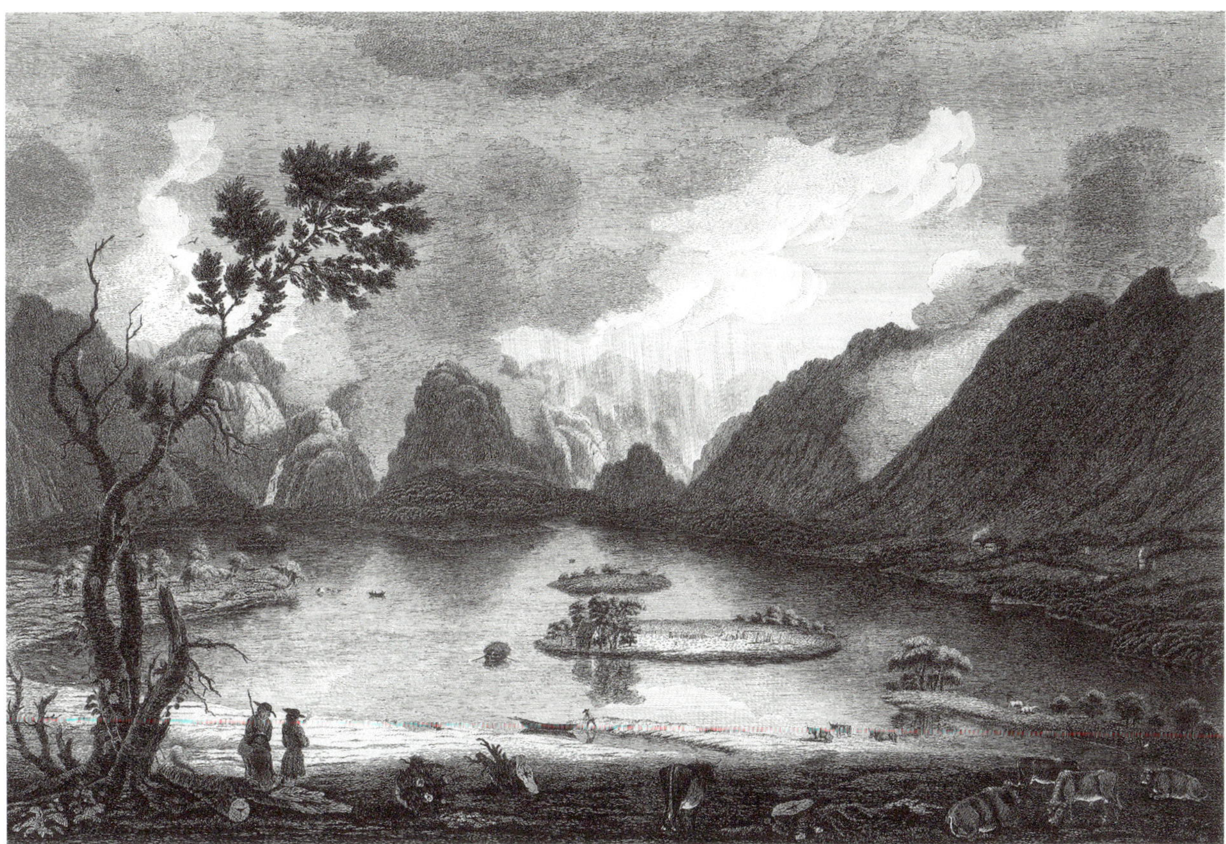

Cat. 6

he describes in the poem, because of 'some late violations of those sacred woods and groves, which had, for ages, shaded the sides of the surrounding mountains, and … the shores and promontories of that lovely lake'. *A Descriptive Poem* is a celebration of the beauty and prosperity of Cumberland, and Dalton praises Sir James for not disdaining his native county 'to bask beneath a southern sun', and for transforming Whitehaven into a thriving port. In this, its original form, it was published in a deluxe quarto volume with extensive notes by his friend the chemist William Brownrigg (1771–1800), who lived in Whitehaven, and who also supplied a laudatory letter to the author. The notes gave detailed descriptions of the mines, and identified some of the places mentioned in the poem. As a poem it is typical of the kind of privately produced lyrical effusion to lords and ladies, stately homes and places of beauty, of the kind so popular at the time. Its lasting interest derives from its status as the earliest published description of the area in verse, and it would become widely anthologised as the area became more popular. SH

6

THOMAS SMITH OF DERBY (*c*.1720/4–67)
A View of Darwentwater &c. from Crow-Park
1761, as reissued in 1767
Etching and engraving, 38.3 × 55 cm
Engraved inscriptions: below, with title and name of artist-engraver; left, 'N.° 1.' and *Publish'd according to Act of Parliam.*[t] *1767.*
Purchased, 1986

Although William Bellers published the earliest large engravings of the Lake District in the early 1750s (see cat. 3–4), Thomas Smith had led the way by painting, engraving and publishing views of similarly dramatic scenery elsewhere in Britain a decade earlier. Smith was one of the first British artists to celebrate the stranger and wilder natural features of his own country, painting views of 'the most extraordinary natural prospects' of Derbyshire and Staffordshire as early as 1743. From the narrow gorges, waterfalls and overhanging cliffs of the Peak District he turned his attention to equally arresting features in the Lake District, publishing *Three Views in the North*

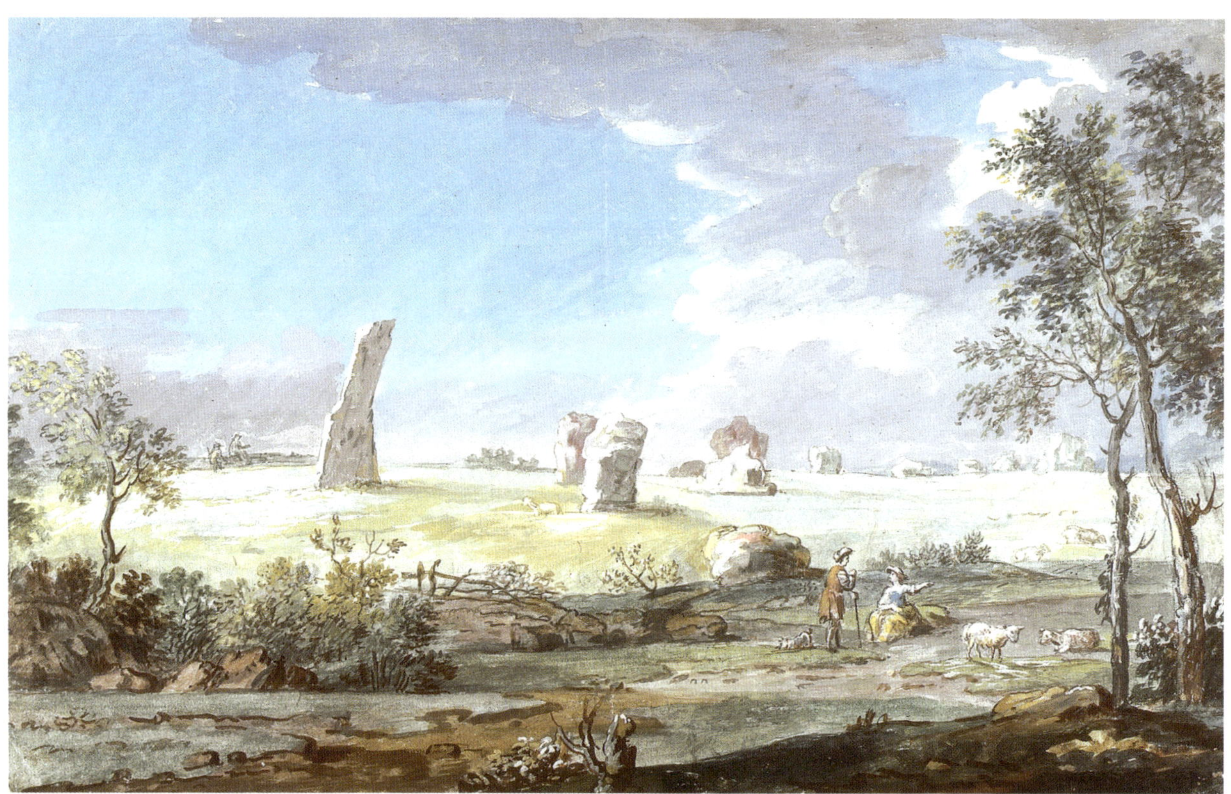

Cat. 7

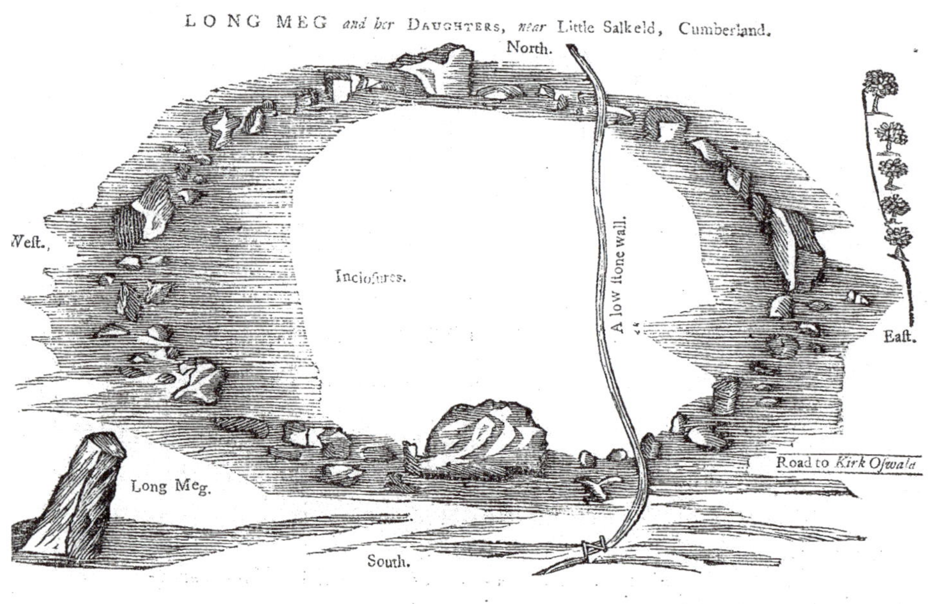

Fig. 11 After George Smith, *Long Meg and her Daughters, near Little Salkeld, Cumberland*, woodcut from the *Gentleman's Magazine*, July 1752.

of England (showing Derwentwater, Thirlmere and Windermere) in 1761. Interest in the Lakes was to be substantially increased by the first publication – in April 1766 – of Dr John Brown's letter describing the vale and lake of Keswick, so it is not surprising that by 1767 the engraved plates of Smith's three views had been acquired by the London print-dealer John Boydell. He republished them that same year as he was entitled to do: under the new legislation of 1767 copyright in an engraving passed automatically to the owner of the engraved plate. Smith's role in the work's genesis is acknowledged in the inscription at lower right.

Crow Park, Smith's viewpoint to the south-west of Keswick, soon became one of the most favoured viewing stations for artists and tourists visiting Derwentwater. In October 1769 Thomas Gray wrote that, 'Smith judged right, when he took his print of the Lake from hence, for it is a gentle eminence, not too high, on the very margin of the water & commanding it from end to end, looking full into the *gorge* of *Borodale*' (Toynbee and Whibley (ed.), 1935, vol. III, pp. 1089–90). These words were quoted in successive editions of West's *Guide*, together with Gray's anguish at the felling of the grove of ancient oaks that adorned the park until 1751; in retaliation for the support given by the Earl of Derwentwater to the Jacobites in 1715 his estates were confiscated and he himself was executed for treason. By the 1760s Crow Park was a rough pasture, large roots in the ground being poignant reminders of the vanished beauties of the glade. CFP

7

LADY MARY LOWTHER (1738–1824)
Long Meg &c from the Gate
1766
Pencil, pen and ink, watercolour and bodycolour, 27.1 × 41.3 cm
Inscribed in the artist's washline mount 'No. 8 / Long Meg &c from the gate'
Purchased with the generous support of the W.W. Spooner Charitable Trust, 2004

Long Meg and her Daughters, the subject of two drawings by Lady Mary Lowther in the Trust's collection, lies north-east of Penrith, less than ten miles from Lowther Hall, the artist's home after her marriage to Sir James Lowther (1736–1802) in 1761. The largest prehistoric stone circle in the north of England, Long Meg originally consisted of some seventy pillars; over half of the sixty or so remaining stones, of diverse shapes and sizes, are still in an upright position. The tallest and most tapering, Long Meg herself, lies well outside the circle, as is clearly shown in Lady Mary's watercolour; modern estimates put its height at about 12 feet. Despite the remarkable nature of the stone circle, few visitors to the Lakes at this time would have sought it out (even Wordsworth, who lived in the area for most of his life, did not go there until 1821, hastily footnoting it for *A Description of the Lakes* in 1822). However, thanks to the library of her father, the third Earl of Bute, Lady Mary is likely to have known that it had begun to attract the attention of antiquarians: in 1752 it had been minutely discussed – and depicted (fig. 11) – by George Smith in the *Gentleman's Magazine* (see also cat. 1–2). This stimulated correspondence about its supposed druidical origins.

Much of the charm of Lady Mary's drawing lies in the fact that the artist has been more selective than usual and included fewer features (compare Hebron, 2008, pp. 23ff.). She has used brighter colours (adding lead white to create 'bodycolour' and achieve opacity); she has also allowed the stones of Long Meg to stand imposingly across the centre of the scene, linking land and sky. Two minute figures – probably visiting antiquarians – are seen against the horizon on the left while a shepherd and shepherdess, taken straight from the world of French rococo painting or a porcelain factory, converse in the foreground. They provide the greatest possible contrast to the crude and primitive antiquities depicted beyond.

Lady Mary would have executed this drawing at Lowther Hall on the basis of on-the-spot studies in a sketchbook. She then finished her work by creating a 'wash-line mount' (i.e. ruling lines in wash on its mount as was then *de rigueur*) and inscribing it with a number and title. This work is her 'No. 8' and contains no inscription apart from the title, but on 'No. 6', also in the Trust's collection (Hebron, p. 26), she recorded, 'Long Megg and her Daughters 73 in Number the Largest stone is 11 feet 6 Inches' and listed the landscape features shown in the background including Lowther Hall itself. Lady Mary's residence there was not a happy one, made tolerable only through diversions such as sketching expeditions and the practice of her art, and the couple went their separate ways after some fifteen years of marriage. CFP

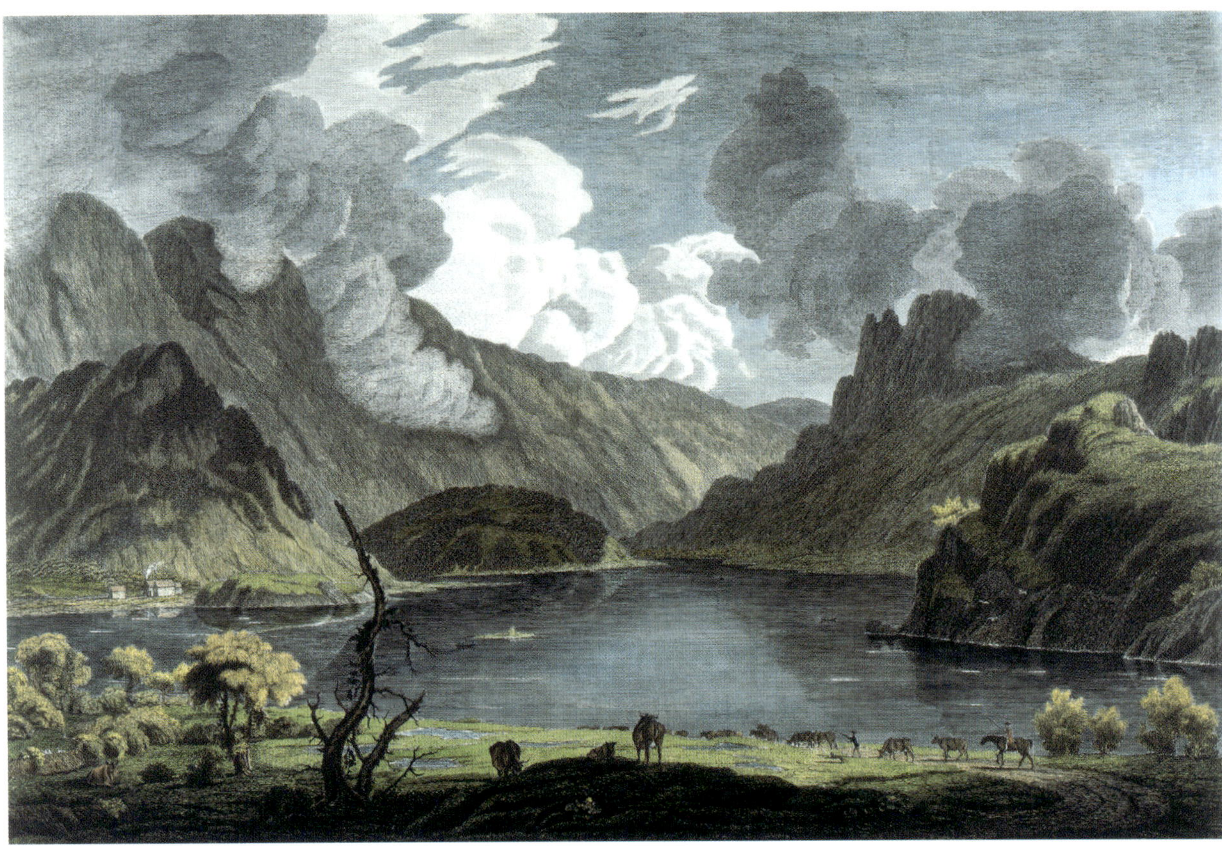

Cat. 8

8

THOMAS SMITH (*c.*1720/4–67)
A View of Ennerdale Broadwater, &c.
1767
Etching and engraving, 38.9 × 55 cm
Engraved inscriptions: below, with title and name of artist-engraver; left, 'N.º 3.' and *Publish'd according to Act of Parliam.*ᵗ *1767.*
Purchased, 1986

When Boydell republished Smith's three Lakes scenes in 1767 (see cat. 6), they were joined by a fourth, this view of Ennerdale, and the set was accompanied by a short text of eight pages describing the features in the prints; hence the numbers that are still just discernible beneath the watercolour washes added to this engraving (e.g. 1 centrally in the lake, 2 just above the cottage on the left).

This is one of the most spectacular early prints of the Lake District, partly for its exaggeratedly jagged peaks and partly for the vast rain-bearing clouds that hurtle through the sky and tumble down the fells. Smith shows Ennerdale Water from the west, looking up the lake to Pillar Fell and the needles of Pillar Rock high above the right-hand shore. The range on the left lies between Ennerdale itself and Crummock Water and Buttermere, its peaks including Red Pike, High Stile and High Crag. The view was originally published as a black and white engraving and must have been awe-inspiring in this form. However, the brilliant green colouring of cat. 8 (added at a much later date) makes a valuable contribution to the scene. As Wordsworth commented of the Lake District as a whole in *A Description of the Scenery of the Lakes* (1822, p. 11), 'The general *surface* of the mountains is turf, rendered rich and green by the moisture of the climate. Sometimes the turf … is little broken, the whole covering being soft and downy pasturage. In other places rocks predominate; the soil is laid bare by torrents and burstings of water from the sides of the mountains in heavy rains; and not unfrequently their perpendicular sides are seamed by ravines.' Smith's print shows an artist's awareness of precisely such contrasts and he neatly rounds off his portrait of Ennerdale by juxtaposing a blackened, blasted tree and a stately procession of cows in the foreground.

The inclusion of Ennerdale in Smith's *Four Prints* is of considerable interest, given the poor quality of the roads at this date and the remoteness of the lake. It was not described in West's *Guide to the Lakes*, being mentioned briefly in a footnote, with Wastwater, Elterwater and Broadwater, as 'not yet noticed by writers' (third ed., 1784, p. xi); West's ignorance is illustrated by the fact that he regarded Broadwater as a separate lake whereas in fact this was an alternative archaic name for Ennerdale Water. It was not until 1797 that Ennerdale featured in a painting at the Royal Academy (no. 651, *Silver Cove at the head of Emerdale Water* by William Green). Green's later watercolour (Abbot Hall Art Gallery, 1812) shows a broadly similar view to Smith's but without any of its exaggeration. CFP

9

JOHN BROWN (1715–66)

A Description of the Lake at Keswick, by a late popular writer

Kendal: 1771

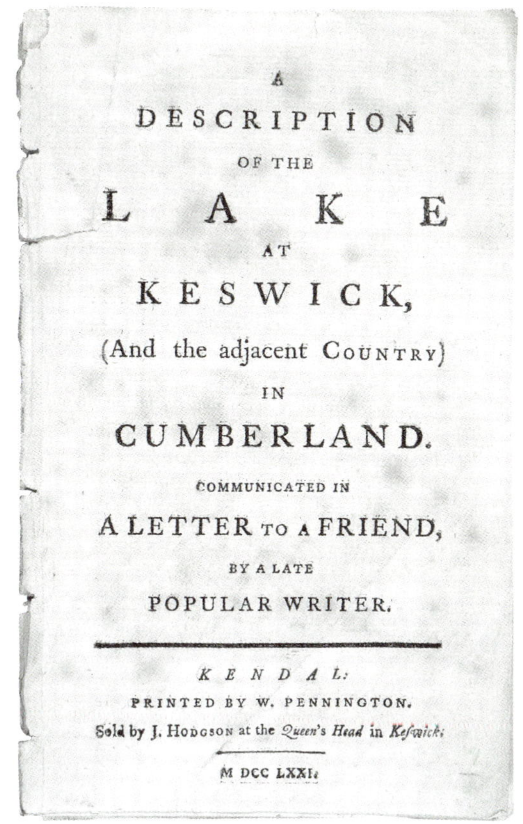
A DESCRIPTION OF THE LAKE AT KESWICK, (And the adjacent COUNTRY) IN CUMBERLAND. COMMUNICATED IN A LETTER TO A FRIEND, BY A LATE POPULAR WRITER.

KENDAL: PRINTED BY W. PENNINGTON. Sold by J. HODGSON at the *Queen's Head* in *Keswick*: M DCC LXXI.

Cat. 9

John Brown was a prolific essayist and sermoniser on moral, religious and political subjects, as well as a minor poet and dramatist. He is best known today, however, for this short prose description (one of the earliest) of Derwentwater. Like John Dalton, Brown had spent his early years in Cumberland, growing up in Wigton. After Cambridge he returned to the area, working as a minor canon at Carlisle Cathedral and, following his ordination, vicar of Morland in Westmorland. He was present in Carlisle during the siege of the city during the 1745 rebellion, and was part of the artistic circle that centred around John Bernard Gilpin. For a while he acted as tutor to Gilpin's son William.

Brown seems to have written his description of Derwentwater in the 1750s as a private letter to Lord Lyttelton. He compares the vale of Keswick favourably with Dovedale in Derbyshire. He describes the cultivated fields, projecting cliffs and more distant mountains that together create the permanent form and character of Derwentwater, and then, in companionable fashion, conducts his reader by boat around the lake, taking him to each promontory and island while pointing out the numerous '*varying* or *accidental* beauties' fleetingly created by the shifting light and weather. He concludes with a walk around the lake by moonlight. Famously, Brown calls upon three artists, Claude, Salvator Rosa and Gaspard Dughet to do full justice to the beauty, horror and immensity of the scene.

The relative brevity of the *Description* meant that it turned up in a variety of forms. It was first published, shortly before Brown's death, in April 1766, in the *London Chronicle*, as 'Description of Keswick in Cumberland, in a Letter from a Gentleman to his friend in London'. It was then issued separately in a series of eight-page pamphlets, the first published in Newcastle in 1767, and then Kendal (as here), Whitehaven and London. It was also short enough to turn up as a footnote. George Pearch printed it as a footnote to Dalton's poem in his *Collections of Poems by Several Hands* (first published 1768) and it was also included in many of the later guidebooks. From its obscure private beginnings 'Dr Brown's letter', as it was known, became one of the most anthologised of all Lakes descriptions. Brown

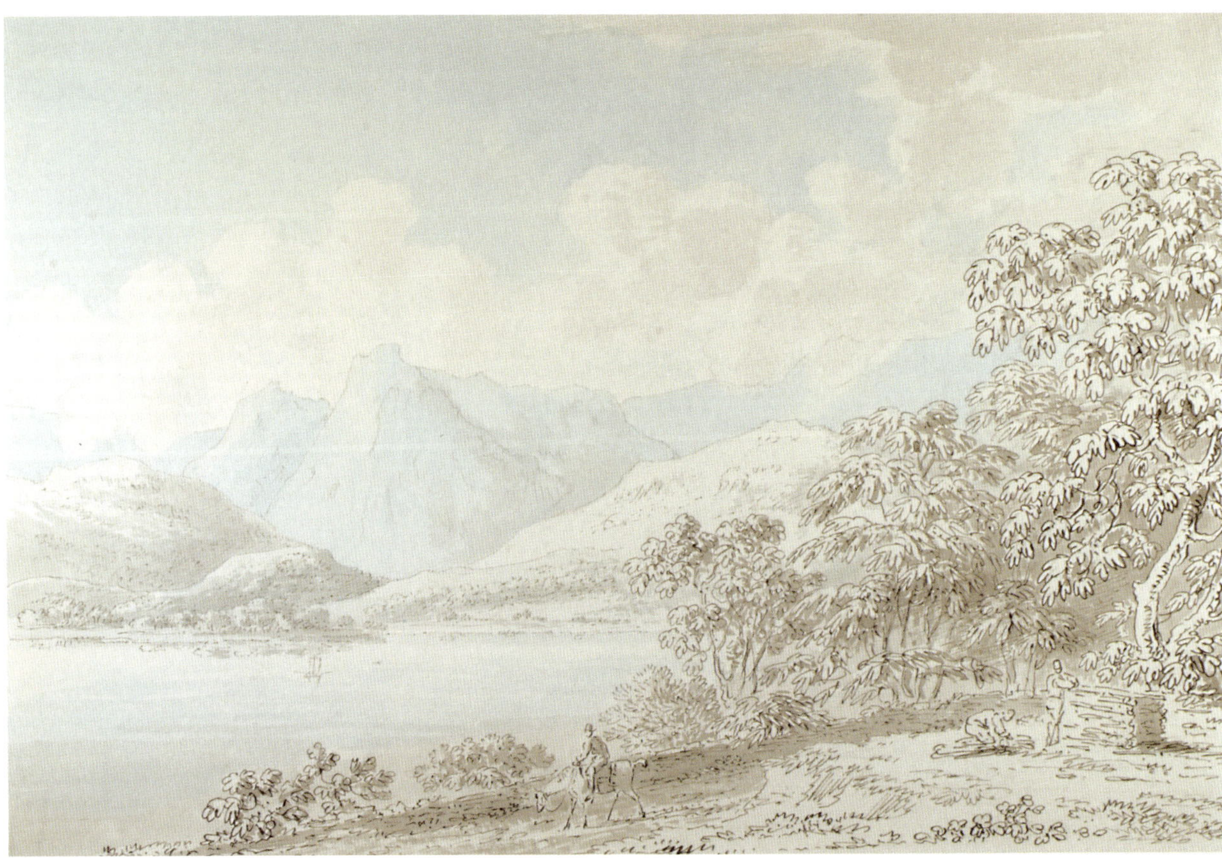

Cat. 10

himself was celebrated as 'the Columbus of Keswick', praised by Wordsworth as 'one of the first who led the way to a worthy admiration of this country'. SH

10

ANTHONY DEVIS (1729–1816)
Winandermeer
c.1770?
Pen, ink and blue wash, 53.5 × 65 cm
Inscribed '(Langdale Pike)', 'Winandermeer' and '3 Miles from Ambleside'
Gift of the W.W. Spooner Charitable Trust, in memory of Robert Woof, 2006

The half-brother of the better-known figure-painter Arthur Devis, Anthony Devis concentrated on landscape painting and produced Lake District scenes that are marked by a unique combination of vivacity and delicacy. The landscape itself is very simply drawn (not always quite accurately) and is lightly tinted in a limited range of colours to create a sense of perspective. Like other artists of the day he developed his own personal shorthand for depicting trees and foliage; he made no attempt at naturalism but managed to infuse them with life and energy through his rhythmically repetitive and wiry outlines. The figures and animals that he characteristically placed in the foreground are invariably well disposed and appropriate to their setting.

Devis often annotated his drawings with the name of his subject or his viewpoint, as in the case of another drawing owned by the Wordsworth Trust, a view of Ullswater from 'House Holm' (an old name for Norfolk Island). In his inscription to cat. 10 he identifies the Langdale Pikes in the distance beyond the head of Windermere and records that his viewpoint was three miles from Ambleside. If his calculation was correct he would have been somewhere near the old farm known as Calgarth Hall. A horseman rides by the lakeside on his way towards Bowness while a couple of woodmen are depicted next to the timber they have felled. CFP

11

WILLIAM HUTCHINSON (1732–1814)
An Excursion to the Lakes, in Westmoreland and Cumberland
London: 1775
Canon H.D. Rawnsley Bequest, c.*1920*

William Hutchinson was a Durham solicitor, but his legal practice, such as it was, left him plenty of time to indulge his antiquarian and literary enthusiasms. *An Excursion to the Lakes* was his second book (after *The Hermitage: a British Story*, 1772). Initially published anonymously in 1774, it described the journey he and his brother Richard had taken the previous year from Bowes to Kendal. Their route took them through Appleby, Penrith, Keswick, Grasmere, Rydal and Bowness. From Penrith and Keswick they went on a number of excursions, including a memorable boating trip on Ullswater, where they listened to the celebrated echoes from the fired cannon, and were entertained by French horns.

The brothers travelled with pens and pencils: Richard sketching, William presumably making the notes on which this account was based. His likeable prose blends descriptions of the scenery with antiquarian and background historical information, opinions on the qualities of the local inns, occasional philosophical and religious meditations, and reflections on the health-giving properties of exercise, fresh air, lack of hurry, and early rising: 'Half mankind know nothing of the beauties of nature, and waste in indolence and sleep the glorious scene which advancing morning presents; – as we passed on, the varied prospect kept attention exerted.'

This tour was first published a year before Thomas Gray's account (cat. 12), and the novelty of the subject perhaps contributed to its popularity. This is the second edition, published in 1775, this time under Hutchinson's name, and soon after the premature death of his brother Richard, who is remembered in the text. Encouraged, perhaps, by the sales of the first edition, this time there were a number of plates, and the typography is rather more elaborate, with separate headings and shoulder notes. A number of errors are silently corrected ('Hull's-water', for instance, becomes 'Ullswater', and 'Basnet' is changed to 'Bassonthwaite'. A subsequent tour of the north-east is appended to the original Lakes tour, although this is markedly more antiquarian in emphasis (Hutchinson's future books would be more antiquarian after this early attempt at landscape description, and he published a two-volume *History of the County of Cumberland, and Some Places Adjacent*, in 1794. SH

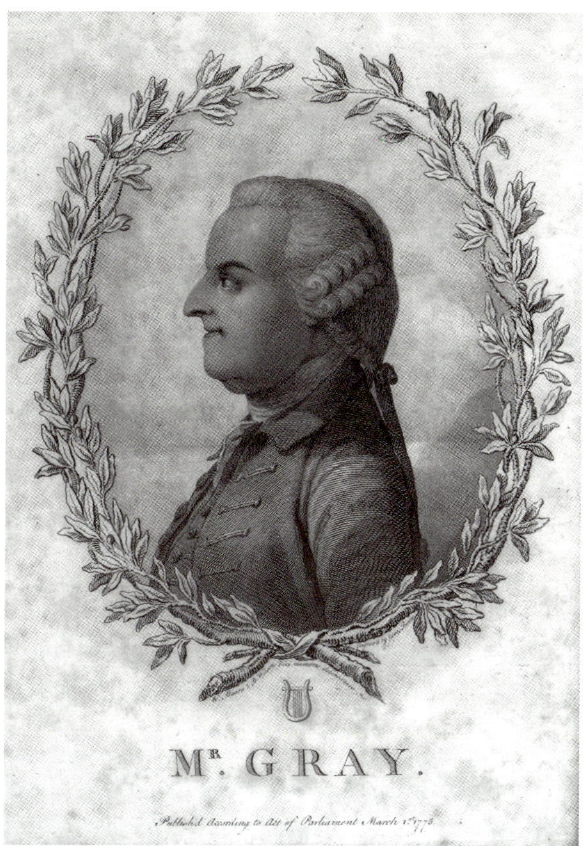

Cat. 12 (frontispiece)

12

THOMAS GRAY (1716–71)
The Poems of Mr. Gray: To which are added memoirs of his life and writings, by W. Mason, M.A.
York: 1775
Purchased, 1990

In his youth Thomas Gray had toured the Alps. In later life he developed a taste for domestic travel, and in 1769 he toured the Lake District. He described his tour in a series of meticulously composed letters to his friend Dr Wharton, who had been unable to join him because of ill health. Gray willingly allowed memories of his Alpine adventures to colour his response to the Lakeland scenery. After an excursion to Borrowdale he wrote: 'the place reminds one of those passes in the Alps, where the Guides tell you to move on with speed, & say nothing, lest the agitation of the the air should loosen the snows above, & bring down a mass, that would overwhelm a caravan. I took their counsel here and hasten'd on in silence.' When not thrilling himself with such sentiments, or complaining about the quality of Lakeland accommodation, Gray provides some wonderfully sensitive responses to the scenery: Keswick and Derwentwater sit in 'the vale of Elysium', Grasmere is 'a little unsuspected paradise.'

Gray, who was reluctant to publish even his poetry, would certainly not have considered sharing his Lake District journal with the general public. On his death, just two years later, it therefore remained in manuscript form, and in the care of his literary executor, the poet and garden designer William Mason. Some knew of its existence: Mason told William Gilpin that he had been looking over it with a view to publication, and Gilpin immediately asked if he could see it. Mason did publish the tour, as part of his 1775 edition of Gray's poetry and selected correspondence (cat. 12). He tidied up some of the phrasing and presented it as a continuous narrative, together with some explanatory footnotes. Mason's only regret was that Gray had not visited the falls at Rydal.

Once published, Gray's tour was immediately popular, and became one of the best-known, and most often quoted accounts of the Lakes. Just a year later Richard Cumberland described it as being 'in every hand', and William Wordsworth admired it for its 'unaffected simplicity'. SH

13

WILLIAM GILPIN (1724–1804)
Observations, relative chiefly to Picturesque Beauty ... on Several Parts of England; Particularly the Mountains, and Lakes of Cumberland, and Westmoreland
London: 1786
Purchased, 1992

OBSERVATIONS,
RELATIVE CHIEFLY TO
PICTURESQUE BEAUTY,
Made in the YEAR 1772,
On ſeveral PARTS of ENGLAND;
PARTICULARLY THE
MOUNTAINS, AND LAKES
OF
CUMBERLAND, AND WESTMORELAND.

VOL. I.

By WILLIAM GILPIN, M. A.
PREBENDARY OF SALISBURY;
AND
VICAR OF BOLDRE, IN NEW-FOREST, NEAR LYMINGTON.

LONDON;
PRINTED FOR R. BLAMIRE, STRAND.
M.DCC.LXXXVI.

Cat. 13

Born near Carlisle, the Reverend William Gilpin was a writer, schoolmaster and amateur artist. In the summer holidays he went on a series of excursions around Britain, including, in 1772, northern England. While travelling he scribbled down 'rough thoughts' and sketches in small notebooks, and on his return he developed his scribbles into prose, and his sketches into finished drawings. His account of the tour he made through northern England was by far his most ambitious. Now in the Bodleian Library, the eight volumes comprise 834 pages of Gilpin's hand-written text and are illustrated with maps, diagrams and plans, and over 150 landscape drawings by Gilpin himself, his nephew William Sawrey Gilpin, and others. Each volume has its own index. Gilpin entitled the work 'A tour through England; more particularly the mountainous parts of Cumberland, and Westmorland: with a view chiefly to illustrate the principles of picturesque beauty in landscape'.

When William Mason saw the manuscript of Gilpin's Lakeland tour, he urged Gilpin to publish it. Gilpin spent large amounts of time experimenting with the best means of reproducing his drawings, working with a number of professional artists, who as a breed he found 'a very tedious set of people to be engaged with'. His tour was finally published in 1786, in two volumes. There were far fewer illustrations than in the original manuscript, and, reproduced in rather flat aquatints, they are not so much identifiable Lakeland scenes, as generalised views that aim to demonstrate Gilpin's picturesque principles (see cat. 48). SH

14

RICHARD CUMBERLAND (1732–1811)
Odes
London: 1776
Purchased, 1987

This 28-page quarto publication contains two odes by the dramatist, poet and essayist Richard Cumberland: 'To the Sun' and 'To Dr. Robert James'. Cumberland visited the Lake District with the Earl of Warwick towards the end of 1775. He went with the recently published edition of Gray's works (cat. 12) in his hand, and 'To the Sun' is his contribution to the incipient body of Lake District literature. Like Dalton's poem, and Brown's letter, it would be widely anthologised.

Why, Cumberland wonders in a prefatory letter 'To Mr. George Romney', did 'this enchanting display of sublime and beautiful objects' only inspire mere prose from Gray's poetical pen? He had, he wrote, just been shown a manuscript 'of the late ingenious Dr. Browne', and he goes on to publish, for the first time, the poem that Brown had originally appended to his prose description of Derwentwater: 'Now sunk the Sun, now Twilight sunk, and Night / Rode in her zenith'. Cumberland's own effusion to the sun (composed, he says, extempore and 'on the spot') celebrates not only the 'sweet fantastick vale' of Keswick, but 'Huge Helvellyn', 'savage Wyborn', 'delicious Grasmeres calm retreat' and 'stately Wyndermere'. In a footnote Cumberland adds a note of competition: 'the Great Lake of Ulswater' is 'a scene of grandeur and sublimity far superior in my opinion to the Lake of Keswick'. This type of comparative judgment would be a standard feature of the genteel appreciation of the Lakes in the years to come.

Cumberland recommends a tour of the Lakes to those who, hitherto, have ignored the delights of domestic scenery in favour of the Alps, the Rhône and the Rhine. Two years earlier William Hutchinson had written that an excursion to the Lakes offered an opportunity for calm and reflection, but clearly this was not the fashion among Britain's youth, for Cumberland here bemoans their 'depravity of taste': 'Whilst they are journeying there is no respite nor repose; their enquiries extend neither to right hand nor left, and seldom further forward than to the next poste; the shortest and straightest road to dissipation and pleasure is their's, all the rest is out of the way.' SH

15

THOMAS HEARNE (1744–1817)
Sketch of Sir George Beaumont and Joseph Farington painting a Waterfall
1777
Pencil, 18 × 19 cm
Purchased with the generous help of the National Heritage Memorial Fund, 1984

16

THOMAS HEARNE (1744–1817)
Sir George Beaumont and Joseph Farington painting a Waterfall
1777
Pen and ink, watercolour and bodycolour, 41 × 28.5 cm
Purchased with the generous help of the National Heritage Memorial Fund and the V&A Purchase Grant Fund, 1984

Cat. 16 is one of the most famous and, at the same time, most surprising images connected with the discovery of the Lakes. In 1777 Thomas Hearne and Joseph Farington, both professional landscape painters, introduced the wealthy amateur artist Sir George Beaumont to the beauties of the area, staying together at one point at the little inn near the falls of Lodore. During their tour Hearne made a pencil sketch of his two companions working at their easels (cat. 15) and shortly afterwards (the exact timing is not known) he developed his sketch into the larger and more detailed work which he bestowed on Beaumont as a memento of their trip (cat. 16); these remained with the Beaumont family until their acquisition by the Wordsworth Trust.

What are the two artists doing? They are painting in oils on canvases tacked on stretchers. They are using palettes, large brushes and mahlsticks (long sticks to support the artist's arm as he paints). But it was rare for artists working in Britain at this date to sketch in oils out of doors. Typically they would have drawn in pencil in a sketchbook and worked up their sketches in watercolour or oils at a later date (the Trust owns examples of sketchbooks used by Farington and Beaumont, as well as ones used by other artists). Painting in oils out of doors was, however, a well-established feature of artistic life in Rome, going back to the seventeenth century. This would have been well known to Farington, a former pupil of Richard Wilson RA who had visited Italy in the 1750s; indeed, one of Farington's early sketchbooks records Wilson himself 'painting from nature' in Hertfordshire (Ruddick, 1977, p. 32). Beaumont

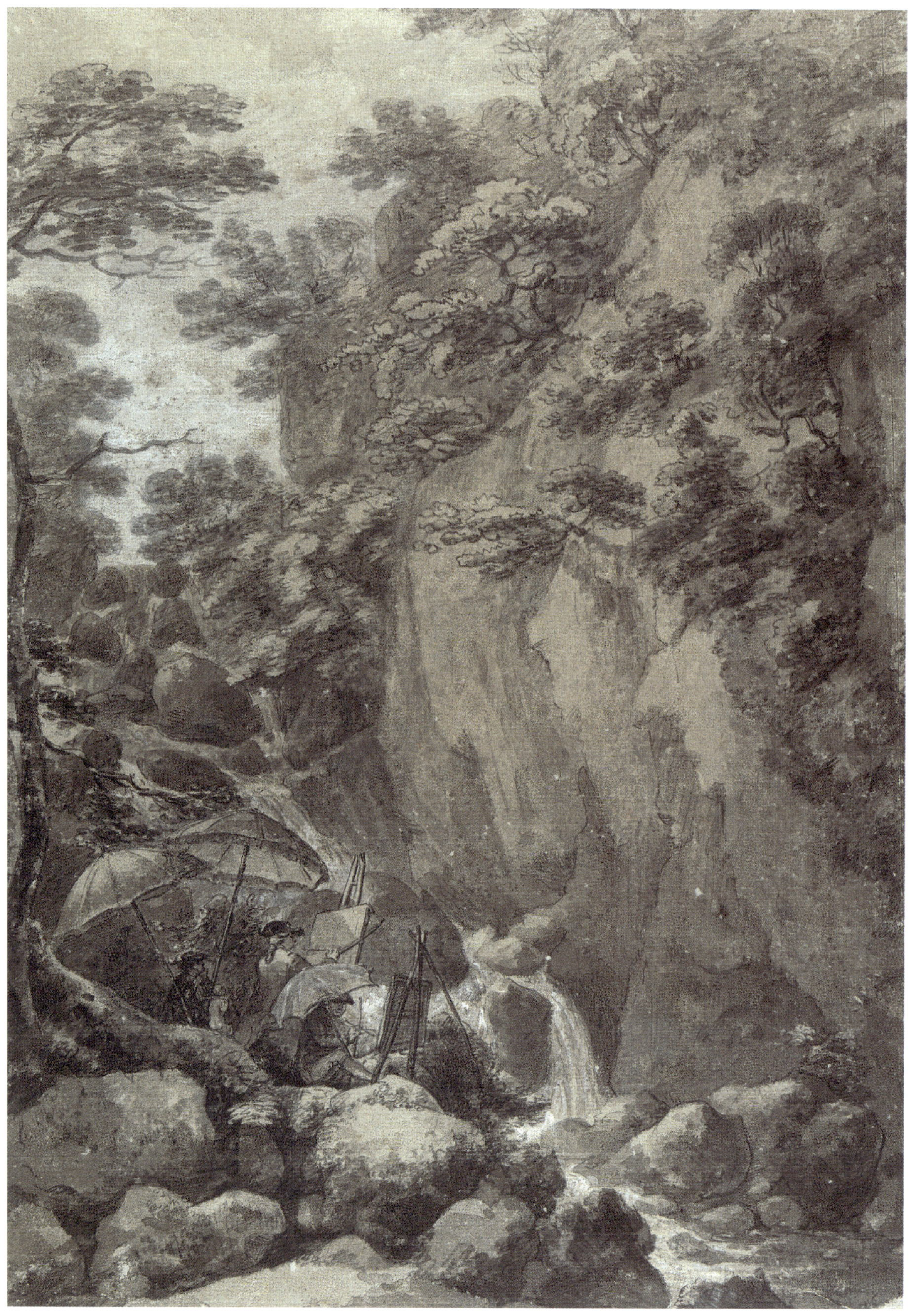

Cat. 16

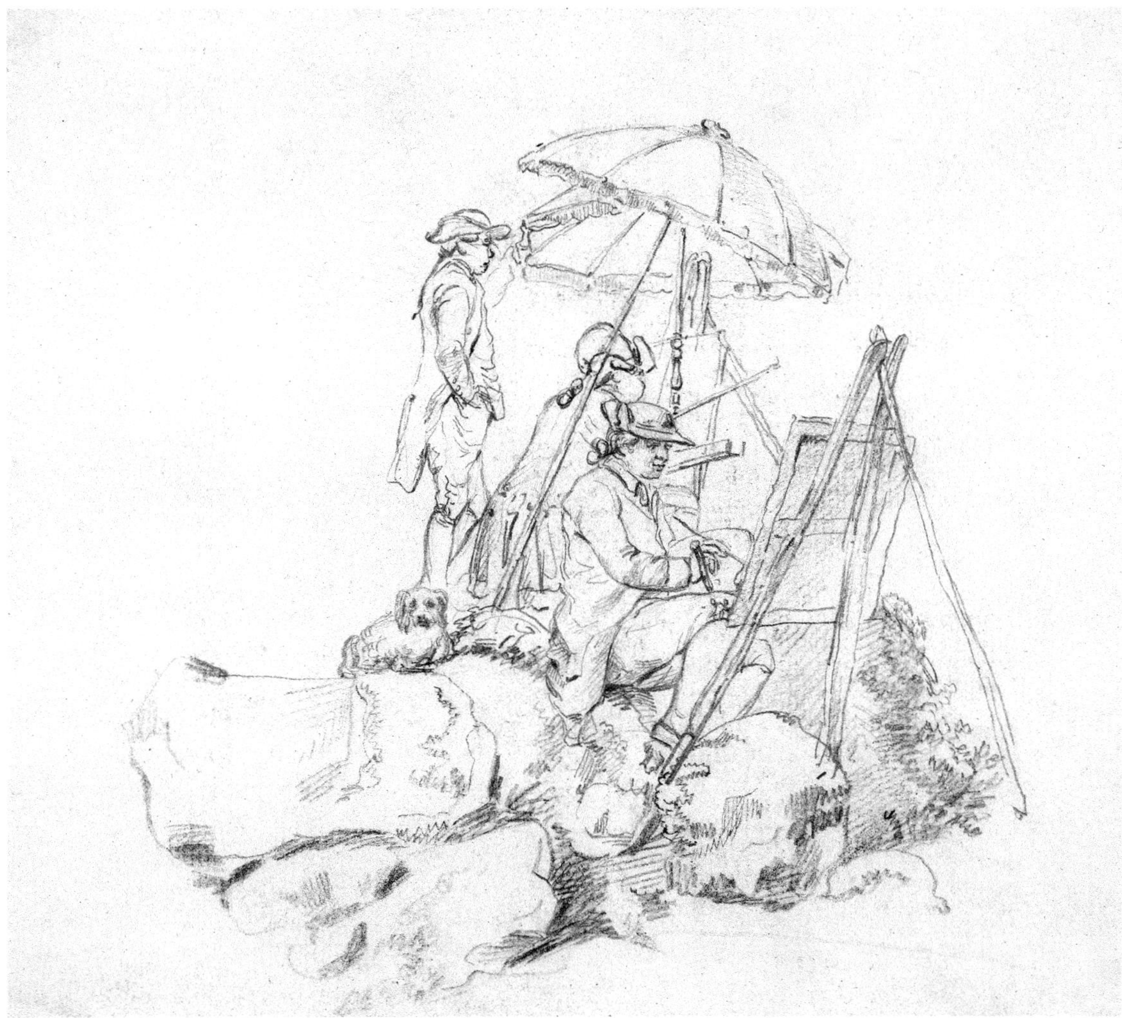

Cat. 15

shared Farington's deeply felt admiration for Wilson, so one can well imagine that he would have delighted in sampling the 'Wilson experience' in the company of two experienced professional advisers.

There is nothing in Hearne's pencil sketch to indicate where it was made and the two painters could theoretically be working almost anywhere. On the other hand, they would only have perched themselves and their easels on a pile of rocks if nothing better were available. The parasols shown in the sketch could be shading the artists and their easels from the sun – it appears, at any rate, to be a balmy day as both the dog and the attendant manservant (useful, no doubt, as the carrier of parasols, paintboxes and easels) seem totally relaxed. Much, however, has changed in the later work. Servant and dog are now huddled together in the shadows, the poses of the artists have been greatly modified, the two parasols have been shifted well to the left and a third, smaller, one added to protect the artist in the foreground. Most crucially, their setting has been included: a narrow chasm, boulders much larger than themselves, towering wooded rocks and a waterfall that is traditionally believed to be Lodore. To all intents and purposes the waterfall is the dominant feature in the scene, all the above changes carefully calculated to enhance its grandeur. However, Hearne has brilliantly captured what it actually felt like to be an artist in the Lakes in the 1770s; he shows Farington and Beaumont as true students of nature, happily engrossed in the pursuit of their art and untroubled by rain, spray or any other discomfort. CFP

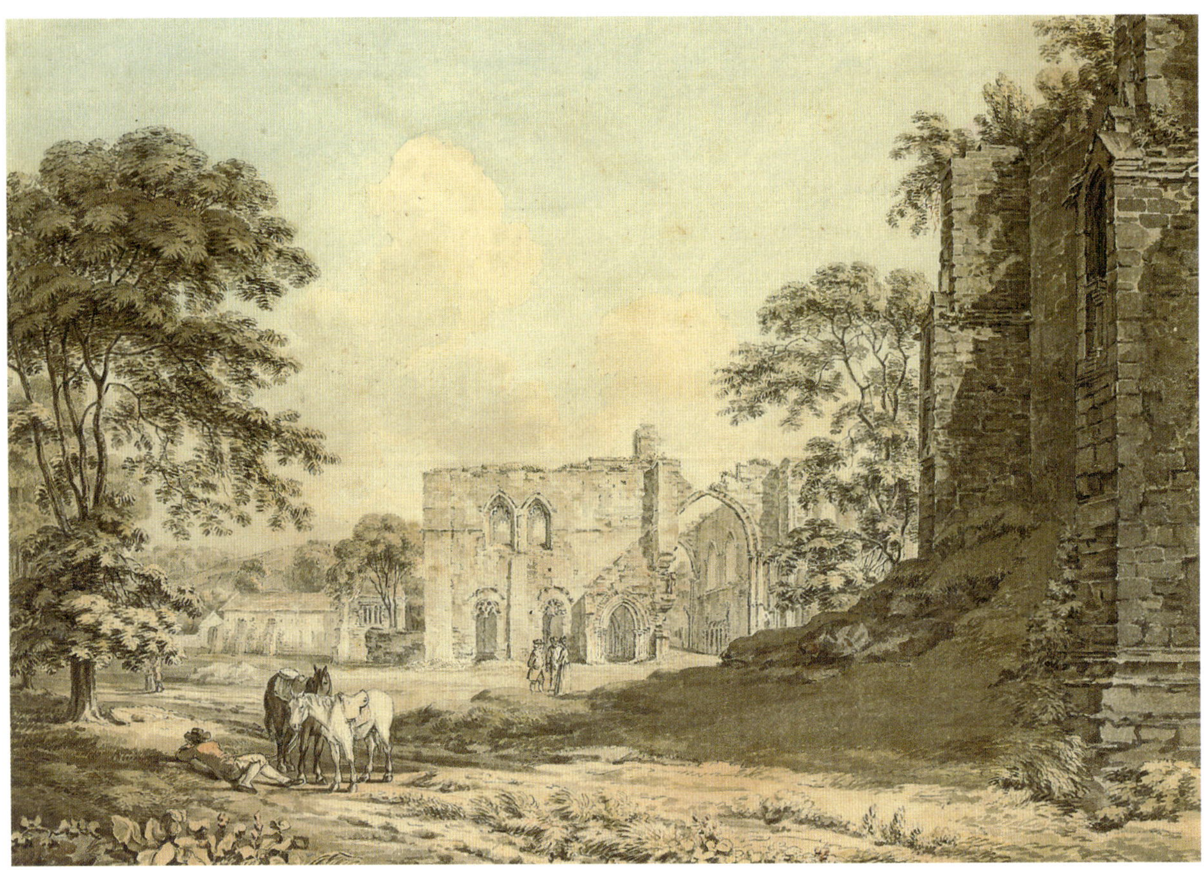

Cat. 17

17

THOMAS HEARNE (1744–1817)
West Aspect of Furness Abbey
1777
Watercolour, 18.5 × 25.4 cm
Inscribed 'T Hearne'
Gift of the W.W. Spooner Charitable Trust, 2008

The eighteenth century witnessed an upsurge of British interest in its antiquarian buildings and relics, fuelled partly by scholarly curiosity and partly by patriotism. Research was actively promoted by the Society of Antiquaries of London, whose origins went back to 1707; it was formally constituted by 1718 and was granted its Royal Charter in 1751. Many artists were involved in its endeavours; Farington regularly attended its meetings and other artist-members included Thomas Hearne, Thomas Daniell RA, the uncle of William Daniell (see cat. 73), and W.F. Wells who engraved the plates for Wilkinson's *Select Views in Cumberland, Westmoreland, and Lancashire* in 1810 (see cat. 62 and figs 31–2 on pp. 114–15).

Hearne's visit to the Lakes in 1777 was undertaken in search of material for his major publishing project, *Antiquities of Great Britain*. This occupied him for much of his career, the work being published in instalments between 1778 and 1786 and again between 1796 and 1806. Hearne made many tours round Britain; produced a total of 84 detailed watercolours on the basis of sketches (in most cases his own); supervised their engraving or executed that work himself; exhibited many of the watercolours in London in 1780 and 1783 to attract support; and wrote the historical letterpress that accompanied the published prints. This was provided not only in English but also in French for the benefit of readers on the continent, foreign markets playing a major role in British print-publishing before the wars of 1793–1815. Although the *Antiquities* was a joint endeavour with the engraver-publisher William Byrne, Hearne himself performed the lion's share of the work as well as being its intellectual guiding force. The long list of its subscribers includes the names of many who feature in this catalogue:

Beaumont, Farington, Daniel Daulby of Liverpool, the Earl of Bute (the father of Lady Mary Lowther), Joseph Pocklington and Joseph Wilkinson. Each of the engravings is inscribed with a dedication to an appropriate local landowner or ecclesiastical dignitary and a delightful personal touch is that the engraving of Cockermouth Castle, based on a drawing of 1777 and published in December 1778, is dedicated to his friend's new wife, Lady Beaumont.

A former Cistercian monastery founded in 1123 and built of local red sandstone, Furness Abbey is the most substantial monastic ruin in the area of the Lakes and has attracted the attention of many artists including Hearne's own contemporaries. *West Aspect of Furness Abbey,* exhibited here, was engraved by William Byrne and his pupil Samuel Middiman and published as the sixth plate of the *Antiquities* on 1 August 1778, with a dedication to Lord George Cavendish, the owner of nearby Holker Hall; *North Aspect of Furness Abbey*, drawn by Hearne after a sketch by Farington, also made in 1777, was published on 15 April 1779, engraved by Hearne himself and William Ellis. (Both these drawings were exhibited, together with others, at the Society of Artists in 1780.) A variant of the present scene, with different lighting effects and figure groups, is in the Victoria & Albert Museum, while the Wordsworth Trust also owns another, entirely different but equally fastidious, view of the west aspect by Hearne. He often repeated his subjects in later life when he had ceased travelling and he was also generous in lending his work to younger artists for study and copying. Both these traits have led to the existence of multiple versions of his works.

Hearne's *Antiquities* was published at a time when there was intense interest in tracing the evolution of Britain's architectural styles from Saxon times to the appearance of the Perpendicular in the fourteenth century. He refers explicitly to such matters in his texts as, for example, in that for *North Aspect* where he points out the 'mixed style of church-architecture' in the abbey and tells the reader that 'the foundation of this religious house was laid whilst the Norman taste in building prevailed; and as it was carrying on (probably under the direction of different architects) the manner of its original design appears to have gradually deviated into that, which is distinguished by the appellation of Gothic.' He then draws attention to the presence in the print of both Norman (i.e. round-headed) features and Gothic (i.e. pointed) ones, enabling the reader to see

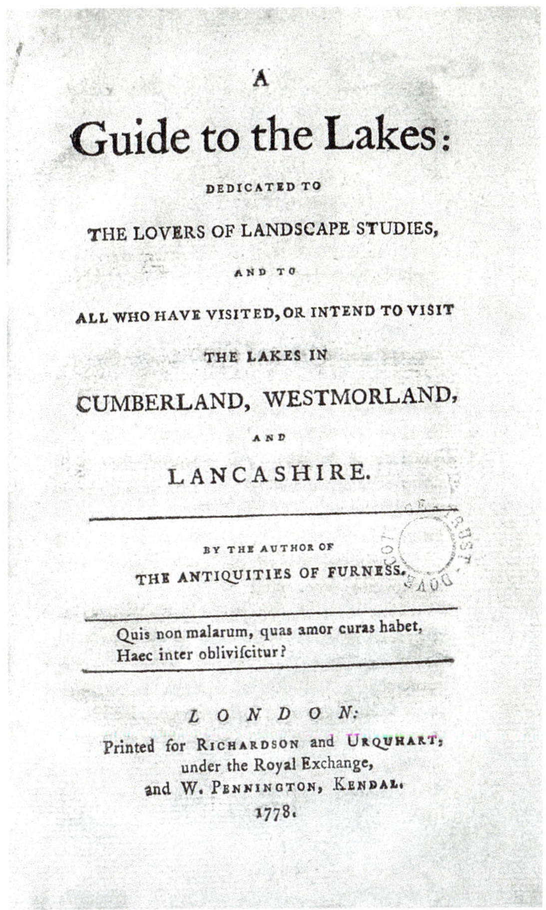
A

Guide to the Lakes:

DEDICATED TO

THE LOVERS OF LANDSCAPE STUDIES,

AND TO

ALL WHO HAVE VISITED, OR INTEND TO VISIT

THE LAKES IN

CUMBERLAND, WESTMORLAND,

AND

LANCASHIRE.

BY THE AUTHOR OF

THE ANTIQUITIES OF FURNESS.

Quis non malarum, quas amor curas habet,
Haec inter oblivifcitur?

LONDON:

Printed for RICHARDSON and URQUHART;
under the Royal Exchange,
and W. PENNINGTON, KENDAL.
1778.

Cat. 18

that his remarks are based on stylistic analysis and the evidence of his own eyes, rather than simply being repeated from earlier written sources. In fact *West Aspect* shows the juxtaposition of Norman and Gothic far better than *North Aspect* since apertures in both styles occur in the same, extremely well-lit, wall in the centre of the scene. CFP

18

THOMAS WEST (1720?–79)

A Guide to the Lakes: dedicated to the lovers of landscape studies, and to all who have visited, or intend to visit the lakes in Cumberland, Westmorland, and Lancashire

London and Kendal: 1778

Thomas West was a Jesuit priest. While serving as a chaplain at Titeup Hall near Dalton in Furness he wrote the *Antiquities of Furness*, published in 1774. He put together his *Guide to the Lakes* after moving to Ulverston. In contrast to the literary appreciations and travel accounts that had so far been published, West's *Guide* was the first book to give practical information to those engaged in, or contemplating, a visit to the Lake District. He advised his readers when to go (June to August was best), what to take (a landscape mirror, a telescope) and which route to take. A tour of the Lakes is recommended to anyone who wished 'to unbend the mind from anxious cares, or fatiguing studies', for they 'will meet with agreeable dissipation and useful relaxation'. 'The contemplative traveller,' he adds, 'will be charmed with the sight of the sweet retreats, that he will observe in these enchanting regions of calm repose.'

West provided substantial antiquarian information where appropriate, but most of his book is concerned with the landscape. He recommended particular viewing points, or 'stations' around the major lakes (only the more remote Wastwater and Ennerdale are left out): 'The design of the following sheets, is to encourage the taste of visiting the lakes, by furnishing the traveller with a Guide', he wrote, 'and for that purpose are here collected and laid before him, all the select stations, and points of view noticed by those authors who have made the tour of the lakes.' These authors included Gray, Hutchinson, and Brown. West published his *Guide* anonymously (the identification 'by the Author of the Antiquities of Furness' did not provide much of a clue as to his identity, since that was anonymous as well), but his modesty did not prevent him from judging the remarks of earlier writers and sometimes opposing them with his own opinions. When writing about Grasmere, for example, he approvingly quotes Thomas Gray's description of the valley from Dunmail Raise, but argues that the view looking north, from Red Bank, was much better. Nor did he wish his readers to follow his own recommendations too slavishly. Instead, he encouraged visitors to approach the landscape critically: 'This Guide will also be of use to the artist in his choice of station, by pointing out the principal objects in a country that abounds in landscape studies, with such variety of scenery. Yet it is not to be presumed, dogmatically to direct, but only to suggest hints, that may be improved, adopted or rejected.'

West's *Guide* was by far the most popular title in Lake District literature up until the 1830s, by which time it had been through more than a dozen editions. Only this first edition was published by West himself, however, for he died just a year after its publication. SH

19

THOMAS WEST (1720?–79)

A Guide to the Lakes: dedicated to the lovers of landscape studies, and to all who have visited, or intend to visit the lakes in Cumberland, Westmorland, and Lancashire ... the second edition revised throughout and greatly enlarged

London and Kendal: 1780

Purchased, 1994

This second edition of West's *Guide* was edited by William Cockin, a writing-master and accountant at Lancaster Grammar School, a poet (see cat. 20), and a friend of George Romney. In a preface Cockin gave a short account of Thomas West's life, and assured the reader that he had been well-qualified to write a guide to the Lakes: his writing might occasionally be repetitious, his antiquarian digressions a little long, and some of his stations 'dubiously pointed out', but the information he gives is 'decently perspicuous and correct'.

Besides making a few minor revisions to the text, Cockin added a long Addenda section providing highlights from earlier Lake District literature, including Brown's letter, an extract from Dalton's poem, Gray's journal, and Cumberland's *Ode*. A frontispiece was added: a view of Grasmere by John Feary, taken, as West had advised, from Red Bank. Any guidebook depends on up-to-date information for its continuing success, and in a concluding advertisement Cockin asked readers to send in any 'useful facts and entertaining descriptions'. SH

20

WILLIAM COCKIN (1736–1801)

Ode to the Genius of the Lakes in the North of England

London: 1780

Gift of Professor Kathleen Tillotson, 1978

Cockin published this poem simultaneously with his edition of West's *Guide*. He even promoted the *Guide* in a footnote: 'Gray, Young, Pennant, and Hutchinson, describe a part of the Lakes and their accompanyments mentioned in this poem; but the most complete and circumstantial account of them may be seen in the new edition of the GUIDE TO THE LAKES just published'. Cockin explains that he does not offer the *Ode* as a literary production; rather, he hopes that it will be read by '*actual tourists*'. Similarly, the *Ode* is an appreciation not only

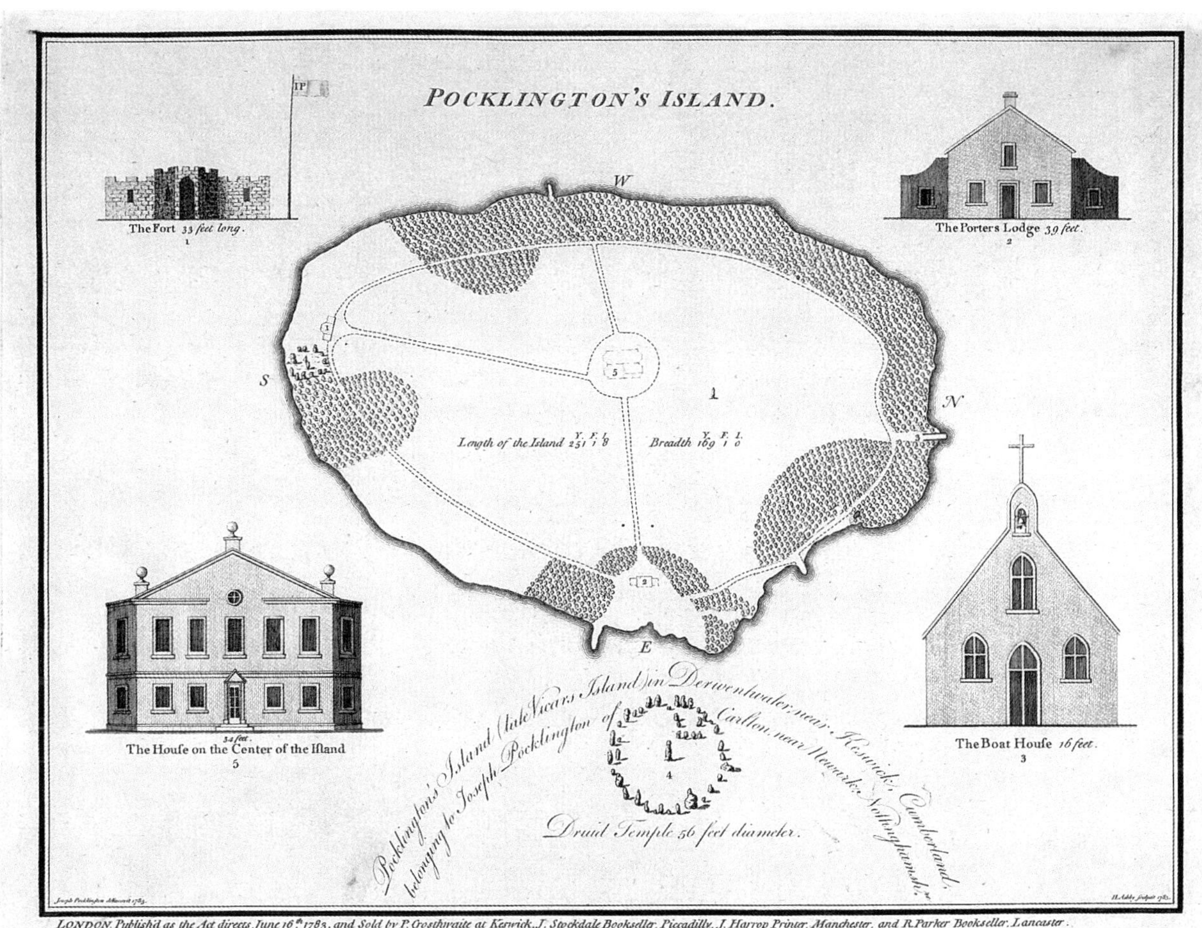

Cat. 21

of the scenery itself, but of the human associations that have embellished and enriched it. It opens with a depiction of the landscape in its original state, before 'these happier days of genuine taste', when its charm was 'felt by few' except the swain, who surveyed it 'with fervour slight'. This is followed by a description of its current celebrity status: 'What wond'ring crouds [*sic*], to trace thy fairy lands, / At Summer's call, in gayest trim appear.' This new attention is welcomed by the landscape, 'whose pleasure is to please'. The shepherd's lot among the mountain retreats is certainly a pleasant one, but not as happy as the life enjoyed by the amateur artist or poet:

> when here some youthful mind,
> Sanguine with hope, and nature's prompt desire,
> With raptur'd eye, and fancy unconfin'd,
> Drinks the deep magic of the muse's lyre:
> And oft with daring fire,
> Himself attempts to make its strings,
> With thrilling tones suggest,
> The high-born images of things,
> That warm the poet's breast.

The poem continues with a roll call of the illustrious dead who were born from the 'happy soil' of the Lake District, and concludes with a hymn of thanks to its divine Creator.

The *Ode* is followed by some 'occasional notes' in which Cockin gives brief biographical details of those named in the poem, and reiterates his recommendation, already given 'in Article 8th of the *Addenda* to the new edition of *The Guide to the Lakes*', that monuments be erected commemorative of those persons of genius who have enriched the area, 'to begin with a memorial of the late Dr. Brown on the borders of *Derwent-water*, and of Mr. Gray near the Lake of Grasmere.' SH

21

PETER CROSTHWAITE (1735–1808)
Seven Maps of the Lakes
London: 1783

Peter Crosthwaite was neither artist nor writer, but he was one of the first Lake District residents wholeheartedly to embrace the commercial possibilities offered by the area's new popularity. After an eventful career as a sailor (he saw active service in the Far East) and a customs officer, Crosthwaite retired to Keswick, and there opened an eccentric museum full of assorted curiosities (see Andrews, 1989, pp. 176–7). In one guidebook he is described as 'Museum curator and Aeolian harp manufacturer'.

Crosthwaite's main publishing venture was a series of 'accurate maps' of the Lakes: 'the matchless Lake of Derwent', 'the Grand Lake of Windermere', 'the beautiful Lake of Ulls-water', 'Broadwater or Bassenthwaite Lake', 'Coniston Lake', 'Buttermere, Crummock & Lowes-Water Lakes'. In each of these maps Crosthwaite identified West's viewing stations, and surrounded the map itself with a number of simple line illustrations of places of interest. The map of Derwentwater, 'in the most delightful Vale which perhaps ever Human Eye beheld', illustrates Crosthwaite church, the 'Bowdar Stone' and 'Lofty Skiddaw'. At the foot of the map is the legend: 'Surveyed &c. by P. CROSTHWAITE Admiral of Keswick Regatta, who keeps the Museum at Keswick & is Guide, Pilot, Geographer & Hydrographer to the Nobility and Gentry, who make the Tour of the Lakes.'

There was nothing cynical about Crosthwaite's salesman's rhetoric, for he took the tourist business very seriously, but there is something undeniably eccentric about his various enterprises. A seventh map (illustrated on the previous page) is of 'Pocklington's Island'. In 1778 Joseph Pocklington, the son of a Nottinghamshire banker, had purchased Vicar's Island on Derwentwater, and renamed it Pocklington's Island. He built a classical villa in its centre, and, around the shore, a series of ornamental buildings: a boathouse in the shape of a church, a small fort, and a mock circle of druid stones. Every year 'Admiral' Crosthwaite devised the mock battles held around the island that were part of the Keswick regattas. SH

22

ROBERT SHERBOURNE (fl. 1775–1810)
Ullswater
1781
Bodycolour, 52.5 × 67.5 cm
Inscribed 'R^t. Sherbourne / 1781'
Gift of the W.W. Spooner Charitable Trust, 2008

At first sight this work seems remarkable for its naïve vision, reflecting its early date and the amateur status of its artist. Little is known of Robert Sherbourne save that he was one of the two illegitimate sons of Admiral the Hon. Robert Digby (1732–1815); his artistic training came presumably from a private tutor. Painted in 1781, cat. 22 predates by five years the publication of the Rev. William Gilpin's *Observations, relative chiefly to Picturesque Beauty ... on Several Parts of England, Particularly the Mountains, and Lakes of Cumberland, and Westmoreland* with its many recommendations on desirable viewpoints and essential features in a scene (cat. 13). However, Sherbourne was not working in isolation. His manner of representing crags and cliffs has elements in common with that of William Bellers (compare cat. 3–4) and his medium – bodycolour – was in regular use at this time. His links with Sherborne Castle in Dorset, home to his father's elder brother – Henry, seventh Baron Digby (and first Earl Digby from 1790) – meant that he was familiar with the work of many Old Masters including Claude Lorrain. Furthermore, the 1770s had seen the start of the transformation of the grounds at Sherborne by 'Capability' Brown, directly inspired by their Claudes; the new landscaping included the creation of a serpentine lake with a cascade and the planting of thousands of trees with foliage of diverse tints. Both these quintessential features of landscape beauty, as disseminated by Brown, are perfectly conveyed in cat. 22, with its curving sheet of smooth water embraced by a landscape of many colours.

If this work does indeed represent Ullswater, as hitherto believed, the view must, presumably, be towards the head of the lake. The diagonal sequence of lumbering shapes near the centre may be intended to represent a waterfall, perhaps Aira Force (though in real life its course and situation are very different). The grassy stepped crags to the right of this are schematic and bear little resemblance to Lakeland fells. CFP

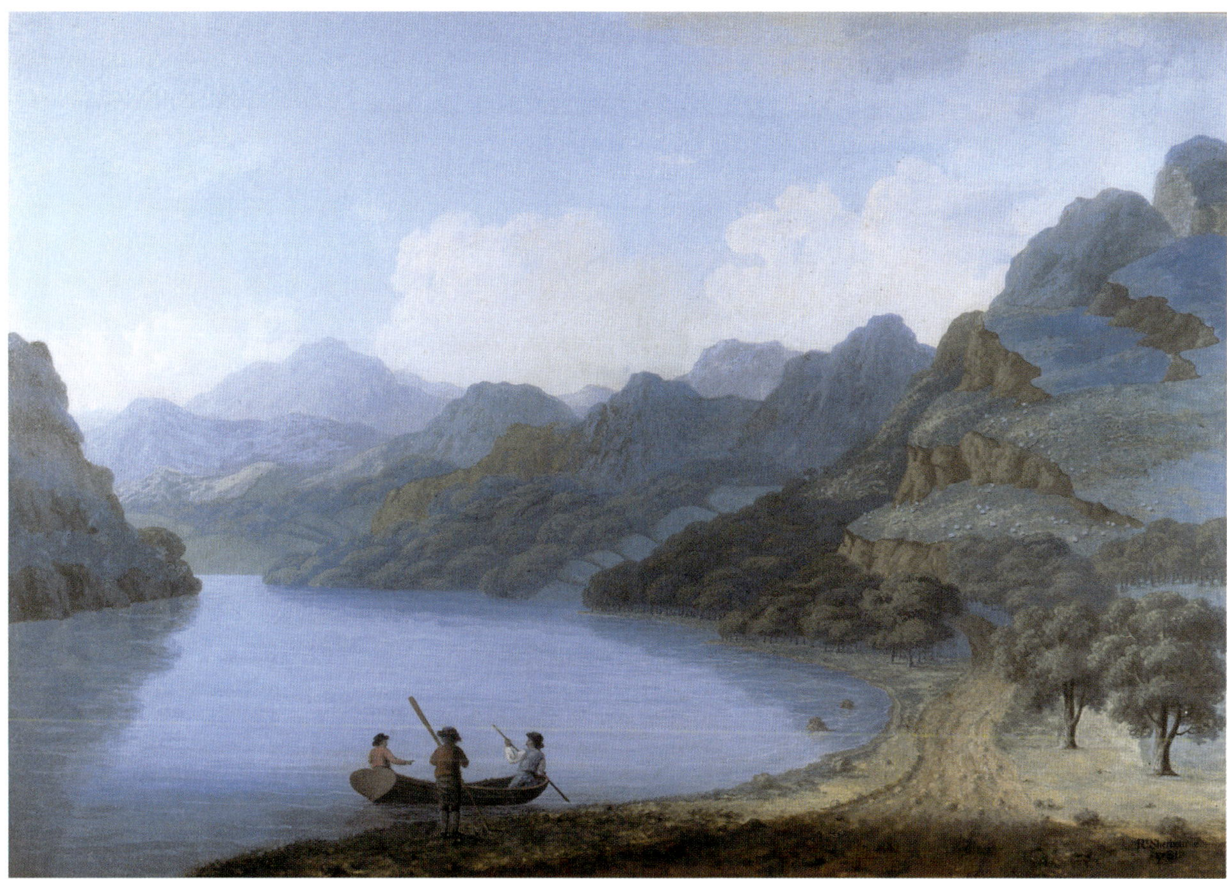

Cat. 22

23

THOMAS GAINSBOROUGH RA (1727–88)
The Langdale Pikes
*c.*1783
Pencil and wash, 26.7 × 41.7 cm
Gift of Charles Warren, 1985

After his youth Gainsborough rarely sketched landscapes from nature, usually preferring to work from his own imagination and from small studio arrangements of cork and coal, sand and clay, mosses, lichens and broccoli. He declared that 'with regard to real Views from Nature in this Country, he has never seen any Place that affords a Subject equal to the poorest imitations of Gaspar or Claude' (Hayes, 2001, p. 30). It is thus not surprising that he drew no sketches from nature during the Lake District tour that he made in the late summer of 1783 at the age of 56 with his Ipswich friend Samuel Kilderbee. However, the grandeur of the Lakes lingered in his mind and the area makes its presence felt in a handful of drawings that were made soon afterwards: cat. 23, evoking the Langdale Pikes as seen from Elterwater; one whose exact source of inspiration was unidentified when it was listed in the catalogue raisonné of Gainsborough's landscapes (Hayes, 1982, vol. 1, plate 192); and one or two others (e.g. Belsey, 2008, no. 1092).

By the time of his tour Gainsborough's taste and interest in landscape was well established; he was concerned not with precise observation and recording but with achieving a personal and poetical response. Breadth, sentiment, energy and rhythmical design were his aims: the capturing of the life and movement that he saw and felt in the natural world itself. He had already depicted generalised mountain features in many of his paintings, including one of those shown at the RA prior to his departure for the north; that exhibit (no. 34, with the typically non-specific title, *Landscape*) is now identified with the *Rocky Wooded Landscape* in the National Gallery of Scotland (composition study in the Cecil Higgins

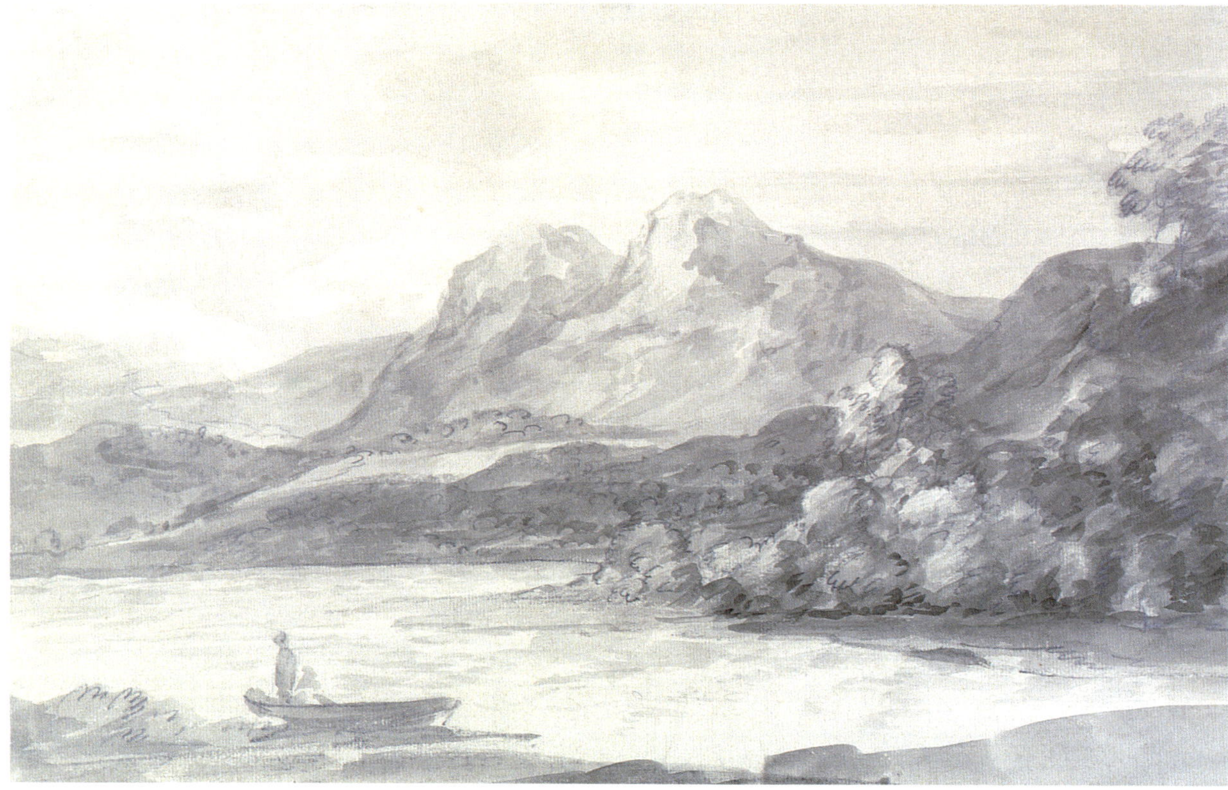

Cat. 23

Art Gallery, Bedford). Despite these over-riding concerns, the Trust's drawing includes an instantly recognisable depiction of the Langdale Pikes: on Pike of Stickle Gainsborough shows the severe dark face of Gimmer Crag and above it Loft Crag veiled in vapour while the massive gnarled heights of Harrison Stickle are distinctively rendered. The boatman standing in the foreground is placed there for effect. Gainsborough regarded such figures as 'a little business for the Eye', serving to 'fill a place (I won't say stop a Gap)' and make the viewer return to the landscape 'with more glee' (Hayes, 2001, p. 40). Gilpin was to introduce just such solitary figures into the illustrations of his *Observations, relative chiefly to Picturesque Beauty* … relating to the Lake District in 1786.

In the months following his tour Gainsborough also made a slightly smaller but far more detailed drawing in chalk and stump. In this study (fig. 12) he made drastic changes to his first composition, transforming it into a powerfully expressed synthesis of mountain scenery: he unified the Pikes into a single, complex mass with a strong diagonal thrust in the opposite direction; he added numerous trees driven by the wind; he reduced Elterwater to a mere tarn, replacing the boatman with a shepherd gazing at his flock of sheep on areas of both low-lying and rising ground; he included clouds racing across the sky above jutting crags and mountain paths; he invented boulders littering the foreground. The painting based on this study (fig. 13) was among those that Gainsborough exhibited at his home, Schomberg House, Pall Mall, in 1784 following his break with the Royal Academy over the display of his work. It was shown there again by his widow in 1789, the year after his death, when it was described in the *Morning Post* as 'painted on his return from the *Lakes*; and though not a portrait of any particular spot, the picture is highly characteristic of that country.' It was bought by the Prince of Wales who presented it to Mrs Maria Fitzherbert and is now in Munich. CFP

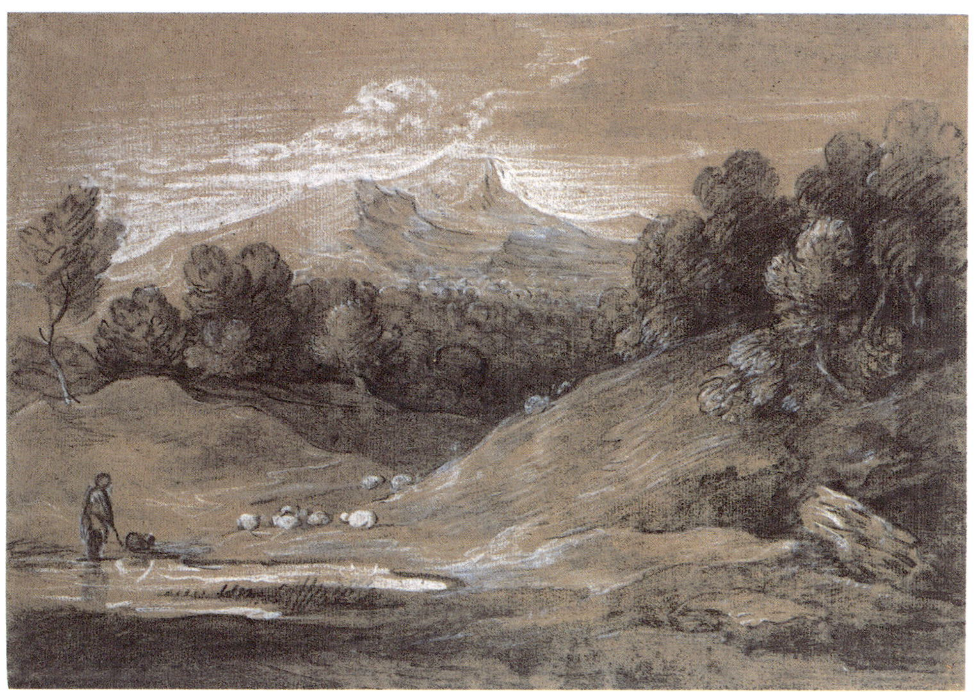

Fig. 12 Thomas Gainsborough, *Upland Landscape with Shepherd, Sheep and Cattle*, chalk and stump, *c.*1783–4 (Gainsborough's House, Sudbury, Suffolk).

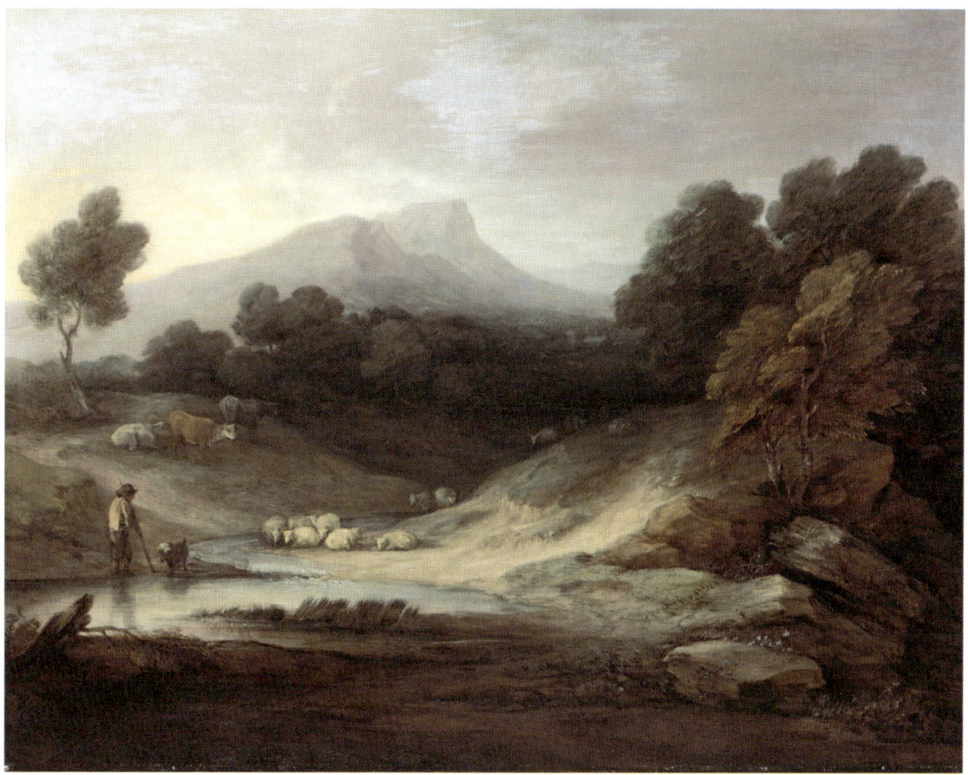

Fig. 13 Thomas Gainsborough, *Mountain Landscape with Shepherd*, oil on canvas, *c.*1783–4 (Bayerische Staatsgemäldesammlungen, Alte Pinakothek, Munich).

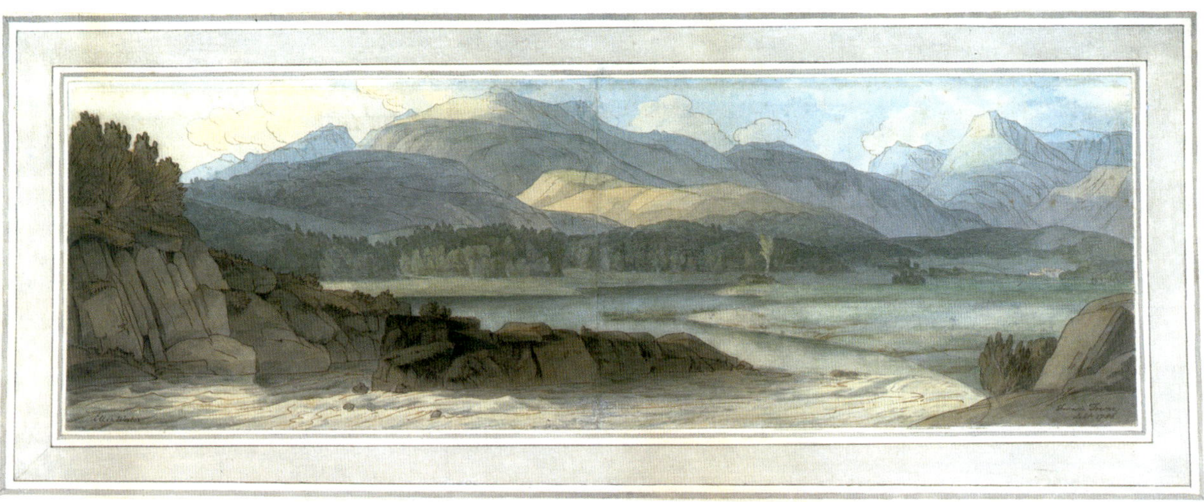

Cat. 24

24

FRANCIS TOWNE (1739–1816)
Elterwater
1786
Pen and brown ink and watercolour, 15.4 × 47 cm
Inscribed 'Elter Water' and 'Francis Towne / del[t] 1786', and on verso 'Elter Water August 12th 1786 / light from the left hand / F. Towne . 19 / London / Leicester Square 1790'
Purchased with the generous assistance of the National Heritage Memorial Fund, 1982

Francis Towne received scant recognition from colleagues and patrons in his own day but is now widely admired for his originality, especially in the depiction of mountain scenery. Among his especially interesting characteristics are his depiction of cast shadows and his habit of annotating his drawings with notes on light effects and sometimes with the hours of the day at which the work was made; this latter preoccupation, during his time in Rome in 1780, has recently been associated with his strict work ethic and his deliberate eschewing of the diversions and frivolity of the metropolis in favour of a simpler life in Exeter among a circle of high-minded non-conformists (Stephens, 2010). His tour of the Lake District in 1786 has been extensively discussed elsewhere (Wilcox, 1997) and it is worth noting here that the inventory of Towne's library at his death included West's *Guide*, which had reached its third edition in 1784, and Gilpin's *Observations* on Cumberland and Westmorland, published earlier in 1786; the latter provided the springboard – and an artistic challenge – for Towne's northern tour in the company of his Exeter friends James White (the uncle of John White Abbott; see cat. 32) and John Merivale.

Towne visited Elterwater on the fifth day of his visit to the Lakes, 12 August, a day on which he also made three drawings of Skelwith Force, the waterfall that carries the waters of the Brathay down to Ambleside and Windermere and which lies close to the viewpoint of this drawing (Wilcox, 1997, pp. 115–16). To create this panoramic view of Elterwater he stationed himself so that he could see virtually the whole of the small lake, looking west towards the vast mass of the Coniston Fells, diverse but unified, and the Langdale Pikes rearing their heads above Elterwater Hall. He drew a pencil sketch using two facing pages of his sketchbook to achieve a wide horizontal format to suit his subject and he also made a note on the verso recording 'light from the left hand'. This enabled him to recreate the light effects that he had seen when he came to work up his sketch in colours at a future date in his studio. There he drew the crisp pen and ink outlines and laid in the flat washes of colour that are the hallmarks of his style and varied little over the course of his career.

In this work the stark portrayal of the desolate fells contrasts superbly with the vitality of the massed stylised trees below, and a similar antithesis is achieved in the juxtaposition of the rough piles of boulders in the foreground with the softly meandering shores of the lake, surrounded with meadows.

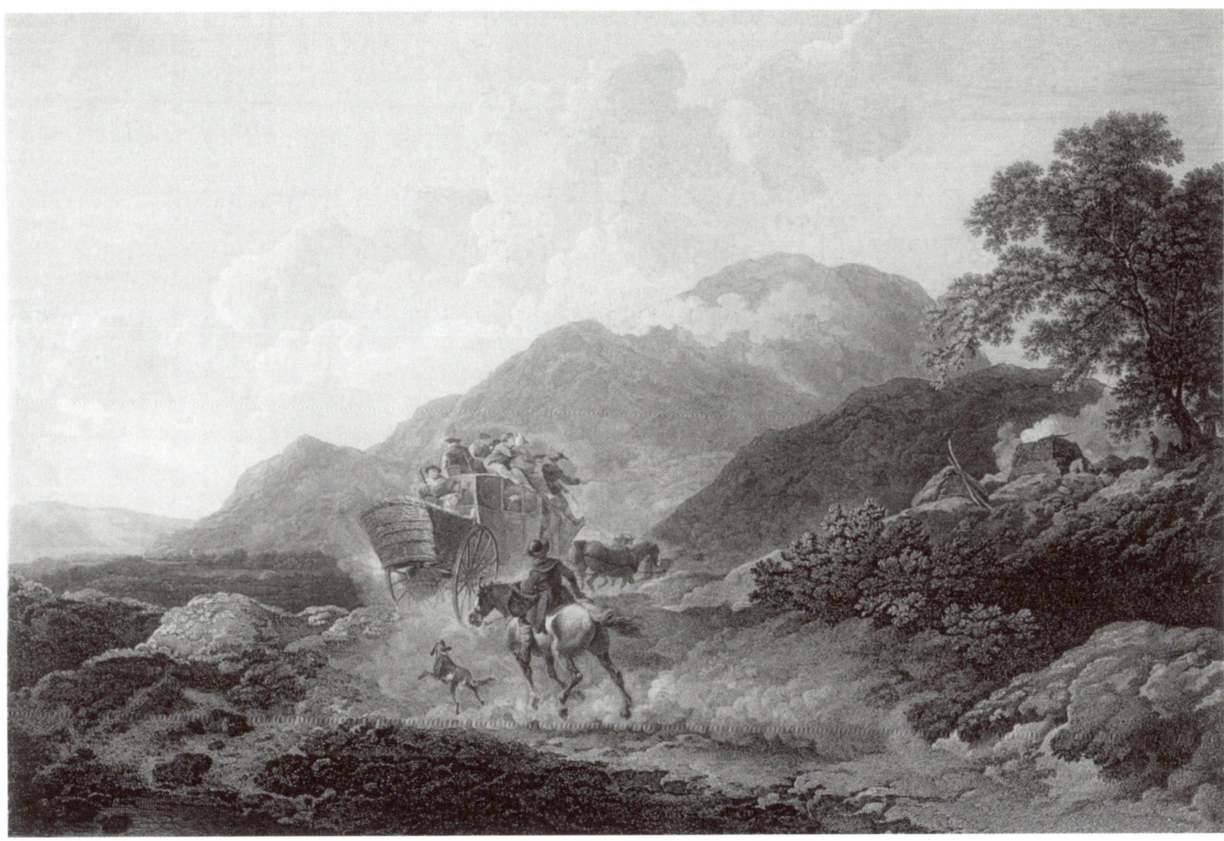

Cat. 25

As Farington remarked in 1803, Towne 'is a man who observes many things' (VI.2082). His powers of observation have rarely been surpassed and his art commands the attention of the viewer in a way that is direct and extremely modern for its date of execution. CFP

25

THOMAS MORRIS and W. THOMAS after PHILIP JAMES DE LOUTHERBOURG RA (1740–1812)
Skiddaw in Cumberland: a Summer's sunset
1787
Etching and engraving, 46.5 × 60 cm
Engraved inscriptions: below, with title and names of artist and engravers (with Morris described as '*Pupil of the late M.*r *Woollett*'; centre, beneath title, *From the Original Picture in the possession of M*r *R. P. Jones*; bottom, *Publish'd as the Act directs Dec.*r *1 1787 by Molteno, Colnaghi & Co. N.*o *132 Pall Mall. London*; left and right, several lines of letterpress relating to Skiddaw in English and French

De Loutherbourg's only visit to the Lake District – in the summer of 1783, probably in friendly rivalry with Gainsborough – inspired an impressive array of works in the Royal Academy exhibitions of the following four years: he showed seven paintings naming places in the area in 1784, six in 1785, two in 1786 and one in 1787. *Skiddaw in Cumberland, a summer evening, with a stage coach* (no. 78) was shown in the first of these years, 1784, with a pendant of identical size but contrasting subject and mood, *A cottage in Patterdale, Westmoreland* (no. 63; both works now in the Government Art Collection). This engraving after *Skiddaw* was published in 1787, the year of De Loutherbourg's final Lakes exhibit, *View of Grasmeer in Westmorland, an evening* (no. 81). It is typical of this artist of many talents that his interest in the Lake District was intense but short-lived.

As the letterpress to the engraving tells the reader, the vast extent of Skiddaw and its great elevation above Keswick led to the belief that it was the highest mountain in Great Britain and, although destitute of volcanic properties, it earned the label of 'the Etna of the North'. However, De Loutherbourg's scene is more than a testimony to its 'Awful Grandeur'. It provides a dramatic illustration of

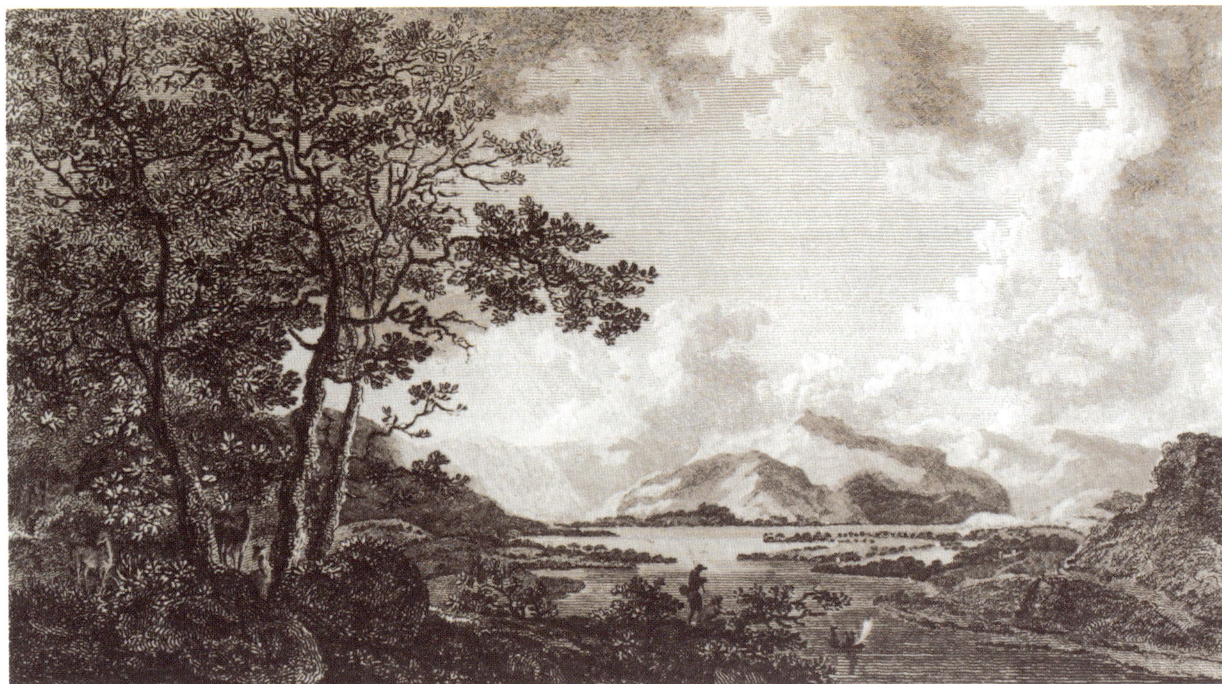

Cat. 26

the realities of travel in the Lake District in the age when horse-drawn carriages jolted their way perilously over stony tracks through the fells, struggling with steep inclines or tediously going round them; we read here that the windings of the road necessitated a 'laborious Ascent of 5 Miles'. Journeys that are today accomplished in minutes on tarmac roads often occupied several hours and were both uncomfortable and dangerous; thus, while the high peaks were awe-inspiring as natural phenomena, the act of travelling carried its own terrors. In portraying Skiddaw as the last and worst obstacle on a mountain road – rather than as a majestic peak beyond the expanse of Derwentwater or Bassenthwaite – De Loutherbourg brilliantly unites and intensifies the two interrelated concepts at the heart of every tour to the Lakes.

Cat. 25 was the work of two engravers, Thomas Morris and W. Thomas, the first of whom mentions conspicuously in the inscription-line that he had been a pupil of the recently deceased William Woollett, the leading English engraver of his day. Woollett's prints had been of the highest quality and financially 'top of the range' – the equivalent of buying a Picasso today – and Morris is here, effectively, claiming to be in the same league. The text below the print, like that for other publications of this period, appears in both English and French (see cat. 17). William Hutchinson's *Excursion to the Lakes, in Westmoreland and Cumberland,* referred to in the final line, is exhibited here as cat. 11. CFP

26

JAMES HEATH after GEORGE BARRET RA (1732?–84)
Uls Water, A Lake in Cumberland
1788
Engraving, 11.1 × 17.6 cm
Engraved inscriptions: below, with title and names of artist and engraver; bottom, *Published as the Act directs June 2.ᵈ 1788 by G. Robinson & Partners*
Gift of Peter Bicknell, 1988

George Barret, a foundation member of the Royal Academy in London in 1768 and one of the most notable and prolific British landscape painters of the eighteenth century, was the first artist to show a painting of the Lake District at the new institution. At its inaugural exhibition, in the summer of 1769, the area went unrepresented, though there were four depictions of mountain scenery (two Scottish landscapes by Barret himself and two Alpine waterfalls by Edmund Garvey). In the second exhibition in 1770, however, Barret exhibited *A study from Nature on the lake at Ullswater, in Cumberland* (no. 9) and he showed further views – of different parts of the area – in 1772 and 1781.

James Heath's engraving after Barret is the only Lake District scene in *A Tour in England and Scotland, in 1785*, published anonymously in London in 1788; all its other illustrations depict Scotland. The author's identity was eventually revealed in the second edition (1791) as Thomas Newte of Tiverton whom Farington refers to in 1816 as 'Captain' (XIV.4802). Although Newte's text reveals that he spent just ten days in the Lakes (9–19 June 1785) and his discussion of the area occupies fewer than twenty pages out of nearly 400, he appreciated its beauties and wrote about them well. Many years later, when Farington was advising the Rev. Thomas Hartwell Horne on his forthcoming visit to the Lakes (see cat. 74), Newte's *Tour* was one of the three books that he lent him; the others were West's *Guide* (cat. 18) and Hutchinson's *Tour* (cat. 11). It is noteworthy that Farington did not equip Horne with any recent publications.

In the text facing Barret's image (p. 65) Newte declares that Ullswater 'has more the appearance of a lake than any of the others, as you can look over, at one view, a greater expanse of water'. This observation is well illustrated in Barret's scene. CFP

27

JOSEPH FARINGTON RA (1747–1821)
and WILLIAM COOKSON (1754–1820)
Views of the Lakes, &c. in Cumberland and Westmorland
London: 1789

28

WILLIAM BYRNE and JOHN LANDSEER
after JOSEPH FARINGTON RA (1747–1821)
North View on the Road leading from Keswick to Ambleside. Taken from the Six mile-stone
1789
Etching and engraving, 25 × 36.5 cm
Engraved inscriptions: below, with title and names of artist and engravers; top right, 'N.° XVIII'; bottom, *London: Published as the Act directs, 1 Jan.ʸ 1789, by* W. Byrne, *N.° 79 Titchfield Street.*

Farington's *Views of the Lakes, &c. in Cumberland and Westmorland* has the distinction of being the earliest volume of engravings dedicated to the scenery of this area and accompanied by descriptive letterpress. A few large engravings had been published earlier, sometimes with a separately available commentary (cat. 3–4, 8, 25), but nothing had appeared to match the scale and quality of this volume with its twenty scenes. As with many such projects at this time, the preparatory work occupied several years, with advance subscriptions being solicited through advertisements in the press and elsewhere. The first six plates were advertised immediately after the Preface to the third edition of West's *Guide to the Lakes* (1784) and the engravings were thenceforth published in instalments or 'parts' with diverse publication dates, ranging from 1 December 1784 to 15 May 1789; the title page of the final volume bears the date 'June 16, 1789'. Several different engravers were employed from the start to assist the chief engraver William Byrne who was himself the publisher.

When Farington produced the drawings on which these engravings were based he had not yet commenced the detailed diary for which he is now famous, so we cannot follow the day-by-day course of events leading up to publication. However, he did record developments following the death of William Byrne in 1805 when his widow had to deal with the remaining stock of engravings and proof impressions as well as the copper plates on which the scenes had been engraved. Several sets of engravings were sold to the museum-owner, map publisher and tour promoter Peter Crosthwaite of Keswick in 1807 for 300 guineas (VII.2693-4; VIII 2942, 3093, 3149). The remainder of the stock, together with the plates, was auctioned in London on 15 June 1808 in a sale where William Havell (see cat. 60) represented Farington but was outbid on every article. Farington received his share of the takings from Byrne's son John a few days later (IX.3238, 3259, 3291, 3295, 3316). One of the interesting facts to emerge from this chronicle is that, in September 1806, *Views of the Lakes* was described as selling 'better than ever' in Keswick (VIII.2852), perhaps reflecting the area's new wave of popularity thanks to artists such as Ibbetson, Glover and, very shortly, Havell himself. And when Farington called on the Crosthwaites in Keswick two years later he was gratified to learn that his *Views* continued to 'sell above all others' (IX.3355).

Farington's twenty views illustrate the most popular sights of the day, focusing chiefly on Derwentwater and the eastern lakes: Ullswater, Grasmere, Rydal and Windermere. The accompanying short texts were provided by an old friend, William Cookson, Wordsworth's maternal uncle, following an approach from Farington in 1784. These

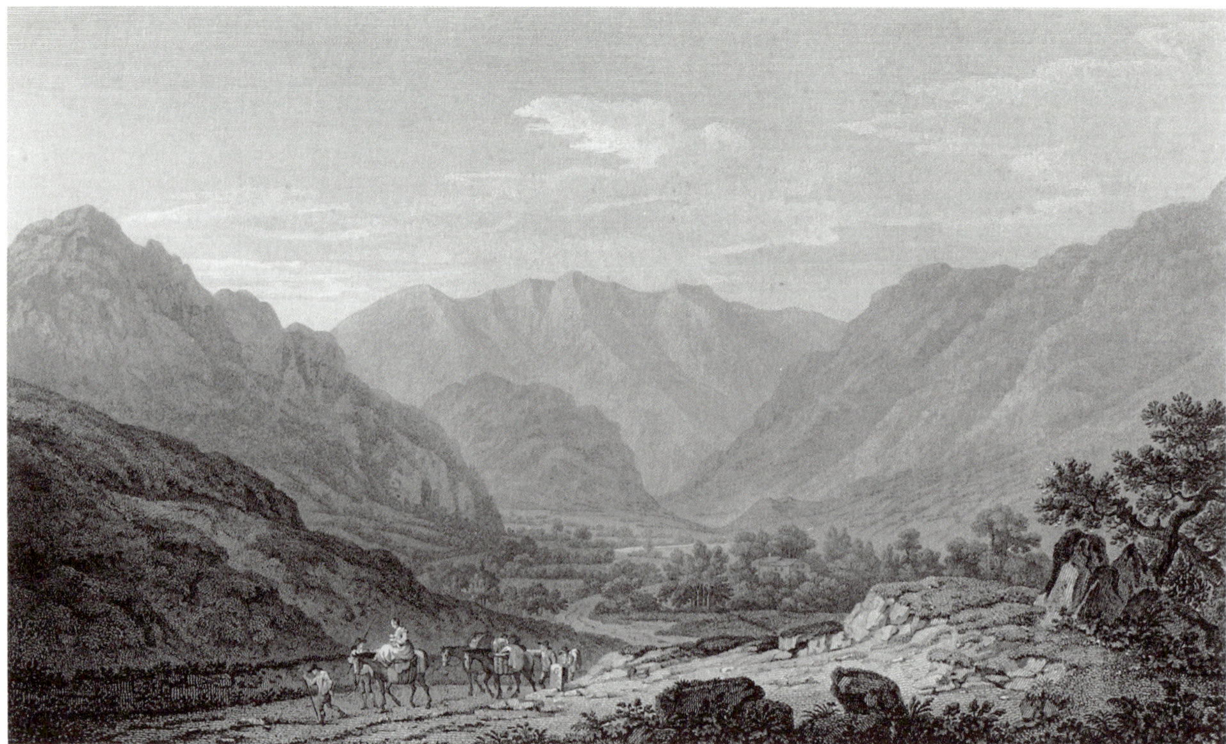

Cat. 28

sometimes incorporated material from authors whose writings on the Lakes were now widely disseminated: thus Gilpin's *Observations* of 1786 is quoted on the 'Palace of Patterdale' while the lower waterfall at Rydal is described in the words of William Mason (who had brought Gray's letters into the public domain in 1775; see cat 12). The texts were printed in both English and French.

Farington's scenes are immensely varied, ranging from groups of buildings (such as Brathay Bridge with the houses of Clappersgate) to wide prospects, or bird's-eye views, over lakes and vales. One of the grandest of the prospects, *North View on the Road leading from Keswick to Ambleside. Taken from the Six mile-stone*, depicts a spectacular valley filled with contrasts and is described, in terms partly derived from West's *Guide* (1784, p. 83), as follows: 'Between lofty Mountains on the right, and Rocks of high and rude Forms on the left, passes the narrow green Vale of Legberthwaite, which is divided into small Inclosures, and peopled with a few Cots. The Vale is terminated by the romantic Rock of St. John; behind which rises Saddleback, a Mountain almost vying with Skiddaw for pre-eminence, and forming a sublime Back-Ground to the Scene.' Against this setting a group of travellers make their way laboriously uphill past the 'six mile-stone' on the right, the men leading horses laden with baskets and barrels, the woman clasping an infant to her breast. CFP

29

?JOHN LAPORTE (1761–1839)
North View on the Road leading from Keswick to Ambleside. Taken from the Six mile-stone
c.1790?
Bodycolour, 46.7 × 67 cm (sight)
Gift of the W.W. Spooner Charitable Trust, 2000

30

?JOHN LAPORTE (1761–1839)
Derwentwater, and the Vale of Keswick from Ashness; Bassenthwaite Lake in the Distance
c.1790?
Bodycolour, 46.7 × 64.8 cm (sight)
Gift of the W.W. Spooner Charitable Trust, 2000

In the 1790s Laporte painted several large bodycolour scenes depicting the Lakes, all of a similar size to cat. 29–30; examples are known in the Fitzwilliam Museum, Cambridge, and the National

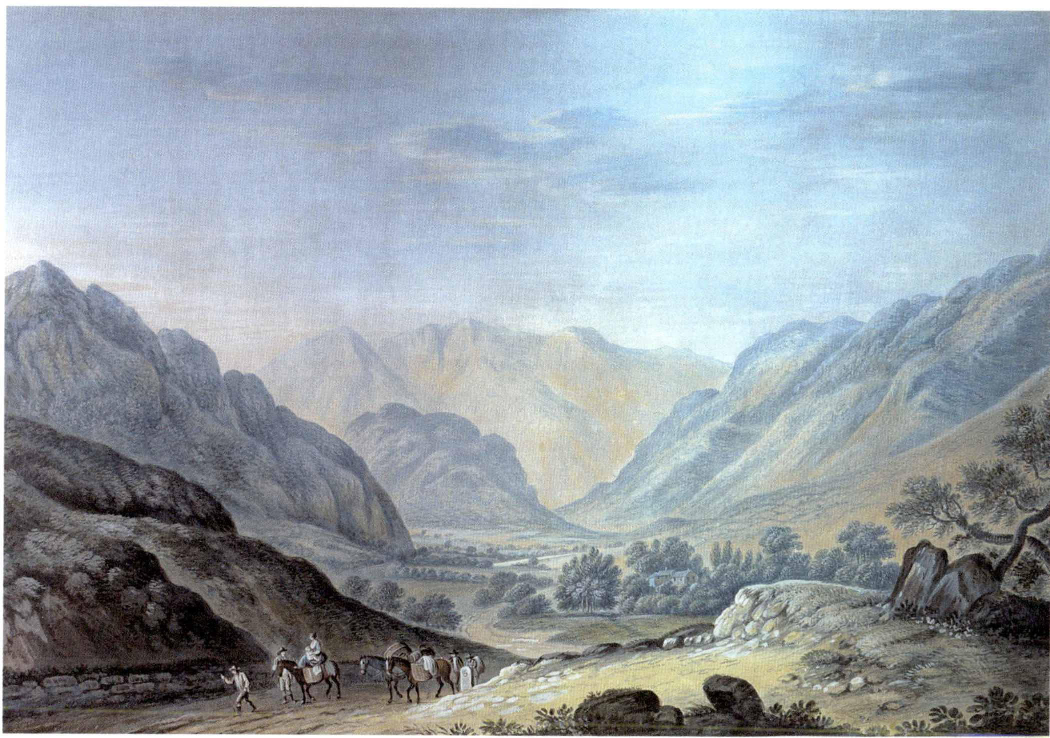

Cat. 29

Gallery of South Australia in Adelaide as well as others reproduced in twentieth-century publications but now untraced. All are highly decorative and well composed, featuring spirited groups of people on and around ferries on Windermere or Derwentwater. They are also marked by considerable liveliness, indicating that they were based on Laporte's own sketches and experiences from his visit in 1790.

Cat. 29–30 are somewhat different in character from the above works. Each corresponds closely to an engraving in Farington's *Views of the Lakes, &c. in Cumberland and Westmorland*, published in London in 1784–9, so they are exhibited here under Farington's titles; from those twenty engravings *North View on the Road leading from Keswick to Ambleside* is displayed here in its own right as cat. 28. Cat. 29–30 cannot have been the sources for the engravings since those would certainly have been drawings provided by Farington. It is equally certain that they are not engravings that have merely been hand-coloured since they are much larger than the prints. It would seem, therefore, that the artist recreated Farington's scenes – on commission from a lake-loving patron, as part of a teaching exercise or perhaps just on speculation. However, he could not have exhibited such works publicly without attracting a charge of plagiarism, which an established and successful artist in Laporte's position would never have risked. When Farington and his engraver-publisher William Byrne spotted a watercolour copy of one of their prints in a shop in Bond Street in 1797 they marched straight in and complained to the proprietor (III.904). Although cat. 29–30 are imposing and colourful, they are somewhat lacking in vitality – an almost inevitable consequence of their being careful enlarged replicas of works by another artist.

Derwentwater, and the Vale of Keswick from Ashness shows a celebrated view that has appealed to many artists and visitors and remains popular to this day; an aquatint from about the same period as cat. 30 is displayed as cat. 42. On a clear day an observer at Ashness Bridge can enjoy an uninterrupted vista of some ten miles along the vale with its two lakes, Derwentwater and Bassenthwaite. In Farington's day Keswick was of only modest size and the most conspicuous building in the view was Crosthwaite church with its tower. The single-arched packhorse-bridge over Barrow Beck provides an attractive foreground feature, echoing the soft arcs of the wooded islands in Derwentwater as well as the angular profiles of the surrounding fells. CFP

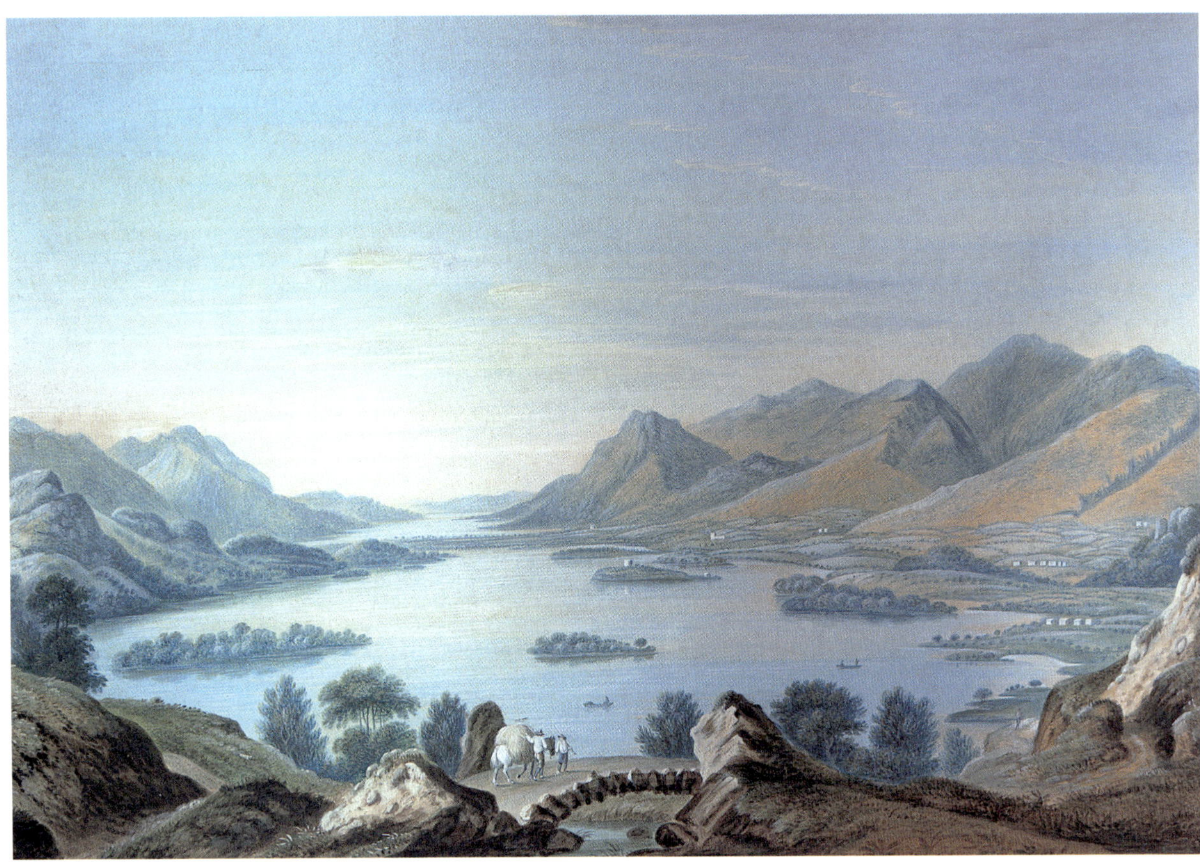

Cat. 30

31

JOHN 'WARWICK' SMITH (1749–1831)
From Mr Parker's Gardens, Coniston Lake
c.1790
Watercolour, 34.6 × 50.4 cm
Gift of the W.W. Spooner Charitable Trust, 2006

By the 1780s Smith was one of the leading watercolourists of the day, with several commissions from the aristocracy to his credit (he probably acquired his nickname through his work for the second Earl of Warwick). In 1788 he received a major commission from John Christian Curwen, the owner (through his wife) of Belle Isle on Windermere, for no fewer than a hundred watercolours depicting the area of the Lakes. In selecting him for this project, Curwen demonstrated his own significance both as one of the most important landowners in the region and as a patron of artists with local connections (Smith had been born near Carlisle and his budding talent had been fostered by the Gilpin family).

The Curwen series was to occupy Smith for several years and demanded extreme ingenuity of composition to avoid a sense of repetition amongst its scenes. Although many are conventional, *From Mr Parker's Gardens* shows how far aesthetic taste had developed since the times when writers longed for the pencil of 'Claude, Poussin or Rosa' to do justice to the enthralling scenery of the Lakes. On Peter Crosthwaite's map of Coniston Water, the estate at Waterhead was the third of the recommended 'stations' from which to view the lake but Smith relegates Coniston itself to second place in both title and composition. He abandons the conventional formulae of painters and theorists, replacing these with a new and original vision based on observation: a stark angular man-made foreground; a mere sliver of lake; morning mists and vapours engulfing the Old Man and the Coniston Fells and hovering round their skirts; abrupt changes of scale between the sundial and the minute lone farm or cottage on the lower ground in the middle distance. The area round the head of the lake is surveyed as if from a viewing platform that has no connection with the

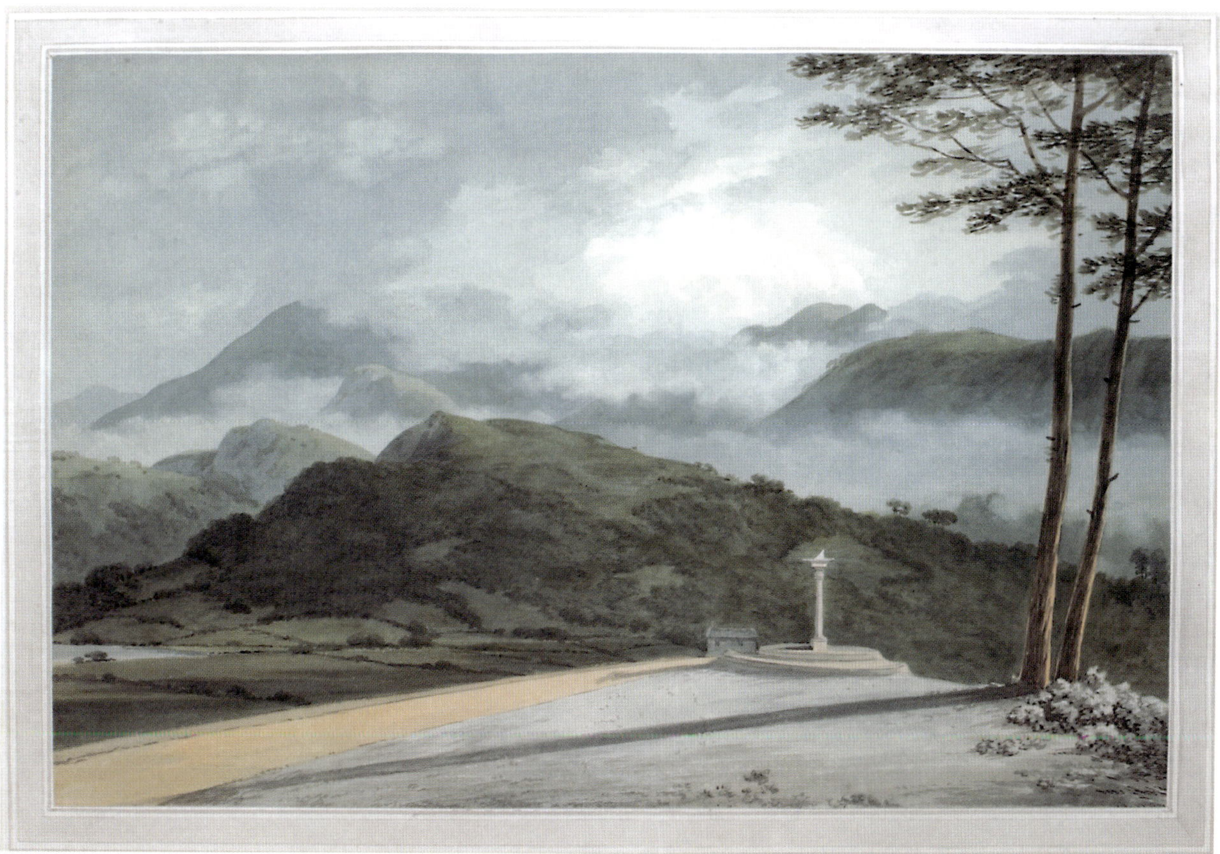

Cat. 31

natural world and this sense of contrast is reinforced by the barrier-like early morning shadow from the trees that bisects the foreground.

Timothy Parker, his wife Ann and their two young children had come to live at Coniston Waterhead following the death early in 1785 of Mrs George Knott (who had inherited it at the age of sixteen from her father William Ford); her husband, a wealthy ironmaster, had predeceased her in January 1784. The Parkers thus became the occupants not only of a newly renovated historic property but also of an enlarged and improved estate that included much of the land at the head of the lake, including the three tarns of Monk Coniston. In 1784 West's *Guide* had noted the 'many beautiful improvements' that George Knott had made to his estate, remarking on the contrast between these and 'the native rudeness of the surrounding hills' which produced 'a most pleasing effect, and are well worth viewing by the curious traveller' (p. 53 note). Smith's drawing enables the modern spectator to share the experience of that 'curious traveller'. CFP

32

JOHN WHITE ABBOTT (1763–1851)
Hill Cragg on Grasmere Lake
1791
Pen and grey ink and watercolour, 19 × 29.5 cm
Inscribed on verso 'Hill Cragg on Grasmere Lake' and 'July 12, 1791'
Purchased with the generous assistance of the National Art Collections Fund, 1977

After Gray's remarks describing Grasmere as a 'little unsuspected paradise' had become widely known through their publication first in Mason's *Memoirs* of his friend (1775; cat. 12) and then, from 1780, in successive editions of West's *Guide* (cat. 18–19), it was depicted by many artists seeking to capture its special charm. Some sought to encapsulate the unity of vale, lake and village in an image from a high viewpoint such as Dunmail Raise to the north (fig. 14) or Red Bank to the south (cat. 49). Others, including Joseph Farington (see fig. 17 on p. 76) and Edward Dayes (cat. 36), chose a low, waterside viewpoint that enabled them to stress the contrast between the

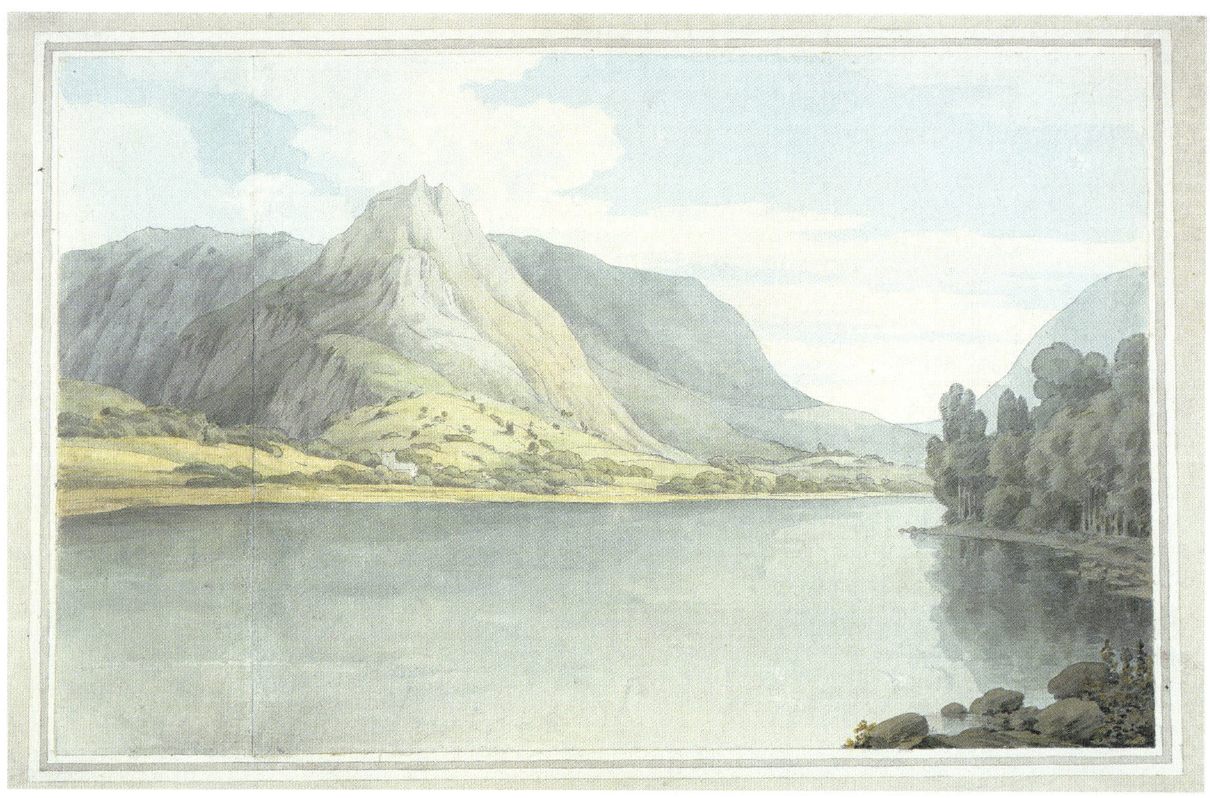

Cat. 32

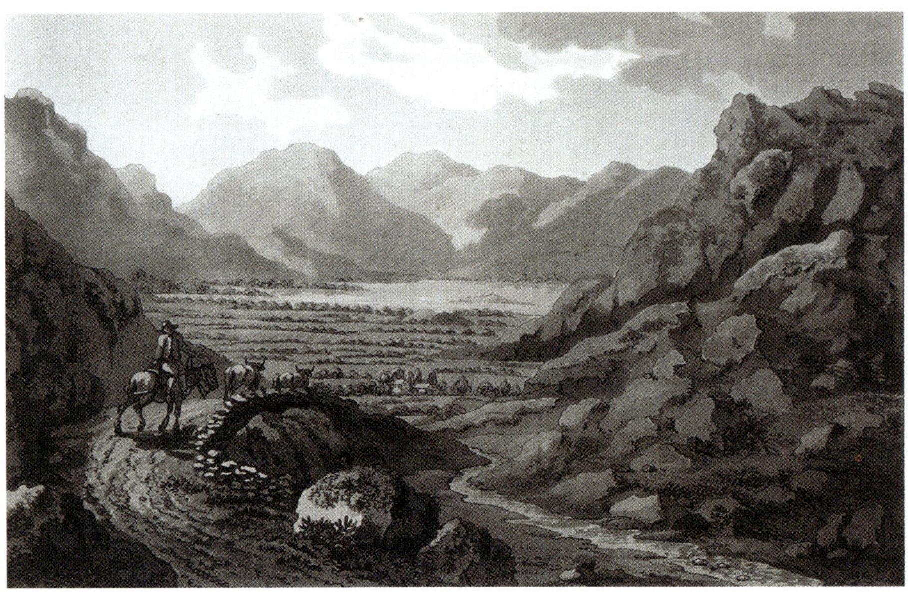

Fig. 14 C. Rosenberg after Peter Holland, *Grassmere from near Dunmail Raise*, aquatint, 1792 (The Wordsworth Trust).

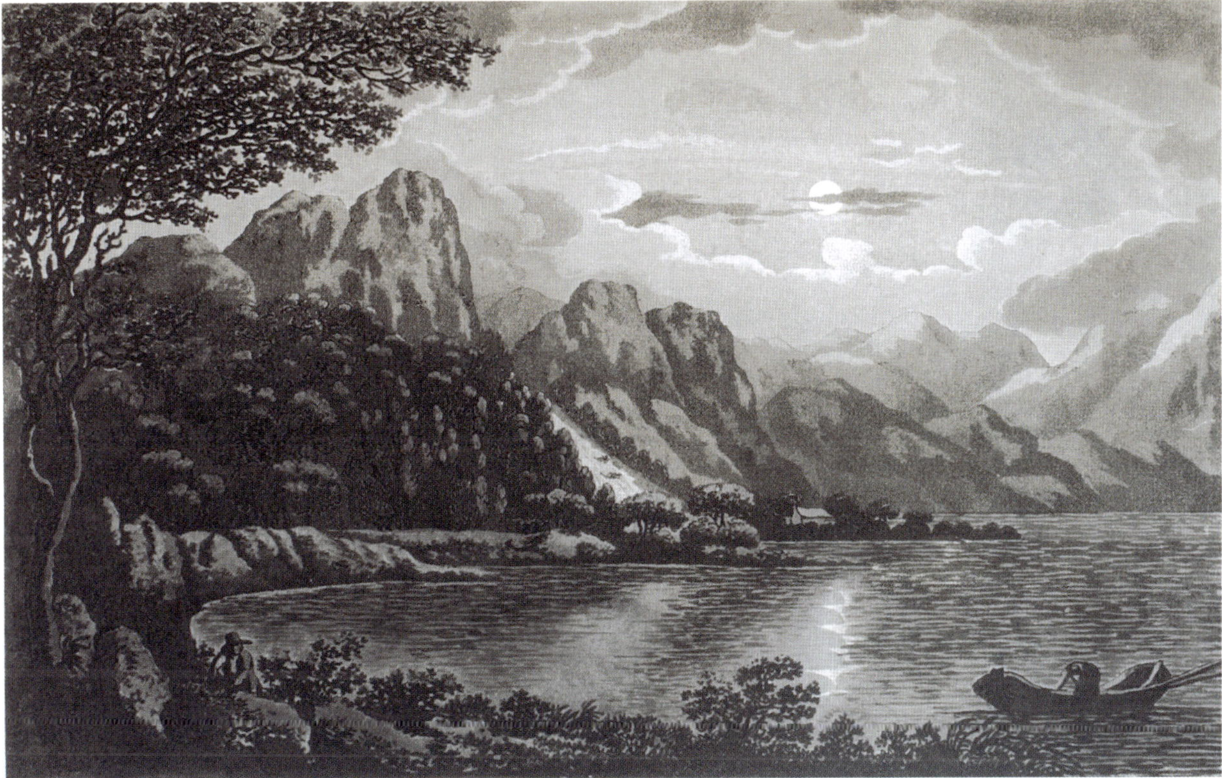

Cat. 33

rugged mass of Helm Crag and the tranquillity of Grasmere Lake. Indeed, Abbott's inscribed title on the verso of this drawing underlines this very point: 'Hill Cragg on Grasmere Lake'. He has stationed himself on the rock-strewn shore of Baneriggs on the eastern side of the lake where the shadowy boulders at his feet answer the chilly landmass diagonally opposite. He does not include the island – which would have introduced a note of liveliness into the composition – but we cannot know whether this was a deliberate choice or simply the result of his misinterpreting his pencil sketch. In any event, despite the exaggerated scale of Grasmere church, the resulting scene is one of stark, uncompromising grandeur more suitable to a remoter and bleaker lake.

Abbott was an amateur artist from Exeter, an apothecary and surgeon by profession, who made just one tour of the Lake District in 1791. He is one of the few identifiable pupils of Francis Towne (see cat. 24) and his style was much influenced by his master. Like Towne he concentrates on grand masses, omitting details he regarded as trivial as well as decorative embellishments; he applies broad washes of colour and crisp outlines in pen and ink that pull the composition together. However, the subtlety and range of Towne always eluded him. CFP

33

C. ROSENBERG after PETER HOLLAND
(fl. 1780–1812)
Lodoar Waterfall
1792
Aquatint, 13.5 × 21.9 cm
Engraved inscriptions: below, with title and names of artist and engraver; bottom, *Published as the Act directs by P. Holland. Aug.st 1.st 1792.*
Rawnsley Bequest, 1959

The first book on the Lake District to consist of aquatint views of the area (as opposed to the generalised scenes that had embellished Gilpin's *Observations*, cat. 13), Peter Holland's *Select Views of the Lakes in Cumberland, Westmoreland & Lancashire* was published in Liverpool in 1792. The new technique of aquatint had first been used in Britain by Paul Sandby RA for a series of twelve views of south Wales in 1775. It soon became popular, thanks

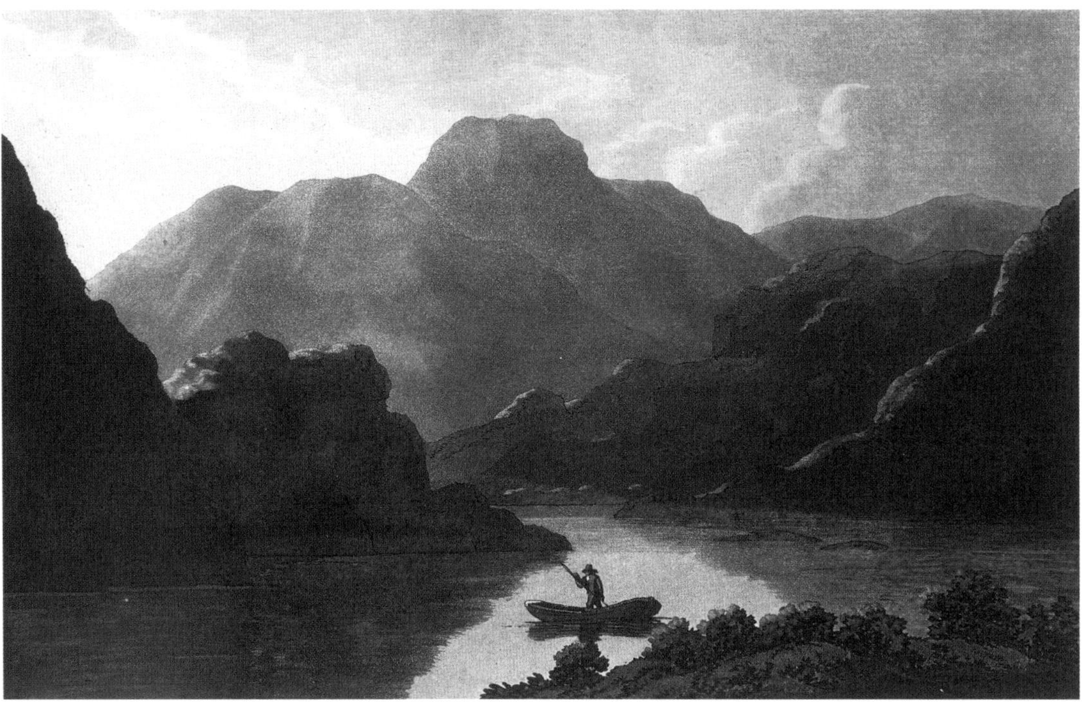

Fig. 15 C. Rosenberg after Peter Holland, *Ullswater from Lyulphs Tower*, aquatint, 1792 (The Wordsworth Trust).

to its ability to reproduce the wash-like quality of a drawing in watercolour, or in pen and ink with monochrome washes, and Sandby followed up his aquatint views of Wales with *The Virtuosi's Museum* (1778–82), covering many parts of England, Scotland and Ireland. The precise details of the transmission of the 'grand secrets' involved in the technique itself remain somewhat elusive but there is no doubt that one of the figures experimenting in this field, as early as 1772, was Peter Perez Burdett, an artist known to both Thomas Chubbard (cat. 43–4) and Peter Holland. The latter's *Select Views* contains a total of twenty-one aquatints, of which the first is an illustrative title-page showing the artist's name and that of the book carved, as it were, into the surface of the Bowder Stone in Borrowdale (see fig. 24 on p. 89). This imaginative approach, coupled with the ability of aquatint to produce an emotionally charged scene, marks out Holland's *Select Views* from more straightforward contemporary publications using line-engraving, such as those by Farington and 'Warwick' Smith (cat. 28 and 35).

In the 1760s Dr John Brown (cat. 9) had recommended that a tour of Derwentwater should be concluded with a walk 'by still moon-light (at which time the distant water-falls are heard in all the variety of sound)'. This advice was reprinted at two separate points in West's *Guide*, first as part of the section devoted to the lake and again in the Addenda, within Brown's letter as a whole (e.g. 1784, pp. 113, 194). The visitor would thus, Brown maintained, enjoy 'a scene of such delicate beauty, repose and solemnity, as exceeds all description'. On the other hand, the visitor might enjoy somewhat different experiences, as can be seen in cat. 33. Here the artist shows Derwentwater from a conventional viewpoint, looking towards Borrowdale, but renders the familiar view sinister by depicting it by night, with a full moon streaked with drifting clouds. The foreground contains furtive figures on both land and water; they may perhaps have been involved in illegal activities since the former glances nervously over his shoulder while the latter crouches down in his boat under a dark cloak to avoid detection. However, the scene is brilliantly lit by diverse sources of illumination: the moon brightens the clouds with its radiance, is reflected in the lake and catches the snow-covered peaks to the right; the torrent of Lodore provides a further source of light, its reflection breaking the surface of the lake in parallel to that of the moon. It is also worth noting that another of the aquatints in the book, *Ullswater from*

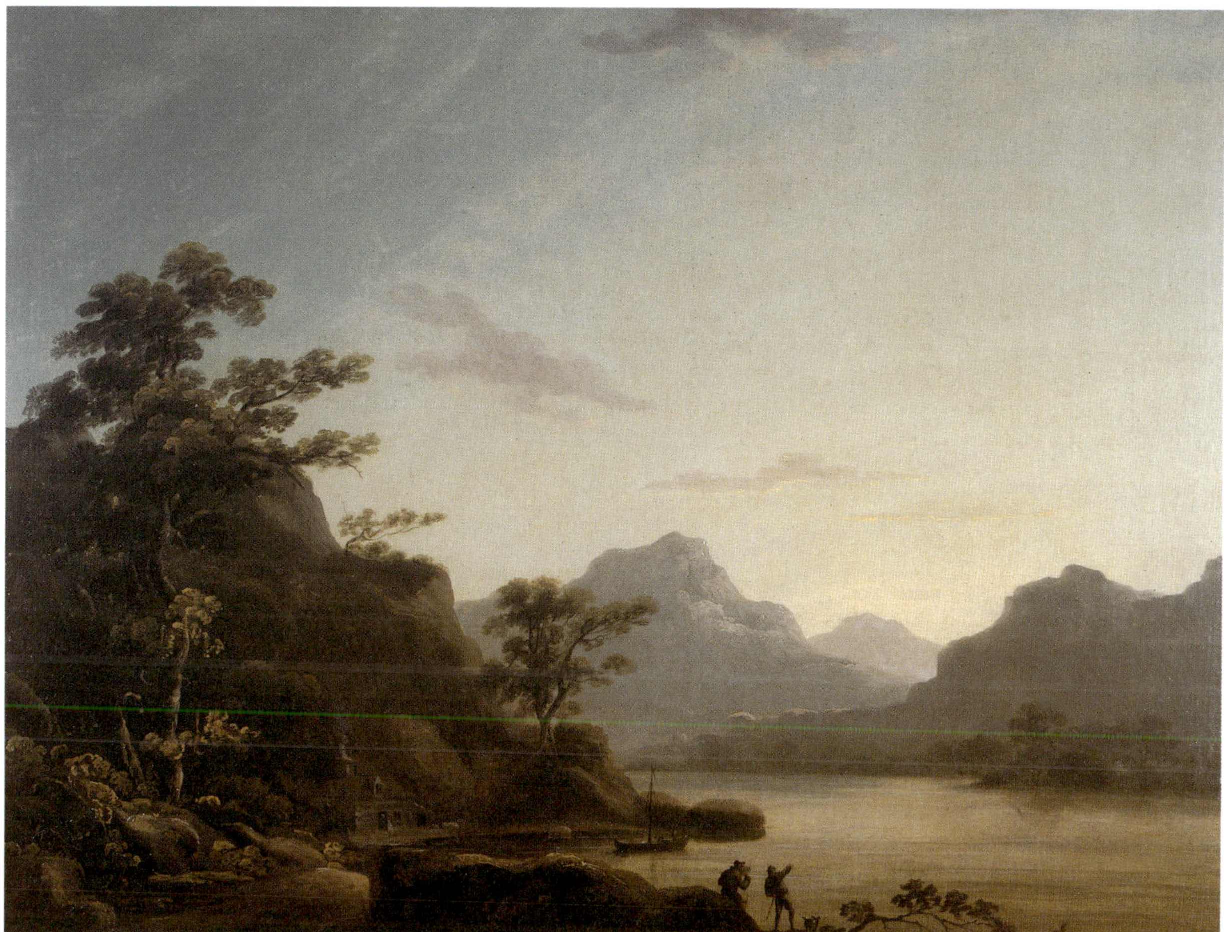

Cat. 34

Lyulphs Tower (fig. 15), shows a solitary boatman surrounded by lofty dark mysterious crags: a situation directly comparable with the experience of the young Wordsworth alone on that lake which the poet later described in *The Prelude*.

Holland dedicated his *Select Views* to his fellow-Liverpudlian Daniel Daulby (see cat. 43–4) who was passionately interested in prints and print-making. He, too, would have known the work of Burdett, whose experiments with aquatint had coincided with Sandby's development of the medium. There can be little doubt that Holland studied the Rembrandt etchings in his friend's outstanding collection and learned much from them about the orchestration of light and shade. At about the same time the young Turner was similarly learning to employ several sources of light in his work under the influence of his great predecessor. CFP

34

THOMAS WALMSLEY (1763–1805/6)
Ullswater, Evening
1792
Oil on canvas, 55 × 72 cm
Purchased with the assistance of the MGC/V&A Purchase Grant Fund, 2001

The Dublin-born artist Thomas Walmsley exhibited four paintings of the Lake District at the Royal Academy in 1792–3 of which cat. 34 is the only one to have come to light in modern times. This captivating work is here identified as the *Ulls-Water, evening* exhibited in 1792 (no. 399) when Walmsley was living in Bow Street, Covent Garden. It shows the view southwards towards the head of Ullswater from close to the tip of Place Fell, the rocky cliffs of the Devil's Chimney occupying the left-hand part of the scene. The two prominent peaks to the right of these rocks represent Birks and Keldas, between which St Sunday Crag is glimpsed in the distance.

As in the slightly later painting of Ullswater by Joseph Wright of Derby from a similar viewpoint (cat. 40), the lake is suffused with evening light but here the similarities end. Walmsley's scene is far more decorative and he introduces a homely, even domesticated, note by showing a cottage nestling under the rocks on the left and he animates the foreground by showing two figures apparently exclaiming over the beauty of the view. He softens the ruggedness of the fells by casting a veil of pink radiance over their rough surfaces but at the same time he intensifies their massive grandeur by introducing feathery wisps of cloud in the sky above, their undersides lit up by the rays of the setting sun. The result is a painting of great charm – but it is also rather more than that. When Coleridge came suddenly upon Ullswater on his first visit to the Lakes in 1799 he exclaimed over the 'noble Promontory' of Place Fell that gives the lake 'the winding of a majestic River'; he described parts of the lake as a 'large Slice of calm silver', 'melted Silver' and 'fused Silver'; he wrote of Ullswater's woods 'shadowy with Sunshine', its 'bare knobbly' cliffs and crags, and the 'bright ruffledness' of the sky (Perry, 2002, p. 15). Walmsley's painting makes it possible for us to understand Coleridge's excitement and suggests that the artist might have enjoyed considerable success had his career not been cut short by illness. It is by works of this quality that he should be judged, not by the rather crude prints after his work that were later produced by the engraver Jukes (cat. 56–7). CFP

35

JAMES MERIGOT after JOHN 'WARWICK' SMITH (1749–1831)
Entrance into Borrodale
1792
Etching and engraving, 32.5 × 46.7 cm
Engraved inscriptions: below, with title and names of artist and engraver; bottom, *Publish'd as the Act directs. June, 1792, by R. Blamire, Strand, London.*

Within a few years of carrying out John Christian Curwen's commission for a hundred views of the Lakes (see cat. 31) Smith brought a selection of similar scenes before a wider public by issuing them as engravings. *Entrance into Borrodale* was published, with nineteen other scenes, in *Views of the Lakes in Cumberland and Westmorland: from original drawings by J. Smith*. These appeared in five numbers between 1791 and 1795, with two separate numbers published in 1792 and the final two being issued together in 1795. The engraver throughout was the French landscape artist and drawing-master James Merigot (fl. 1772–1816) who had recently moved from Paris to London.

Unlike Farington's *Views of the Lakes* published in the 1780s (cat. 27–8) Smith's *Views* had no accompanying letterpress. The selection naturally included a depiction of 'Belle-Isle Lodge' itself, complete with appropriate words dedicating the entire series to its owner, Curwen, in the very first number.

The engraved series gives an excellent idea of Smith's range as an artist as well as reflecting current tastes among visitors. Besides such well-established sights as Windermere and Derwentwater and the falls at both Lodore and Rydal, it also included Wythburn (Thirlmere) and Elterwater in the first number and Loweswater and 'Broad Water at the upper end of Paterdale' (i.e. Brothers Water) in the last. Many of Smith's images achieve breadth and balance by using the compositional formula of foreground, sidescreens and graduated recession that had been perfected by Claude Lorrain in the seventeenth century. However, he could also employ very different schemes. In *The Ferry on Windermere Lake*, for instance, the horse-ferry and its users are rhythmically spread out across a horizontal band of water, parallel to the picture-plane, as though carved on a neo-classical frieze (fig. 16).

Other scenes are marked by abruptness and irregularity. *Entrance into Borrodale* is one of the finest of this type, using sharp contrasts of lighting combined with angular forms to portray the desolate and dangerous terrain. These qualities were far less in evidence in the original watercolour made for Curwen in which the rocks on both sides were almost rectilinear, that on the right occupying a third of the watercolour. Smith's second depiction, however, was filled with the dramatically intersecting diagonals that mark the final engraving, further refinements of light and shade being added along the way by the engraver Merigot. This scene has been selected here partly for its own merits and partly so that it can be directly compared with the small watercolour copy made by the Liverpool landscape artist Thomas Chubbard about five years after its publication (cat. 44). CFP

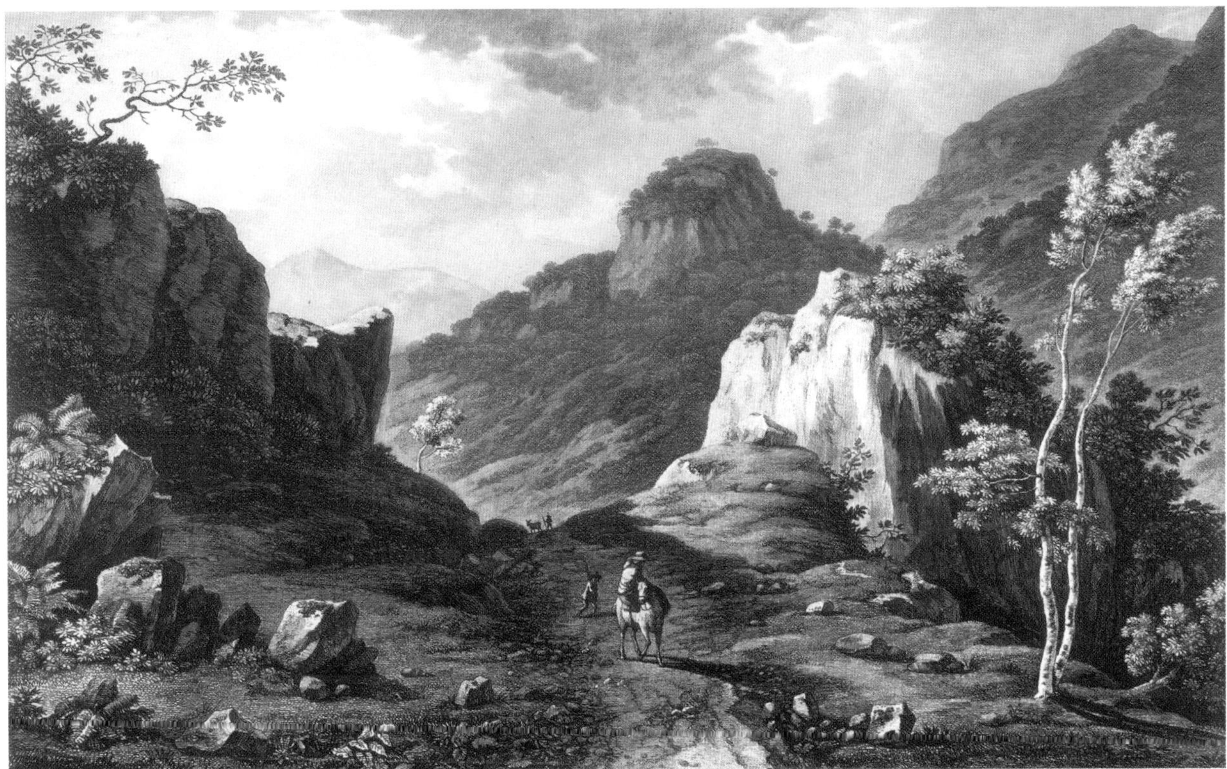

Cat. 35

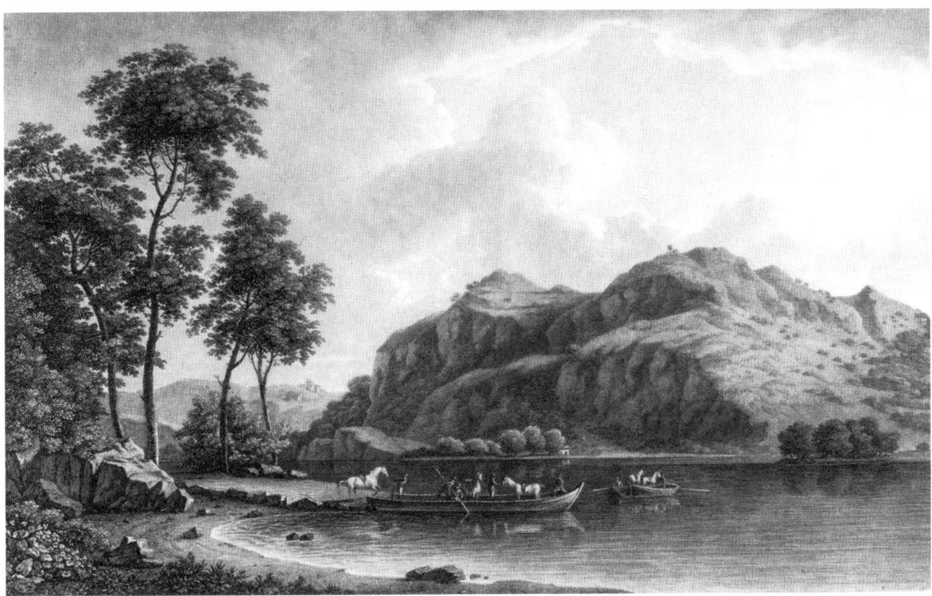

Fig. 16 James Merigot after John 'Warwick' Smith, *The Ferry on Windermere Lake*, etching and engraving, 1792 (The Wordsworth Trust).

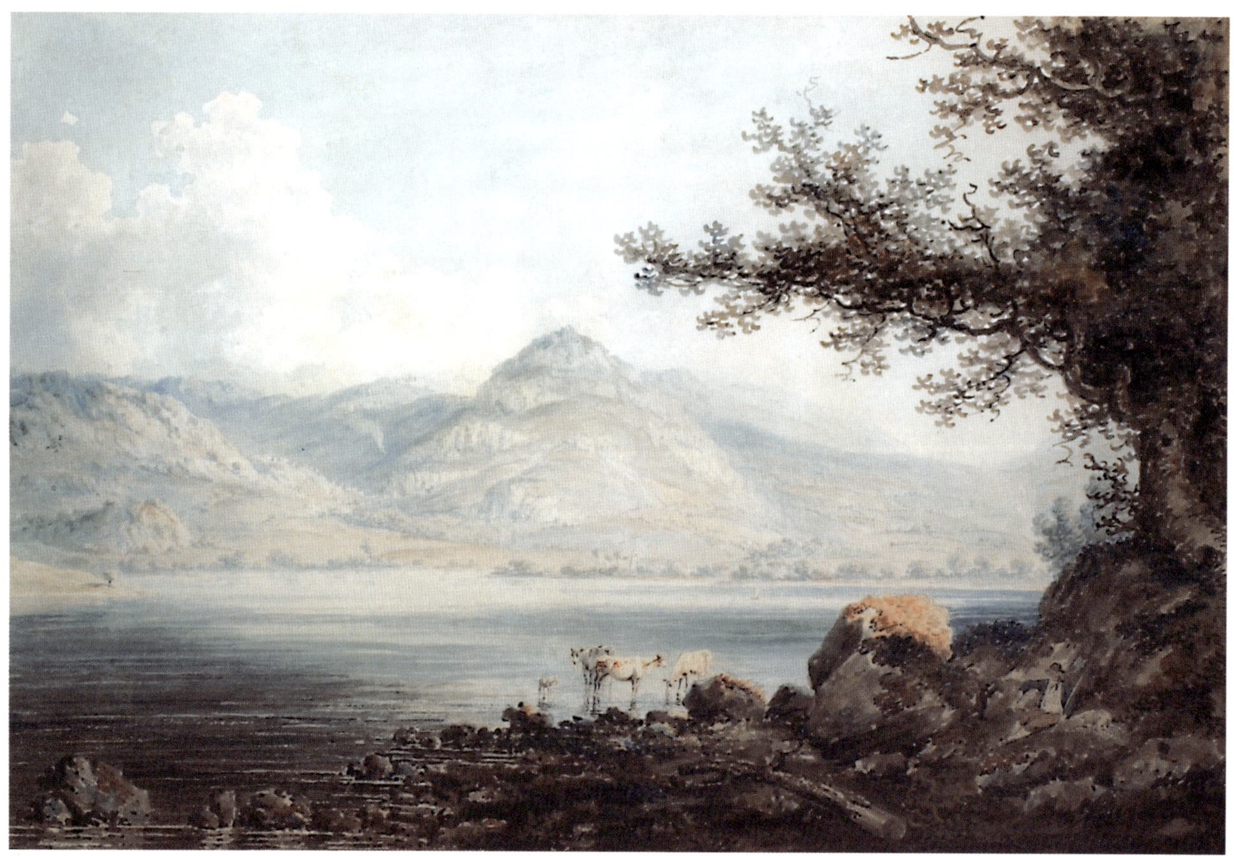

Cat. 36

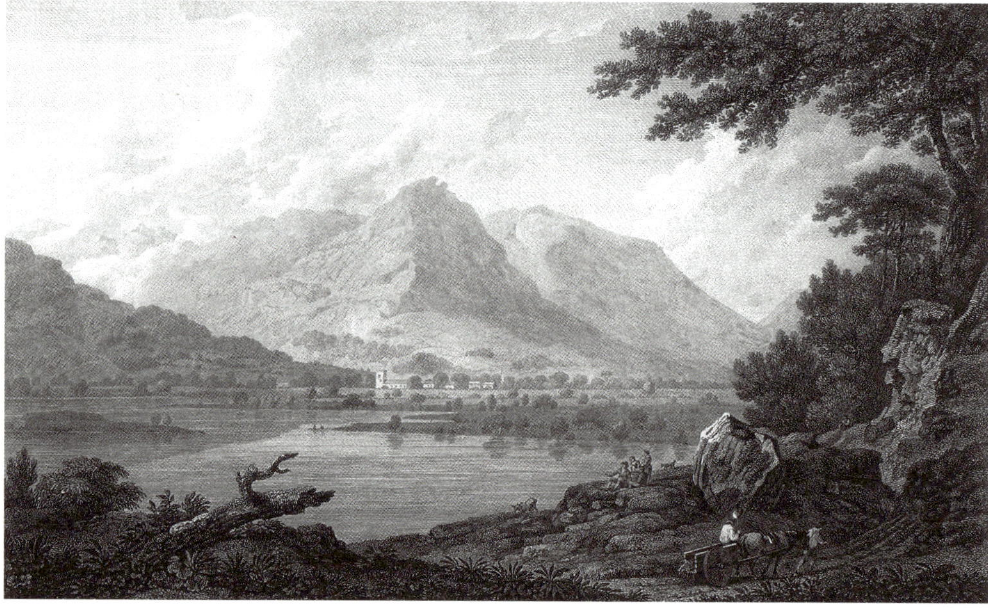

Fig. 17 Benjamin Thomas Pouncy after Joseph Farington, *Grasmere*, etching and engraving, 1785 (The Wordsworth Trust).

36

EDWARD DAYES (1763–1804)
Grasmere Lake, Westmorland, with Cattle watering
1792
Watercolour, 33.3 × 48.3 cm
Inscribed on washline mount 'Edw[d.] Dayes 1792'
The National Trust, on long-term loan to The Wordsworth Trust

Unlike many other professional artists who visited the Lakes in the 1780s Dayes worked only in watercolour, so while Gainsborough, De Loutherbourg and Wright of Derby (for example) were producing oil paintings of the area, Dayes was creating and exhibiting what were known as 'tinted drawings'. These were pencil drawings enriched by successive washes of watercolour, with distinctions between light and shade being introduced first, followed by richer tints of positive colour. The strongest accents were added in more saturated (i.e. less diluted) colour, applied with brushes that were firm enough to permit stylised drawing that was almost a form of calligraphy; sometimes pen and ink would also be used. In many cases Dayes' 'tinted drawings' are almost monochrome, relying on varying tones of blue and grey with flourishes of black ink; others, such as the present example, are far more varied, resulting in greater naturalism and liveliness.

Dayes' viewpoint on the shore of Baneriggs was broadly similar to that of Farington's engraving in his 1789 *Views of the Lakes* (fig. 17) which was also adopted by Abbott in his watercolour of 1791 (cat. 32) with which it may be usefully compared. (None of these artists was working in isolation, of course, and many of the compositional devices used by Dayes were the common currency of the age; one of the criticisms voiced about Abbott in his own day was that he had not spent enough time studying works of art to familiarise himself with such devices.) Although Dayes places Helm Crag virtually in the centre of his scene there is nothing symmetrical or monotonous about it, thanks to his intricate and irregular foreground. He creates the illusion of distance not through absence but through presence: the ingredients close at hand – the cattle refreshing themselves in the water, the encrusted boulder and gnarled old tree – all serve to emphasise the extent of the lake between the viewer and Helm Crag. He evokes the calm, light-reflecting surface of the lake not through uniformity of washes but through variety: his innumerable multi-coloured bands of light and shade appear to shimmer in the heat. Finally Dayes presents a landscape that is inhabited: he shows the smoke of a bonfire on the hillside left of Helm Crag while the farmer who has brought his cows down to the lake is depicted resting, staff in hand, in the shade at lower right. It was through study of well-composed, imaginatively integrated landscapes by living artists such as this that the young Turner was to develop his own talents in the 1790s. CFP

37

FERDINAND BECKER (fl. 1780–1825)
Scale Force near Buttermere
*c.*1795?
Pen and wash, 18.5 × 11.5 cm
Inscribed 'Scale force / near Butter / mere'
Purchased, 1994

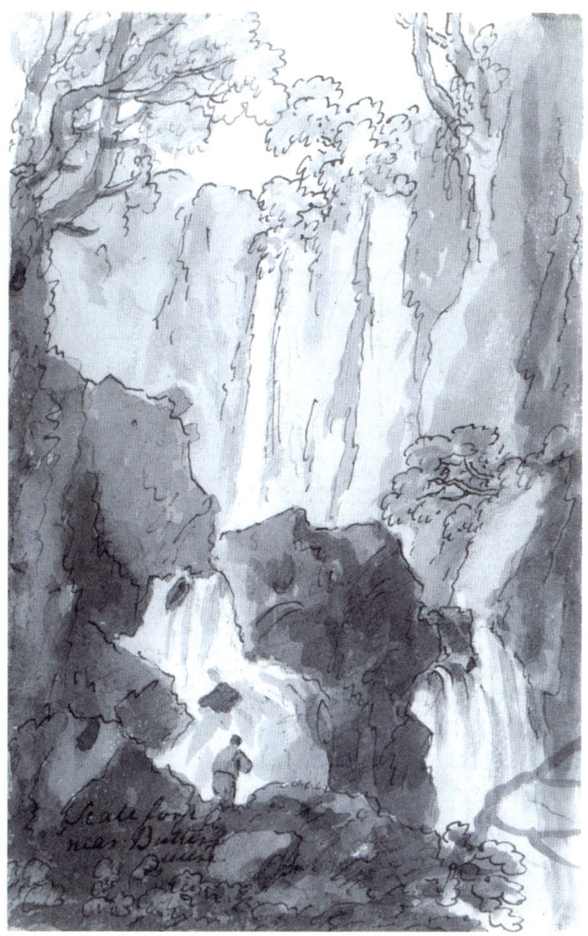

Cat. 37

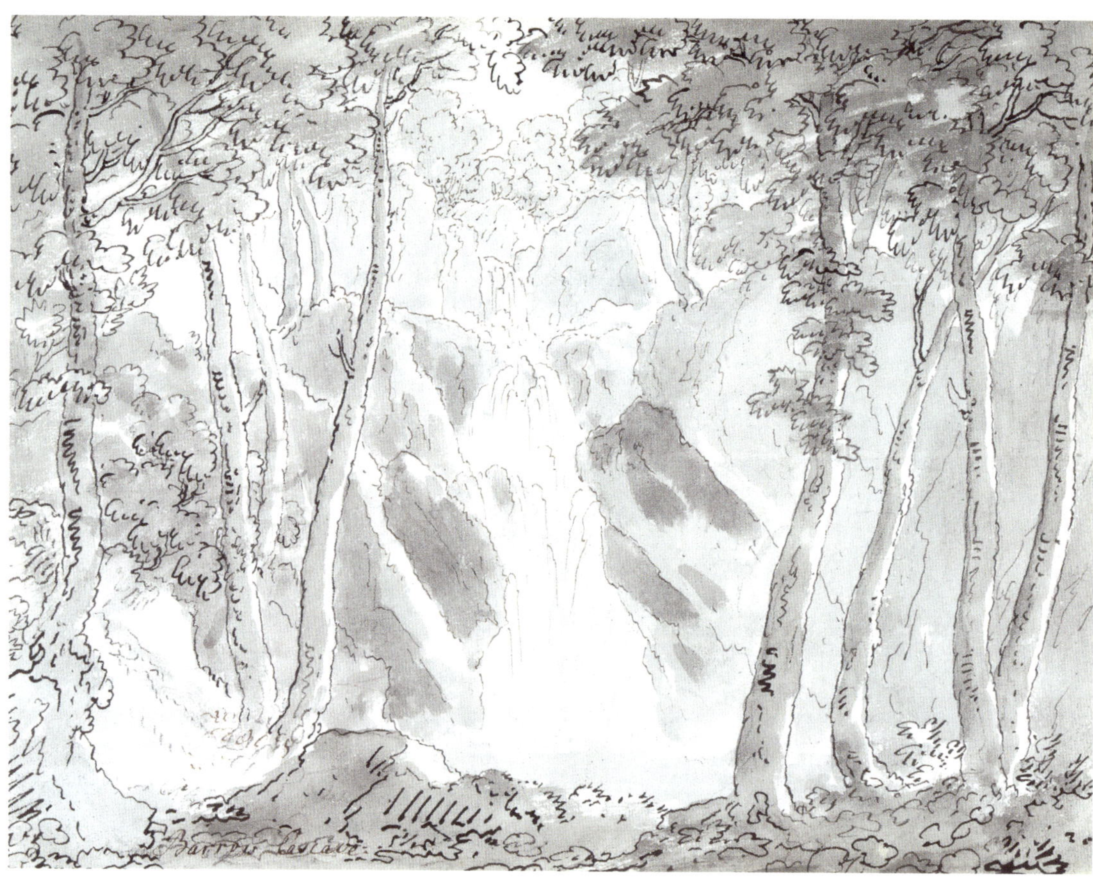

Cat. 38

38

FERDINAND BECKER (fl. 1780–1825)
Barrow Cascade, Derwent Water
*c.*1795?
Pen and grey wash, 23 × 29.3 cm
Inscribed 'Barrow Cascade' and 'Derwent Water'
Purchased, 1994

In the autumn of 1796 the drawing-master Ferdinand Becker held an exhibition of a hundred of his own works at his residence, 17 Queen Square, Bath, which included, according to the *Bath Chronicle* for 10 November, subjects from the Cumberland lakes as well as scenes in North Wales and Monmouth. The artist had evidently visited the Lake District by the summer of that year, if not earlier: a dating which is consistent with his interest in Barrow Cascade (cat. 38). Many of Becker's ink and wash sketches are known from his various visits to different parts of Britain including a long tour in Wales in 1808. The best of his drawings have an energy and verve that makes them extremely engaging and some, like cat. 37–8, are among the most vivid depictions of the Lakes in this period. His style characteristically combines wiry ink outlines and flourishes with swift, schematic and blotchy washes indicating light and shade.

Scale Force, the longest uninterrupted chute of water in the Lake District, falls into the south-western end of Crummock Water so Becker's inscribed title describing it as 'near Buttermere' may well refer to Buttermere village rather than Buttermere Lake. He has chosen to represent it not from a distance (so that much of its descent of 125 feet could be shown) but from close at hand near its highest point where it lies 'concealed within the bosom of the cliff' (West, 1784, p. 134); it is as though the artist, like the figure in the foreground, had reached it after an arduous struggle among rocks and trees. The presentation of a waterfall in this manner was not, by any means, an invention of Becker's; he was merely following the taste of the time (codified by Gilpin) which demanded overhanging trees, jagged rocks

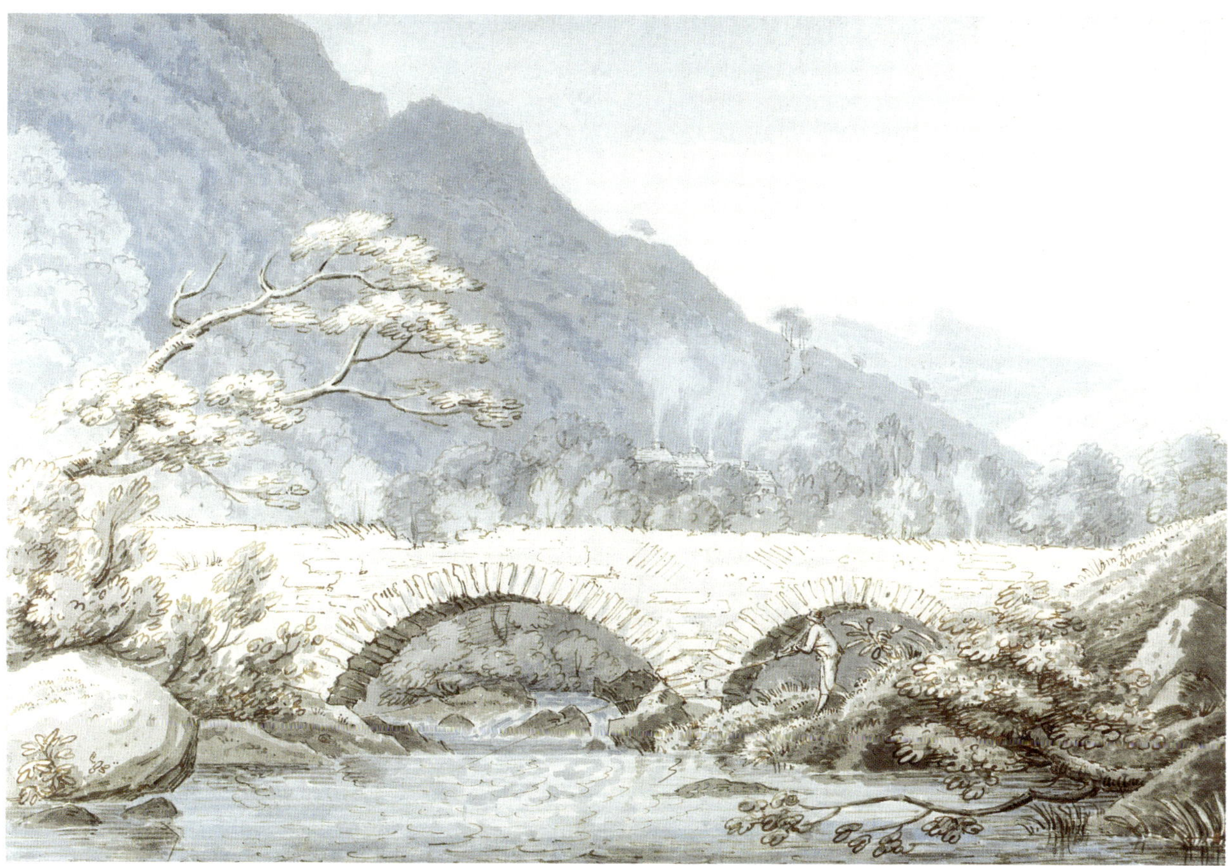

Cat. 39

dividing the cascade, a strategically placed figure or group of figures, and the water flowing out of the picture at lower right. Doubtless Becker searched out viewpoints for his on-the-spot pencil sketches that provided most of the above *desiderata* and later made the necessary adjustments to achieve a good composition.

Unlike Scale Force, Barrow Cascade is not an entirely natural phenomenon. When the retired Newark-on-Trent banker Joseph Pocklington built 'Barrow Cascade House' overlooking Derwentwater in 1787–97 he 'improved' the modest waterfall of Barrow Beck in its grounds so that he could enjoy the sight of a spectacular cascade from his dining room window. There was an element of competitive imitation in this landscaping project; the cascades in the grounds of Rydal Hall, the property of a long-established local family, the Le Flemings, were already much admired, especially since the lower cascade – with its own specially built viewing station – had been extolled by Mason in the 1770s (see cat. 74). Barrow House is today a youth hostel and by walking behind the house it is still possible to reach a viewpoint similar to Becker's. The beauty of this drawing lies in its contrast between the foaming cascade amid dark boulders and the airy grace and elegance of the soaring birch trees. CFP

39

THOMAS SUNDERLAND (1744–1823)
Ulpha Bridge
*c.*1795–1800
Pencil, pen and ink and blue and grey watercolour, 31.9 × 45.5 cm
Gift of the W.W. Spooner Charitable Trust, 2008

Many of Sunderland's most successful watercolours depict sights that lie not far from his home near Ulverston at the northern end of the Furness peninsula. The village of Ulpha is situated in the Duddon valley beneath the great mass of the Dunnerdale

Fells. In Sunderland's day it had an inn, the Travellers' Rest, where Coleridge spent a night on his epic fell-walking excursion in 1802, and a few farmhouses (shown by Sunderland amongst the trees, with smoke rising from their chimneys); a short way north of the bridge stands Ulpha Kirk while a few miles to the south lie the medieval ruins of Old Hall.

The Duddon valley was much loved by Wordsworth who visited it innumerable times from his boyhood onwards. He celebrated it in his sequence of thirty-four Duddon sonnets, begun in 1806 and first published in 1820 in the volume that contained his *Description of the Scenery of the Lakes* (cat. 79). Like Wordsworth, Sunderland evokes a wild, unfrequented and sometimes mysterious vale, the river winding between rough copses, its course strewn with rocks, its buildings redolent of past ages. The shadowy hillside that dominates the scene shows the influence of the poetic, slightly melancholic Alpine watercolours painted by J.R. Cozens in the 1780s, which were executed in a similar range of muted greys and blues. However, Sunderland brings a note of vivacity to his scene through the use of pen and reddish brown ink for the features he places so dramatically in the foreground: the stylised trees and bushes, the old and somewhat damaged stone bridge and the sprightly fisherman on the shore. The twentieth-century Cumbrian poet Norman Nicholson has written of the Duddon valley near here as 'flittering, twittering, rippling, restless, hunting, dodging, never-still', the landscape in autumn 'as fiery and challenging as a red-haired girl' (1963, p. 51). Sunderland's drawing captures some of that magic. CFP

40

JOSEPH WRIGHT OF DERBY (1734–97)
Ullswater
1795
Oil on canvas, 44.4 × 52 cm
Purchased with the generous help of the National Art Collections Fund and the funds administered by the Victoria & Albert Museum for the Museums and Galleries Commission. The Wordsworth Trust also has a special debt to other contributors including Mr and Mrs Harry Djanogly, the John Paul Getty Jr General Charitable Trust, Mrs Henry Luce III and the Luce Foundation, Mrs and Mrs Eugene Thaw, 1992

Wright's visits to the Lake District in 1793 and 1794 resulted in a total of some ten oil paintings of which around half are now untraced or known only through copies (see cat. 41). At least three of these depicted Ullswater, including the works described in Wright's account book as follows: 'A large picture of Ullswater' (1795–6; unsold and later described as 'large and romantic' and showing the head of the lake from Lyulph's Tower); 'A smallish picture of Ullswater Sun set [sold] to M^r. Hardman, £42' (1795); and 'A View upon Ullswater morning' (sold to Mr Norris for £36 15s. in about January 1796). Since the Wordsworth Trust's *Ullswater* undoubtedly shows the head of the lake from the eastern bank and at sunset, it cannot be the first or third of these; the question to be addressed is whether it is the second painting or a replica or variant of that work.

In the autumn of 1796 Farington paid a visit to the north of England. On 27 October he recorded in his diary: 'Wm Hardman I called on & saw His new room. He has in his different rooms, now hung, 48 pictures. – A picture lately painted by Wright is "an effect on Ullswater", there is no figure in it.' To this remark he appended a quick memorandum of the composition (fig. 18) and further jottings, many linked by lines to the point referred to. On the left he writes 'all brownish shade' and 'all white light'; on the right 'yellowish tree' and '& brown', 'It is less than a 3/4 [i.e. smaller than 3 feet by 4] & He had 40^gs for it' [i.e. £42]; and, finally, beneath his sketch, 'Whole picture of a leathery colour.' When Farington's diary was published by Yale University Press in 1978-98, the page containing this entry (III.682) was immediately followed by a reproduction of the Trust's *Ullswater* (then in the collection of R.D. Plant), implying, though not actually stating, that it was the work referred to. There are, however, significant differences between them: in the contour of the fells on the left; the presence of a figure in a boat in the foreground; and the absence of the trees on the right.

In the catalogue of Wright's work published in 1968 Benedict Nicolson postulated that the *Ullswater* sketched by Farington was now untraced while the painting in the Plant collection was a separate work. This may not be correct. The Plant/Wordsworth Trust's *Ullswater* is unusual in shape as well as unsatisfactory in its truncated composition and it is hard to believe that Wright would have painted such an ill-proportioned scene. It may be better to postulate that Farington failed to identify the minute figure in the 'leathery' foreground and that the painting has been trimmed at some stage in its history; it must

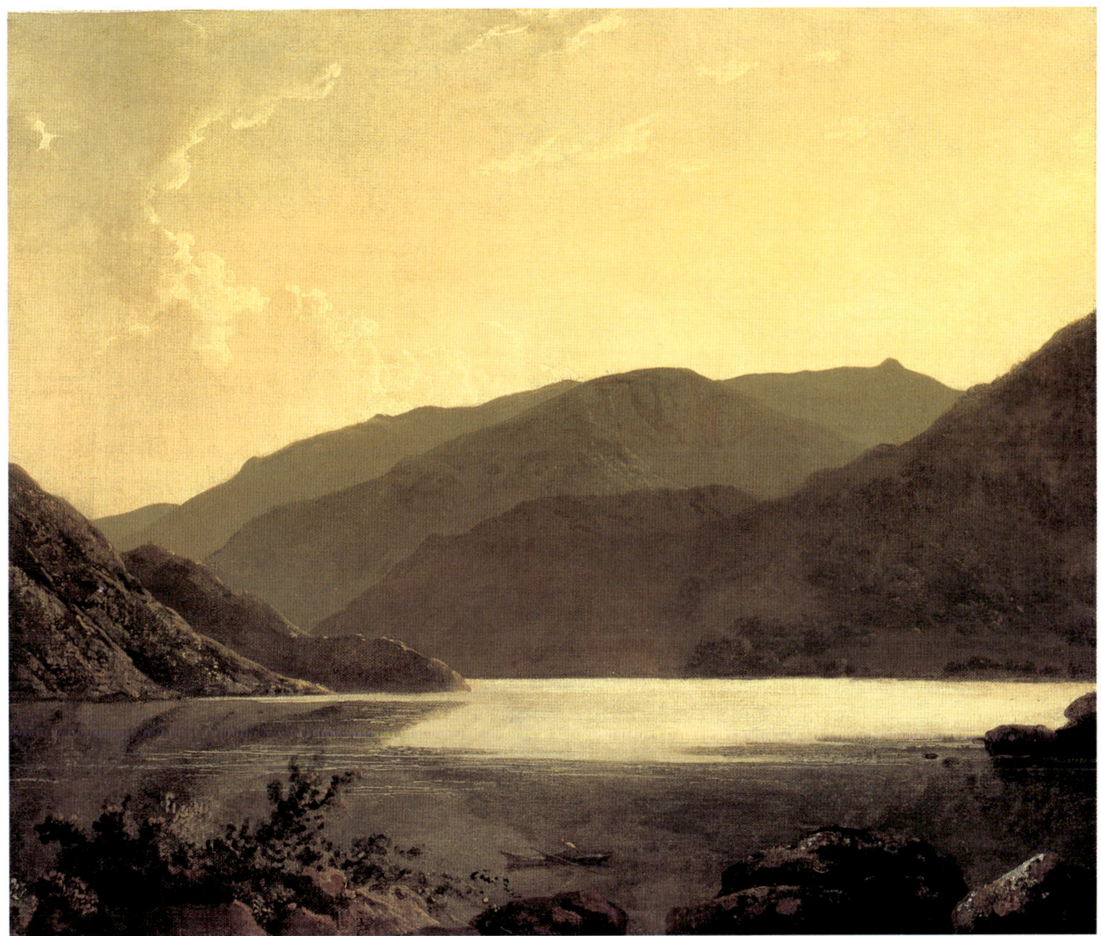

Cat. 40

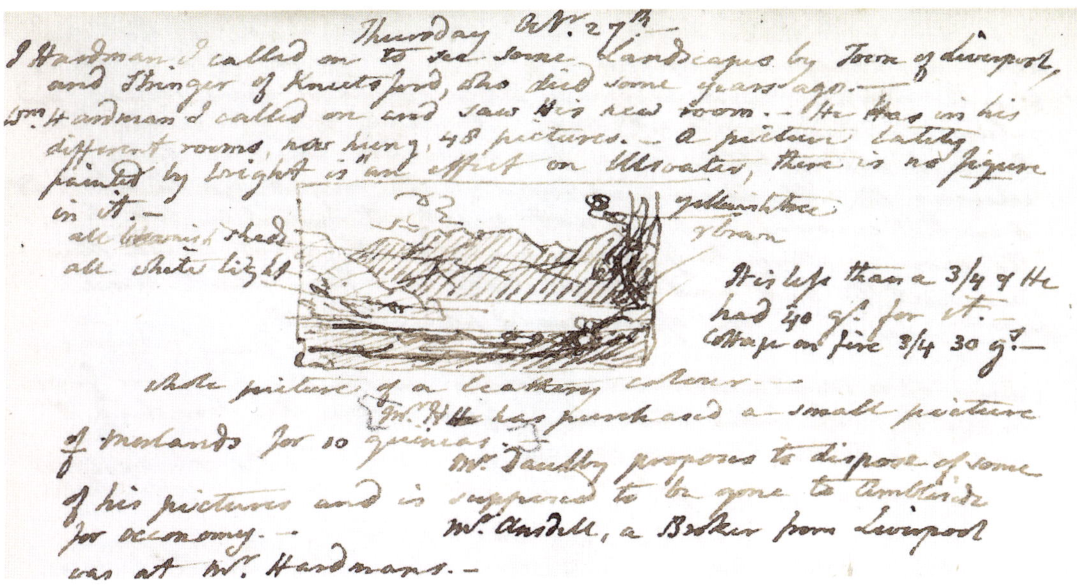

Thursday Octr. 27th
J Hardman I called on to see some Landscapes by Tom of Liverpool, and Stringer of Knutsford, who died some years ago.—
Wm. Hardman I called on and saw his new room.— He has in his different rooms, now hung, 48 pictures.— A picture lately painted by Wright is "an effect on Ullswater, there is no figure in it.—
all brownish shade
all white light
yellowish tree
& brown
It is less than a 3/4 & He had 40 gs. for it.
Cottage on fire 3/4 30 gs.—
Whole picture of a leathery colour—
Mr. H. He has purchased a small picture of Morlands for 10 guineas.—
Mr. Daulby proposes to dispose of some of his pictures and is supposed to be gone to Ambleside for oeconomy.— Mr. Ansdell, a Broker from Liverpool was at Mr. Hardmans.—

Fig. 18 Joseph Farington, entry for 27 October 1796, including a sketch of cat. 40 in its original form (Diary, vol. 4, The Royal Collection).

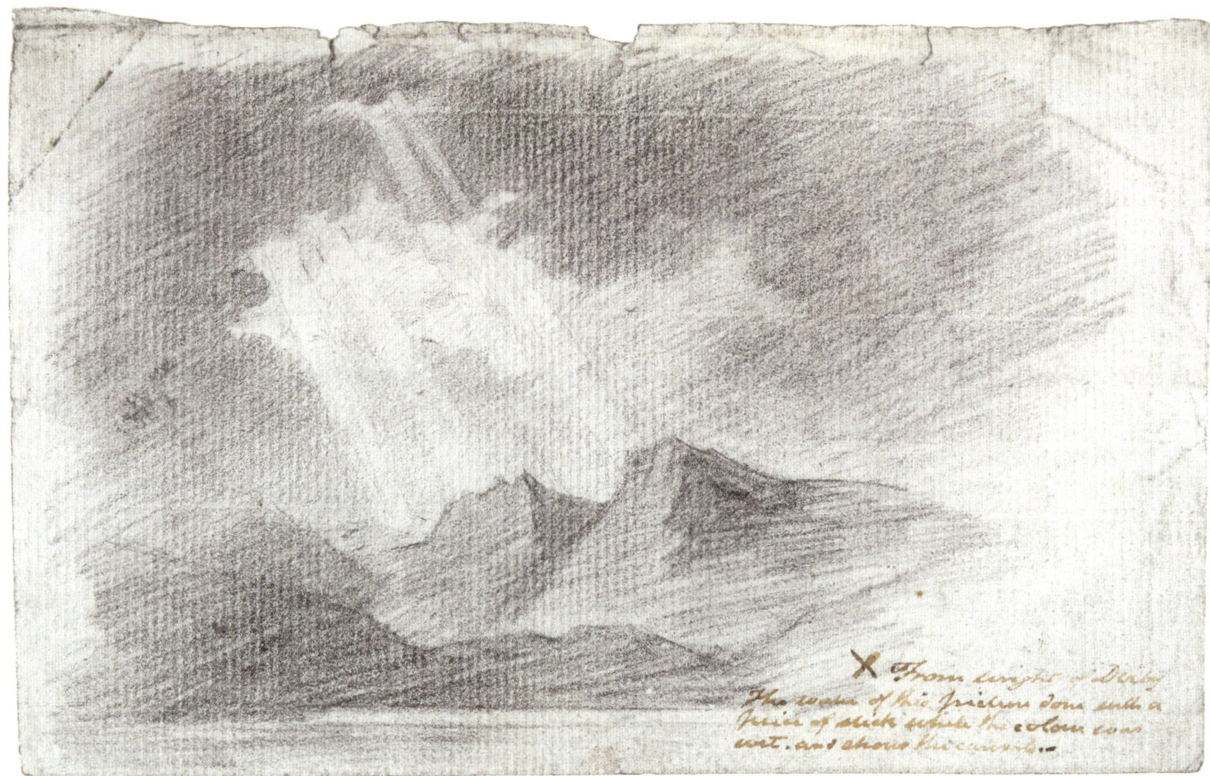

Cat. 41

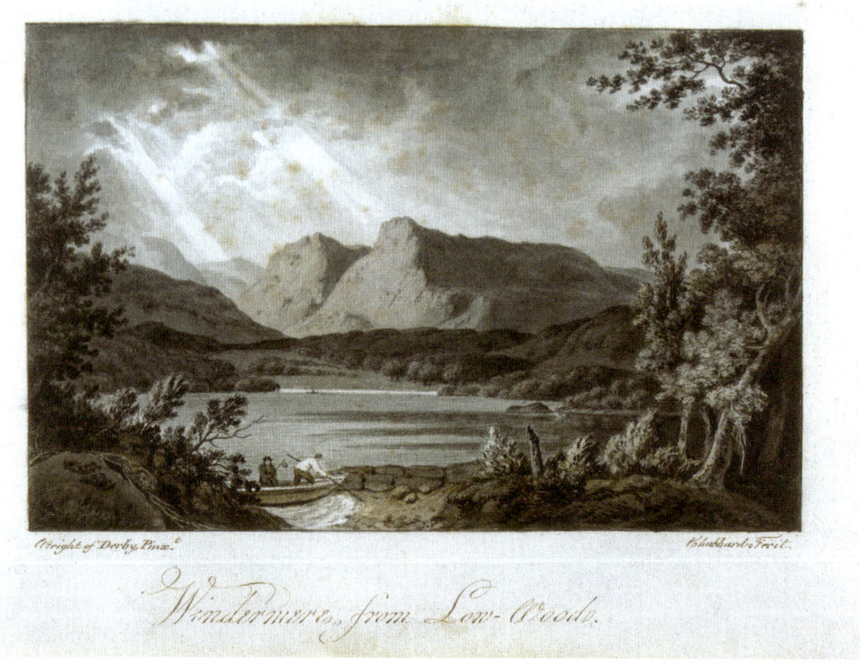

Fig. 19 Thomas Chubbard, *Copy of Wright's 'Windermere from Low Wood'*, pen, ink and watercolour, *c.*1796–8 (The Wordsworth Trust).

originally have been the same size as Wright's other 'smallish' Lake District views such as his view of the cascade at Rydal Hall (Derby Art Gallery).

Many earlier commentators have spoken of the deeply elegiac nature of this painting, linking this supposed quality to claims that it was Wright's last work. It was, however, by no means his last painting; that distinction belongs to the large, unfinished and unsold, view of Ullswater abandoned a year or so later, in October 1796 when his eyesight was too poor for him to continue. In its original state the 1795 *Ullswater* must have been far less elegiac than it now appears; Wright's concern was, as ever, with the effects of light, and the twilight gleam of the lake, fully surrounded on all four sides by extensive areas of shade and shadows, must have been truly breathtaking. CFP

41

After JOSEPH WRIGHT OF DERBY (1734–97)
The Langdale Pikes
c.1795–1800
Pencil on laid paper, 9.8 × 15.3 cm
Inscribed 'X From Wright of Derby / The water of this picture done with a / piece of stick while the colour was / wet and shows the cascade'
Peter Bicknell Bequest, 1997

This tiny study, apparently torn from a notebook, relates to one of the oil paintings that resulted from Wright's visit to the Lakes in 1794 with Thomas Moss Tate of Liverpool and was recorded in his account book as 'Windermere with Langdale pikes sold to Mr. T.M. Tate, £42'. The artist also mentions the painting in a postscript to a letter to another friend and patron, John Leigh Philips, written on 29 May 1795: 'My friend T. Tate has bought a picture I painted soon after my return from ye. Lakes of Langdale Pikes seen from Low wood. When I have put a figure in, pushing off a boat, it is to be sent to Manchester for your inspection' (Nicolson, 1968, vol. 1, p. 267).

That work itself, evidently painted in 1794–5, is now untraced but a copy in oils, of similar size (78.7 × 57.1 cm), was recorded and illustrated in Nicolson's catalogue of Wright's work (vol. 1, fig. 114). More interesting in the context of the present exhibition, however, is the small watercolour copy by Thomas Chubbard in one of the albums of Lake District scenes assembled by Daniel Daulby (see cat. 43–4). Despite its limited size and some discolouration in the sky, this copy (fig. 19), gives an excellent idea of the grandeur of Wright's original painting as well as including all its important features known through the above-mentioned copy in oils. It is, in fact, superior to the latter in its precise record of the very strong light effects – the diagonal shafts of sunlight raking the fells like searchlights – that are such a feature of the annotated pencil sketch.

So what was the function and status of this sketch? On the one hand, it could theoretically be a record of the Pikes made from Low Wood by Wright himself in 1794. It is, however, more likely to have been drawn by someone studying the oil painting in Tate's collection in Liverpool (as Chubbard and Daulby did) and wishing to record its central feature and, from an artistic point of view, its most significant area. The inscription was clearly made by someone privy to Wright's actual working methods while engaged on the painting, narrowing the range of possible artists to a person within his own circle. CFP

42

SAMUEL ALKEN after B. ROGERS (fl. 1790–1803)
The Lake & Vale of Keswick, with a distant view of Basinthwait Lake
1796
Aquatint, 30.2 × 42.4 cm
Engraved inscriptions: below, with title and names of artist and engraver; bottom, *May 10, 1796. Published as the Act directs, by B. Rogers, Drawing Master, Stafford.*
Peter Bicknell Bequest, 1997

Several collections of aquatints devoted to the Lakes were published by different artists following the appearance of the first, Peter Holland's *Select Views* (cat. 33), in 1792. The Cheshire-born John Rathbone, now settled in London, published twelve (each accompanied by text) in 1795; the same year saw the publication of the sixteen prints after drawings by John 'Warwick' Smith and John Emes that were designed to be bound with West's *Guide*. In 1796 six aquatints, larger than any of the above, were published in Stafford by the artist and drawing-master B. Rogers.

Rogers' view of the vale of Keswick from the fells near Ashness Bridge is broadly the same as that published as an engraving by Farington in his 1789 *Views of the Lakes* and later copied in bodycolour (cat. 30). Compared to both those versions, the aquatint is

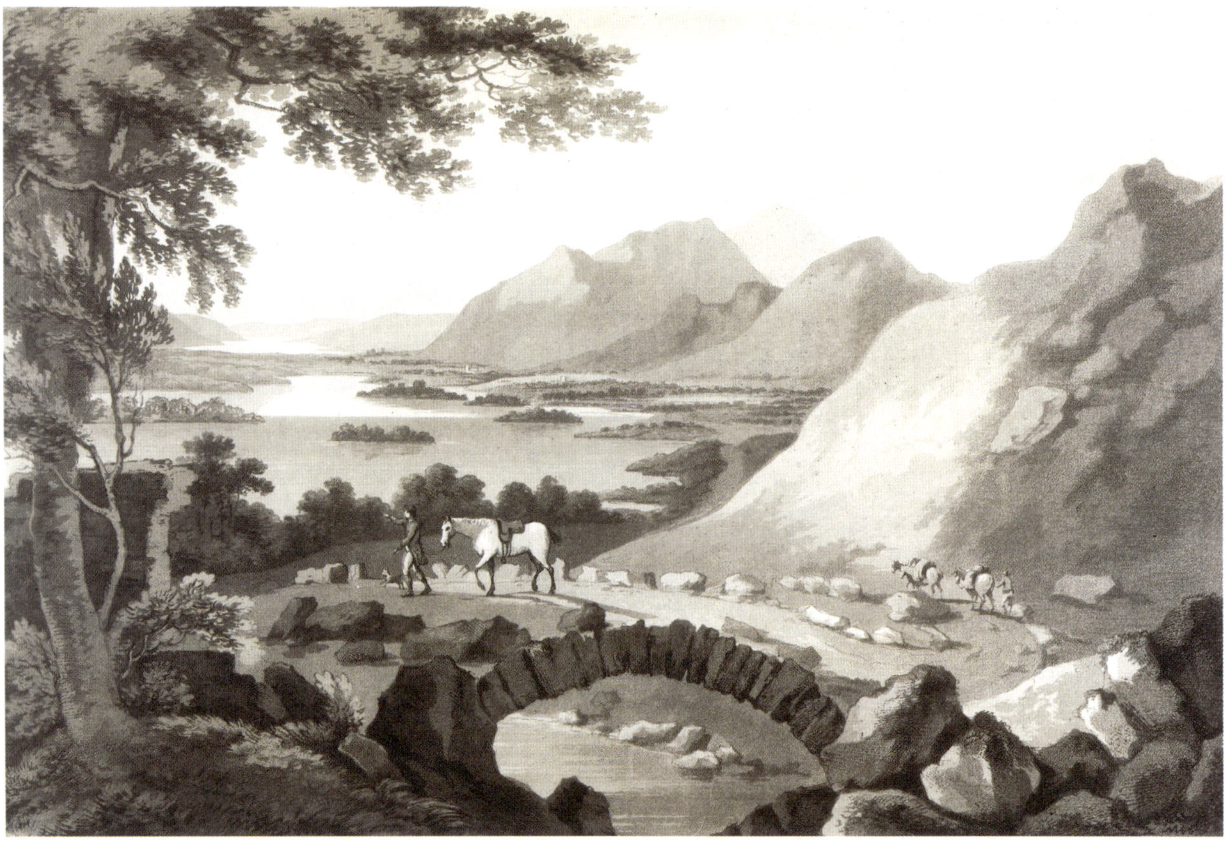

Cat. 42

more compact in format and the artist makes the view even narrower by using the device of a spreading tree, like a side-screen or curtain, to enhance the sense of recession down the vale. A framing tree such as this was by now part of the British artist's stock-in-trade of compositional motifs, adopted from the example of the Old Masters, in particular Claude; such trees can be seen elsewhere in this exhibition, in works by Barret and Dayes for example (cat. 26, 36), not to mention the amateur Elizabeth Wharton (cat. 66). It remains today a standard ingredient in photographs and postcards of the Lake District, including those showing the view from Ashness Bridge.

With its clear outlines and distinct areas defined by gradations of tone, aquatint is well suited to the rendering of landscape watercolours and it can be seen from this example that its simplicity and economy can match the grandest of scenes. CFP

43

THOMAS CHUBBARD (1738–1809)
Haws-water, with Bampton
*c.*1796–8
Watercolour, 10.8 × 16.9 cm
Inscribed 'T. Chubbard del. et fecit,' and 'Haws-water, with Bampton.'
Purchased with the generous assistance of the Art Fund, 2000

This album of prints and drawings and its companion (cat. 44) were compiled for Daniel Daulby (1745/6–98), an important northern art-lover and member of a prominent brewing family, at about the time he came to live at Rydal Mount, 1796. The albums are similar in appearance, though different in size, and both carry Daulby's engraved bookplate. As Liverpudlians, both Daulby and the professional artist closely involved with the albums, Thomas Chubbard, were able to pay visits to the Lake District much earlier than the 1790s (Chubbard exhibited Lakes subjects in 1774 and Daulby had summer sojourns at Rydal Mount from 1783 onwards)

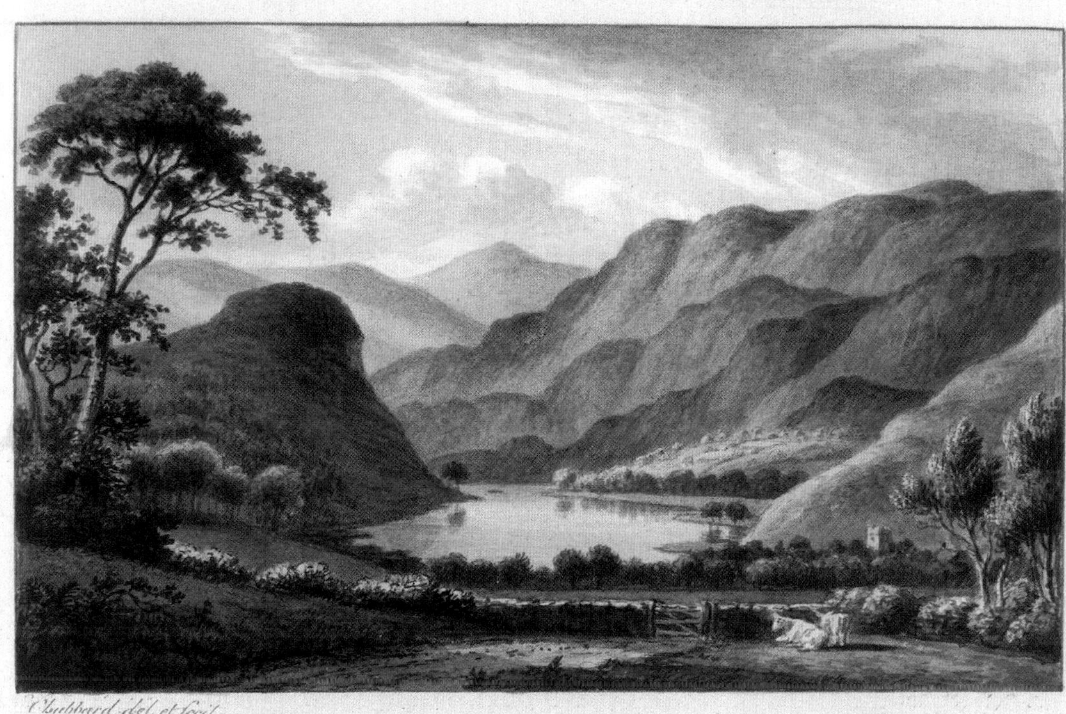

Cat. 43

but the albums provide their own clues regarding their date of compilation.

The present album begins with a collection of aquatints, a medium in which both Daulby and Chubbard were deeply interested, beginning with twenty-two from a book dedicated to Daulby himself, Peter Holland's *Select Views of the Lakes in Cumberland, Westmoreland & Lancashire* of 1792 (see cat. 33). These bear no date lines and do not appear in exactly the same order as in the printed volume; they must be early impressions, given to Daulby by Holland. The first, showing the Bowder Stone, is the illustrated title-page that followed the highly ornate engraved title-page bearing the dedication to Daulby while the last (inscribed by hand 'Glencoyne Beck Ulleswater' but listed in the album's index as 'Ulleswater from Styboar Cragg') must have been an unused image; the drawing for this and at least one of the other prints was owned by Daulby. After the Holland scenes come four prints from the series of twelve published in 1794–5 by another artist known to (and collected by) Daulby, John Rathbone (*c.*1750–1807) who had been based in Lancashire until 1785. The final sixteen prints were those advertised in the fifth edition of West's *Guide to the Lakes* (1793) as being 'of a proper size to bind with the Guide'; they were produced in 1794–5, chiefly by the engraver Samuel Alken, after drawings by John 'Warwick' Smith.

The final ten pages of this album are the most personal and noteworthy. These bear watercolours by Thomas Chubbard of views that had not been recorded in the aforementioned aquatints, and were less familiar to tourists, including Bassenthwaite, Ennerdale, Haweswater, Aira Force, Brothers Water and Esthwaite Water. Some were developed from drawings by Daulby himself or by Holland, while the final two views have sources from further afield. The penultimate page records the 1795 painting of Windermere and the Langdale Pikes by Wright of

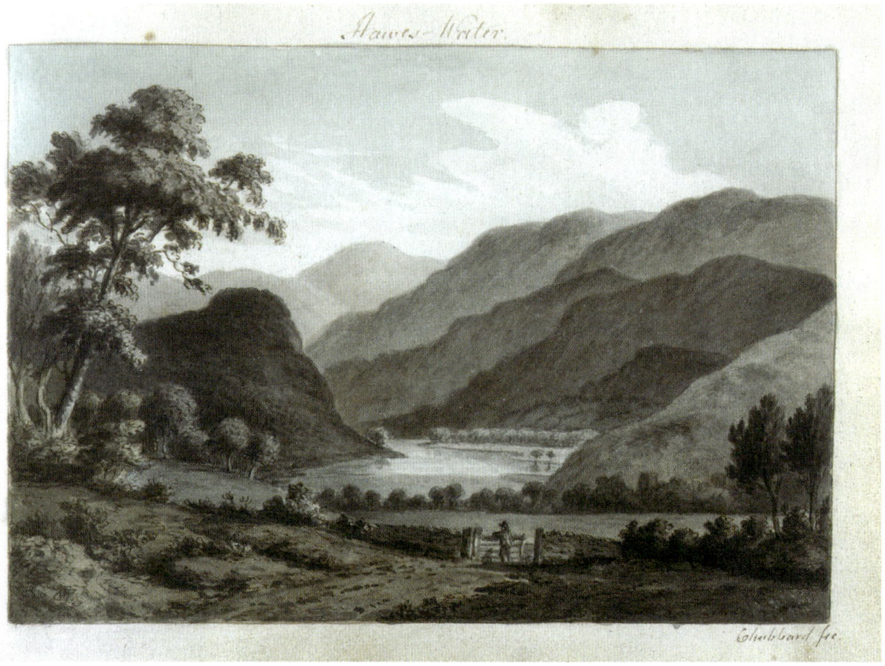

Fig. 20 Thomas Chubbard, *Hawes-Water*, pen, ink and watercolour, *c.*1796–8, from the smaller Daulby album (The Wordsworth Trust).

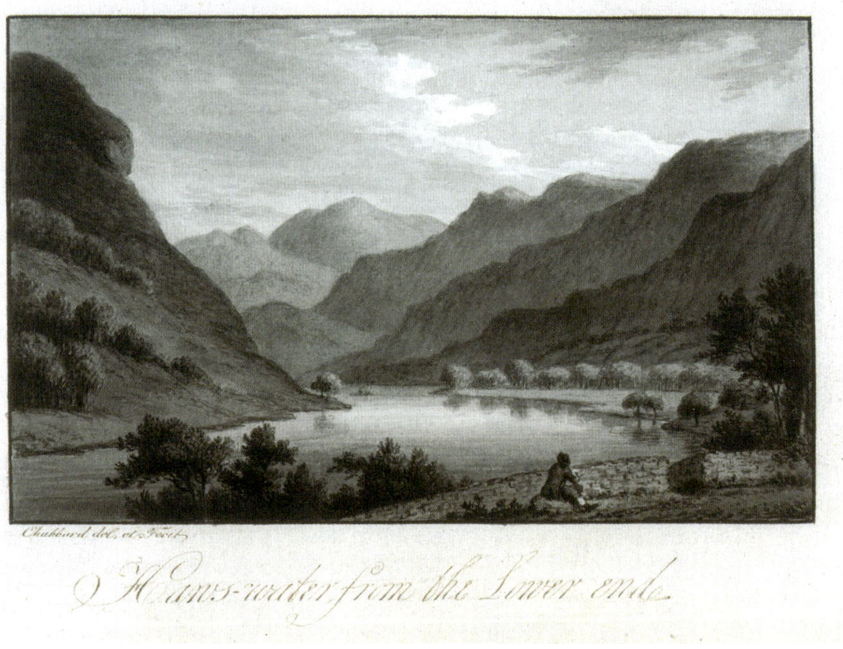

Fig. 21 Thomas Chubbard, *Haws-water, from the Lower end*, pen, ink and watercolour, *c.*1796–8, from the larger Daulby album (The Wordsworth Trust).

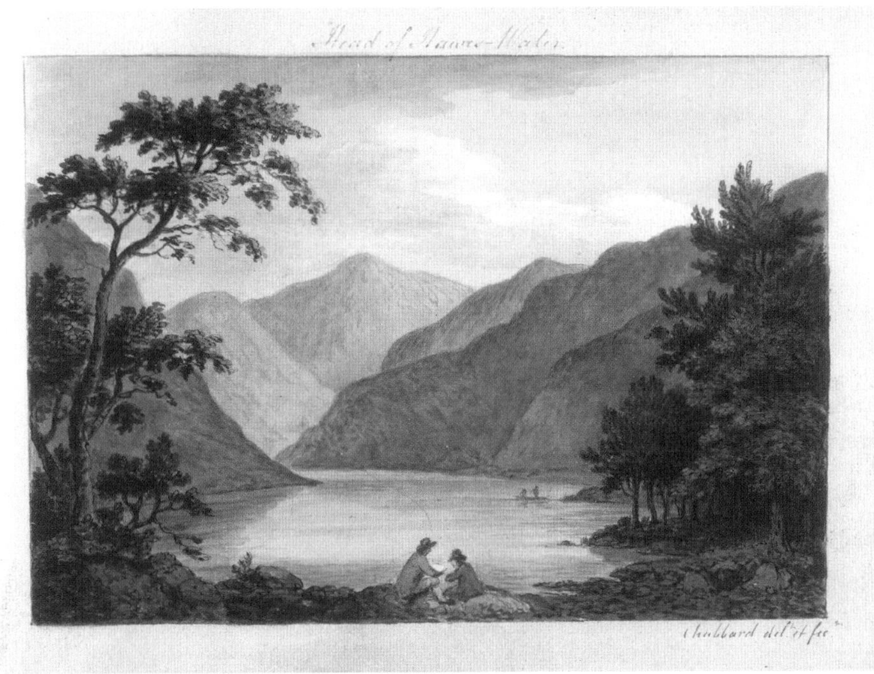

Fig. 22 Thomas Chubbard, *Head of Hawes-Water*, pen, ink and watercolour, *c*.1796–8, from the smaller Daulby album (The Wordsworth Trust).

Derby that then belonged to his friend Thomas Moss Tate of Liverpool and is also partially recorded in an anonymous small sketch in the Wordsworth Trust's collection (see cat. 41 and fig. 19 on p. 82). The last scene is copied from *North Aspect of Furness Abbey* by Joseph Farington which had been engraved in Hearne's *Antiquities of Great Britain* (see cat. 17). In all these cases the watercolour is presented on the page with inscriptions beneath, exactly as if it were in fact a print after a drawing or painting, e.g. 'Holland del' or 'Wright of Derby pinxit' accompanied by 'Chubbard fecit'.

The album is displayed here to show a drawing of Haweswater, a lake which Daulby had discovered in the summer of 1794 when he wrote to Farington that there were 'two fine views' of it (I.233). The album, in fact, contains three views of the lake, though – as will appear – the second and third are very similar. Each is repeated with minor foreground variations in the smaller Daulby album (compare cat. 43 and fig. 20). These are of special interest, partly because Haweswater is comparatively little visited even today, and partly because the lake has undergone so many changes since the 1790s. The small 8-shaped natural lake that Chubbard and Daulby admired is now a much larger man-made reservoir supplying water to the Manchester area; this was created, following an Act of Parliament in 1919, by building a large hollow buttress dam to hold back the waters of Haweswater Beck at the northern end of the lake. The village of Mardale was evacuated in the 1930s and the dam completed in 1941; the area of lake was increased three-fold, the water-level being raised by around ninety feet, covering farms, cottages, inn and church alike.

Of even greater significance, however, is the fact that Chubbard's Haweswater views correspond closely to the descriptions of the lake published in 1795 by Mrs Ann Radcliffe. Daulby's library contained not only all Mrs Radcliffe's novels but also her *Journey made in the Summer of 1794, through Holland and the Western Frontier of Germany*. He and Chubbard would have been especially interested in this since it included over a hundred pages devoted to 'Observations during a Tour to the Lakes of Lancashire, Westmoreland, and Cumberland'. Mrs Radcliffe describes how she travelled from Lancaster to Kendal and then made her way to Bampton and Haweswater over the Shap Fells; this is followed by over six pages devoted to the lake itself, the first object of interest in her 'Observations'. Chubbard's first view, *Haws-water, with Bampton* (cat. 43), shows the small northernmost part of the lake ('Low Water') and echoes her words on reaching the first expanse of the lake when approaching from 'Bampton vale': 'Its eastern shore, rising in a tremendous ridge of rocks, darkened with wood to the summit, appears to terminate in Wallow-crag, a promontory of towering height, beyond which the lake winds from view. The finely broken mountains on the west are covered with heath, and the tops impend in crags and precipices; but their ascent from the water is less sudden than that of the opposite rocks, and they are skirted by a narrow margin of vivid green, where cattle were feeding, and tufted shrubs and little groves overhung the lake and were reflected on its dark surface … the narrow perspective was closed by dark and monstrous summits' (p. 400). In his second and third views, figs 21–2, Chubbard records the views that greeted travellers as they passed 'The Straits' under Wallow Crag and reached the large southern area known as 'High Water'; Mrs Radcliffe describes the experience as follows: 'the rocks unfolded and disclosed the second expanse, with scenery yet more towering and sublime than the first. … Harter-fell reared his awful front … and shut in the scene. … Among the fells of this dark prospect are Lathale, Wilter-crag, Castle-crag and Riggindale, their bold lines appearing beyond each other as they fell into the upper part of the lake. … Kidstow-pike is pre-eminent among the crowding summits beyond the eastern shore…; on the west High-street, which overlooks the head of Ullswater, is the most dignified of the mountains' (pp. 400–1).

Mrs Radcliffe was not the first writer to praise Haweswater; Arthur Young's description of 1770 was reprinted in successive editions of West's *Guide* from 1780 onwards. However, the parallels between Chubbard's views and Radcliffe's descriptions are repeated in several other drawings in this album, including his views of Bassenthwaite from Ouse Bridge (Radcliffe, pp. 461–2), Esthwaite and Hawkshead (pp. 478–9) and Furness Abbey (pp. 487 ff.). Even his copy of Wright's view of Windermere from Low Wood reflects her description of the stupendous light effects on the Langdale Pikes and other fells as seen from a little further south, above Calgarth (pp. 473–4). One cannot help wondering: did Chubbard and Daulby, at one stage, dream of producing their own illustrated, interleaved, personal copies of Mrs Radcliffe's 'Observations'? CFP

44

THOMAS CHUBBARD (1738–1809)
after JOHN 'WARWICK' SMITH (1749–1831)
The Entrance into Borrowdale
c.1796–8
Pencil, ink and watercolour, 12.6 × 17.9 cm
Inscribed 'Smith del[t].', 'The Entrance into Borrowdale' and 'Chubbard fec[t].'
Gift of Beatrice Thornely, 1947

The second and smaller of the two Daulby albums, though superficially similar to the first (cat. 43), differs from it in several important ways. To begin with, it contains no prints; it is simply an assemblage of watercolours and pencil drawings. These are extremely varied in subject and are put together in a far more random way than the prints and watercolours of its systematically organised counterpart: the second half of the album includes not only views of the Lakes but also ones from many parts of Britain including – in this order – North Wales, Derbyshire, Sussex and Cheshire. Amongst these are interspersed seven diverse Lakes scenes.

The album opens with a magnificent calligraphic title-page, declaring itself to be *Select Views, Chiefly of the Lakes; Drawn by Thomas Chubbard*. This is hand-drawn in pen and ink but mimics the title-page of a printed book; not just any book but Peter Holland's *Select Views of the Lakes*, which had provided the starting-point of the larger album. Chubbard's title-page was the work of the same calligrapher as Holland's, Charles Graham. This is followed by a landscape showing Borrowdale with the river Derwent and the Bowder Stone in imitation of the first aquatint in Holland's book (figs 23–4); Chubbard must have planned to have his title inscribed on the Bowder Stone in similar fashion but this work was never carried out.

All the watercolours are the work of Chubbard but many are copies of a painting, drawing or print by another artist. His main sources for the Lake District views were Holland, Farington, Barret and 'Warwick' Smith while two of those depicting Wales were copied from works by Peter Perez Burdett and an artist given simply as 'Evans'. All the artists are credited in inscriptions beneath the scenes; like those in cat. 43, these follow the style of print inscriptions. Another source for Chubbard was Daulby himself, for both Lakes views and ones of Bedgellert, Basingwerk Abbey and Capel Curig as well as the Cheshire properties Speke Hall, Hooton

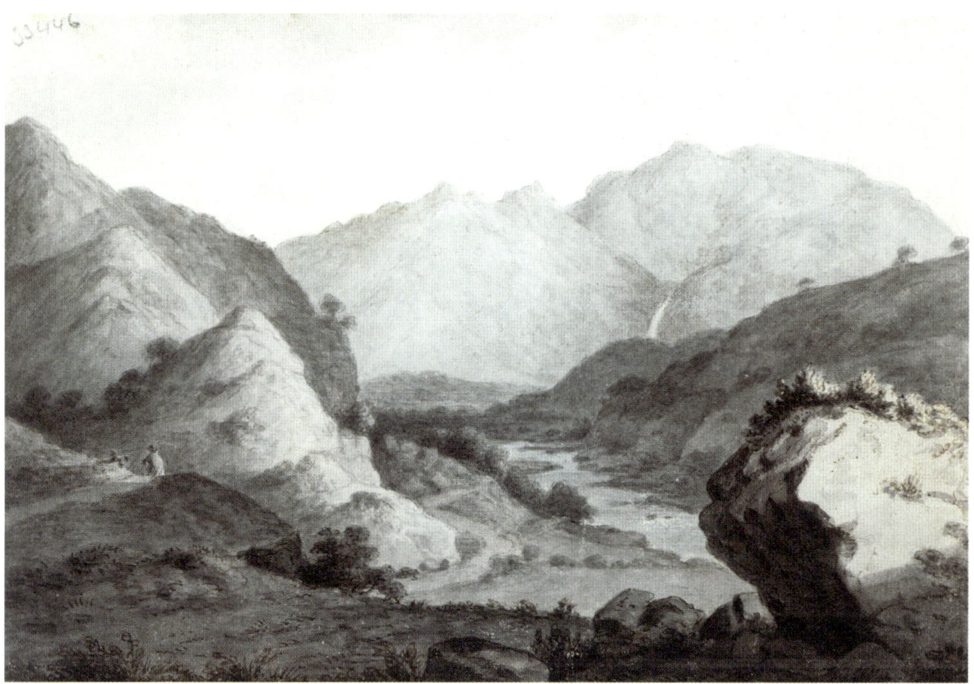

Fig. 23 Thomas Chubbard, *Bowdar Stone, Borrowdale*, pen, ink and watercolour, *c.*1796–8 (The Wordsworth Trust).

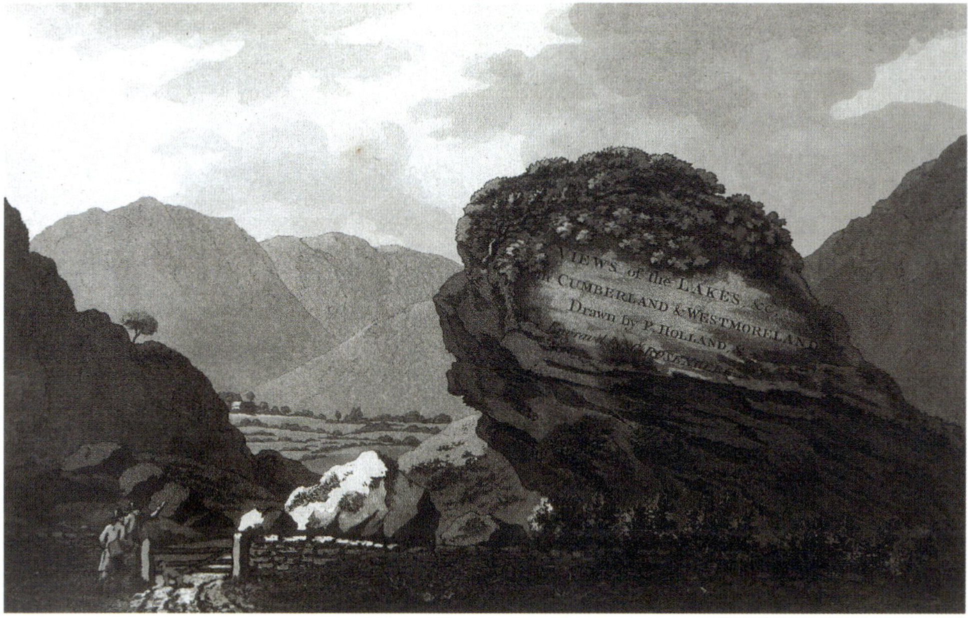

Fig. 24 C. Rosenberg after Peter Holland, *Bowdar Stone in Borodale*, aquatint, 1792 (The Wordsworth Trust).

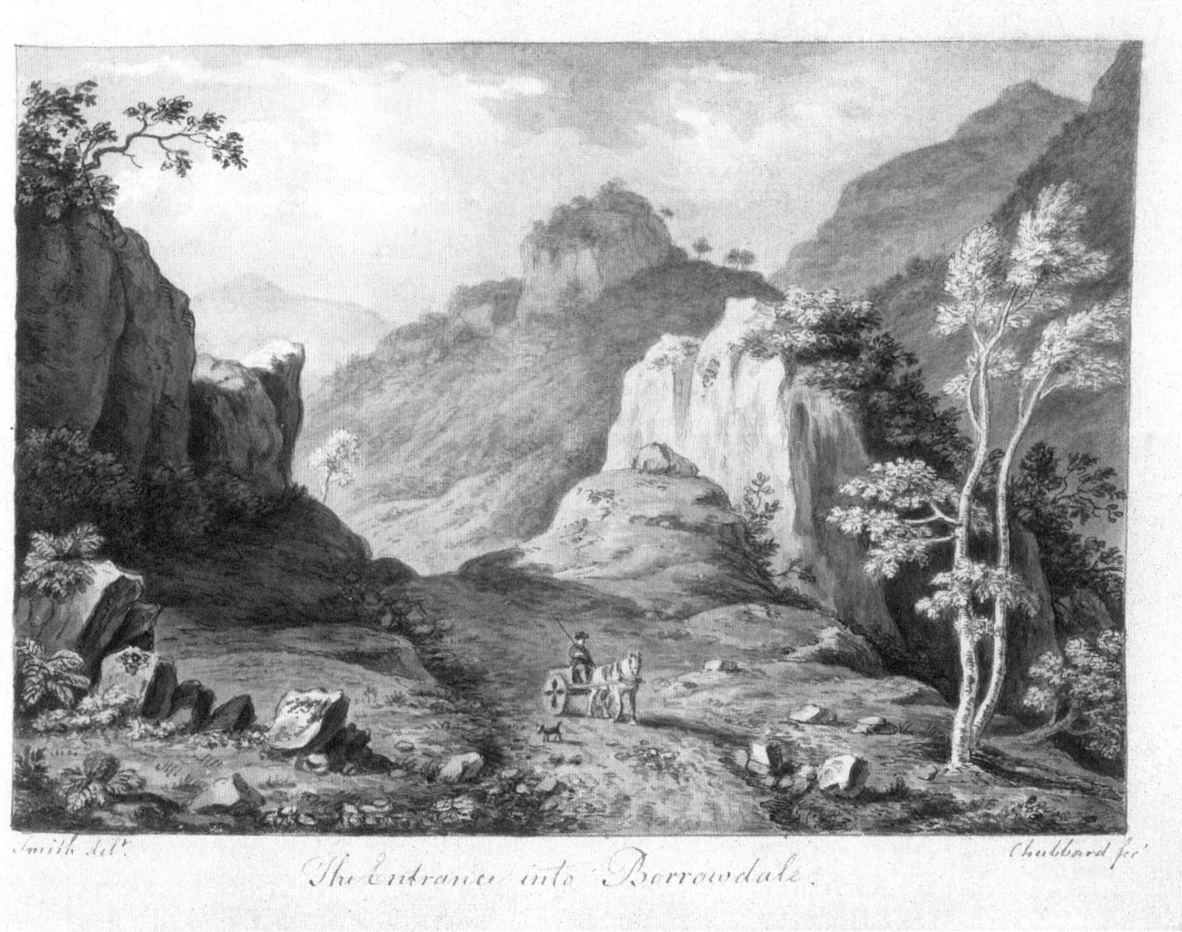

Cat. 44

Hall, Poole Hall and Rock Savage (Daulby had contributed a view of Hooton to William Watts' *Seats of the Nobility and Gentry* published in 1779–86). The index to the book shows that further drawings after Daulby were planned, showing the Wrekin, Ellesmere and Beeston Castle. These were not executed, being replaced by three views of Haweswater similar to those in cat. 43 (see figs 20 and 22 on pp. 86–7).

Eight of the pencil drawings in the album depict the area near Rydal Mount where Daulby spent the last period of his life – from around the middle of 1796 to the beginning of March 1798. Of these just one, showing Pelter Bridge, is inscribed as the work of Daulby and bears the date 'Novr 17th 1796'; either he or Chubbard began to strengthen its outlines in pen but then abandoned it (fig. 25). Its view is almost identical to that shown in an aquatint published by Rogers of Stafford (see cat. 42) earlier that year, save that it shows Rydal Hall clearly among the trees on the right. Nothing could be more natural than that Daulby, installed at Rydal Mount, should have wished to depict his new environment and enlisted Chubbard's help in this endeavour: to join him in sketching out of doors and to spend winter evenings working up sketches and washing in effects. Sadly, none of these fascinating records of Daulby's residence at Rydal was properly developed.

The contents of the album show that Chubbard felt thoroughly at home when translating prints and drawings by other artists into watercolours on a much smaller scale. One of the most successful examples of this is the watercolour selected for exhibition, his copy of Merigot's engraving of 1792 after John 'Warwick' Smith's *Entrance into Borrodale* which itself is on display (cat. 35). The reduction in scale led inevitably to some pruning of details (the tiny figures at the top of the rise at the centre, for example)

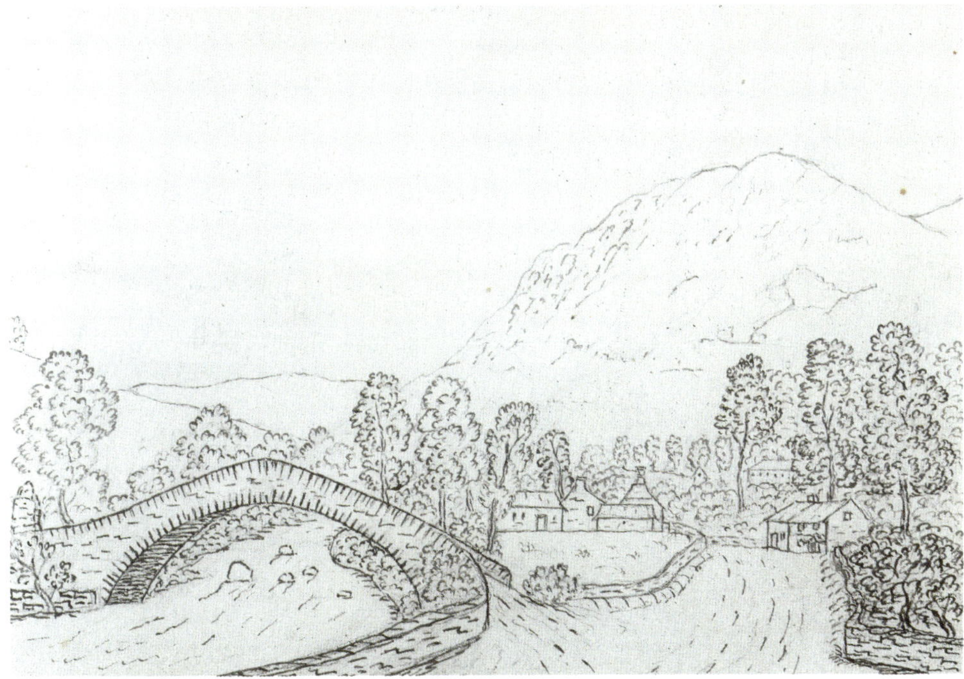

Fig. 25 Daniel Daulby, *Pelter Bridge Rydall*, pencil, pen and ink, dated 'Nov.[r] 17.th 1796' (The Wordsworth Trust).

and Chubbard chose to alter the central figure from a lady riding side-saddle to a much more rustic and typical sight, a farmer driving his cart. More importantly, though, he succeeds in capturing the spirit of Smith's work: the fearsome scenery of Borrowdale with its winding boulder-strewn paths and the crags that led to its entrance being described as 'the Jaws of Borrowdale'. CFP

45

FRANCIS NICHOLSON (1753–1844)
Skiddaw from across the Lake of Derwentwater
c.1798?
Pencil and watercolour, 30 × 41.9 cm
The National Trust, on long-term loan to The Wordsworth Trust

In 1798 – four years after he had first visited the Lake District – Nicholson was invited to send some of his drawings on approval to the art-loving Walter Fawkes of Farnley Hall near Leeds, already a patron of John 'Warwick' Smith and later to be an intimate friend and patron of Turner. Several of Nicholson's nine drawings gave immediate satisfaction and were praised for their 'clearness and transparency': two of Windermere were described as 'most beautiful', one of Bowness as '*Perfection*' and that of the Bowder Stone as 'one of the most beautiful drawings I ever saw'. A drawing that may have been cat. 45 produced a slightly less enthusiastic comment: 'Skiddaw perfect, the water in one part has a line, and one line does the mischief, that gives the water rather more convexity than it ought to have.' Nevertheless Fawkes was delighted with his new acquisitions, complimenting Nicholson on the improvement in his work, and before the end of the year he had commissioned him to produce further drawings, depicting Ullswater and Honister Crag (Davies, 1931, pp. 16–17).

Although nearly all Nicholson's work was devoted to subjects in the north of England, Wales and Scotland, he only exhibited fourteen Lake District scenes at the Society of Painters in Water Colours between 1806 and 1814 including just one of Derwentwater, *View above the Fall of Lowdore on Derwentwater* (1810, no. 121). This was the year that he included no fewer than seven Lakes subjects among his exhibits: apart from depicting several of the most popular lakes, including Windermere and Grasmere, he also painted less spectacular views such as the mill at Ambleside and Loughrigg Tarn.

Cat. 45 shows Skiddaw from across Derwentwater, with low cloud swirling round its

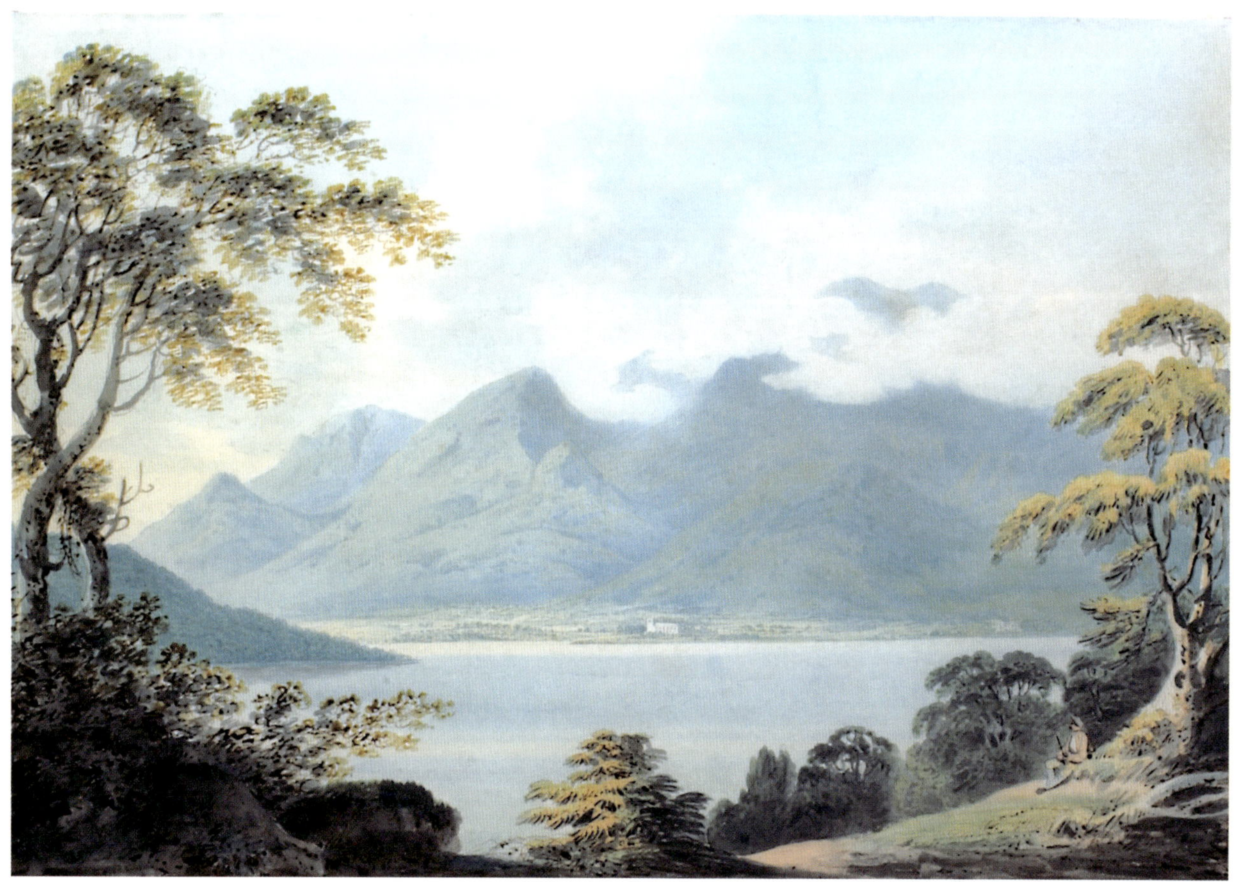

Cat. 45

summit, creating the illusion of an almost symmetrical profile, much lower than can be seen in clear weather. Below this, beyond the smooth expanse of water, Crosthwaite church is shown nestling at its feet. The foreground is conventionally framed with stylised trees, the light pleasantly catching their leaves (those on the left are painted with Nicholson's characteristic dabs and curling touches of superimposed colours); a grassy bank on the right provides a convenient resting place for a walker to enjoy the view on a fine summer's day. Taken overall, the watercolour is highly decorative, providing an image of Derwentwater that is beautified rather than profound, awe-inspiring or startling. It would have enhanced any drawing-room around 1800 and as an advertisement for a tour to the Lakes it would have had few competitors. CFP

46

SIR GEORGE BEAUMONT (1753–1827)
Borrowdale
1798
Pencil and grey wash, 16.7 × 21.6 cm
Inscribed 'Borrowdale Aug / 24'

Beaumont's sketch of Borrowdale comes from a sketchbook used on his visit to the Lakes in 1798, one of the many visits he made to the area following his first in 1777 when, himself an amateur artist, he was accompanied by two slightly older professionals, Thomas Hearne and Joseph Farington (see cat. 15–16). By 1798 Beaumont and his wife were so enamoured of the Lake District that, while staying in Keswick, they bought land above Brathay, near Loughrigg Tarn, with a view to building their own house there for summer sojourns. The idea was abandoned, however, after a few years and the land resold; on future visits they continued to rent houses or stay with friends and acquaintances as before.

Day after day during these visits Beaumont would go out sketching and return with a haul of pencil sketches, each carefully labelled and dated. The Wordsworth Trust owns a large number of those made between June and August 1798, as well as many others made in 1799 and 1800. As can be seen from the present sketch, Beaumont's work in the open air was brisk and schematic: a good vantage point having been selected, he outlined distant contours and lightly characterised their surfaces, he noted trees and bushes by loops and squiggles, and recorded darker or shadowed areas with quick, regular diagonal hatching. Several sketches like this could be made comfortably on each excursion. Later, at home and perhaps by lamplight, he would add monochrome washes to provide atmosphere and a sense of perspective, and later still the sketches were carefully laid down in albums with fresh inscriptions of dates and places.

Beaumont had sketched in this manner since he first received instruction as a schoolboy at Eton and from private masters in the vacations and he continued to sketch thus, deriving pleasure from the activity of drawing just as he did from studying and buying works by professional artists. His own style changed little and remained essentially that of an amateur; in this drawing, for example, despite his additions of hatching and washes, it is hard for the viewer to make three-dimensional sense of the piled-up rocks on the left or the smaller dark mass on the right. Beaumont himself was well aware of his limitations – and he was also an imaginative and generous (if sometimes fickle) patron to those he favoured. Having made the acquaintance of the young Thomas Girtin, one of the rising stars in the art of watercolour, at about this time, he commissioned him to transform some of his own recent sketches into larger, finished works (see cat. 47). CFP

47

THOMAS GIRTIN (1775–1802)
Borrowdale
*c.*1801
Pencil and watercolour, 31 × 47.1 cm
Purchased with the generous help of funds administered by the Victoria & Albert Museum for the Museums and Galleries Commission and the National Heritage Memorial Fund, 1984

Girtin's transformation of Sir George Beaumont's view of Borrowdale (cat. 46) is one of eight or nine known examples of the young artist being commissioned by the baronet to turn an on-the-spot record into a work of art. It is immediately obvious to the viewer that Girtin's watercolour is larger, subtler and more colourful and also that it is by no means a faithful copy; if the viewer wished to know the artist's exact subject and precise viewpoint it would be necessary to carry a copy of Beaumont's sketch on a field trip rather than Girtin's watercolour. Girtin's brief was to transform a topographical record (an accurate depiction of a particular spot) into something more substantial and meaningful as well as

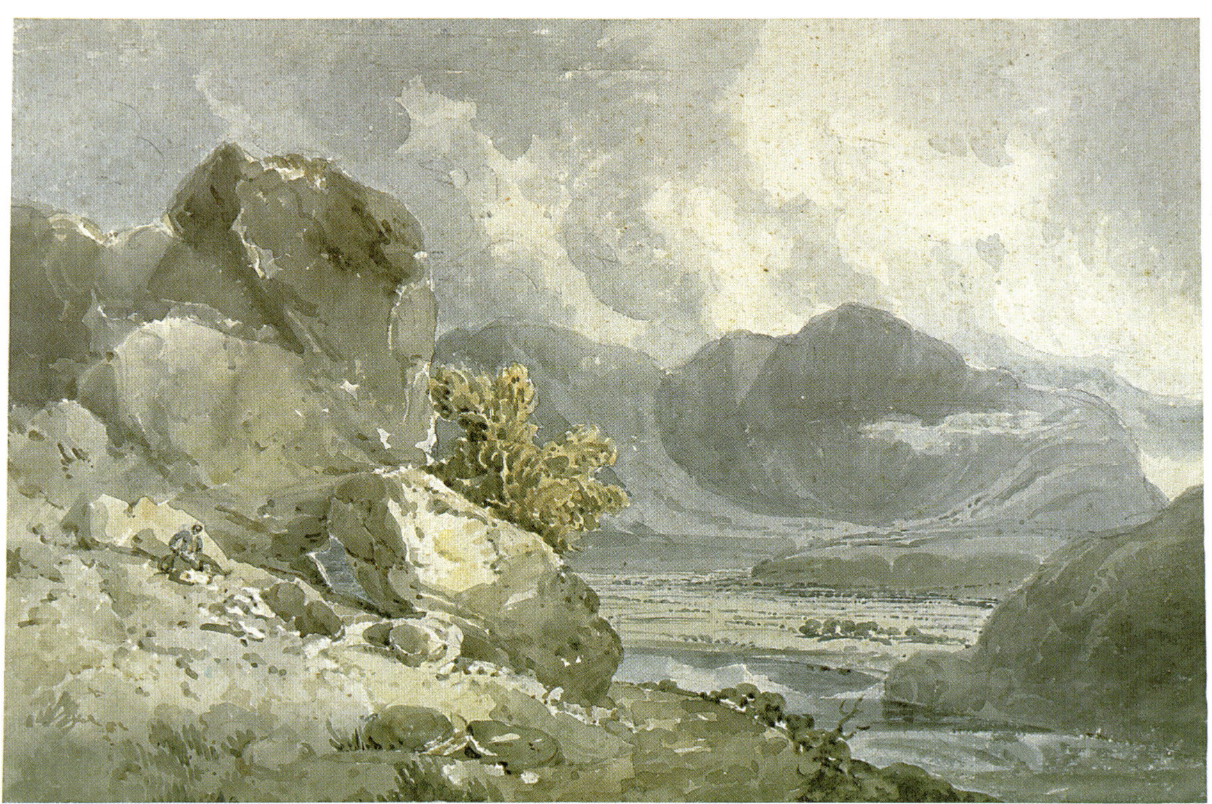

Cat. 47

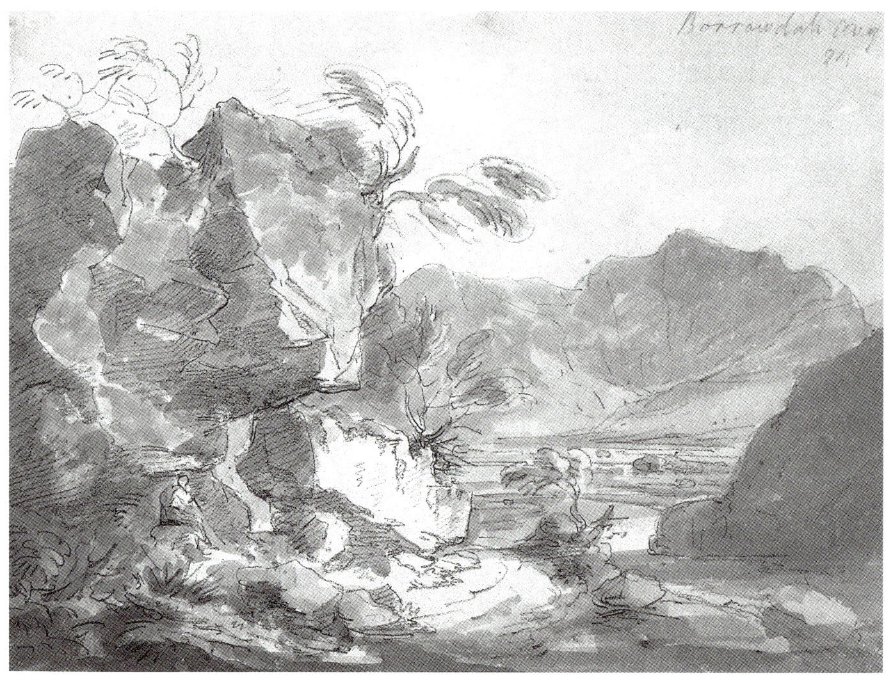

Cat. 46

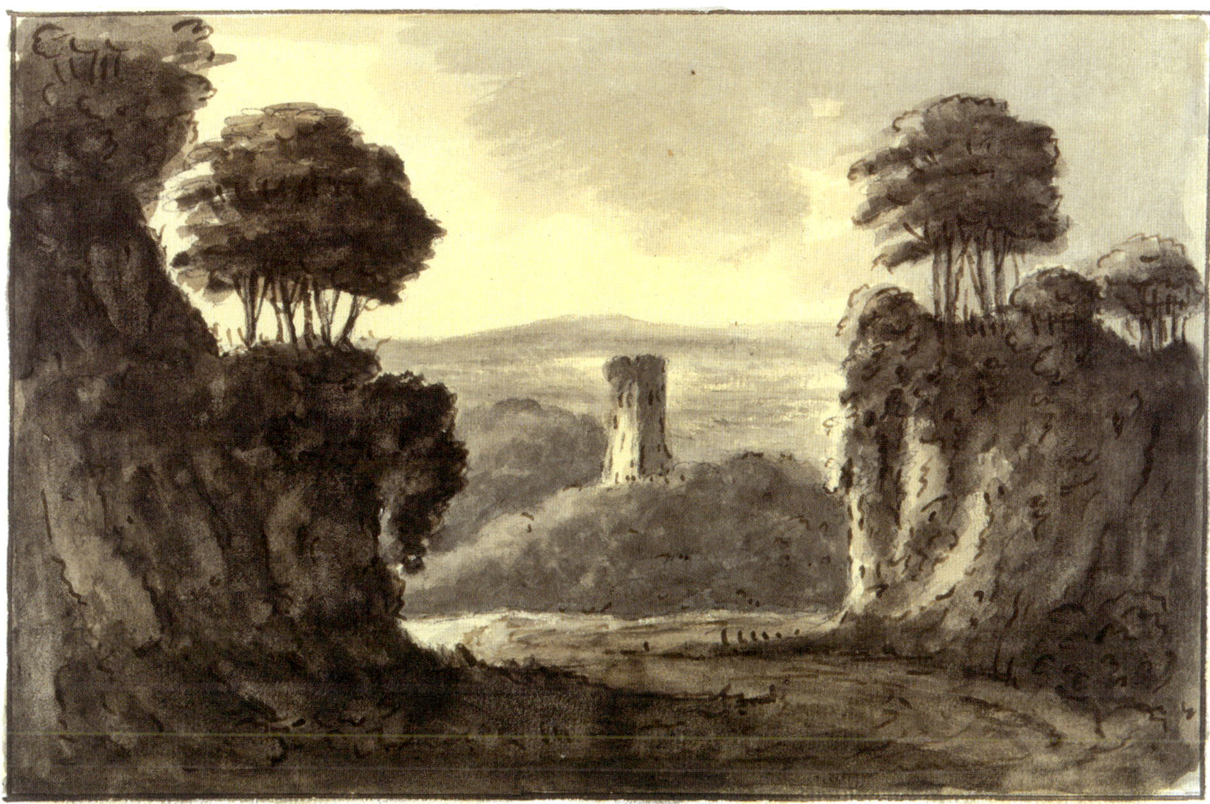

Cat. 48

more professionally executed: a mountain landscape inspired by the Lake District. This he brilliantly fulfilled, despite never having visited the area. His familiarity with other upland areas in Britain (notably North Wales and Yorkshire), combined with prolonged study of the work of earlier artists (especially the Alpine views of J.R. Cozens), enabled him to produce a scene that is infused with poetry and grandeur.

First and foremost, Girtin eliminates a lot of Beaumont's detail and concentrates on presenting clearly defined areas, each with its own character and significance. He rearranges and simplifies the towering heap of boulders on the left, for instance, and removes its distracting fringe of wind-swept vegetation. He opens up the vale in the middle distance and punctuates it with trees and bushes, thus creating a vista of countless small enclosures beneath the range of uncultivable grey peaks beyond. The latter he develops and reshapes into a typical 'bowl' gouged out by glaciers, with trails of white cloud hovering within the bowl – these again suggest the immense scale of what is shown. Part of the scene is bathed in light, making it credible that the figure on the left is enjoying a period of repose; however, the mass of shifting clouds and the shadows in the foreground are portents of a probable storm. Out of Beaumont's record of particulars Girtin thus extracts a quintessential Borrowdale view that every lover of the Lakes can recognise, even though it has never actually existed. CFP

48

WILLIAM GILPIN (1724–1804)
Landscape with a Tower
1801
Pencil, pen and ink and wash and bodycolour on laid paper, 15.2 × 22.8 cm
Inscribed on the verso '23 November 1801 / W Gilpin'
Peter Bicknell Bequest, 1997

Through his extensive writings, circulated in manuscript from the 1770s, and his numerous publications, from the early 1780s onwards, the Rev. William

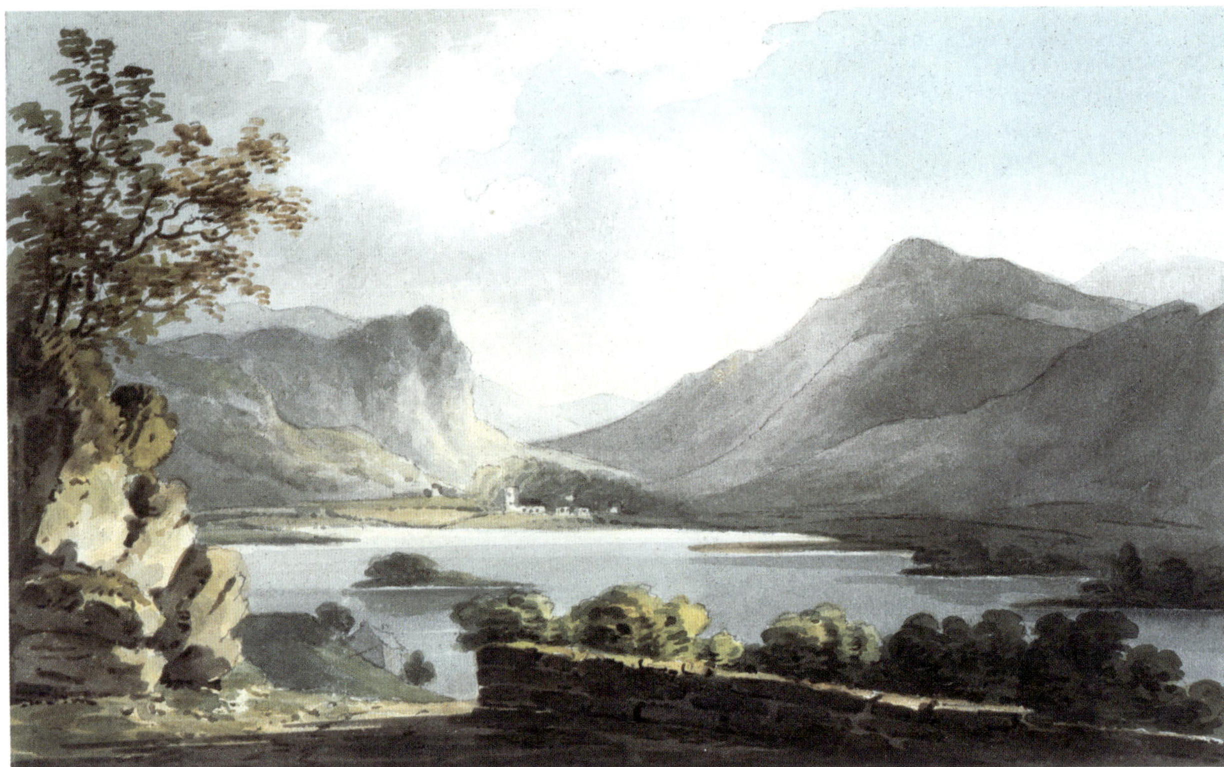

Cat. 49

Gilpin exerted a deep and long-lasting influence on public understanding and appreciation of the British landscape (see cat. 13). He himself continued to make drawings of what he called 'mountain scenes' until the end of his life, this term denoting imaginary combinations, 'where one part relates to another, and the effect of a whole is produced', rather than portraits of actual views, where the objects may be grand in themselves but are 'huddled together, confused, without connection'. As he remarked when describing the 'majestic scenes' between Ambleside and Keswick, mountainous countries most commonly present the latter type of view (which he termed 'a scene of mountains') but this particular road was an exception, the mountains being 'naturally combined into scenes' and 'marked with the great lines of composition' (Gilpin, 1786, vol. 1, pp. 160–1).

Landscape with a Tower is a good example of what Gilpin classified as a 'contracted valley', illustrating this term with one of his oval aquatints (1786, vol. 1, plate VI). 'These scenes are generally decorated with a river; but sometimes only with a road', he writes, and the emphasis is on the foreground rather than the distance. The abruptness of the transition between foreground and distance can be adjusted by varying the size, shape and relative positions of the side-screens; these may also be permitted to intersect, considerably reducing the distant view. The screens in this example consist of variegated and tree-crowned hanging rocks that stand like portals guarding a deep but narrow vista. As in the works of many of the Old Masters, to whom Gilpin often made overt reference, the middle distance is enhanced by a ruined tower, a reminder of man's presence and intervention in the landscape in earlier centuries. CFP

49

?JAMES BOURNE (1773–1854)
Grasmere from Red Bank
c.1802?
Watercolour, 12.8 × 20.3 cm
Rawnsley Bequest, 1959

This watercolour, and eleven others, comes from the Wordsworth Trust's copy of *Interesting Views of the Lakes*, an undated printed text of 67 pages describing what had become 'a fashionable excursion' for those whose circumstances permitted them to quit 'the hum, and busy haunts of men' (a phrase adapted from Milton). The wording of the title-page suggests that the artist James Bourne was responsible for both text and illustrations and there are references in the text to the latter, in phrases such as 'the annexed drawing'. A few other copies of the printed text are known, each interleaved with full-page watercolours, while there are apparently no copies with any form of engraving apart from a generalised lakeland vignette in aquatint on the title-page. The watercolours in the various copies are effectively replicas of the same scenes, with the Wordsworth Trust's copy containing the largest known number (the British Museum copy, for instance, contains only six while that in the Victoria & Albert Museum has nine; another copy, with twelve scenes, is in the Armitt Museum, Ambleside). This may suggest that a select few of Bourne's aristocratic patrons were each furnished with a semi-unique item or, perhaps, that he simply produced hand-illustrated copies of *Interesting Views of the Lakes* on commission. The attribution of the illustrations to Bourne has been queried by several scholars on the grounds that they lack the rigour and stylistic hallmarks of his later watercolours when he worked largely in monochrome; others, however, have accepted the attribution, regarding such differences as the result of their early date in the artist's career. If they are not by Bourne, they must be the work of someone who was not only a professional artist but also a very close associate.

Although Bourne spent much of his artistic career in London, his origins lay in Lincolnshire and he dedicated his *Interesting Views* to an eminent 'fellow countryman', Lord Yarborough (1749–1823), an important patron of the young Turner in the years round 1800. The tone of Bourne's dedication, missing from the Wordsworth Trust's copy but present in the British Museum copy, suggests that he, too, craved Lord Yarborough's patronage, hoping to attract his attention through the dedication of his 'first public effort'; there is, unfortunately, no evidence that he succeeded. The ensuing text describes a tour of some seven or eight days which probably contains elements of Bourne's own experiences; he refers to the activity of sketching as well as to the Keswick blacklead merchant, Mr Ladyman, who supplied pencils to tradesmen and artists in both England and Scotland. Bourne's tour itself was made in 1798 but the publication and its watercolours date from some years later. The Wordsworth Trust's group of watercolours includes one of Bassenthwaite drawn on paper bearing a watermark of 1801.

At one point the narrative describes a journey from Windermere up to Keswick, noting that Rydal Hall had been 'lately much improved, by the addition of an elegant new front, built in a good style of architecture'. From here the writer took the 'neat white bridge' into the bye-road instead of using the customary route, the turnpike to Grasmere. This deviation enabled him to enjoy views of the lakes of Rydal and Grasmere from the south and west, the climax of his description being reached when he comes over 'Grasmere Hill' (Loughrigg) and sees the whole of Grasmere vale extending before him. The accompanying watercolour of the view from Red Bank below Loughrigg (cat. 49) matches his words perfectly: 'a sweeter or more lovely prospect no one could ever behold, wherever his course may have been, either in the luxurious plains of Italy, or the sequestered vales of Switzerland.' Bourne then proceeds to quote Gray's now-famous description of 'this admirably happy vale', which had described the view from the opposite end of the lake. CFP

50

WILLIAM PICKETT after PHILIP JAMES DE LOUTHERBOURG RA (1740–1812)
Lake of Wyndermere
1805, as reissued in 1822
Aquatint with hand-colouring, 30.2 × 38.7 cm
Engraved inscription: below, with title
Peter Bicknell Bequest, 1997

This engaging scene first appeared in *The Romantic and Picturesque Scenery of England and Wales*, the second volume of aquatints after 'drawings made expressly for the undertaking' by De Loutherbourg, which appeared in 1805. The eighteen aquatints were the work of William Pickett, with hand-colouring by John Clark, and they were accompanied by texts in French and English. Both this and De Loutherbourg's earlier collection of 1801, *Picturesque Scenery of Great Britain*, were published by Robert Bowyer. A later edition of the 1805 volume, with the imprints and signatures removed, was issued in 1822,

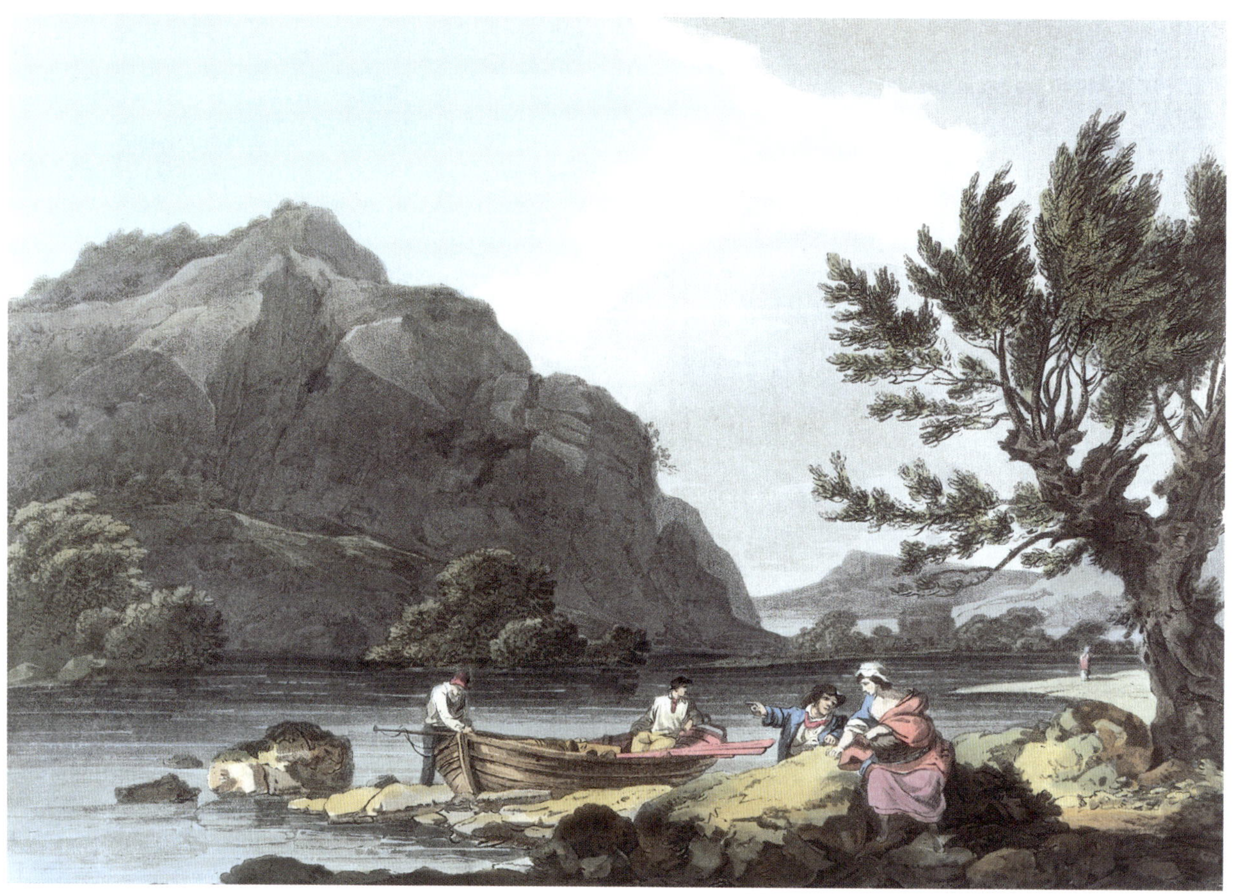

Cat. 50

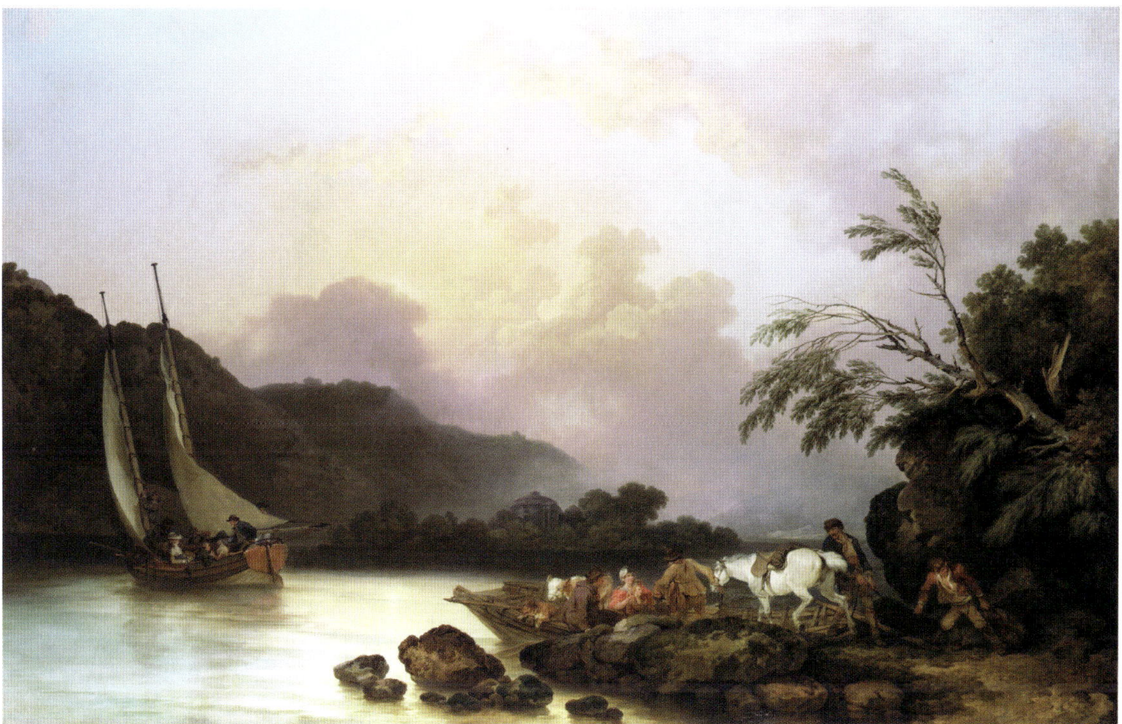

Fig. 26 Philip James de Loutherbourg, *View of Winandermeer, near the ferry, a sun-set*, oil on canvas, 1786, now known as *Belle Isle, Windermere, in a Calm* (Abbot Hall Art Gallery, Kendal).

ten years after De Loutherbourg's death, and it is likely that cat. no. 50 comes from this later publication.

The composition of the aquatint is similar to that of one of De Loutherbourg's Royal Academy exhibits of 1786 (no. 204), *View of Winandermeer, near the ferry, a sun-set,* now in Abbot Hall Art Gallery, Kendal (fig. 26). The left-hand part of the scene is dominated by the wooded crags of Claife Heights while in the right foreground a boat is drawn up on a rocky shore, the ferry landing-place on the east side of Windermere just south of Belle Isle. In both scenes Belle Isle itself and its picturesquely sited house, built in the 1770s and resembling a circular classical temple, are clearly depicted. Here the similarities end, however. In the painting the country folk cramming themselves and their animals into the boat on the shore afford a distinct contrast to a group of elegant ladies and gentlemen enjoying the beauties of the lake from a sailing boat. The aquatint has no such message to proclaim. The landing-place simply provides an attractive setting for a group of local people, including a gaily attired girl being encouraged to embark by a handsome youth. CFP

51

JAMES HEATH after J.M.W. TURNER RA (1775–1851)
Patterdale
1805
Engraving, 11.8 × 17.6 cm
Engraved inscriptions: below, with title, names of artist and engraver, and *London, Published May 1. 1805, by J. Mawman, Poultry.*

In 1804 Turner was commissioned to produce three watercolours for engraving in *An Excursion to the Highlands of Scotland and the English Lakes* written by Joseph Mawman and published by the author himself the following year; by then Mawman was both publisher and joint editor of the *Critical Review*. His tour, made in July 1804 in the company of another Londoner William Salte, had taken him from London to Edinburgh via York and Durham. They then crossed to Glasgow for a short tour as far north as Inverary before returning to London using a more westerly route. Arriving at Penrith from Carlisle, they headed for Keswick whence they made two excursions (the first to Patterdale, the second to Borrowdale and Buttermere) before travelling on to Ambleside, Kendal and Lancaster.

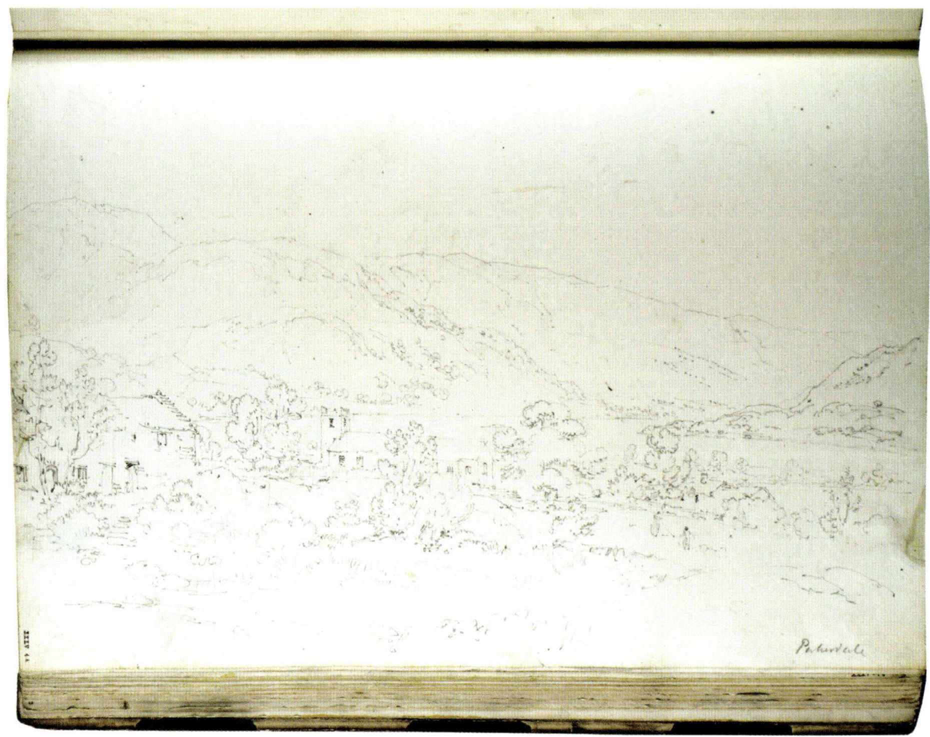

Fig. 27 J.M.W. Turner, *Patterdale Old Church, looking north to the Lake*, pencil, 1797 (Tate Britain, London).

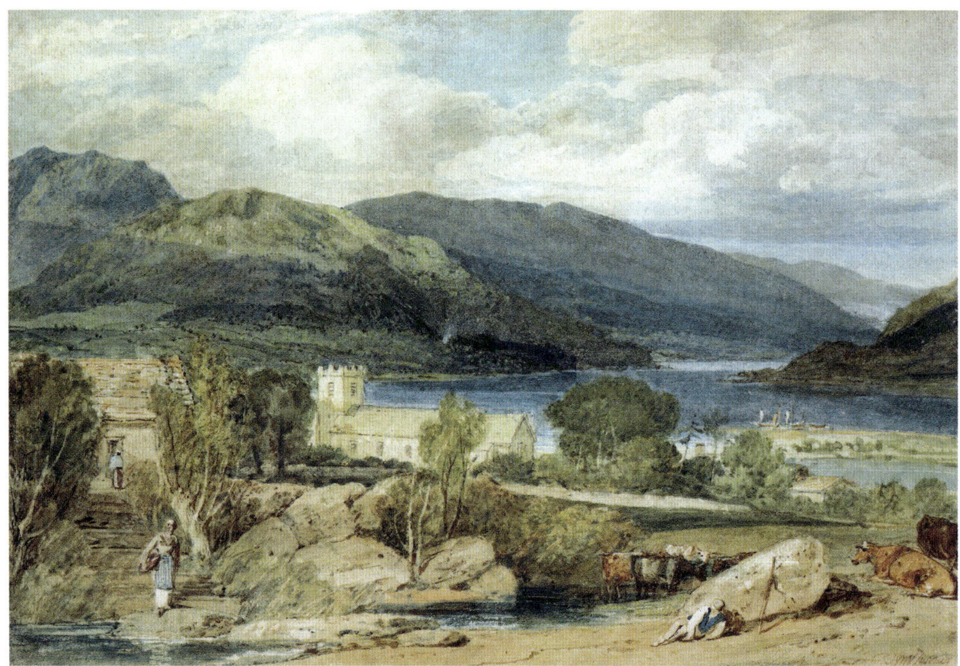

Fig. 28 J.M.W. Turner, *Patterdale*, watercolour with pen, *c.*1804–5 (private collection).

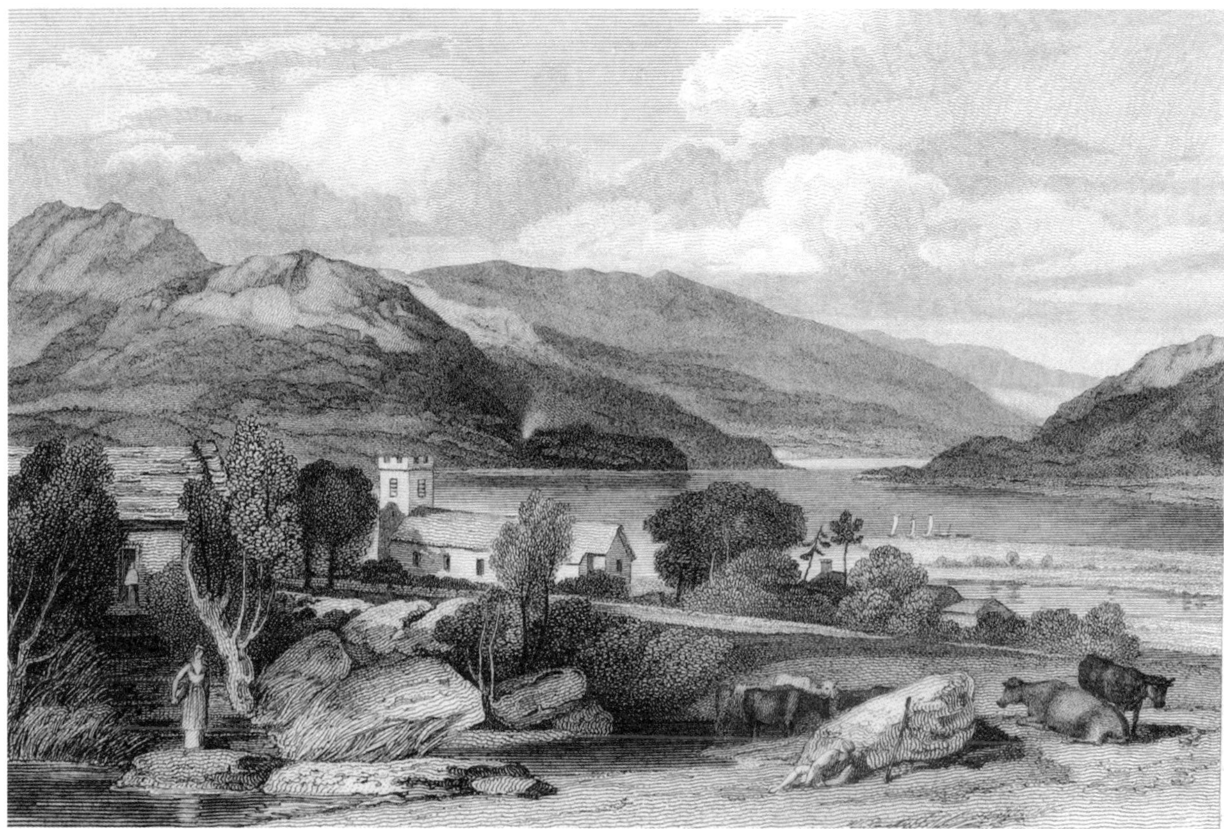

Cat. 51

By this date Turner was a well-established artist with an ever-increasing circle of patrons for his watercolours and oil paintings and he had already contributed views for engraving in numerous publications. Mawman's commission resulted in the earliest engravings after Turner depicting Scotland and the Lake District: *Inverary*, *Loch Lomond* and *Patterdale*. All were the work of James Heath, a leading engraver of the day and the father of Charles Heath, promoter of Turner's most important publishing projects in the 1820s and 1830s. Turner had first visited the Lake District on his northern tour of 1797, making sketches at Patterdale in the sketchbook he entitled '*Tweed and Lakes*' (fig. 27). That tour inspired several outstanding watercolours and imaginative paintings including *Morning amongst the Coniston Fells*, exhibited with a quotation from Milton at the Royal Academy in 1798 (Tate). His watercolour of Patterdale (fig. 28), measuring 19.7 by 28.6 cm and based on the above sketch, is necessarily more straightforwardly topographical in nature, as befitted a book illustration, but it is brilliant in its colouring and contains warm rich afternoon light effects. Many of Turner's views in the Lake District can still be enjoyed by modern tourists but this is, sadly, not the case here. His viewpoint is now inaccessible and, in any case, Patterdale church was completely rebuilt by Anthony Salvin in 1853, two years after Turner's death.

Mawman's choice of Patterdale for his only Lake District illustration seems to have been governed simply by his recollection of the pleasure of his visit. In the adjacent text (pp. 209–10) he recalls: 'In our rambles about Patterdale, from a rising ground behind the village, we caught a beautiful view of the lake (as represented in the annexed plate) with the interesting fore-ground of a quiet and romantic groupe [*sic*] of cottages scattered round the church, and the fine woods of Gowbarrow, contrasted with the gigantic and naked precipices of Place-fell on the opposite side of the water, in the distance.' Throughout Mawman's brief visit to the Cumbrian Lakes, he inevitably made constant comparisons with those of the Highlands: 'There the seeping

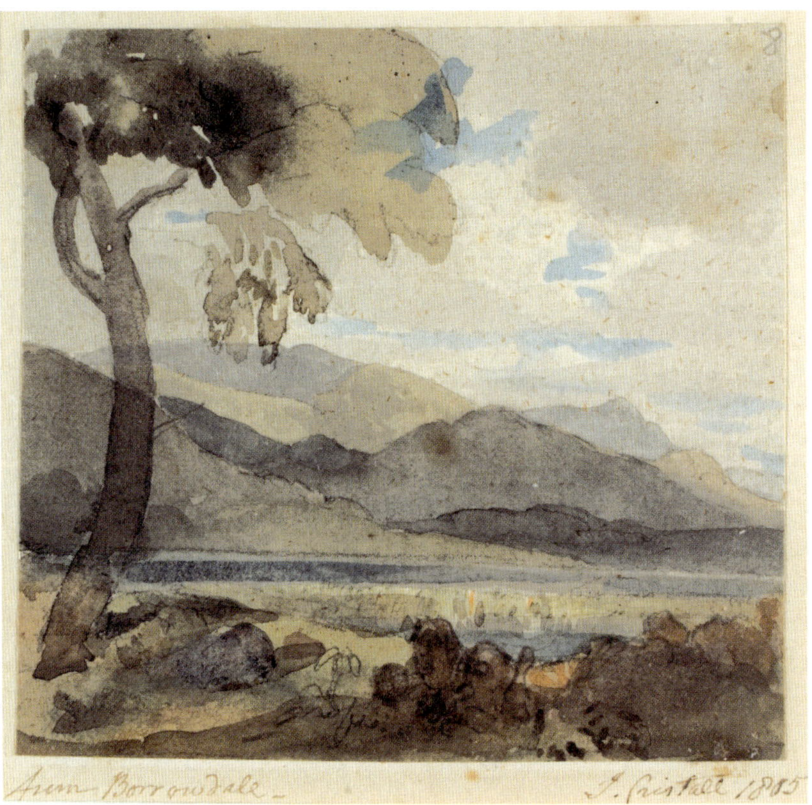

Cat. 52

nakedness, unbroken by vegetation or brushwood, gives an awful idea of wildness and desolation; here [Ullswater] the eye is refreshed by the intervention of trees, villages and scattered habitations; the general scenery is less sublime, and the picture is beautified and enriched by occasional luxuriancy' (pp. 205–6). Turner's scene is filled with just such refreshment for the eye, with habitations scattered among its trees and sailing boats drawn up on the lakeshore. The foreground subject – a lightly clad reclining herdsman gazing at a girl coming to a stream with her pitcher – seems at first sight more fitted to the lakes of northern Italy than those of Westmorland but this, too, echoes Mawman's sentiments when he reached Buttermere: 'We were much struck with the appearance of the females about these lakes. … All walked gracefully, all had an air of superiority which sat easy upon them; and an impressive beauty, with few exceptions, characterizes the whole race' (pp. 227–8). It was wholly characteristic of Turner that he illustrated diverse features from his reading as well as uniting and blending ingredients from several different sketches. CFP

52

JOSHUA CRISTALL (1768–1847)
From Borrowdale
1805
Watercolour, 10.7 × 10.7 cm
Inscribed 'from Borrowdale' and 'J. Cristall 1805'
Gift of Robert Ponsonby, 2005

53

JOSHUA CRISTALL (1768–1847)
Borrowdale
1805
Watercolour, 11.2 × 17.2 cm
Gift of Charles Warren, 1982

In July 1805 Cristall paid his only visit to the Lake District, encouraged by the recent success of his works at the first exhibition of the recently formed Society of Painters in Water Colours and spurred on by the popularity of the Lakes subjects of another member of the group, John Glover. His tour is documented in a number of sketches, some in pencil, some (like cat. 52–3) in colours. Although

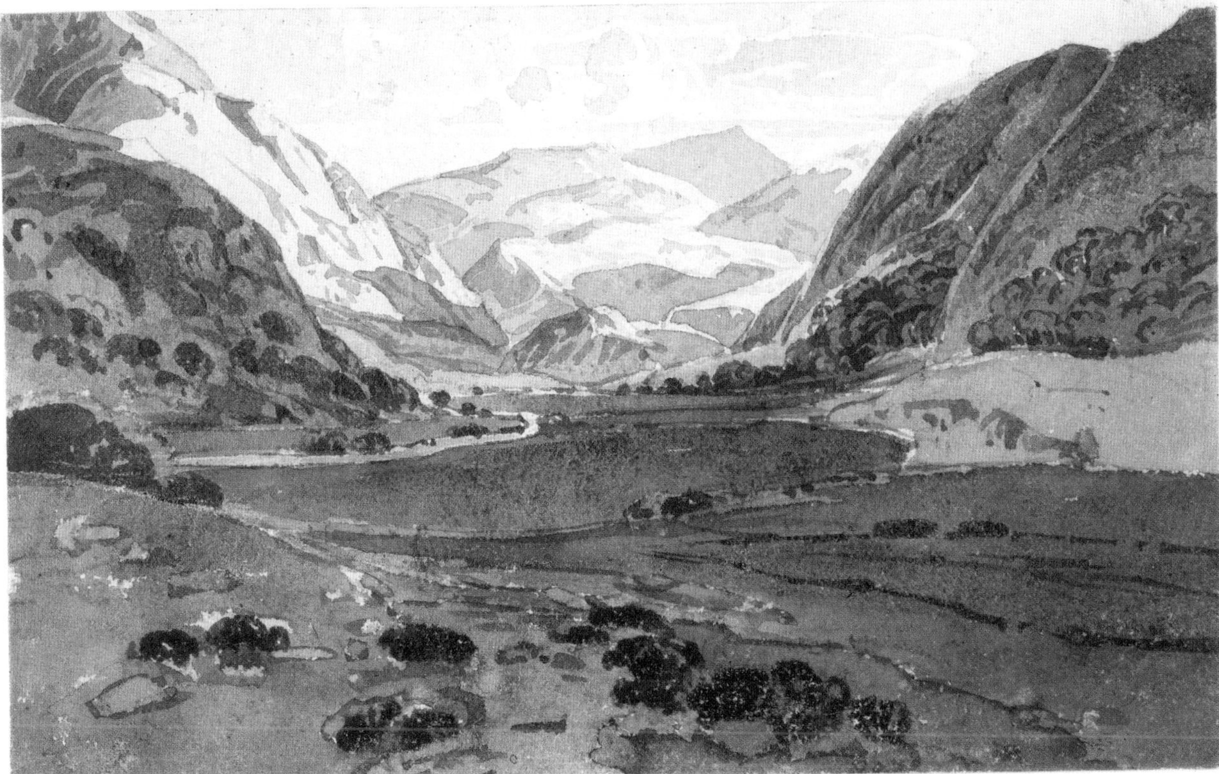

Cat. 53

Cristall was principally a painter of figure-subjects, his tour resulting in many exhibits with titles like *A Well near Ambleside* (SPWC 1806, no. 83) and *Girl at a Well – Scene in Cumberland* (SPWC 1821, no. 60), the wildness of Borrowdale and its fells evidently held a strong fascination for him. He worked up his on-the-spot sketches into several finished watercolours exhibited at the SPWC: *View near Buttermere, Cumberland* (1811, no. 29), *View near Rosstwaite, Cumberland* (1813, no. 134) and *Rossthwaite, Cumberland* and *Wastdale Head, Cumberland* (1814, nos 120, 188). The influence of Lake District scenery may also be felt in the backgrounds of some of his subject-pictures.

Both these two sketches show a keen eye for effective composition. The title of *From Borrowdale*, inscribed by the artist himself, is a very loose one, perhaps suggesting that Cristall saw the view just before or just after a visit to Borrowdale. It has recently been identified by David Hill as showing part of the view across Derwentwater from the lakeside area now occupied by Mary Mount, just north of the Lodore falls. On the left Cristall includes the north end of Catbells while Swinside is in the centre, the high ground between, and beyond, them being Heavy Side, part of Grisedale Pike. To the right of Swinside he shows the eastern escarpment of Lorton Fells but, rather surprisingly, he does not include Skiddaw, which would probably have been visible further to his right; he evidently did not want to embrace a more panoramic view. The sketch may well have been coloured out of doors, an activity that was becoming popular in the early nineteenth century; several of Cristall's exhibits in 1806 were described in the catalogue simply as 'studies from nature' and may have been comparable to this but more fully developed. He appears not to have known – or did not wish to record – the names of the peaks that confronted him; it was enough to record their visual appearance. The number '8' at top right suggests that this sketch was part of a numbered sequence.

Cat. 53, once known simply as 'A mountain landscape' but identified by the late Charles Warren as *Borrowdale*, also shows a view with a mountain backdrop but in a different way. Its composition, leading

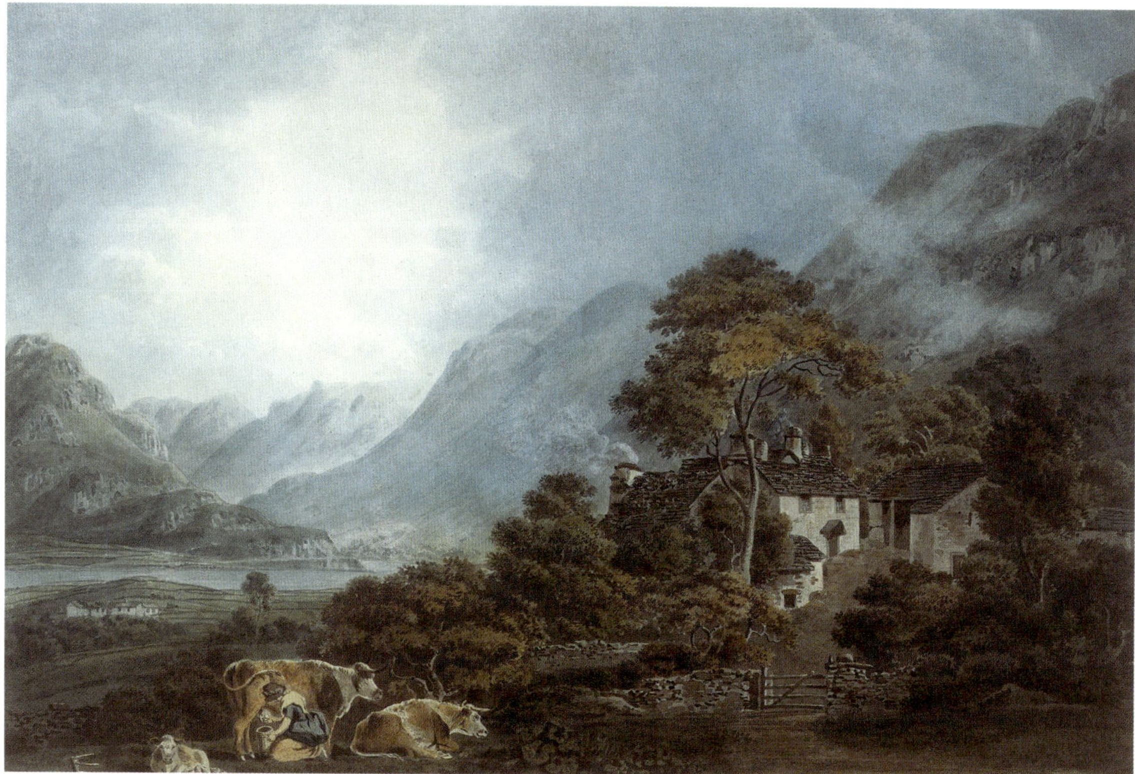

Cat. 54

the eye along serpentine curves towards peaks that seem literally piled upon each other, wonderfully captures the excitement of exploring a valley so untamed and untravelled that it seems almost to belong to another planet. Its subject was identified a few years ago as a view looking towards Glaramara (see Hebron, Shields and Wilcox, 2006, p. 52) but this idea has been challenged by several scholars; the Trust awaits further opinions as to its true subject. The application of paint shows elements that Cristall learned from his contacts with John Varley: an emphasis on the rough grandeur and massiveness of the fells and the way their appearance is transformed by the fall of light on their surfaces. CFP

54

ROBERT SEATON (1785/6–1808)
Crummock Water
1805
Watercolour, 31 × 45 cm
Inscribed on verso with artist's name and the date 1805
Purchased with the generous help of the funds administered by the Victoria & Albert Museum for the Museums and Galleries Commission, 1992

Seaton appears to have been a promising artist. Like many late eighteenth-century painters he combined an interest in landscape with a focus on buildings and domestic incidents; parallels may also be drawn with work closer to his own time such as that of Ibbetson (cat. 69). As a Cumberland man, Seaton had ample opportunity to study the beauties of his own area and showed considerable talent for evoking them but he became ill and died before realising his potential.

Seaton's view of Crummock Water is taken from the north, looking towards the grotesque forms of Rannerdale Knotts above Hause Point on the left. As West's *Guide* says of the old road here (Buttermere Hause), the lake 'serpentizes round the rock, and under a rugged pyramidal craggy mountain.' The right-hand side shows Mellbreak followed by High Stile and thereafter the peaks beyond Buttermere including Great Gable. In the foreground Seaton depicts one of the farms on the lower land beneath Raven Crag; the solidly constructed buildings of this farm, well sheltered by trees, together with the nicely placed group of cattle and attendant milkmaid provide a strong contrast to their 'murky neighbours', the uninhabitable and inhospitable fells. CFP

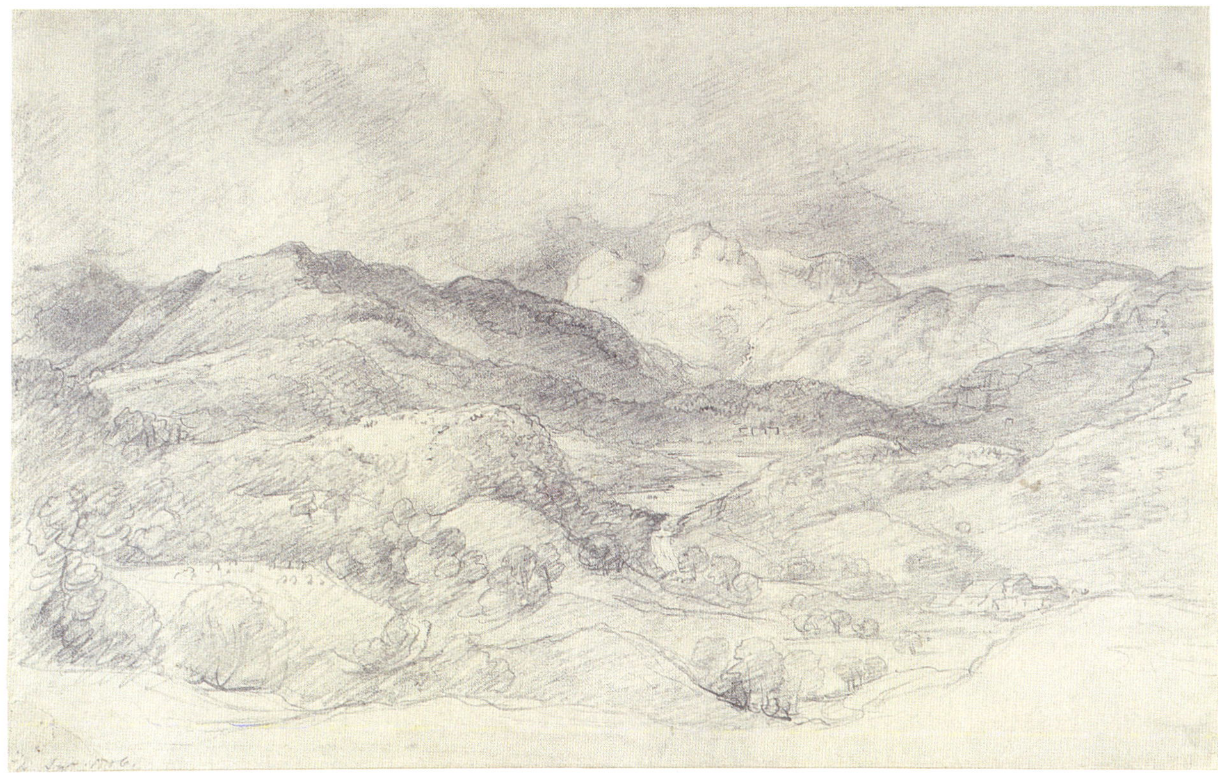

Cat. 55

55

JOHN CONSTABLE RA (1776–1837)
The Langdale Pikes
1806
Pencil, 23.9 × 38 cm
Inscribed '4 Sepr. 1806'
Purchased, 1985

This is one of the earliest of the hundred or so sketches that Constable made on his only visit to the Lake District, a visit that has received detailed attention in an earlier publication of the Wordsworth Trust (Hebron, Shields and Wilcox, 2006). Constable had arrived in Kendal by 1 September when he sketched its castle; the following day, while lodging with George Gardner (a Kendal lawyer and the son of his friend the pastellist Daniel Gardner), he drew Whitbarrow Scar and Scout Scar (R06.186-9 in Graham Reynolds' 1996 catalogue of Constable's work). Constable and Gardner are known to have lodged at a cottage in the grounds of Storrs Hall on Windermere for a few days before the former arrived at Brathay Hall on 8 September to stay with the Hardens; this sketch – and one showing Skelwith Bridge, probably dated 7 September (R06.191) – were apparently made on excursions from Storrs.

Constable's viewpoint was some two hundred feet above the river Brathay near Skelwith Fold, looking north-west towards Elterwater which lies almost at the centre of the composition. His view embraces a diversity of terrains, from the pale rugged peaks of the Langdale Pikes through dark wooded slopes down to flat cultivated land including a field of haystacks at lower left. All are rendered with his characteristic pursuit of breadth and naturalness, his technique consisting of a mixture of rounded, almost scribbled, outlines and carefully modulated diagonal hatching that vividly suggests distance in the landscape as well as shapes and textures. Amid such contrasts Elterwater itself appears no more than a tranquil pool while the turbulent waters of Skelwith Force hurtle forward energetically towards the viewer; its white mass would have been a conspicuous feature in the scene. Signs of habitation are provided by three tiny rectangles beyond the water's edge, indicating Elterwater Hall, and some farm buildings at lower right.

The Langdale Pikes feature prominently in several other pencil sketches. Notable among these is one drawn from a very similar viewpoint on

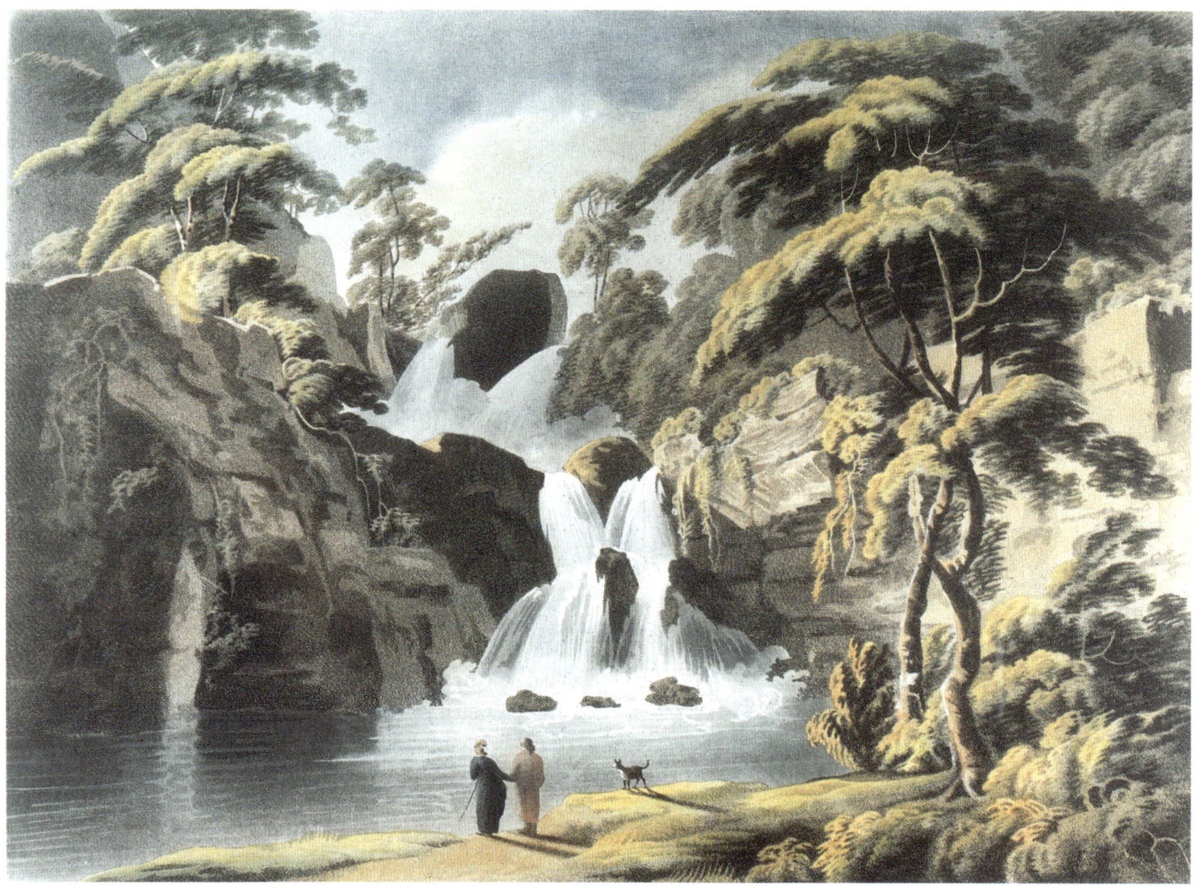

Cat. 56

13 September, a day when Jessy Harden recorded that 'the gentlemen went out sketching' (presumably Harden himself, Constable and the Irish artist Richard Shannon who was also at Brathay) and the ladies then followed them to Skelwith (R06.193). An undated drawing (R06.279) shows the Pikes from Low Wood, already a celebrated Windermere viewpoint, which also includes Brathay itself in the middle distance. A more perfunctory, and more elongated, sketch (R06.274) is on the verso of the coloured drawing that was the basis for cat. 72, proving that the sheet of paper (fig. 38 on p. 129) was in use during the tour itself.

When Constable visited the Lakes he was – at the age of thirty – still struggling to make a name for himself. He was largely engaged in painting portraits, despite his yearning to be a landscape painter, and he was still dependent on his family. His seven-week tour was suggested and financed by his mother's brother David Pike Watts, a recent occupant of Storrs Hall, and it was not until after the death of both Constable's parents, in 1815 and 1816, and the sale of the family home in East Bergholt in 1818 that he at last achieved independence. Constable never felt at ease amid 'the solitude of mountains', to use the phrase of his first biographer C.R. Leslie; although he drew some remarkable watercolour studies including the Trust's *Helvellyn* (Hebron, Shields and Wilcox, 2006, no. 44, somewhat disfigured by the inscription on its verso), few finished paintings resulted from his tour. CFP

56

F. JUKES after THOMAS WALMSLEY (1763–1805/6)
Upper-fall at Ridal, Westmorland
*c.*1801–8
Aquatint, 33 × 41.5 cm
Engraved inscriptions: below, with title and names of artist (*From the Original Drawing by T. Walmsley*) and engraver

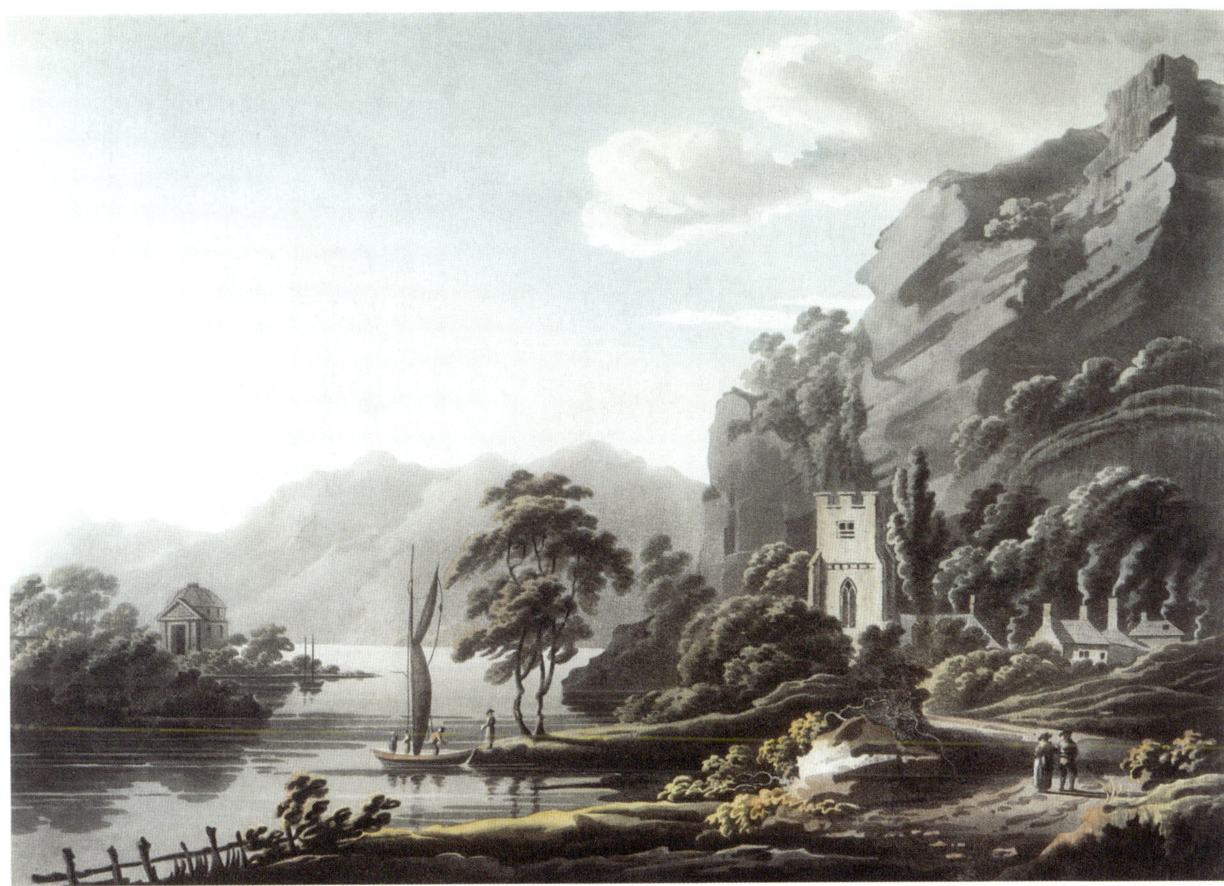

Cat. 57

57

F. JUKES and G.F. SARJENT
after THOMAS WALMSLEY (1763–1805/6)
Bowness on Windermere
1808
Aquatint, 36.3 × 46 cm
Engraved inscriptions: below, with names of artist (*From a Painting in Water Colours by Walmsley*) and engravers; centre, dedication, '*To the most Noble Charles Duke of Norfolk / This View of* BOWNESS ON WINDERMERE, *is with the / utmost deference and respect, inscribed by his Graces very obedient Servants*' followed by '*Sarjent*'; bottom, 'London, Published April 10, 1808, by Jukes / & Sarjent, N.° 10, Howland Street.'
Peter Bicknell Bequest, 1997

Thomas Walmsley delighted in waterfalls and cascades, painting many in England, Wales and his native Ireland. However, anyone looking at cat. 56, a depiction of the upper cascade in the grounds of Rydal Hall, might well wonder if he had ever visited the Lake District. It bears very little truth to Cumbrian reality, resembling, instead, a scene in a distant land, or perhaps on a tropical island, with exotic trees of unimaginable height and the vast buildings of a vanished empire engulfed in a deluge of biblical magnitude. The figures in the foreground – and their accompanying dog – are posed in a highly theatrical way, with excessively long shadows that are unrelated to the lighting elsewhere in the scene. In fact, Walmsley did visit the Lakes, probably in 1790, and his depictions of it were deemed sufficiently good by the great arbiters of taste, the selection committee of the Royal Academy, to be accepted for its prestigious exhibitions in 1792 and 1793; the high quality of such works can be seen in cat. 34. It seems possible that he was prevented by illness from supervising the work of the engraver when Jukes and Sarjent produced cat. 56–7.

Fantasy also pervades the engraved depiction of Bowness and Belle Isle on Windermere (cat. 57). Almost every ingredient in the scene is wrongly placed or exaggerated and the result is more suitable

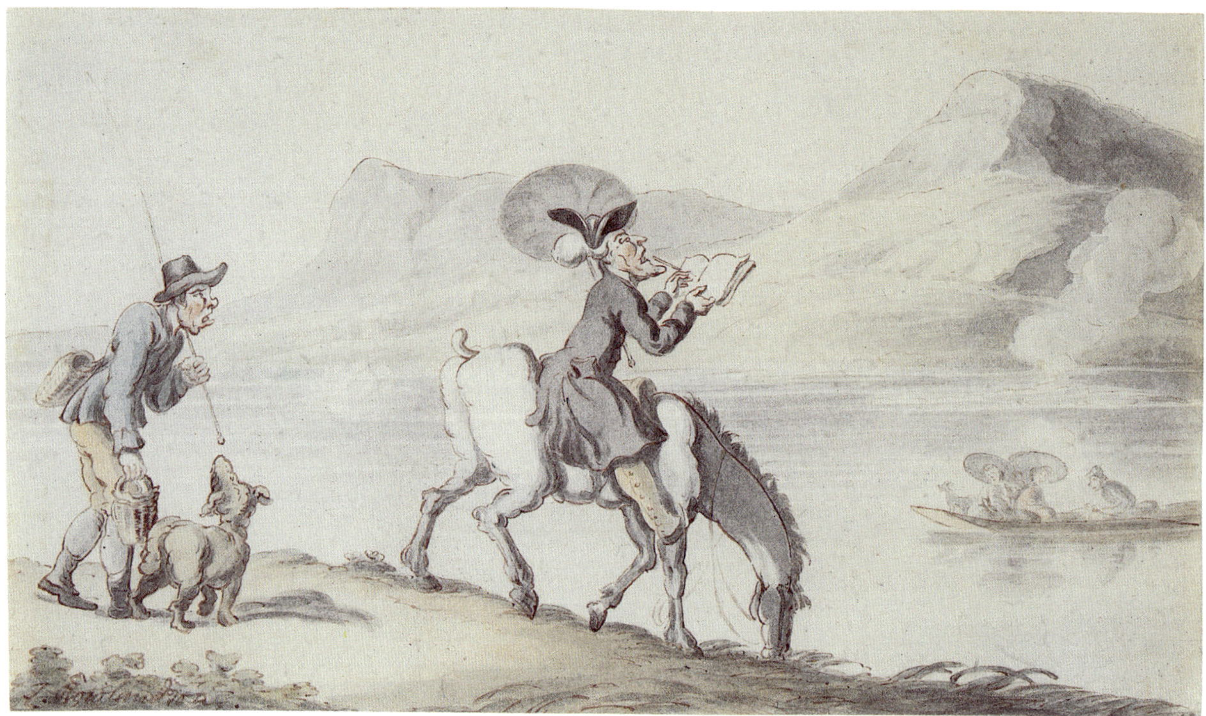

Cat. 58

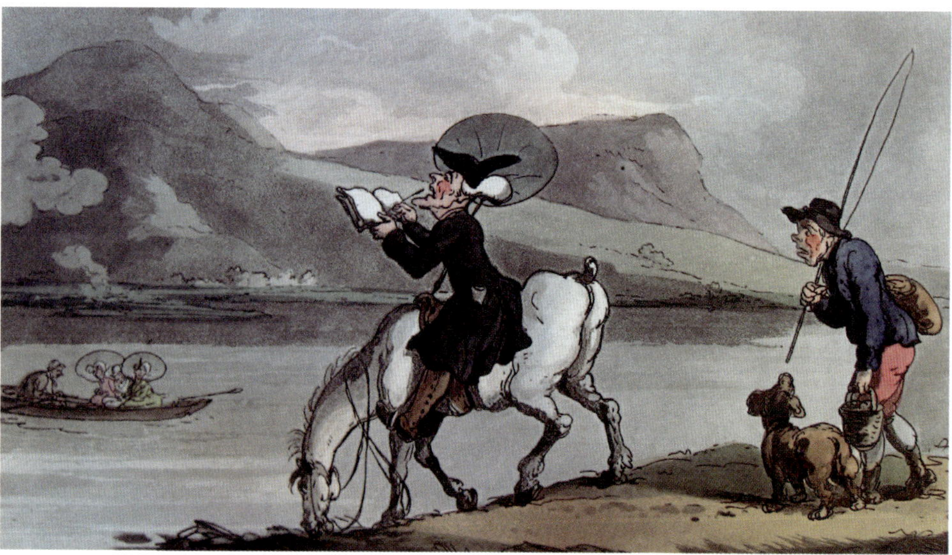

Fig. 29 Thomas Rowlandson, *Doctor Syntax sketching the Lake*, aquatint, 1812 (see cat. 59).

for a theatrical backdrop than for a record of the Lake District. However, there was clearly a market for such scenes in the early nineteenth century. Four views of the lakes by Walmsley, engraved by Jukes, were advertised (along with ones by other artists) in the eighth edition of West's *Guide* (1802) and were available from its printer, William Pennington in Kendal, and from other booksellers. Not all visitors to the Lakes could afford to take home high-quality prints by the likes of Farington or John 'Warwick' Smith and Walmsley's scenes must have given pleasure in many a modest home. CFP

58

THOMAS ROWLANDSON (1757–1827)
Doctor Syntax sketching the Lake
*c.*1810
Watercolour, 11 × 19 cm
Purchased with the assistance of the MGC/V&A Purchase Grant Fund and the National Art Collections Fund, 1992

59

WILLIAM COMBE (1742–1823) and
THOMAS ROWLANDSON (1757–1827)
The Tour of Doctor Syntax in Search of the Picturesque, a poem
London: 1812
Gift of Pamela Middleton Murray, in memory of Raymond Disley (1913–1982), 1982

The Tour of Doctor Syntax was first published in instalments in the *Poetical Magazine* from 1809 to 1811. Every month Rowlandson drew an illustration, which was passed to Combe by the publisher, Ackermann. Combe's brief was to write lines that incorporated Rowlandson's scenes, while building up, month by month, an overall narrative. The work proceeded fruitfully in this manner for two years; throughout this time, artist and poet never met.

The poem narrates the adventures of Dr Syntax, an impoverished schoolmaster, and his horse Grizzle, on their journey to the Lakes. Syntax's motives are financial: he tells his wife in the opening canto:

> —*I'll make a* TOUR,—*and then I'll* WRITE *it.*
> You well know what my pen can do,
> I'll prove it with my pencil too:—
> I'll ride and *write*, and *sketch* and *print*,
> And thus create a real mint;
> I'll *prose* it here, I'll *verse* it there,
> And *picturesque* it ever'y where.

Dr Syntax eventually reaches Keswick, where he prepares to work on the drawings that he hopes will earn him his fortune. Cat. 58 is Rowlandson's original watercolour for his illustration of Syntax sketching the lake. Seated on Grizzle he attempts to draw the scene, watched by a bewildered fisherman, and, from a boat, a group of fashionable tourists. Out of it Combe created the following episode:

> Along its banks he gravely pac'd,
> And all its various beauties trac'd;
> When, lo, a threat'ning storm appear'd:
> Phoebus the scene no longer cheer'd:

Syntax valiantly continues to sketch through the storm, until the fisherman advises him that ''tis all in vain / To take your prospects in the rain'. Syntax agrees, but before he can return to the inn Grizzle trips, and throws him into the lake. The day ends with Syntax back at the inn, working up his sketches.

Otherwise, the Lake District hardly features in the *Tour*; indeed, neither Rowlandson nor Combe ever visited the area. The *Tour* is really a light-hearted satire on picturesque touring in general, and William Gilpin in particular (the father of the picturesque had died in 1804). The popularity of Rowlandson's aquatints and Combe's verses did much to improve the fortunes of the *Poetical Magazine*. Their curious manner of working eventually produced thirty aquatints and ten thousand lines of verse. Inevitably, the narrative rambles, and Combe admitted that it barely deserved to be called a poem. Cat. 59 is the first complete edition of the *Tour*, for which Combe made a number of improvements, ironing out repetitions and inconsistencies. SH

60

WILLIAM HAVELL (1782–1857)
The Beck at Ambleside after Much Rain
1808
Watercolour, 32.3 × 26 cm
Originally inscribed 'The Beck at Ambleside after much / Rain, sketched from a Window / in year 1808 by W[m] Havell'
Purchased with the generous help of the funds administered by the Victoria & Albert Museum for the Museums and Galleries Commission, 1990

Already an accomplished and successful painter, Havell was stimulated to visit the Lake District by the attention aroused by the watercolours of an

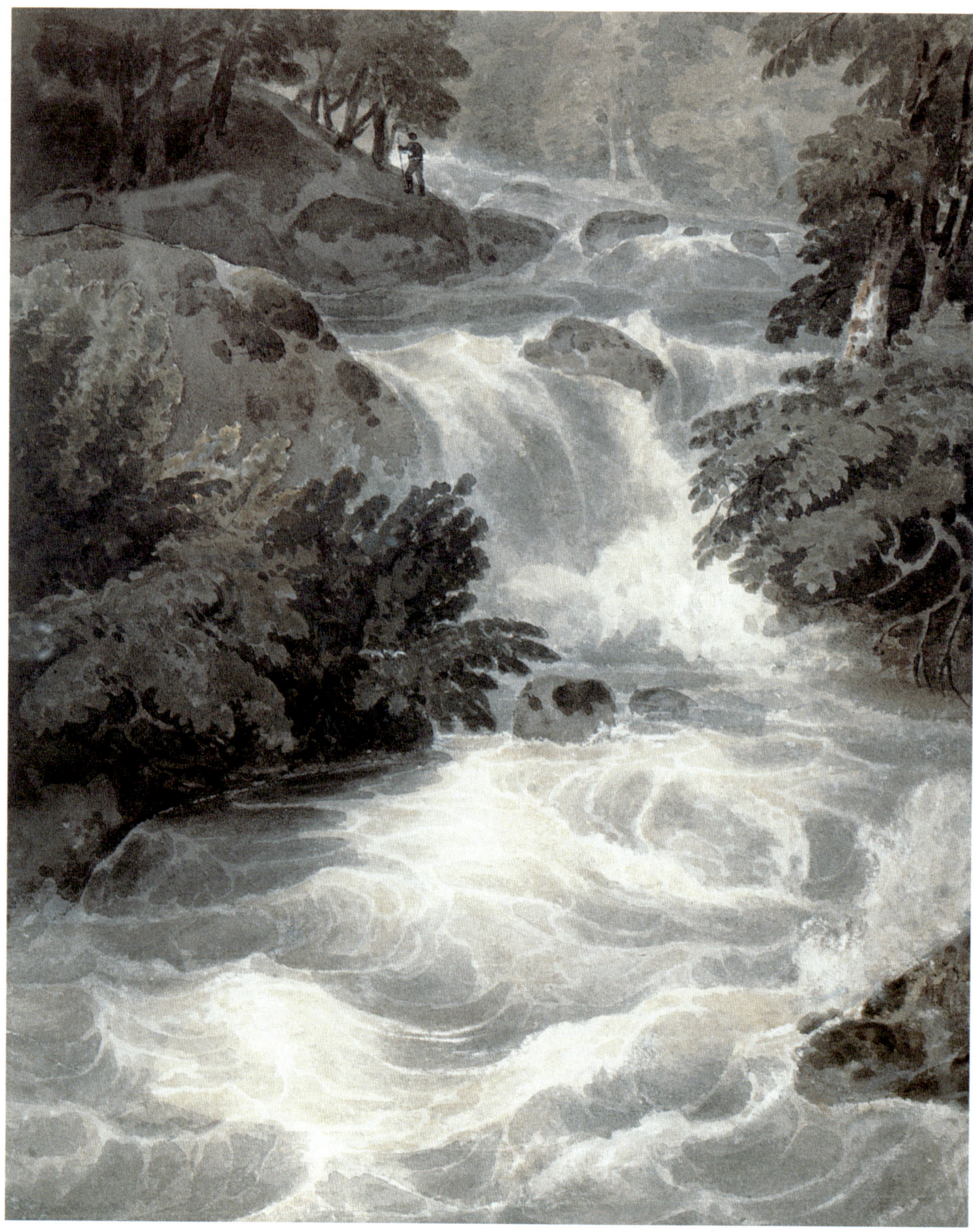

Cat. 60

older colleague: John Glover (see cat. 68) had shown nine views of the Lakes at the second exhibition of the newly formed Society of Painters in Water Colours in 1806 and twelve the following spring. In August 1807 Havell set off for the area – not for a brief summer tour but for a lengthy stay that would enable him to become thoroughly acquainted with the landscape and its life. He rented a house in Ambleside for six months, presented a letter of introduction (from the Scottish artist H.W. Williams) to the Hardens at Brathay, and settled into a regular routine. He sketched out of doors, using not only pencil and watercolour but also oil paints on prepared paper, as did his companion at the start of his visit, Ramsay Richard Reinagle (cat. 65). Many of Havell's contemporaries (including Turner) were experimenting with this type of work during this decade and he himself had already done so in the Thames valley in 1805.

This depiction of Stockgill Force in Ambleside, however, was drawn in the more traditional media of pencil followed by watercolour and, as the inscription tells us, the artist was not out of doors but at a window; this was obviously in one of the old houses at the foot of Peggy Hill that still provide good views of the cascade today. His viewpoint enabled him to gaze straight at the water from a much closer and more comfortable station than is usually possible in the Lakes. He thus had the opportunity to trace the stages of its journey from the point where the beck comes into view tumbling over rocks between the trees: the water divides into white streams pouring between dark boulders; it then tumbles and splashes, swirls, froths and eddies, its whiteness enhanced by the grey boulders and green foliage on either side. One of Havell's contemporaries remarked on the 'depth and harmony of effect' in his Lake District work which made it 'nearer to reality than the compositions of any of his compeers' (quoted in Roget, 1891, I.295. The truth of this comment is well illustrated in cat. 60, which is either Havell's SPWC exhibit of 1809, *The Beck at Ambleside, after Much Rain* (no. 334) or a preparatory study for that work.

The previous year Havell had exhibited *The Beck, near Ambleside* (SPWC 1808, no. 253), a much larger and more sophisticated work in a squarer format, which had been bought from the exhibition by Sir Thomas Gage for 15 guineas and is now in The Hepworth, Wakefield. In that work the beck is integrated into a classically organised landscape composition dominated by rocks and trees and enlivened by foreground figures bathing in a pool; its Ambleside origins are scarcely recognisable. In the Wordsworth Trust work Havell focuses single-mindedly on Stockgill Force itself, making no attempt to confine it within a conventional framework. CFP

61

PAUL SANDBY MUNN (1773–1845)
At Troutbeck, Westmorland
1809
Watercolour, 29.6 × 25.7
Inscribed 'P.S. Munn / 1809'
Gift of the W.W. Spooner Charitable Trust, 2006

The subject of this watercolour is Townend Farm, Troutbeck, which straddles the lesser of the two roads from the Kirkstone Pass down to Bowness on Windermere. It is well known to visitors to the area today, having belonged to the National Trust since the 1940s, but it has long been a standard subject for artists, partly for its own sake and partly because it lies close to good viewpoints over the head of Windermere towards the Langdale Pikes. In 1805 Jessy Harden described Troutbeck as 'famous for its picturesque cottages', the village often featured in works shown at the Society of Painters in Water Colours and Munn would have known the watercolour of almost exactly the same view by Ramsay Richard Reinagle, painted around 1807–8 (fig. 30). The present scene is likely to be one of the two works entitled *At Troutbeck, Westmorland* shown by Munn at the SPWC in 1811 (nos 77 and 308).

On the left, sheltered by the trees, is the farmhouse, parts of which date back to the late sixteenth century; facing this across the lane stands its seventeenth-century barn with a gallery. Between them Munn shows an encounter, perhaps between members of the Browne family who owned the farm for over three centuries: a woman weighed down with pails, a girl with a swill made of plaited oak under her arm, and a youth taking care of a small boy, still too young to help on the farm. The subject is a humble and charming one, very different from the grand views of mountains and lakes that had been the preoccupation of artists in the Lake District a decade earlier.

Although Townend today presents a whitewashed face to the world, the evidence of artists shows that in the early nineteenth century its stone walls

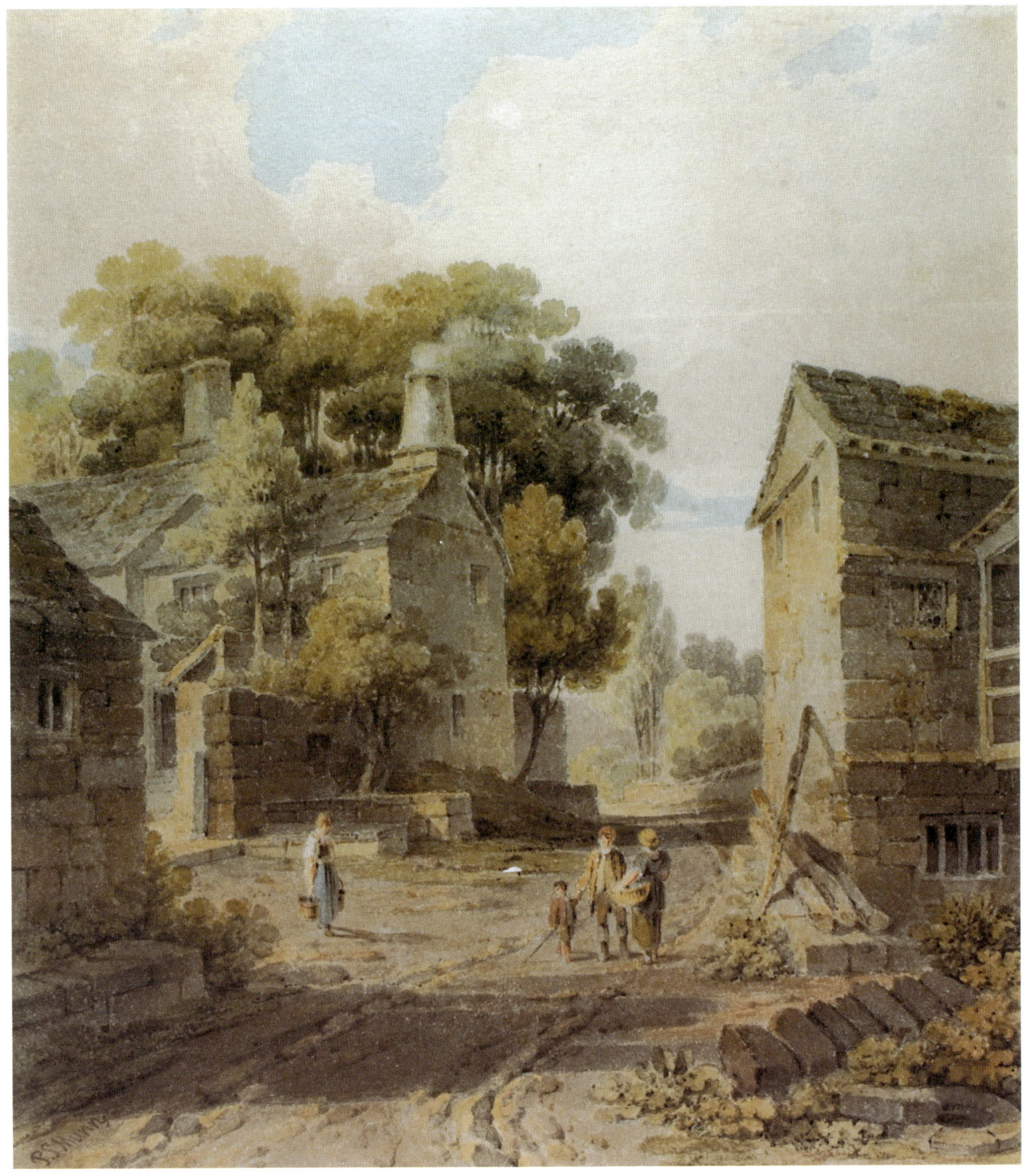

Cat. 61

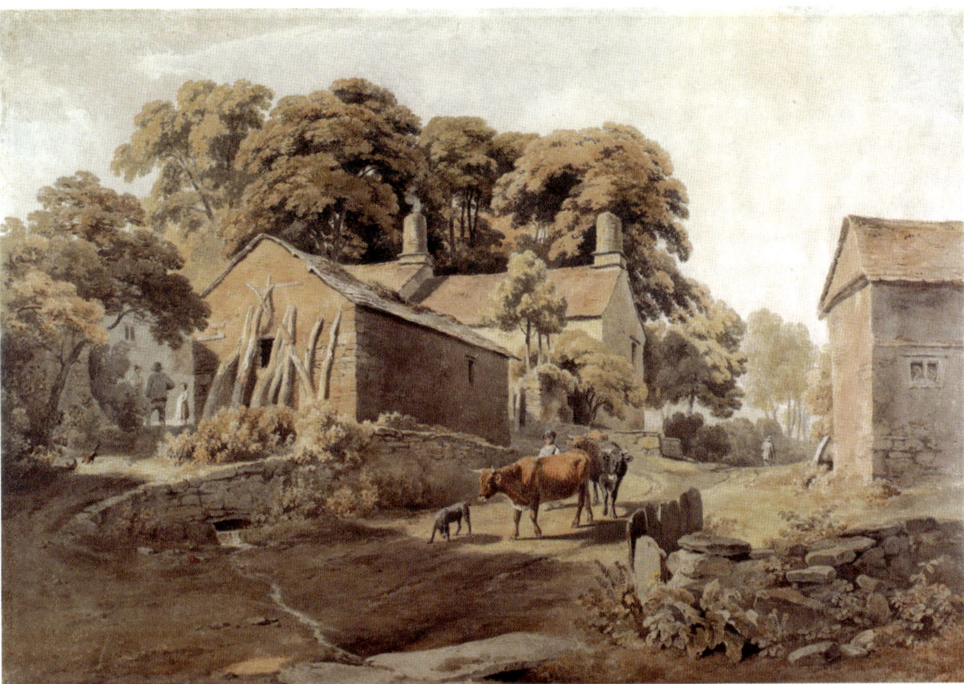

Fig. 30 Ramsay Richard Reinagle, *Farmstead near Ambleside*, watercolour, *c.*1807–8 (Birmingham Museum and Art Gallery).

remained in their natural state and colouring. It was at that time an almost perfect example of the precept attributed by Wordsworth to Sir Joshua Reynolds and perhaps known to the poet from conversations with Sir George Beaumont: 'if you would fix upon a colour for your house, turn up a stone … and see what is the colour of the soil where the house is to stand, and let that be your choice' (*Select Views*, 1810, p. xxv). Wordsworth's comments on chimneys are also pertinent: 'Nor will the singular beauty of the chimneys escape the eye of the attentive traveller. … Of a quadrangular shape, rising one or two feet above the roof; which low square is often surmounted by a tall cylinder, giving to the cottage chimney the most beautiful shape in which it is ever seen' (pp. xviii–xix).

Munn's penchant for cottages and farmhouses was evident from his first Lake District exhibits at the RA in 1799 when he showed three such works (*Cottage in Westmorland*; *Cottage at Kirkerdale, between Keswick and Buttermore*; *Cottage, the Grange Barrowdale, Cumberland*; nos 420, 977, 984) alongside three more broadly based topographical views (nos 595, 603, 884). In 1808 over fifty of his studies of rural architecture were etched for publication by his pupil Francis Stevens. CFP

62

JOSEPH WILKINSON (1763–1831)
Langdale Chapel, Vale of Langdale
*c.*1809
Pencil and watercolour, 23.7 × 38.1 cm
Purchased, 1994

Langdale Chapel was situated between Elterwater and Great Langdale, beneath Thrang Crag and close to the passage into the Thrang slate quarries, and was described by Wordsworth in his letterpress to Wilkinson's *Select Views* as a 'sequestered and simple place of worship'. It was replaced by the present church building that serves the village of Chapel Stile in the second half of the nineteenth century but its churchyard remains, including the memorial to Owen Lloyd, the son of Wordsworth's friend Charles Lloyd who was born at Old Brathay in 1803 and was vicar here from 1829 to 1841; Wordsworth composed his epitaph later that year.

As can be seen from this watercolour, Wilkinson's enthusiasm for drawing was not matched by any remarkable skill. For the plate of Langdale Chapel in his *Select Views*, he supplied William Frederick Wells with a strongly drawn pencil sketch that differs in a number of details from the watercolour but

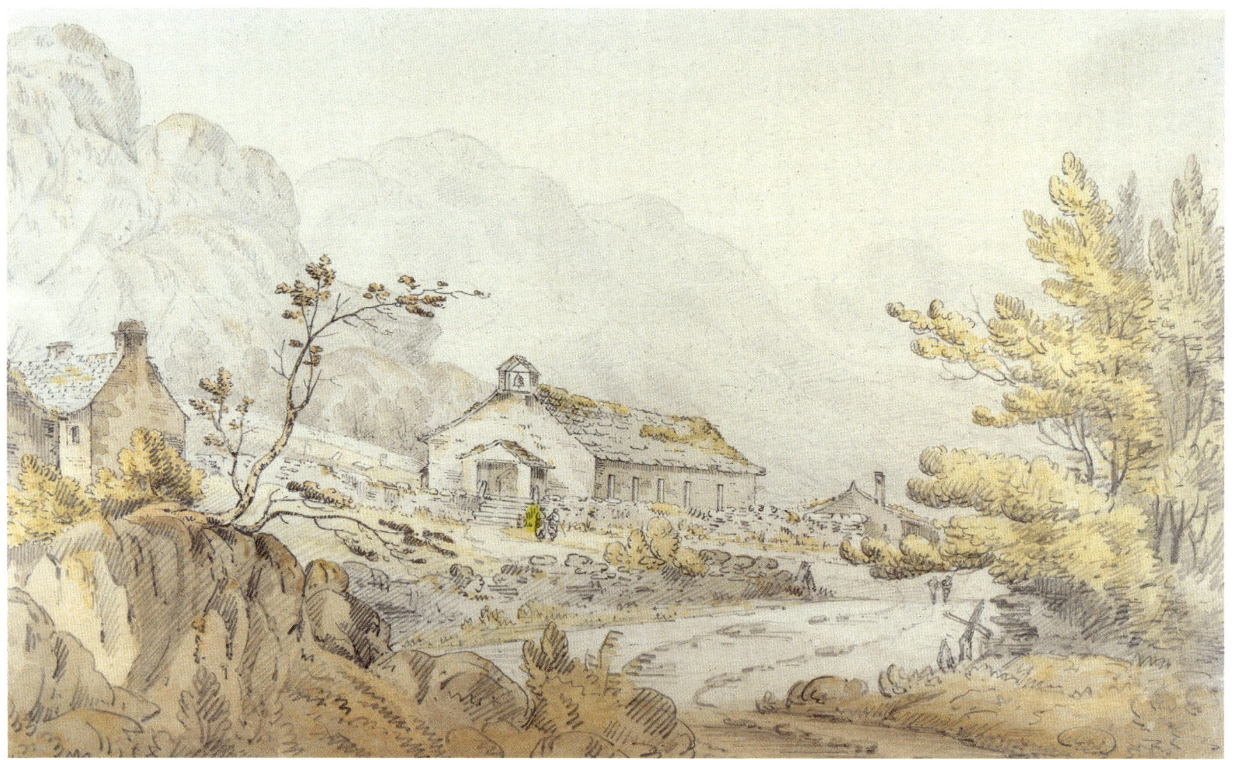

Cat. 62

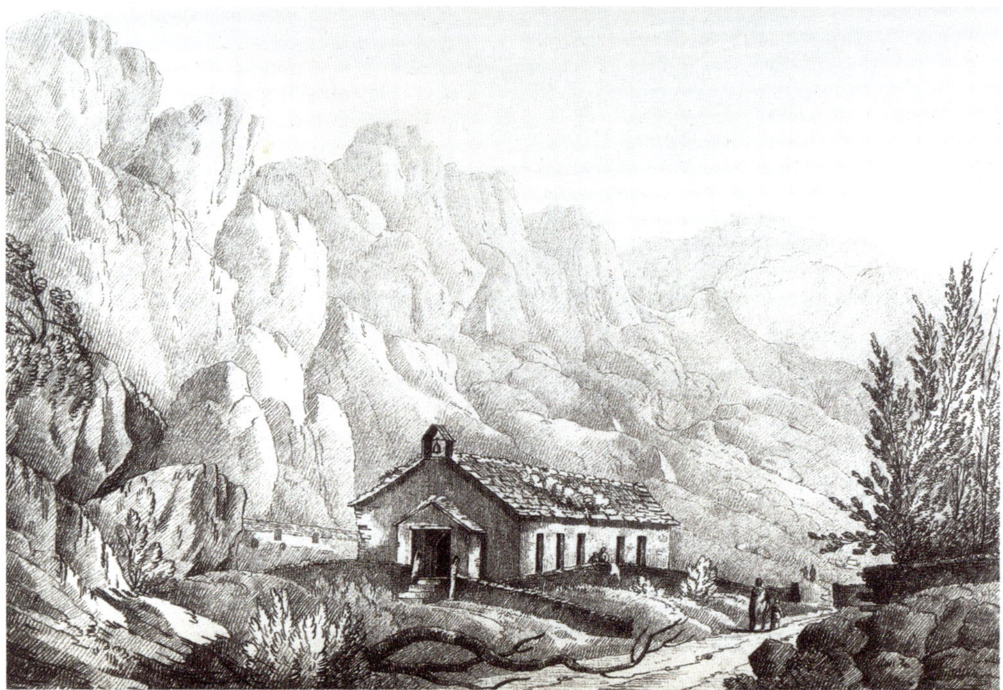

Fig. 31 W.F. Wells after Joseph Wilkinson, *Langdale Chapel, Vale of Langdale*, soft-ground etching, 1810 (The Wordsworth Trust).

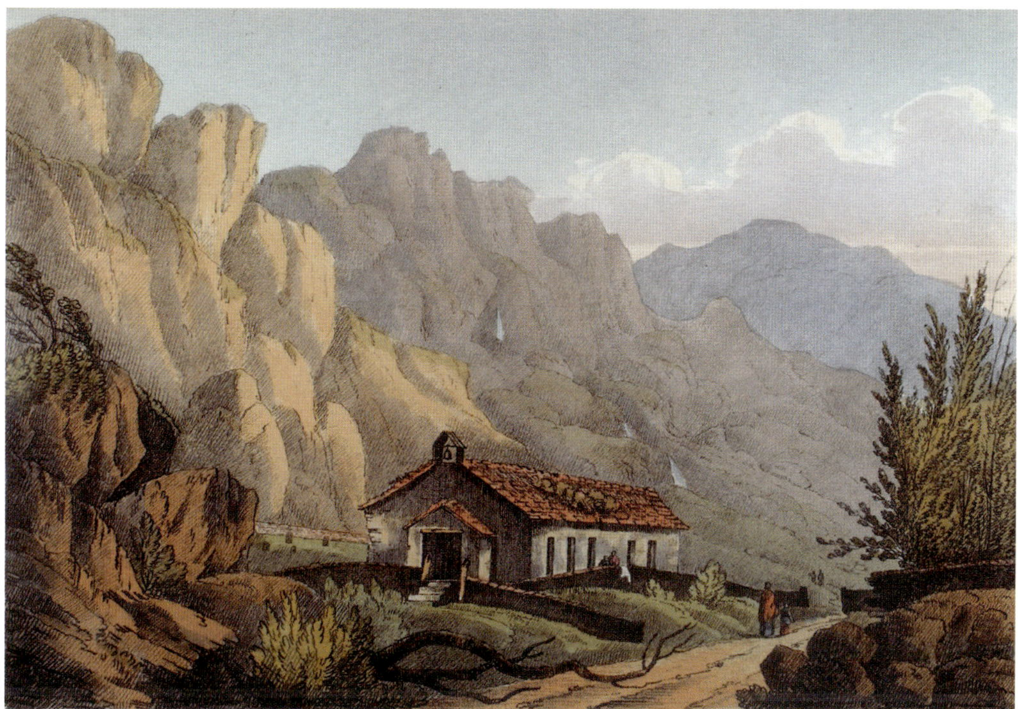

Fig. 32 W.F. Wells after Joseph Wilkinson, *Langdale Chapel, Vale of Langdale*, hand-coloured soft-ground etching, 1810, as issued in 1820 (The Wordsworth Trust).

resembles it in capturing the simplicity and isolation of the tiny chapel, crouching beneath its backdrop of crags. These qualities are also adequately, if conventionally, conveyed in the monochrome soft-ground etching by Wells, an established and respected professional artist and etcher as well as a drawing-master who had been the prime mover behind the foundation of the SPWC in 1804. Wells' forty-eight etchings were published in twelve monthly parts between January and December 1810 by the London publisher Rudolph Ackermann, being also reissued in 1821, and were available in both plain and coloured versions (figs 31–2). It was when colouring was introduced into the depiction of *Langdale Chapel* that things went seriously wrong. Ackermann's assistants had no idea about the natural colours or building materials of the Lake District and transformed the chapel from an edifice of stone and slate into a whitewashed, red-tiled chapel more suited to the Alps or the Apennines than to Westmorland. It was against just such disfigurements of the landscape that Wordsworth protested in his successive remarks on the scenery of the Lakes and his disparaging phrases about Wilkinson's volume are well documented and well known (see p. 139). CFP

63

WILLIAM PAYNE (1760–1830)
Bowder Stone South
1810
Pencil, 20.5 × 30.9 cm
Inscribed 'Bowder Stone South', 'Borrowdale Aug 26', 'Henderson's Band', 'Green', 'Castle Crag'
Gift of the W.W. Spooner Charitable Trust, 2008

This sketch belongs to a group of dated and annotated pencil drawings that Payne made during his visit to the Lakes in the summer of 1810. The Wordsworth Trust owns eleven of these, ranging in date from 19 August (inscribed *Winandermere near Lowood Inn*) to 29 August (two drawings inscribed *Derwent Water North* and *Derwent Water South*). They demonstrate the high quality of Payne's draughtsmanship, an aspect of his work that was crucial to his early career as a surveyor with the Board of Ordnance but is all too easily forgotten by those who think of him simply in terms of his later career: as a fashionable drawing-master and the inventor of simple processes for aristocratic amateurs. In their survey of British painters published in 1866 the Redgrave brothers criticised him for 'failing to refill

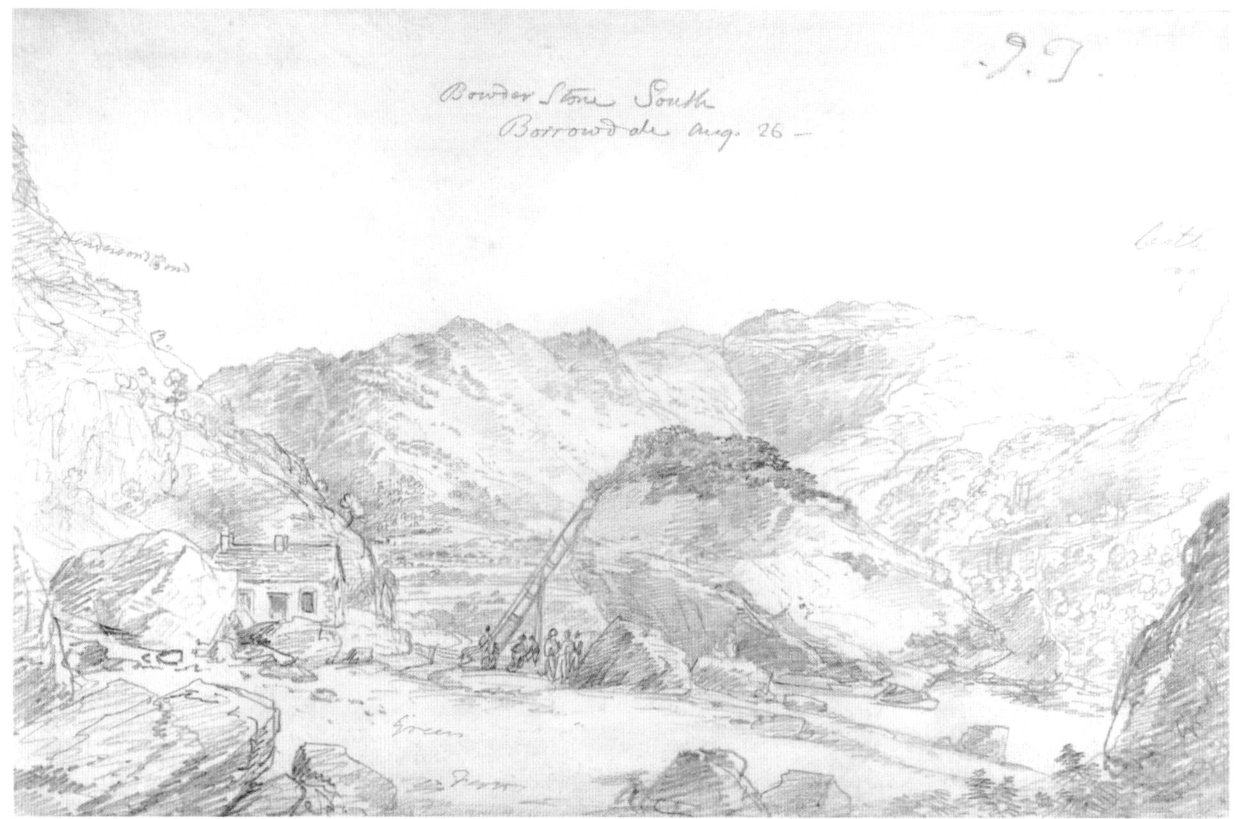

Cat. 63

and refresh his mind by studying from nature' and degenerating into 'the merest mannerist' (p. 153); they were evidently unaware of the carefully executed private sketches that lay behind the exhibited works.

Sometimes regarded as an 'erratic boulder' (i.e. one driven from its original site by ice) but now firmly identified as the largest surviving fragment of a prehistoric rockfall from the adjacent Bowder Crag, the Bowder Stone lies close to the river Derwent south of the village of Grange in Borrowdale (see figs 23–4 on p. 89). Today it is approached by a rough side-track but in earlier times it lay directly on the main route up Borrowdale. In 1798 the surrounding land was bought by Joseph Pocklington who had earlier bought – and sold in 1797 – Vicar's Island in Derwentwater (today known as Derwent Isle) and built Barrow Cascade House just north of Ashness Bridge (see cat. 38). Recognising the interest to visitors of such an extraordinarily vast boulder amidst what West's *Guide* had described as a 'labyrinth of embattled obstacles', Pocklington cleared and levelled the land round the Bowder Stone, lowering the ground-level in its immediate vicinity; he also built a small cottage to house an elderly lady as custodian and erected a ladder on the east side of the rock for enterprising tourists. Both these 'improvements' to the site are clearly recorded in Payne's sketch but his viewpoint obscured Pocklington's other additions to the west: a minute mock chapel or hermitage (no longer extant but recorded in works by William Green) and a 'druid' stone. Pocklington added a final touch of excitement by improving the boulder itself which lies on one edge 'like a ship on its keel' as West's *Guide* had put it: he enlarged a hole at its base so that (for a fee) tourists could 'improve their luck' by lying down beneath the colossal overhang and shaking hands with the custodian through the aperture. He recorded its measurements (62 feet 6 inches long by 36 feet high with a circumference of 89 feet), estimating its weight at over 1,771 tons. Subsequent misreadings and generalisations increased this over the years to 'nearly 2,000 tons' but recent professional re-examination of the stone itself has reduced the calculation to 1,253 tons. It remains one of the most popular tourist attractions in the Lake District – not only for its geological interest and incomparable setting but also as a superb site for the sport of 'bouldering', a source of sublime thrills for younger visitors in the twenty-first century.

Payne's annotations vary from factual data that would aid him if he developed his sketch into a finished work ('Green' to remind himself that the foreground path was composed of grass rather than earth) to the names of the eminences just south of the Bowder Stone: Andersonband Crag (misheard from his guide as 'Henderson's Band') and Castle Crag. A store of such detailed and annotated 'working drawings' was an invaluable resource for the artist and such on-the-spot sketches, when they survive, are equally invaluable today as dated records of particular places. Payne's careful drawings, executed in the very year that saw the first publication of Wilkinson's *Select Views* with its commentary by Wordsworth, are precious documents in the history of the Lake District. CFP

64

THOMAS JAMESON (1789–1827)
Derelict Cottage in Ambleside, with Wansfell in the Distance
*c.*1810
Pencil, 18 × 26.8 cm
Purchased with the generous help of the funds administered by the Victoria & Albert Museum for the Museums and Galleries Commission and the National Art Collections Fund, 1991

Thomas Jameson spent part of his childhood in the south of England (his younger brother Robert being baptised in Hampshire in 1796) but by 1800 his parents had returned to the north. His father Thomas was the son of the rector of Egremont while his mother Mary was the elder daughter of the Rev. Joseph Sympson of Wythburn, a good friend to the Wordsworths during their years at Dove Cottage. After the death of young Thomas's father in 1800 the family remained close to the Sympsons; Mrs Jameson lived in Ambleside (then a very small town of fewer than 550 inhabitants), taking in lodgers and striving to educate her four children without succumbing to poverty.

Thomas's talent for drawing was evident while he was still in his teens. It was spotted by George Arnald ARA whose visits to the Lakes led to several RA exhibits and engravings after his scenes from 1803 onwards, including *Buildings at Ambleside: A study* (RA 1809, no.73) and one may postulate that both Arnald and other visiting artists lodged with Mrs Jameson. Thomas soon came to the notice of John Harden of Brathay who, in 1809, paid for him to go to London in the hope that he might make a living there as a drawing-master. Within a year, however, he had abandoned this idea and embarked on his future career of teaching and following both grandfathers into the church. His surviving oeuvre of pencil drawings and watercolours is extremely varied in both subject and technique, reflecting the experiments of a somewhat isolated young man with limited access to works of art. Harden believed he would benefit from visiting exhibitions and galleries in London and he himself expressed his pleasure at having seen works there by the great Dutch landscape painters of the seventeenth century, Jacob van Ruisdael and his pupil Hobbema; however, he also declared that he thought he ought to study nature rather than works by contemporaries such as Turner and Havell (Farington, *Diary* IX.3456). Among the twenty or so works by Jameson held by the Wordsworth Trust, some (fig. 33) have an almost visionary intensity similar to that later shown by Samuel Palmer in his Shoreham period (the mid 1820s). Others show a sensitivity to the natural world – akin to that of Constable – which he was able to preserve when a small sketch was developed into a larger, more finished work (fig. 34).

It is tempting to link Jameson's drawing *Derelict Cottage in Ambleside* with the poverty that he undoubtedly saw around him on his walks around the area, the poverty just kept at bay by his own family, the poverty that Wordsworth described in many works from the 1790s onwards including 'The Ruined Cottage' (eventually incorporated in *The Excursion*, published in 1814). He must also have known the drawings of his Ambleside neighbour, William Green, who depicted not only well-kept cottages and farmhouses but also cottages, barns and other rural buildings that had fallen into decay. Green often showed such buildings in his soft-ground etchings – a medium perfectly suited to the reproduction of pencil drawings – which were issued in a series of publications from 1808 onwards. Jameson would naturally have been stimulated to imitate the etchings in pencil drawings of his own, reserving watercolour for entirely different subjects such as his extensive landscape views around Ambleside and Rydal. CFP

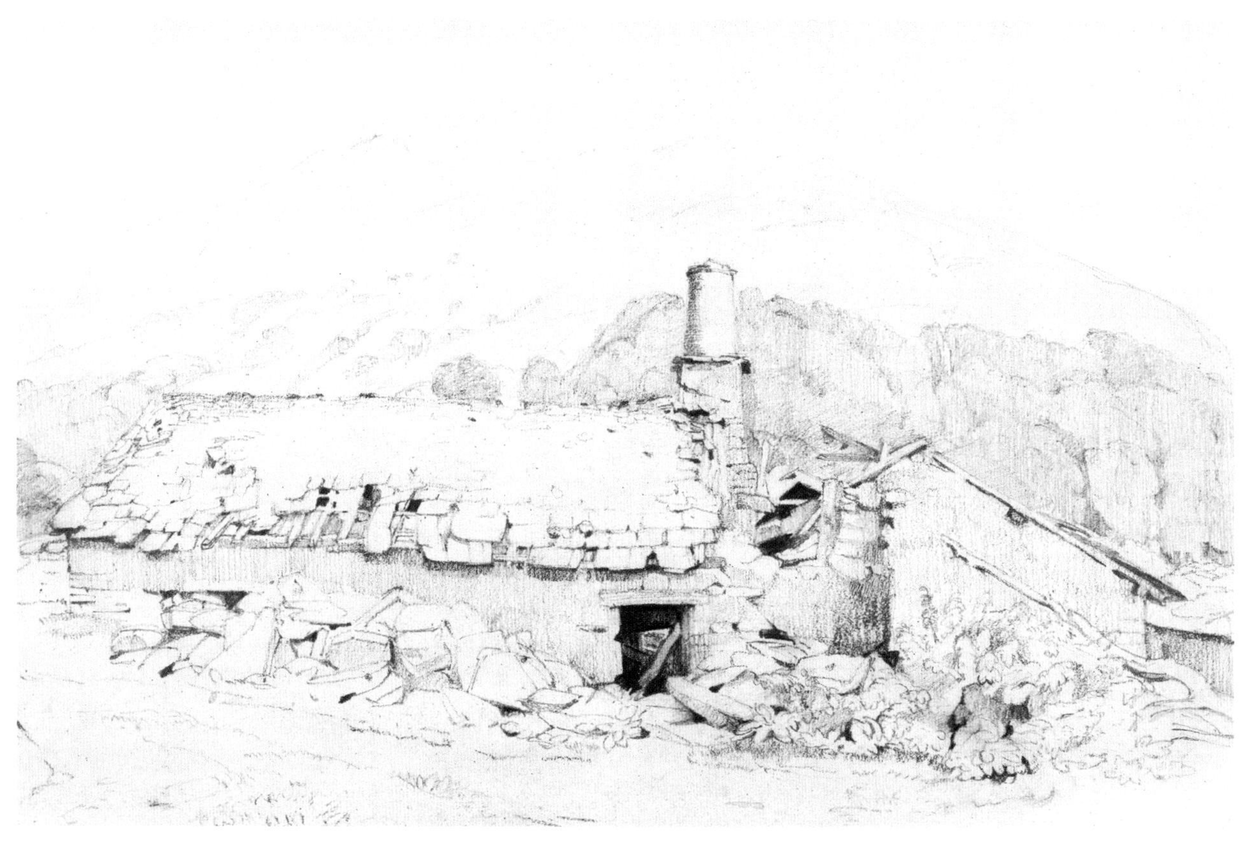

Cat. 64

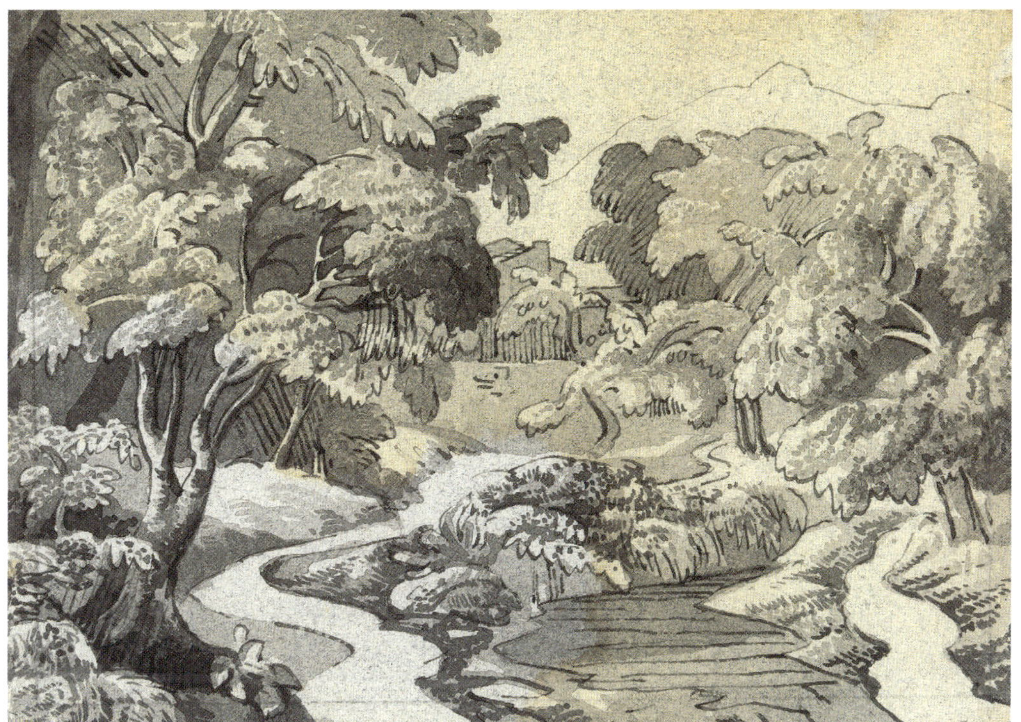

Fig. 33 Thomas Jameson, *River and Path, with Wansfell behind*, pen and ink and wash, *c.*1809 (The Wordsworth Trust).

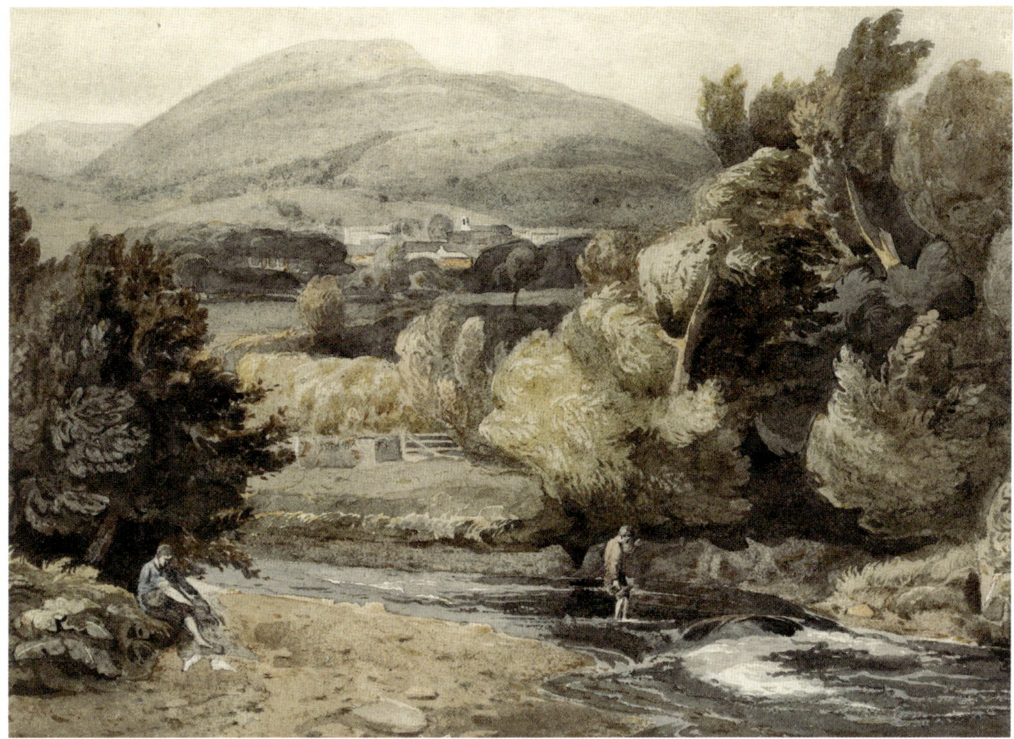

Fig. 34 Thomas Jameson, *Ambleside*, watercolour, *c.*1808–10 (British Museum).

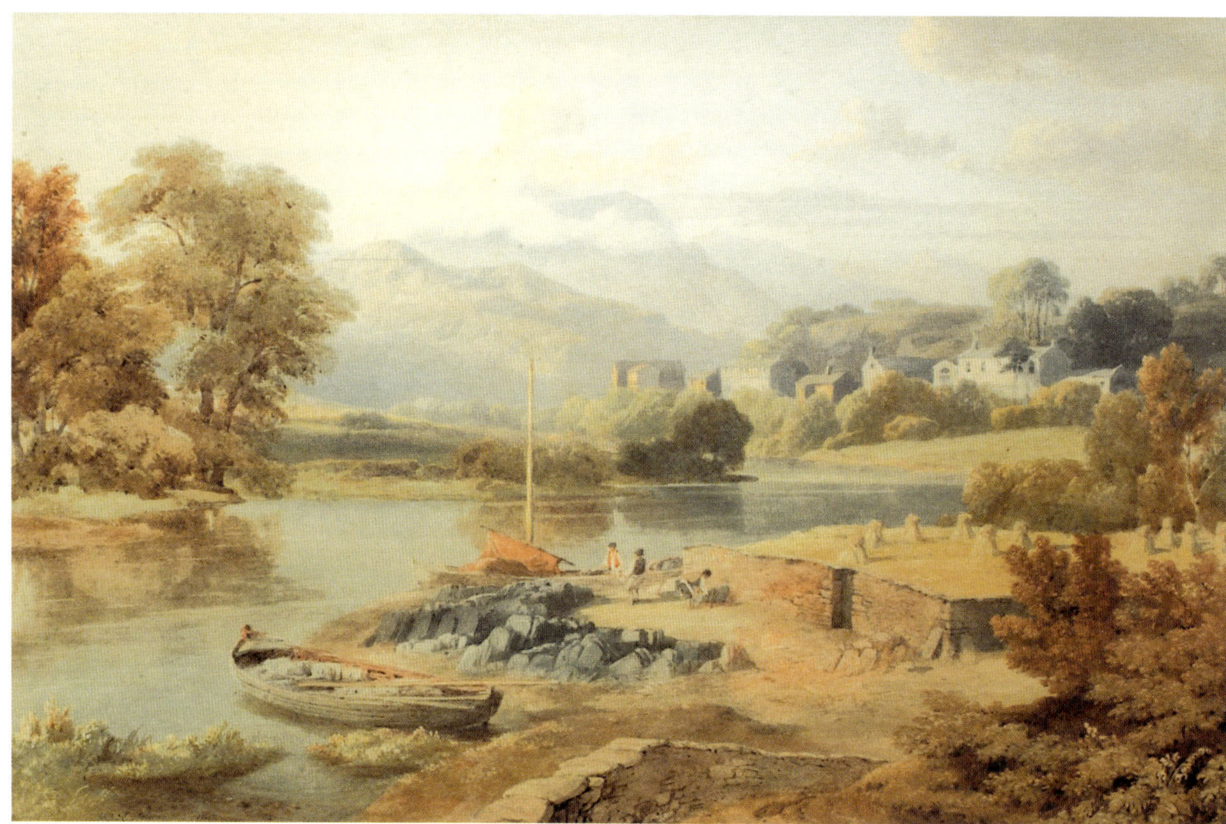

Cat. 65

65

RAMSAY RICHARD REINAGLE (1775–1862)
The Slate Wharf and Village Clappersgate on the River Brathy near Windermere. Morning
c.1810–11
Watercolour, 32.2 × 48.2 cm
Title inscribed on paper affixed to backing board
On long-term loan to The Wordsworth Trust

In 1810 Reinagle exhibited a very similar work to this at the Society of Painters in Water Colours entitled *A Slate Wharf, with the Village of Clappersgate, and Coniston Fells, near the Head of Windermere – Forenoon* (no. 111, now in the Laing Art Gallery, Newcastle upon Tyne). These were inspired by his tour of 1807 when, in the company of William Havell (cat. 60), he became well acquainted with the environs of Ambleside. Here they visited the Hardens at Brathay and made drawings in their grounds, Reinagle greatly impressing Jessy Harden with his well-known facility of execution.

The hamlet of Clappersgate lies at the foot of Loughrigg, close to the north end of Windermere, and facing the confluence of the Rothay and the Brathay immediately prior to the mingling of their waters with the lake. This area has served as the quay for the head of the lake since Roman times (the lake itself having inadequate depth here), the quantity of goods handled at the quay reaching its peak in the late eighteenth century. Slate was one of the main commodities passing through, mostly arriving from the quarries at Elterwater and at Thrang in Great Langdale, with an average of 1,500 tons a year being unloaded and reloaded for transport down Windermere to the wider world. Incoming material at the wharf at this date included gunpowder for use in the quarries. Although Reinagle shows a quiet moment on a hot summer morning, the slate wharf must often have been a hive of activity; the buildings of Clappersgate housed essential services including a blacksmith's and a saddler's – not to mention three public houses! CFP

66

ELIZABETH WHARTON (1757–1829)
Windermere, from the Ferry Inn
1811
Pen and ink wash, 23.1 × 36.9 cm
Inscribed 'E.W.', Aug.[t] 16.th 1811.', 'Windermere, from the Ferry Inn.'
Purchased, 1996

67

ANONYMOUS
Windermere, from the Ferry Inn
1811 or earlier
Pen and ink wash, 25.5 × 43.4 cm
Purchased, 1996

These drawings come from an album that includes a manuscript note about its provenance and its principal artist, Elizabeth Wharton. Perhaps not surprisingly the note, written in the nineteenth century, mentions her two brothers – Robert Wharton Myddleton of Old Park (the eldest son who inherited not only the Wharton estate near Spennymoor where Elizabeth was born but also wealth from his mother's relations, the Myddletons) – and Richard Wharton, MP for the City of Durham. What it fails to mention is that she was the daughter of Dr Thomas Wharton, the intended guide and companion of the poet Gray on his Lake District tour of 1769 and the recipient of his famous letters that describe it.

Elizabeth's album contains sixteen drawings, mostly in pen and ink wash and in most cases dated and initialled. They range in date from 14 to 20 August, beginning at Lowther Castle and ending at Brough Castle, with depictions of Ullswater, Coniston, Windermere, Borrowdale, Buttermere, Crummock Water and Derwentwater recorded for the intervening days. It would clearly have been impossible for her to have travelled so extensively round the Lakes and completed these drawings on the dates indicated; the album is, rather, a 'virtual tour' and the dates must be those on which she regarded her drawings as 'finished' and literally 'signed them off'. Since the Whartons and the Lonsdales were on intimate terms and the drawings include an interior of Lowther Castle (*The Corridor at Lowther*, dated 14 August), it is likely that Elizabeth was a guest at the castle during August and devoted her leisure hours – or evenings – to the creation of the album: either working up sketches made some time earlier or, as in the example discussed here, making copies of drawings by another artist. She would have had most congenial company, the four daughters of Lord Lonsdale (especially Lady Mary) also being enthusiastic draughtswomen and often receiving advice from Farington; indeed, he called on them in London in July 1811 and advised Lady Mary on the painting materials she should take to the country (XI.3966). In August 1811 Lowther Castle was reaching the end of a five-year period of rebuilding to the designs of Robert Smirke who had been recommended to Lord Lonsdale by Sir George Beaumont among others. Thus in her maturity as well as in her childhood, Elizabeth was in touch with major players in the history of the Lake District.

The chief interest of Elizabeth's drawings lies in their associations rather than in any distinction as works of art. Although several of the drawings in the album have charm or historical interest, they are essentially the work of a lady amateur, now in her mid-fifties; almost inevitably, they are executed with care and attention to detail rather than with spontaneity and vivacity. Their style is also somewhat conservative for their date of execution. In just one instance, *Windermere, from the Ferry Inn*, the album contains alternative versions of the same scene, which may usefully be compared with each other. Cat. 67 is by a hand other than Elizabeth's and served as her model: it is the work of a more competent artist, perhaps a drawing-master who had left it at Lowther for just that purpose. Elizabeth's first attempt at a copy was almost finished when it was wrecked by some domestic accident and abandoned. She then embarked on a second version that reached completion and was duly dated and initialled (cat. 66). Throughout this drawing, Elizabeth's work is timid and tentative – both in what she depicts (or does not depict) and how she recreates the various ingredients. By contrast with her model, her tree serving as side-screen is rigid and inorganic while the adjacent wall is described with undue emphasis and regularity; the surface of her lake is no more than a painted patchwork, her boat a mere symbol, while the foreground shore and the island are both uninhabited.

The viewpoint of all these drawings (on the west side of Windermere, reached via the village of Sawrey) was extremely popular among artist-visitors, 'the isthmus of the ferry point' having been recommended in West's *Guide* as the first 'station' for viewing the lake. From the ferry point visitors

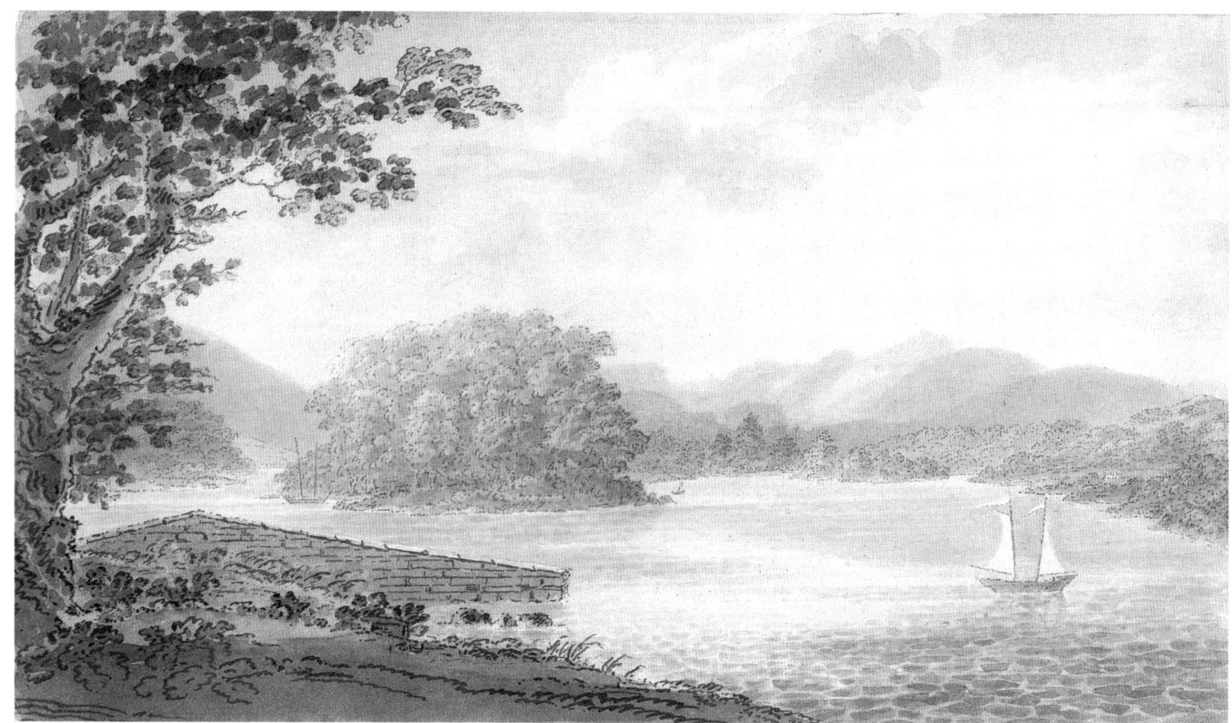

Cat. 66

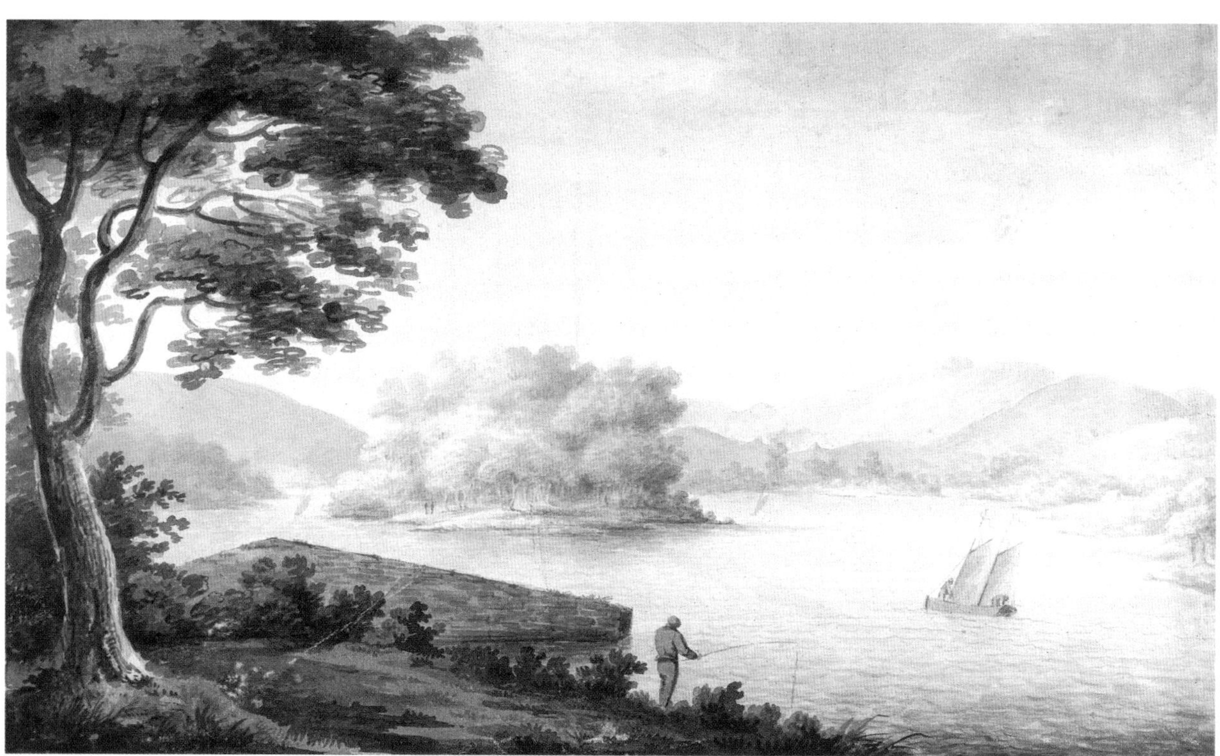

Cat. 67

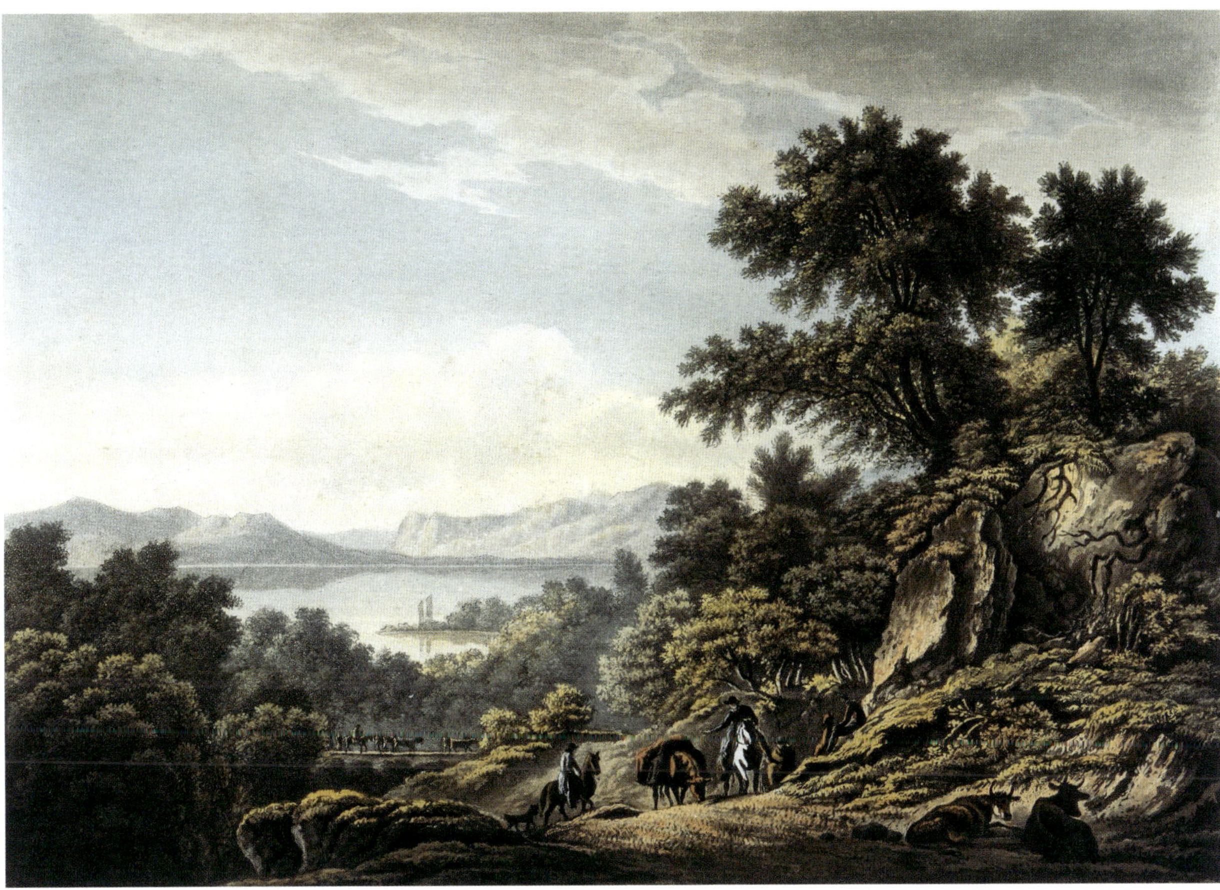

Cat. 68

could enjoy views both northwards (as here) to the fells above Ambleside or south towards the foot of the lake. It is tempting to connect Elizabeth's drawings with a viewpoint just north of the ferry itself which West describes in these words: 'Here a charming picture will present itself in an elegant stile. The island from this stand appears with much variety of shore. ... A sweeter picture than this the lake does not furnish. – The artist will find a proper stand on the inside of the stone-wall' (1784, pp. 58-9). CFP

68

JOHN HASSELL after JOHN GLOVER (1767–1849)
Windermere
1813
Aquatint, 26.5 × 35 cm
Engraved inscriptions: below, with title and *From an original drawing by J. Glover, in the possession of – Shawe, Esq.*[1]
Peter Bicknell Bequest, 1997

John Glover's depictions of the Lake District in the first two decades of the nineteenth century were enormously influential. They stimulated younger artists to visit the area (see cat. 52–3, 60, 65) and introduced its beauties to an ever-increasing audience. While the works themselves were shown at the annual exhibitions of the Society of Painters in Water Colours from 1805 onwards, they were also reproduced in books of instruction for aspiring amateur artists who could not afford a private drawing-master such as Glover himself or William Payne (cat. 63). The methods advocated in such books varied according to the practices of their authors but, by and large, they relied on the copying of predetermined scenes, taking the pupil stage by stage through the different processes of drawing and colouring. The illustrations in such books were typically in aquatint, the ideal medium for this purpose.

This aquatint after Glover's *Windermere*, showing the head of the lake and the Langdale Pikes, comes from one of the best of these books. It was written and published by John Hassell: first issued in parts over a two-year period, it was then available as a single volume in 1813. *Aqua Pictura. Illustrated by a Series of Original Specimens from the Works of … all the Most Approved … Draftsmen, with their Style and Method of Touch, in Progressive Examples* contained specimens from sixteen contemporary artists (including several of those featured in the present exhibition) with each scene being presented in stages and accompanied by verbal instructions for its replication by the student. Glover's *Windermere* was presented in four stages of execution: as a simple etched outline of the composition; with monochrome grey washes carefully articulating light and shade; with a pale tinted yellow wash to add warmth to the scene; and finally with a variety of tints. The text on the facing page gave detailed advice as to which pigment to use for which ingredient in the scene (down to such things as the drapery of the panniers on the horse), with every reference to every pigment being followed by an inch-long colour sample of that pigment: words are thus interspersed with floating patches of indigo, Indian red, Indian ink, yellow ochre, gamboge, light red, burnt terra sienna, grey, madder and lake, creating an effect that would today – in some quarters – be regarded as 'art' in its own right.

A long-established practitioner of aquatint, John Hassell (1767–1825) worked with many artists and contributed to numerous publications. In 1795 he had been responsible for twelve aquatints based on paintings by John Rathbone, published as *Select Views of the Lakes of Cumberland and Westmoreland, &c engraved in Aquatinta*; four of these, showing Lodore, Skiddaw, Thirlmere and Ullswater, are pasted into the larger of the two albums belonging to Daniel Daulby (see cat. 43). CFP

69

JULIUS CAESAR IBBETSON (1759–1817)
Buttermere Bridge and Church, from the Fish Inn
*c.*1813
Oil on canvas, 33.7 × 44.4 cm
Purchased with the generous assistance of the National Heritage Memorial Fund, 1981

This painting dates from several years after Ibbetson had left the Lake District and returned to his native Yorkshire. There he continued to paint Lakes subjects, either repeating previous scenes or producing new works based on sketches made during his years in Ambleside and Troutbeck (1801–5).

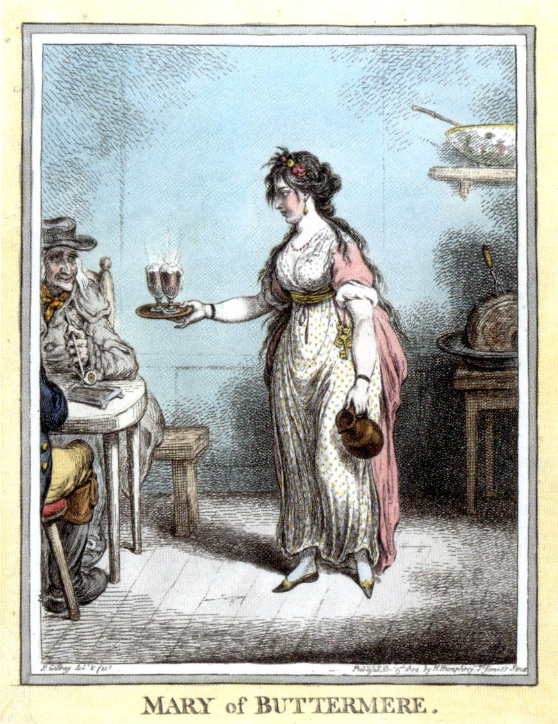

Fig. 35 James Gillray, *Mary of Buttermere*, coloured etching, 1802 (The Wordsworth Trust).

The pencil sketches on which the present work is based (Burkett and Slowe, 1982, nos 44–5) were made about 1803, a time when the tiny village of Buttermere was notorious throughout the country. In 1802 the famously beautiful daughter of the landlord of the Fish Inn, 'Mary of Buttermere' (fig. 35), had been duped into marriage by a criminal posing as an aristocratic suitor; in 1803 John Hatfield, bigamist and forger, was sentenced to death and Mary returned to the Fish Inn.

Ibbetson's painting shows Buttermere village from the Fish Inn, which provided an excellent view of the bridge over Mill Beck, today's rebuilt Bridge Inn and the diminutive chapel perched on the hillside with the steep winding track leading to Newlands Hause. The ensemble had long appealed to visiting artists; a tiny work drawn by Girtin, well before the Fish became noteworthy (fig. 36), is a copy of an anonymous and untraced work of the 1790s. The Wordsworth Trust owns a nineteenth-century watercolour by Lady Beresford, showing the same ensemble, and a pencil drawing by George Shepherd of the buildings clustered round Mill Beck seen from the opposite direction and thus including the façade of the Fish Inn, Ibbetson's viewpoint.

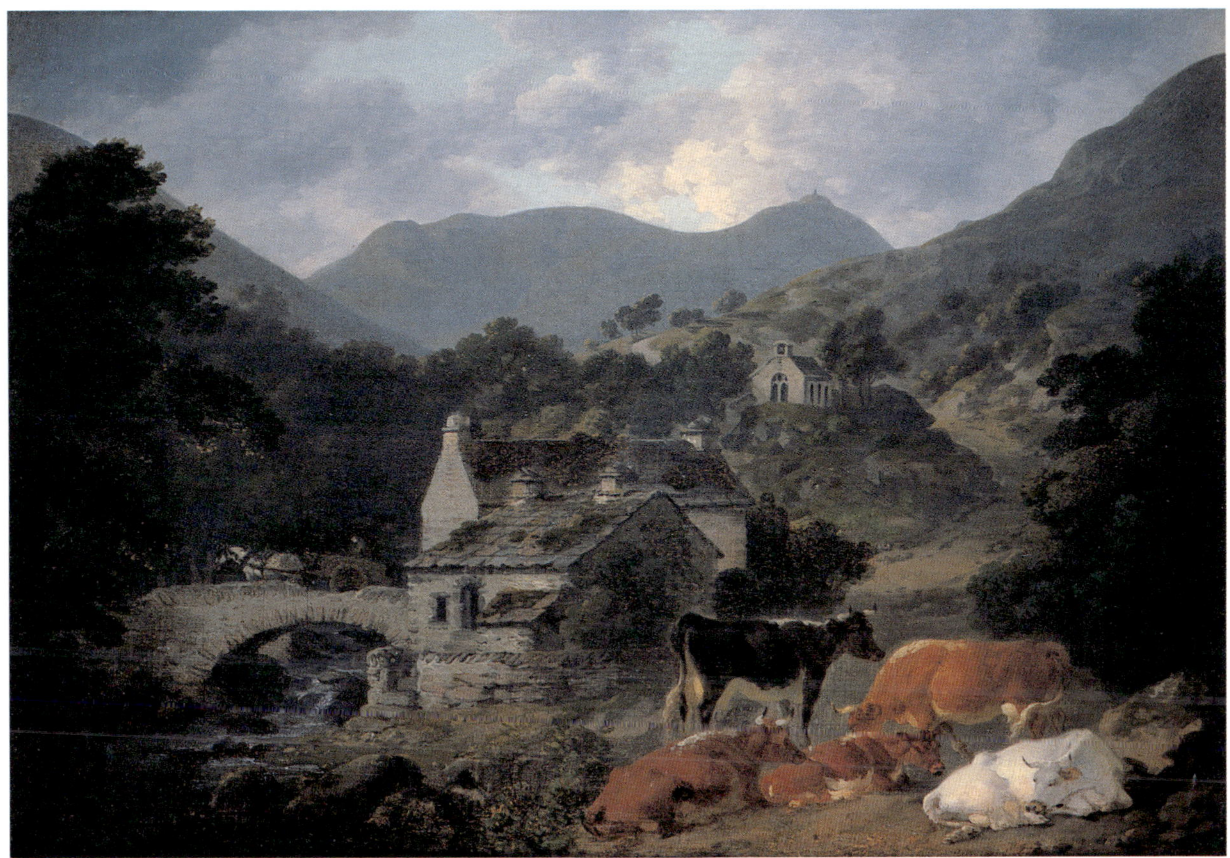

Cat. 69

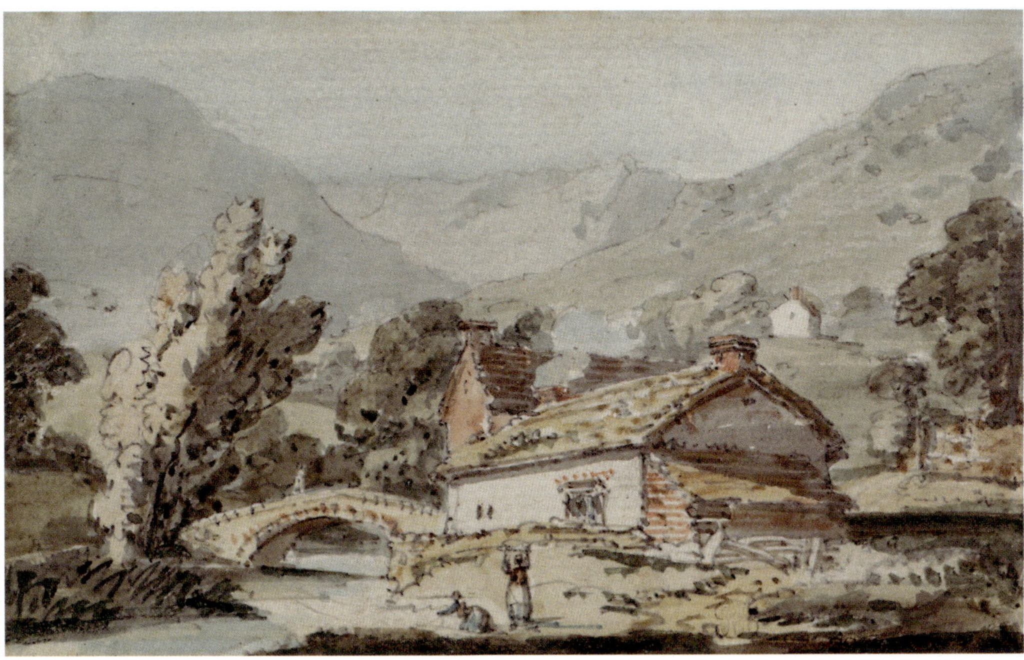

Fig. 36 Thomas Girtin, *Buttermere Bridge*, pencil and watercolour, *c.*1797 (Tate Britain, London).

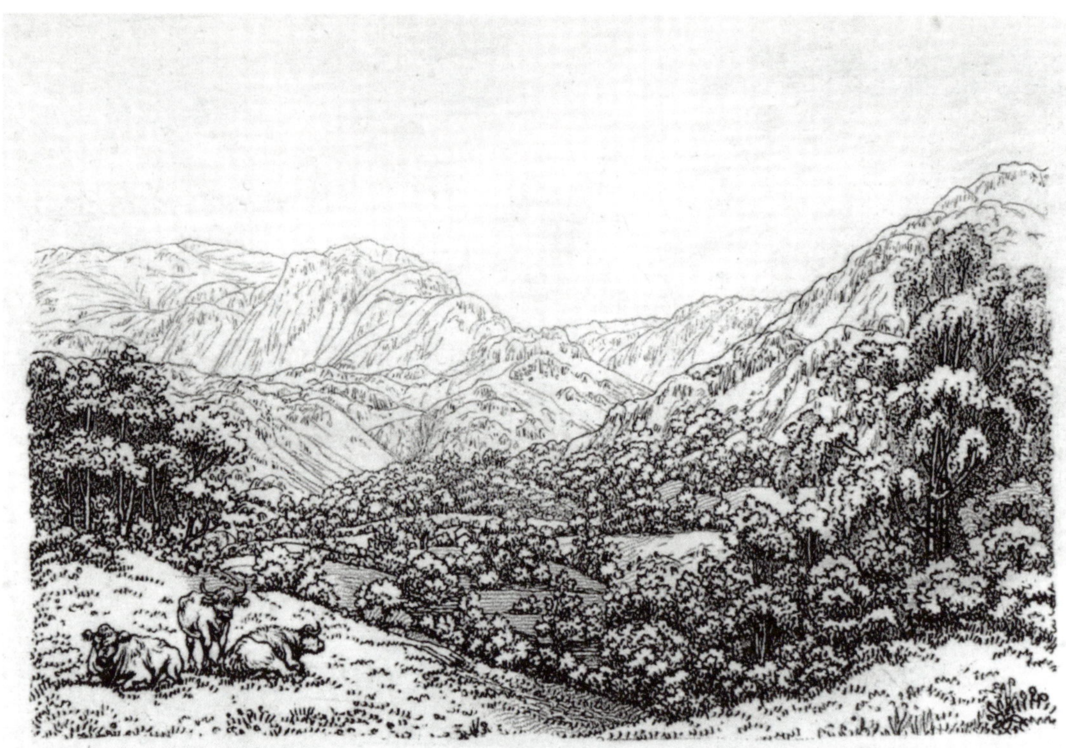

Cat. 70

Ibbetson also provides a grand evocation of the fells to the east. These are presented with the breadth and imagination that Gainsborough and De Loutherbourg had brought to Lake District subjects some thirty years earlier rather than as a precise topographical record. The third ingredient in the work, the group of cattle in the foreground, is typical of Ibbetson's concerns. He had a long-standing interest in seventeenth-century Netherlandish art, including the small paintings of peasant life by David Teniers and Nicolaes Berchem, which were very popular in Britain in the early nineteenth century; Ibbetson made frequent use of their rustic motifs to animate his own paintings of contemporary England just as David Wilkie (1785–1841) was doing in his depictions of peasant life in Scotland. He was also influenced by the work of the seventeenth-century Dutch landscape artist Aelbert Cuyp and in cat. 69 he enlivened the monotonously coloured landscape foreground with a carefully posed group of cows of sharply contrasting hues, very much in the manner of his predecessor. Some years after this painting he published a selection of similar groups in *Six Etchings of Cattle, From Nature.* CFP

70

WILLIAM GREEN (1760–1823)
Easedale from Butterlip How
1814
Soft-ground etching, 14.4 × 21 cm
Engraved inscriptions: below, with title; bottom, *Published at Ambleside, Aug.t 1, 1814, by W.m Green.*

71

WILLIAM GREEN (1760–1823)
Easedale from Butterlip How
1814
Soft-ground etching and wash, 14.4 × 21 cm
Engraved inscriptions: below, with title; bottom, *Published at Ambleside, Aug.t 1, 1814, by W.m Green.*

From 1800, when he settled in Ambleside, until his death in 1823 the Manchester-born Green, a surveyor by training, was almost totally occupied in depicting and recording the area in which he lived. While other artists came and went, exhibiting their work in London or other cities, Green was the 'artist-in-residence' in the Lake District – going out sketching from nature in summer, working up his views in winter, displaying his work at his own home, selling

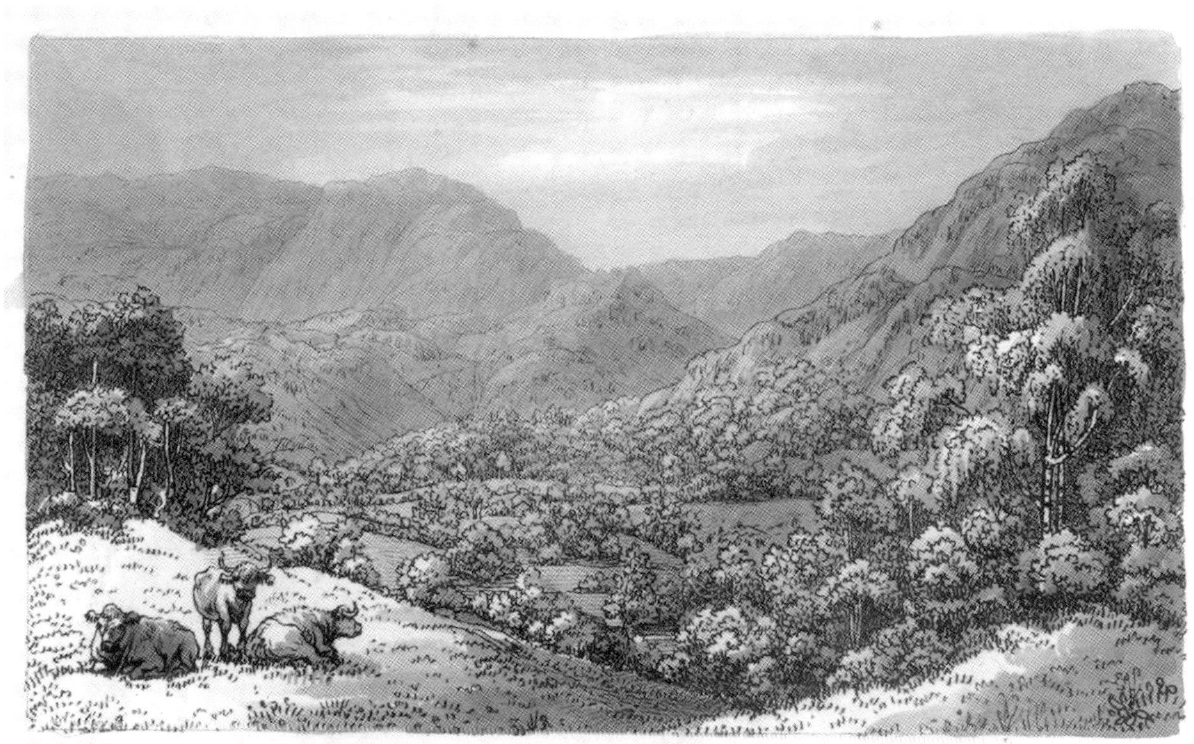

Cat. 71

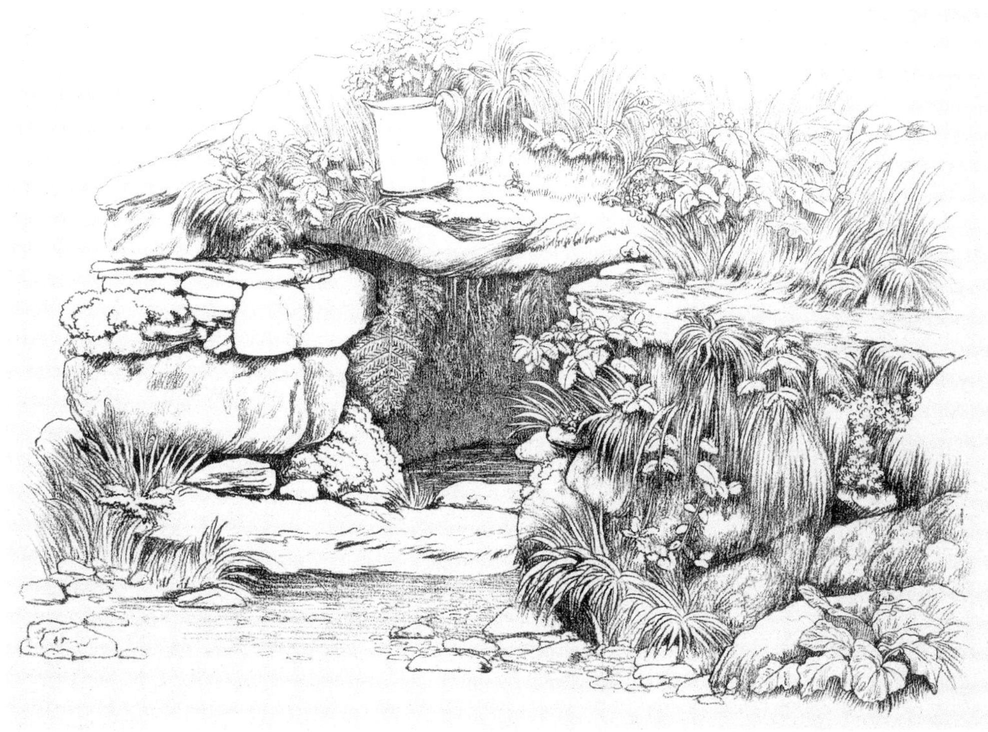

Fig. 37 William Green, *Well at Skelgill*, soft-ground etching, 1809 (The Wordsworth Trust).

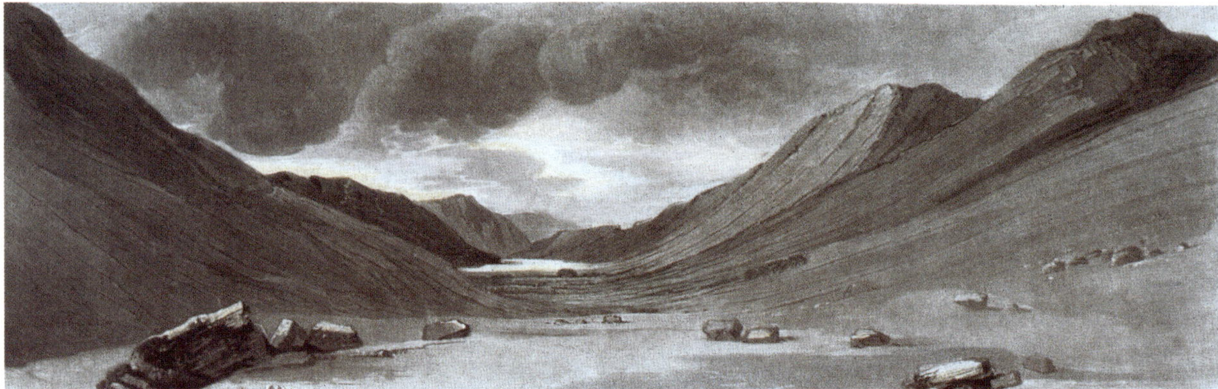

Cat. 72

artists' materials, giving drawing lessons. He catered unashamedly for the tourist market, publishing a succession of collections of his own drawings that provided both an introduction to the scenery of the Lakes and a souvenir of the region. These he etched himself, often presenting them in different states (with and without tinted washes, probably done by his daughters, as in cat. 71; in sepia and in colours). The collections of prints were often large in number – seventy-eight 'studies from nature' appearing together in 1809, sixty studies in 1810, for example; his lifetime's work runs into hundreds of scenes. To accompany the studies Green sometimes published small books, or 'descriptions', containing information on the features illustrated. Some of this material – and much else – appeared in the culmination of his writing, *The Tourist's New Guide, containing a Description of the Lakes, Mountains, and Scenery, in Cumberland, Westmorland, and Lancashire, ... being the Result of Observations made during a Residence of Eighteen Years in Ambleside and Keswick*, published in two volumes in 1819.

Easedale from Butterlip How was the 24th of the *Sixty Small Prints* published in 1814 with an accompanying 'description' of some thirty pages. It has been selected here in deliberate preference to Green's more dramatic and more conventional subjects (prints which were often of the highest quality) partly for the very modesty of its subject, its focus on a charming pastoral valley that does not cry out for attention. One of Green's special qualities was that he often focused on small, mundane things – the stones on a path; a group of foxgloves; a spring with a cup standing near, ready for use (fig. 37). Easedale lies very close to Grasmere, being reached by the footpath near Easedale Beck to the south of Helm Crag, and it was well known to the Wordsworths and their friends as it is to many visitors to Grasmere today. In one of the shortest of the 'descriptions' to this group of studies Green wrote simply, 'Easedale is a romantic and secluded valley branching out of Grasmere; and Easedale Tarn, which will be found by following the frothy stream, is engulphed in precipitous mountains, with large rocks projecting from their sides.' CFP

72

HENRY DAWE AFTER JOHN CONSTABLE RA (1776–1837)
Helvellyn
1815
Mezzotint, proof state, 23 × 40 cm
Engraved inscriptions: below, with title and names of artist and engraver; bottom, *Wythburn Lake, Cumberland. This view is taken from the elevated part of the valley, on the road leading from Grassmere to Keswick, near Dunmail Raise. To the North in the extreme distance, rises Saddleback, and on the right is Helvellyn.*
Gift of Peter Bicknell, 1990

This mezzotint is Constable's only engraving of the Lake District, mountain scenery being conspicuously absent from his important print series, *English Landscape*, and its origin is somewhat obscure. It certainly lies partly in the painter's long-standing friendship with the engraver Henry Dawe's elder brother since in 1815 Constable was heavily occupied in helping George Dawe with the landscape background of

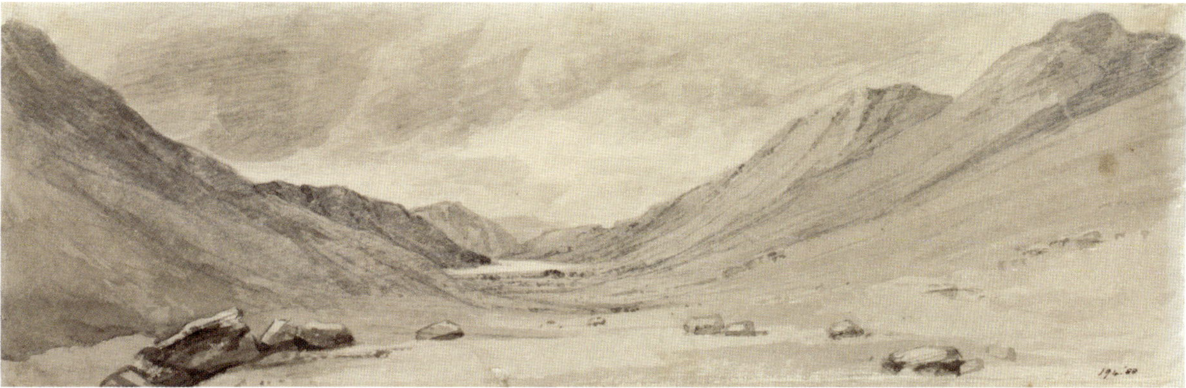

Fig. 38 John Constable *Leathes Water*, pencil and wash, *c.*1815 (Victoria & Albert Museum, London).

his life-size portrait of the celebrated actress Eliza O'Neill in the role of Juliet (RA 1816, now untraced); this kept him busy for the whole of June when he often worked up to fourteen hours a day in Dawe's studio. However, the final mezzotint bears the publication date of 1 May, suggesting a period of collaboration with Henry Dawe in April or even earlier. This seems, on the face of it, somewhat surprising, given that in 1815 Constable submitted no fewer than eight works to the Royal Academy exhibition (his largest number to date and the maximum permitted), making this April an exceptionally busy month.

It has been suggested that in presenting Leathes Water in a barren and inhospitable vale, inspiring awe and anxiety, Constable may have been deliberately challenging the attempt of William Green in one of his etchings in *Sixty Small Prints* of 1814 to present it as leafy and Arcadian (Hebron, Shields and Wilcox, 2006, pp. 145–6). On the other hand, it is possible that its mood reflects Constable's own state of mind in the spring of 1815. His mother was taken ill suddenly at the beginning of March and died before the month was out. It was only a few weeks since she had urged him in a letter to pursue the 'Fame and Gain' that had so far eluded him; now he was unable to attend her funeral in Suffolk through pressure of work in London. His thoughts must inevitably have turned to his mother's family and to his maternal uncle, David Pike Watts, who had long been his guide and mentor, the driving force behind his visit to the Lake District in 1806 (see cat. 55). The mezzotint may perhaps be seen as an elegy.

The subject of the print is given on the Wordsworth Trust's proof as 'Helvellyn' but when it was finally published it bore the title 'Leathes Water, or Wythburn Lake, Cumberland'. Accompanying letterpress below the image informed the viewer, 'This view is taken from the elevated part of the valley, on the road leading from Grassmere to Keswick, near Dunmail Raise. To the North, in the extreme distance, rises Saddleback, and on the right is Helvellyn.' In Constable's day the names 'Wythburn Water' and 'Leathes Water' were both used for parts of the lake that was enlarged to become Thirlmere reservoir after the valley was transformed by the engineers of Manchester Corporation Water Works in the years after 1890. The format of the view is admirably suited to its subject. While many of Constable's sketches of Borrowdale are squarish in form, echoing the confined spaces of that valley, it was not unusual for him to use an elongated horizontal composition for wider prospects and broader vales.

Constable made several sketches in this area in 1806 but the mezzotint is based on a drawing (fig. 38) that is far more careful and precise than most of these; this may have been drawn – or completed – after the tour itself. A detailed drawing rather than a sketch would, in any case, have been required for the use of the engraver. Mezzotint, with its rich texture and ability to produce a full range of tones between the lightest and darkest areas, was uniquely suited to Constable's concerns. A small series of mezzotints after his paintings was proposed in 1824 but never materialised; when he came to produce his *English Landscape* series in 1829–32 he deliberately chose mezzotint over the more modern medium of lithography urged on him by his friend John Fisher.

Mezzotint was rarely – if at all – used for depictions of the Lake District but it had long been the English medium of choice for prints after portraits; this connection, once again, links *Helvellyn* closely to Constable's intimate relationship with both George and Henry Dawe whose father, Philip Dawe, had been one of the most celebrated mezzotinters of his age. CFP

73

WILLIAM DANIELL RA (1769–1837)
Distant View of Whitbarrow Scar, Westmoreland
1816
Aquatint, 22.7 × 29.9 cm
Engraved inscriptions: below, with title and name of artist-engraver; bottom, *Published by Messrs Longman & Co Paternoster Row & W. Daniell 9 Cleveland St Fitzroy Square, London Feby 1, 1816.*
Purchased, 2000

In 1813 William Daniell and his friend Richard Ayton made the first of their journeys round the coast of Britain that led to one of the grandest topographical publications of the early nineteenth century. The publication of *A Voyage round Great Britain* took over ten years from 1814 to 1825; it ran to over 800 pages of text and over 300 aquatints, spread over eight volumes. Daniell, already a well-established topographical artist, was the instigator of the project and was to be responsible for all the illustrations while the considerably younger Ayton was to act as his travelling companion and compose the accompanying text. However, this arrangement only lasted until 1815 when the difference in their temperaments led to Ayton's withdrawal; thereafter Daniell continued single-handed, necessarily at a slower pace, and brought the work to a conclusion.

A Voyage round Great Britain takes the reader on a clockwise tour, beginning and ending at Land's End. It contains just a few images relating to the Lake District, all appearing in the second volume, but both Daniell and Ayton made original contributions to the portrayal of the area. The first plate, *Distant View of Whitbarrow Scar, Westmoreland* shows the view across Morecambe Bay toward 'fertile and beautiful' country, 'broken along the coast by some rugged and barren hills, detached from the main chain, and advanced to the sea. … These hills, which are all composed of grey limestone, are roughened on their summits by piles of bare and broken rock, and are strikingly contrasted with the decorated and graceful landscape which they interrupt.' In more recent times the writer Norman Nicholson has graphically described Whitbarrow Scar as a 'white land-slide' (1963, p. 43).

Continuing round the coast, Daniell depicts Castle Head on the Kent estuary and Piel Castle and then, moving north along the Cumberland coast, Ayton tells of a Wordsworthian experience: 'I remember going up to a clergyman of a considerable parish to condole with him on the poverty-stricken condition of his flock, when he stopped me to say that I might spare my commiseration as there was not one of them who was not as well provided for as he desired. He admitted that I, as a stranger, might be excused for judging otherwise, but attributed those external marks of want and suffering that had influenced my opinion to another cause than that of necessity. There being no great sources of wealth in the county to tempt the greediness of adventurers from other parts of the kingdom, the natives are not disturbed in the enjoyment of their peculiar usages by the interference of strangers, and cling to many antiquated forms which a more enlarged communication with society might have taught them to despise. … They live quietly among themselves, keeping one another in countenance, by an equal observance of the same common fashions, with no intruders to shame them into changes by better examples. But if their confined knowledge of the world shuts them out from some advantages, it defends them too against many evils. Together with some coarseness, they retain a great moral simplicity, which keeps their passions in order, and would be ill exchanged for a little more refinement in the economy of their homes.'

Further north, Whitehaven and Maryport are both depicted, while the text moves into an extended account of the author's visit to Lord Lonsdale's coal-mines at Whitehaven. He obviously found this one of the most extraordinary experiences of his entire tour. Descending by basket down the mineshaft, walking more than four miles underground and under the sea, terrified by strange noises and echoes and always conscious of 'possible danger which gave intensity to my interest in every thing that I heard and saw', Ayton concludes his account with a plea for Parliament to intervene and regulate the terrible hardship suffered by the women and young children employed in the mines. 'The estimation in which

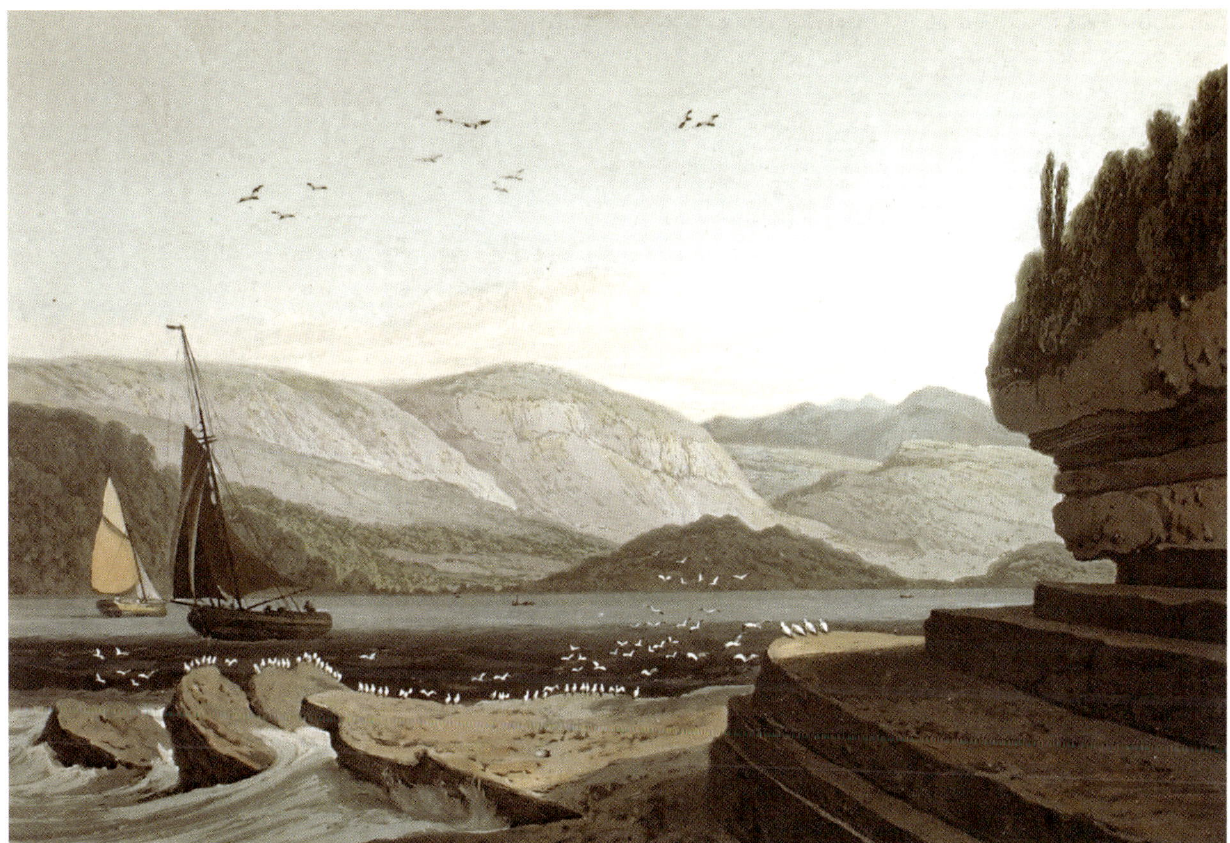

Cat. 73

women are held is one test of the civilization of a people; and it is somewhat scandalous, in a country of gallant men, to see them sacrificed to the rough drudgery of coal mines. If there were nothing but the filthiness of their occupation to complain of, it would be no extravagant refinement to feel that their sex should preserve them from it; it is not a little offensive to see them changed into devils in their appearance, but it is afflicting indeed to witness the perversion that takes place in their moral character. … We must have coals … but we may have them through the intercession of a little humanity and liberality, without this lavish waste of morality.'

As for the children, few of whom were more than eight years old and several considerably younger, Ayton writes: 'We have lately raised a cry that will save thousands, in a distant country, from the pains and the ignominy of a miserable slavery, and should not behold with unconcern any thing that bears the stamp of slavery at home. … Surely some legislative interference is required to restrain so barbarous and unwarrantable an exertion of power – to prevent the exposure of children to loathsome and unhealthy occupations, at least till they are of an age to give their consent. The cries of the little beings condemned to the mines have never, I imagine, reached the ears of their noble proprietor; and if he should hear of their condition through my means, and secure their release, I shall have been accessary [*sic*] to an act of charity that I shall remember with pleasure through life.' Although 1819 saw a Factory Act regulate child labour in textile factories, nothing was to be done in relation to mines until a Royal Commission of 1840 led to the Mines Act two years later which prohibited the employment underground of females and children under ten. CFP

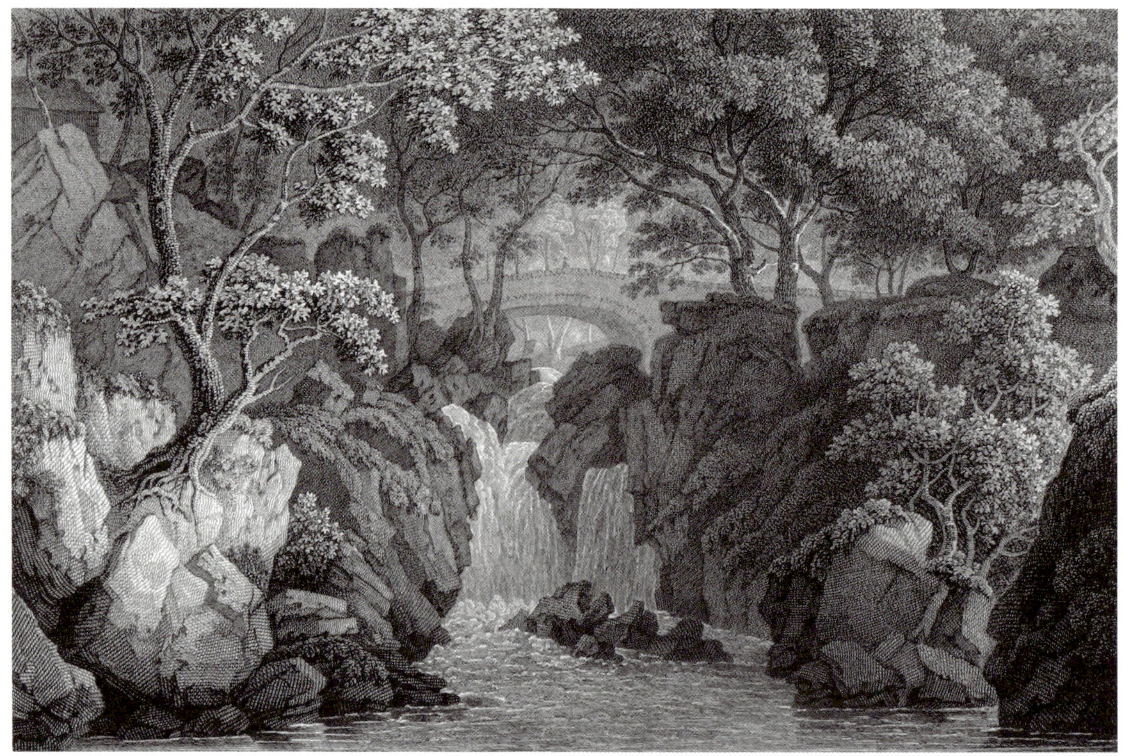

Cat. 74

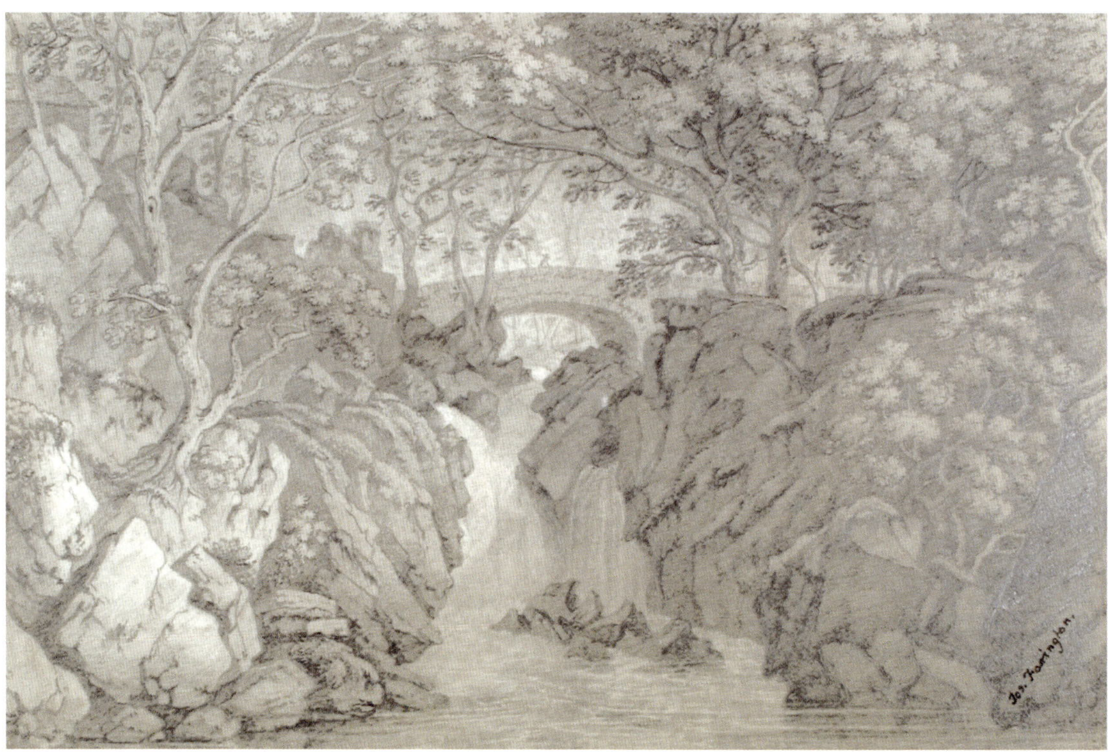

Cat. 75

74

SAMUEL MIDDIMAN after
JOSEPH FARINGTON RA (1747–1821)
Waterfall at Rydal
1816
Etching and engraving, 15.2 × 22.3 cm
Engraved inscriptions: below, with names of artist and engraver
Purchased with the generous assistance of the John R. Murray Charitable Trust, the W.W. Spooner Charitable Trust, the Warren Bequest, John Dobson and David McKitterick, 2006

75

JOSEPH FARINGTON RA (1747–1821)
Waterfall at Rydal
*c.*1814
Pencil, 15.1 × 22.6 cm
Inscribed 'Jos. Farington.'
Purchased, 1986

Some twenty years after the publication of Farington's *Views of the Lakes* (see cat. 27–8) he was involved in events that eventually led to the publication of a further book of engravings after his northern drawings: *The Lakes of Lancashire, Westmorland, and Cumberland*. This is often wrongly described as a new edition of the former work but it was no such thing; it arose from different circumstances and contains a new set of scenes accompanied by a completely different type of letterpress by a freshly commissioned author.

In the summer of 1807 Farington made an arrangement with Daniel and Samuel Lysons that he should assist them with the Cumberland volume of *Britannia Depicta*. This was the series of engraved illustrations to *Magna Britannia*, the mammoth survey of Britain that was being produced county-by-county in alphabetical quarto volumes while the nation was engaged in war against France. The following spring it was agreed between Farington and the publisher-bookseller firm of Cadell & Davies that he should make 12–14 drawings each for the Cumberland and Derbyshire volumes that very summer and he took advantage of his visit to the north to make some fresh sketches: in October he visited Whitehaven, Workington and Maryport as well as returning to Borrowdale. By the end of February 1809 he had completed 22 drawings for the two counties and work began almost immediately: within a month Samuel Middiman had called to collect the first of the many drawings he would engrave for the project and soon other engravers were presenting themselves at Farington's door. Over the ensuing months he recorded all their visits: choosing and collecting drawings, showing etchings and impressions and final proofs. However, May 1810 saw the first major delay which was caused, in part at least, by Farington himself: not only did he criticise the accuracy of some of the drawings in the Cornwall volume (leading to their replacement) but he pointed out that Cornwall was a relatively unknown county – as well as an extremely picturesque one – and required extra illustrations. It was soon decided that *Cornwall* and *Cumberland* were to have 20 plates apiece.

A year later, in May 1811, Farington made two new proposals to Davies: first, that there should be yet further plates in the Cumberland volume (there were ultimately to be 28); second, that it would be a good idea to publish some of these very same engravings, together with others depicting Westmorland, in a separate and quite independent volume, *Views in Cumberland and Westmorland*, aimed at the growing number of tourists now visiting the area. Davies readily agreed that such a book would suit the new tourists. The inclusion of Lancashire was approved early in 1812 and further drawings were given out for engraving; later in the year this was halted, however, for *Britannia Depicta*.

By the following year two decades of war were taking their toll on the British print-publishing industry and in February 1813 Cadell & Davies announced that, in view of 'the dull state of trade', they would not proceed with the *Views* volume. They would, however, seek to complete the illustrations for *Cumberland*, continuing to pay Farington's fee (£240 per annum) and using only his selected engravers. Middiman, Hay, Pye and Scott accordingly proceeded with their work, along with Woolnoth, John Landseer and John Byrne (the son of William Byrne, the publisher of Farington's earlier *Views of the Lakes* who had died in 1805) and there was, once more, almost daily contact between Farington and his engravers. *Cumberland* was eventually published, as the fifth volume of *Britannia Depicta*, in July 1816 and Lysons proudly presented a copy to Queen Charlotte. The days of *Britannia Depicta* itself, however, were numbered and the sixth volume, reaching Devonshire, was to be the last.

Meanwhile, the volume intended for tourists to the Lakes had been reprieved in 1814, following the abdication of Napoleon and the prospect of

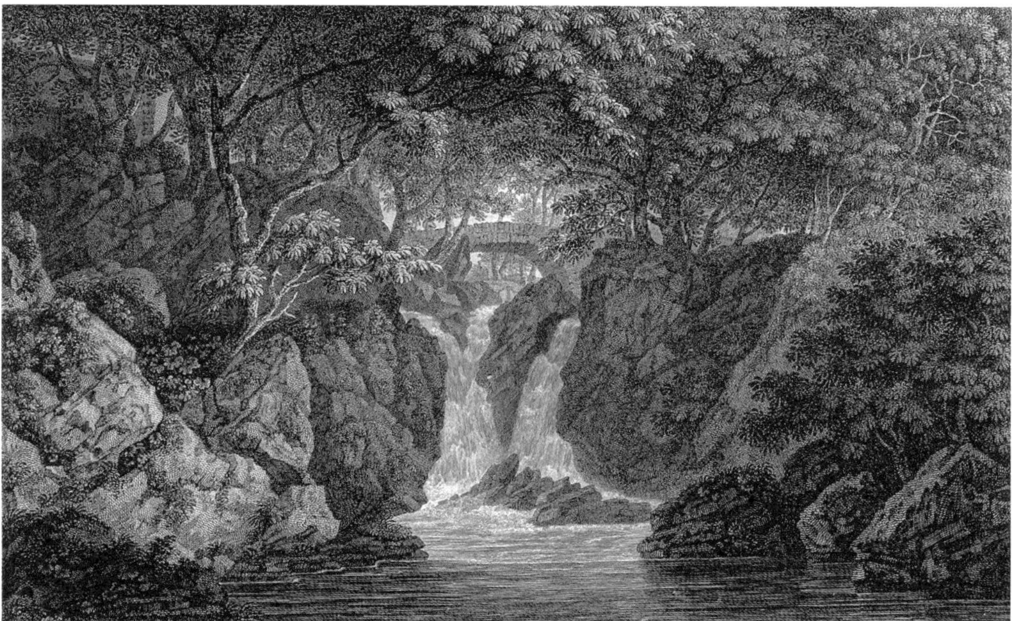

Fig. 39 Benjamin Thomas Pouncy after Joseph Farington, *The Lower Water-fall at Rydal*, etching and engraving, 1788 (The Wordsworth Trust).

a more robust economy; this, too, saw publication in 1816, Farington receiving the first-delivered copy on 21 August. It contained 43 engravings (26 being the same as those in the *Britannia Depicta* volume), which were inserted at appropriate places in the 96-page narrative of a tour – newly made and newly written – by the Rev. Thomas Hartwell Horne (1780–1862). The book's final title, *The Lakes of Lancashire, Westmorland, and Cumberland*, reflects the sequence of its contents, Lancaster having been the starting point of the author's tour. Horne, who had never visited the Lakes, had introduced himself to Farington in February 1816, proposing to write an accompaniment to his engravings based only on the study of books and prints. The artist, however, firmly maintained that first-hand knowledge was essential while the publishers, equally predictably, were resistant to the probable expense of a tour. Farington's offers of assistance eventually secured his case and Horne duly made a tour in early May, taking with him not only impressions of the recently engraved scenes but also the artist's suggestions, itinerary and three books dating from many years earlier (West's *Guide* and the accounts by Newte and Hutchinson: cat. 18, 26, 11). In June Farington read and approved Horne's manuscript (requesting that references to William Green and his rival productions should be excised) and the following month he visited the printer to check the printed pages.

The Wordsworth Trust's copy exhibited here is a particularly fine example of the book and is inscribed in Farington's own hand, 'First Impressions that were taken of the Plates after they were completely finished. Three sets only were taken off before the titles were engraved' and 'This is to be considered a very rare set of Impressions.' When he called on Cadell & Davies in July 1816 he was distressed to notice that some of the impressions of the plates in the half-bound sets of *Cumberland* were of poor quality but he received the reply that the best impressions had been set aside for use in his forthcoming book devoted to the Lakes. This must have gratified him, as did the comments of his friend Robert Smirke soon afterwards, praising the close relationship between engravings and narrative (something that was lacking in the contemporary joint publication of William Daniell and Richard Ayton; see cat. 73).

Waterfall at Rydal depicts one of the most celebrated sights on the tourist route through the Lakes: the lower fall in the grounds of Rydal Hall as seen from a specially built summer-house. Farington had included this subject in his *Views of the Lakes* in the 1780s (fig. 39) but for his new venture he made a new drawing (cat. 75); there are numerous small differences from the earlier engraving in its water,

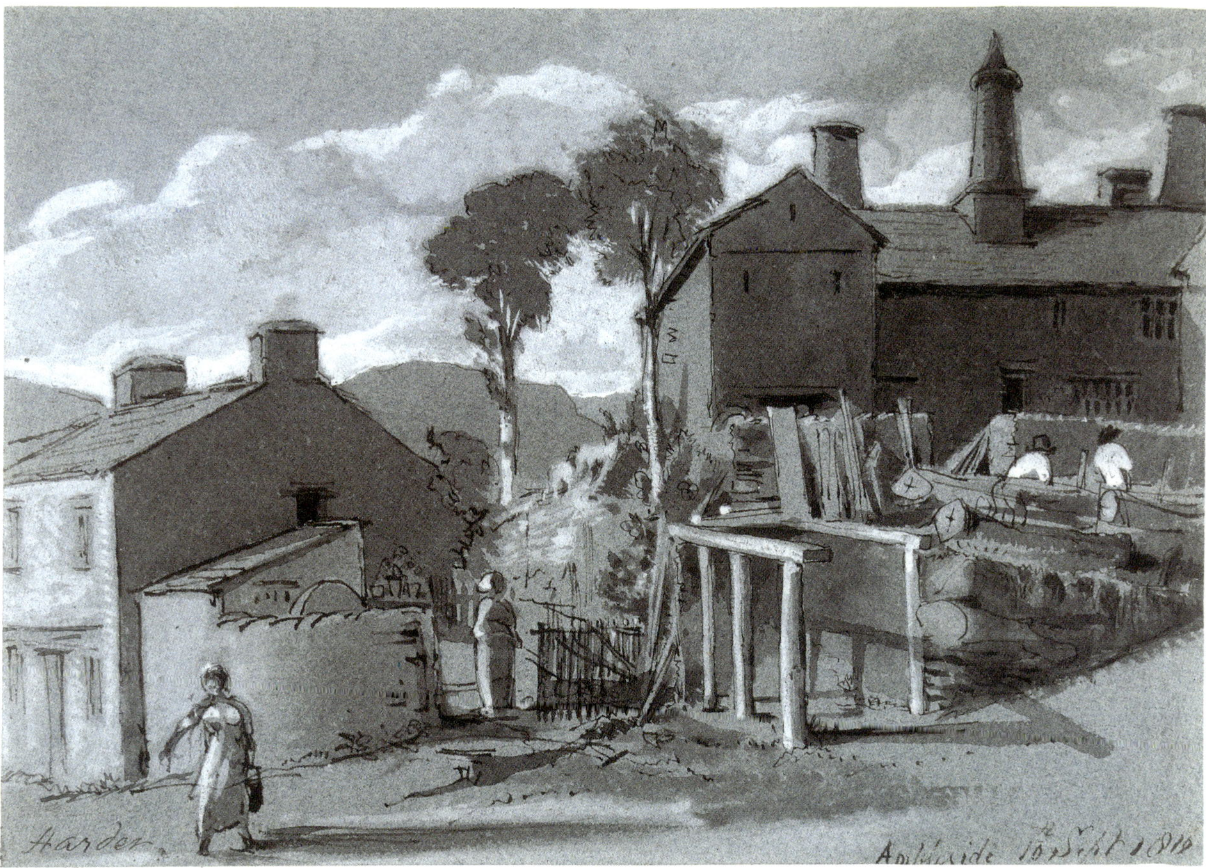

Cat. 76

rocks and foliage as well as in contrasts of light and shade. Horne's account of his tour includes frequent quotations not only from the long-established prose authorities on the Lakes but also from Wordsworth's *Excursion*, published as recently as the summer of 1814. To accompany *Waterfall at Rydal* he cites some well-chosen words from Gilpin: 'The water falls within a few yards of the eye, which … has a long perspective view of the stream, as it hurries from the higher grounds; tumbling, in various little breaks, through it's rocky channel, darkened with thicket. … The dark colour of the stone, taking still a deeper tinge from the wood, which hangs over it, sets off to wonderful advantage the sparkling lustre of the stream; and produces an uncommon effect of light.' This is inevitably followed by another oft-cited passage that had made the view famous. In 1775 Gray's editor Mason had pronounced that, 'Here nature has performed every thing in little that she usually executes on the largest scale. … This little theatrical scene might be painted as large as the original, on a canvas not bigger than those usually dropped in the opera house.' However, Horne's comments are not entirely derivative and, in deference to Farington's artistry, he remarks that the dramatic effect of the fall is still further increased 'if anyone happens to cross the rustic bridge, as happened when our view was taken'. CFP

76

JOHN HARDEN (1772–1847)
Ambleside
*c.*1818–19
Pen and ink, wash, bodycolour, 17.4 × 24.2 cm
Inscribed 'Harden', 'Ambleside' '10th Sept 1818' (or '1819')
Gift of Peter Bicknell, 1981

John Harden made over a thousand drawings and watercolours, from the 1790s until the year of his death, simply for his own pleasure and that of his family and friends. As a man of independent means he did not have to sell or exhibit his work for a living; he was an amateur in the true sense of the word. Many of his works – perhaps the best known – depict aspects of life at Brathay Hall where he and his family lived, apart from occasional absences, from the summer of 1804 to the early 1830s: he shows domestic interiors with social and household activities such as music-making, board games and card-playing, women reading, writing or sewing. He also made many landscape studies and depictions of rural life that provide a lively and valuable record of the Lake District in the early nineteenth century.

Although nothing is known of Harden's art training in his youth in Ireland, he later numbered many professional painters among his friends, entertaining those who visited the Lakes and joining them on sketching excursions. Farington looked over his sketchbook when they met in Bath in 1801; Constable stayed with him in 1806; Reinagle showed him the art of sketching in oils on prepared paper when he came to Brathay in 1807; and there were numerous other contacts with artists including, on a fairly regular basis, William Green in Ambleside. Through his wife Jessy, a former pupil of Alexander Nasmyth, Harden met Scottish artists ranging from the great portrait painter Sir Henry Raeburn to landscape painters such as H.W. Williams. In Dublin, Edinburgh and London he visited exhibitions of modern art and collections of Old Master paintings and his own drawings of Brathay shows its walls copiously hung with framed watercolours and paintings. Few contemporary references to Harden's own drawings survive but when the painter George Arnald remarked in 1808 that Harden 'draws & tints from nature as well as anybody', Farington did not dissent (IX.3491, 3276).

Like many artists, both professional and amateur, Harden drew in a variety of media, often using pen and ink, watercolour washes and white bodycolour as in this view of Ambleside. His subject was the group of buildings collectively known as How Head, situated high up in the oldest part of the little town. How Head today includes the earliest lived-in dwellings in Ambleside, parts of the ensemble dating back to the sixteenth century. Just to the right of Harden's scene lay St Anne's church where he and his wife were to be buried in 1847 and 1837 respectively. (This served the part of Ambleside 'above Stock', a stone building replacing a timber structure in 1812; the present parish church of St Mary's, on lower land near the river Rothay, was not begun until 1850.) Harden's viewpoint must have been an upstairs window in one of the houses to the rear of How Head; he shows part of its rear elevation with the lane outside its garden wall being used for the splitting of timber into planks – presumably for immediate use in a nearby house. To the left is seen the first of the cottages lining the steep incline of Fairview Road. The time of day is late afternoon so the woman in the foreground, bearing a heavy pail, casts a long shadow, as do also the wooden poles forming the enclosure near the centre. Harden emphasises the contrasts of light and shade in his scene with a masterly command of his media: he presents the shaded areas, such as How Head itself, as severely monotonous and devoid of detail while he subtly differentiates the whiteness of everything in the scene that catches the light – the clouds, a woman's dress or bonnet, the trunks of the trees, the men's shirts.

Harden is unlikely to have signed this work simply with his surname, so it is probable that this sheet has been trimmed on the left, removing the word 'John' or 'J'. In the lower right-hand corner the final digit is hard to read but possible years for the drawing are 1818 and 1819. CFP

77

WILLIAM WESTALL ARA (1781–1850)
Skiddaw
1820
Aquatint, 25.5 × 33 cm
Engraved inscriptions: below, with title and name of artist-engraver

By 1819 the topographical artist William Westall had depicted a wide range of scenery, from Australian and Oriental sights derived from his travels of 1801–5 to landscape and architectural subjects from many parts of Britain. He had also developed a great love of the Lake District, paying regular visits to Keswick, and enjoyed the friendship of Robert Southey. His first aquatints of the Lakes, after his own drawings, concentrated on Derwentwater and its neighbourhood, presenting the area in a dozen highly varied scenes of great beauty as well as technical mastery (see figs 5 and 8 on pp. 12 and 18 above). These were published in groups of four at six-monthly intervals beginning in July 1819. It was originally envisaged that he should proceed to make further depictions of other lakes in Cumberland and Westmorland but the project was abandoned after the first group of four Windermere subjects appeared in the spring of 1821; thus the proposed *Views of the Lakes* developed

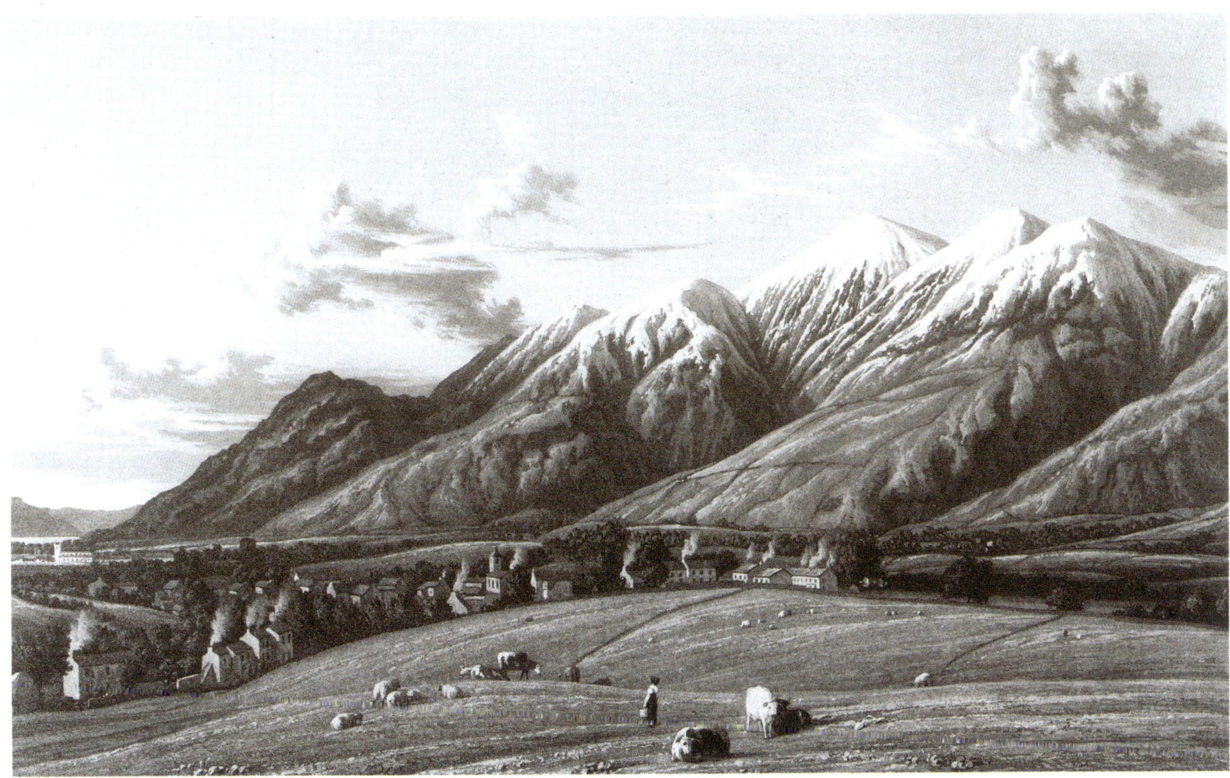

Cat. 77

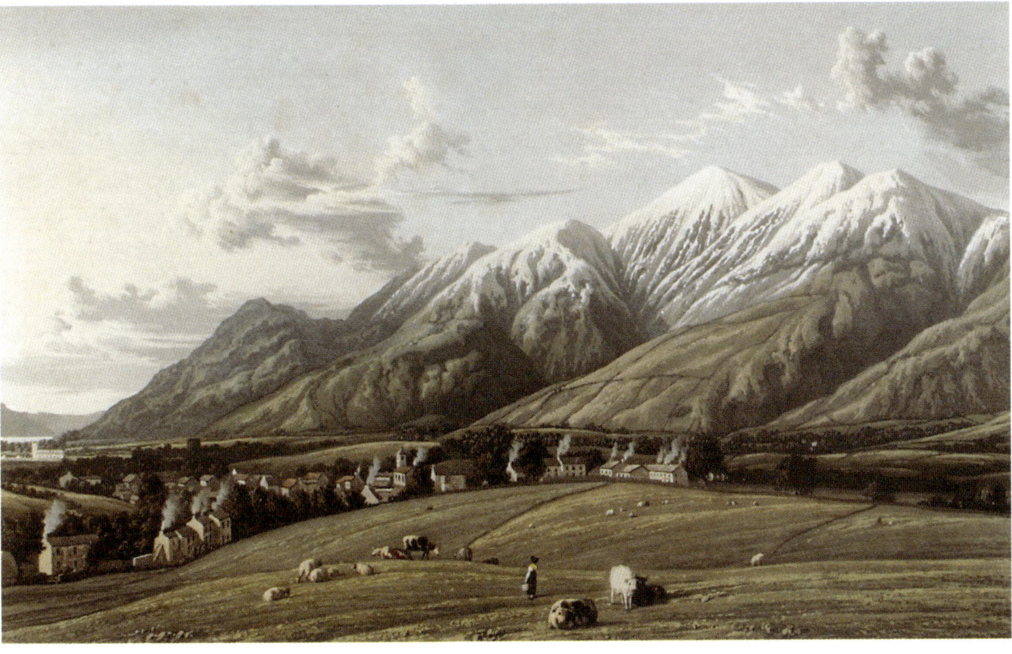

Fig. 40 William Westall, *Skiddaw*, aquatint, 1820 (The Wordsworth Trust).

no further than *Views of the Lake and of the Vale of Keswick*. These were available in both uncoloured and coloured versions (fig. 40).

Westall's scenes were accompanied by a brief descriptive account of Derwentwater which was provided, free of charge, by Southey and was intended (as Sara Hutchinson put it in a letter to John Monkhouse on 15 October 1820) to be useful '& not like Wm's Preface to Wilkinson's the only part of the Publication worth any thing.' Both Wordsworth and Southey used the word 'faithful' to describe Westall's depictions of the Lakes, regarding them essentially as portraits rather than anything more profound. Sara Hutchinson was more forthcoming – in her letters to the artist – describing some of the scenes as 'exquisite' and 'above praise'. The final aquatint in the Derwentwater sequence, *Skiddaw*, embodies all these qualities. While the foreground, with Crosthwaite church and the meadows around Keswick, is presented simply and unpretentiously, the snow-capped peaks of Skiddaw are distinguished not only by their majesty but also by the originality of the artist's vision. Apart from Westall, few painters of his day chose to visit the Lake District in the winter months and depictions of the fells covered with snow are thus rare. His presentation of a recent snowfall on the mighty peaks of Skiddaw, with its icy claws reaching deep into the crevices and crannies of the slopes below and a limpid sky with trailing clouds above, is unlike anything in previous British art. Its closest parallels are to be found in Oriental painting. Just as the experience of the Alps had enriched the work of earlier artists in the Lakes such as Towne and 'Warwick' Smith, so too did Westall's experiences on the other side of the world. CFP

78

JOSEPH WILKINSON (1764–1831)
Select Views in Cumberland, Westmoreland, and Lancashire
London: 1810
Purchased from the estate of Margaret Goalby, with the support of the Friends of the National Libraries, Arco British Ltd, the Binks Trust, and the Roger and Sarah Bancroft Charitable Trust, 1996

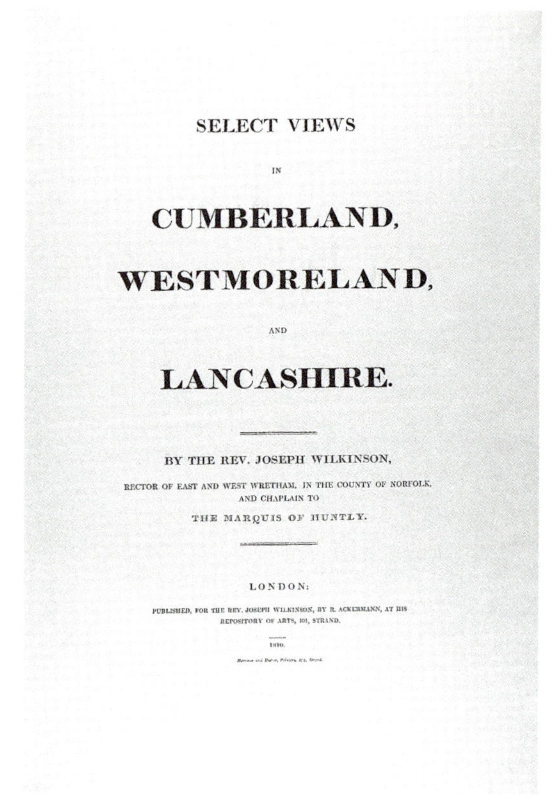
SELECT VIEWS
IN
CUMBERLAND,
WESTMORELAND,
AND
LANCASHIRE.

BY THE REV. JOSEPH WILKINSON,
RECTOR OF EAST AND WEST WRETHAM, IN THE COUNTY OF NORFOLK, AND CHAPLAIN TO
THE MARQUIS OF HUNTLY.

LONDON:
PUBLISHED, FOR THE REV. JOSEPH WILKINSON, BY R. ACKERMANN, AT HIS REPOSITORY OF ARTS, 101, STRAND.

1810.

Cat. 78

Joseph Wilkinson was married to the niece of William Brownrigg, who had supplied the explanatory notes for John Dalton's *Descriptive Poem* in 1755. He and his wife looked after Brownrigg at Ormathwaite, near Keswick. In 1804 Wilkinson left the Lake District to work as a clergyman in Norfolk, but he remained attached to its landscape, as evinced by this large-scale publication. It was issued monthly by Ackermann's Repository in twelve sets of four plates each. Priced at half a guinea a set, it was expensive, and not widely circulated. And of its few purchasers, fewer still would have known that the long, anonymous introduction, a prose description of the Lake District, was by William Wordsworth.

One subscriber, Sir George Beaumont, was a friend of the poet, and knew that he was the author. 'I am very happy that you have read the Introduction with so much pleasure', Wordsworth wrote to Lady Beaumont from Grasmere on 10 May 1810, 'and must thank you for your kindness in telling me of it.' He himself thought parts of it 'well-done', but unfortunately his opinion of Wilkinson's views was not high. 'The drawings, or Etchings, or whatever water similar to that which Carver so beautifully describes when he was floating alone in the middle of the lake Erie or Ontario, and could almost have imagined that his boat was suspended in an element as pure as air, or rather that the air and water were one.

As to the shores, it will be understood that those of the lakes in this country are endlessly diversified; in some places mountains, that admit of no cultivation, descend abruptly into the water; in others the shore is formed by gently sloping lawns and rich woods, with the interposition of flat and fertile meadows between the margin of the lake and the mountains; in many places they are beautifully edged with a rim of blue gravel; here and there are found, bordering the lake, groves (if I may so call them) of reeds and bulrushes, or water-lilies lifting up the orb of their large leaves to the breeze, if it be stirring, while the white flower is heaving upon the wave.

The Islands are neither so numerous, nor so beautiful, as might be expected from the account which I have given of the manner in which the level areas of the vales are so frequently diversified by rocks, hills, and hillocks, scattered over them: nor are they ornamented, as are sometimes the islands of the lakes in Scotland, by the remains of castles or other places of defence, or of monastic edifices. There is however a beautiful cluster of islands at Winandermere; a pair of pleasingly contrasted at Rydale; nor must the solitary green Island of Grasmere be forgotten. In the bosom of each of the lakes of Ennerdale and Devock-water is a single rock which owing to its neighbourhood to the sea, is

Fig. 41 Wordsworth's pencilled revisions to the introduction to *Select Views* (cat. 78).

they may be called, are, I know, such as to you and Sir George must be intolerable' he told Lady Beaumont. 'You will receive from them that sort of disgust which I do from bad Poetry'. He assumed that Sir George Beaumont had subscribed to it as a favour to himself: 'and Wilkinson', he tells Lady Beaumont, 'though not superabundant in good sense, told me that he saw it in that light.'

Cat. 78 is a presentation copy inscribed by Joseph Wilkinson on the front end-paper: 'William Wordsworth Esquire: from his faithful and obliged friend Joseph Wilkinson'. It contains Wordsworth's pencilled revisions to the text, which was republished in 1820 (see cat. 79) and which would eventually form the principal part of his *Guide to the Lakes*. SH

79

WILLIAM WORDSWORTH (1770–1850)
The River Duddon, a Series of Sonnets: Vaudracour and Julia: and other Poems. To which is annexed, A topographical description of the country of the lakes
London: 1820
Gift of William Knight, 1898

The introduction Wordsworth wrote for Wilkinson's *Select Views* first appeared under his name in 1820, as part of this volume, *The River Duddon, A Series of Sonnets*. 'This Essay,' ran the explanatory advertisement, 'which was first published several years ago as an Introduction to some Views of the Lakes, by the Rev. Joseph Wilkinson, (an expensive work, and necessarily of limited circulation,) is now, with emendations and additions, attached to these volumes; from a consciousness of its having been written in the same spirit which dictated several of the poems, and from a belief that it will tend materially to illustrate them.'

The River Duddon was Wordsworth's most popular publication to date, and although the 'topographical description' was described as an 'annex' it made up around a third of the volume. Two years later it was published separately as *A Description of the Lakes in the North of England*, with a fold-out map and an added section at the end entitled 'Directions and Information to the Tourist'. The first edition of five hundred copies quickly sold out, and a second edition, of 1,000 copies, was printed with some revisions the following year. A third edition was published in 1835 with the title *A Guide Through the District of the Lakes in the North of England, with a Description of the Scenery, etc. For the Use of Tourists and Residents*. For this edition, the 'Directions and Information for the Tourist' was moved to the front of the book, and an itinerary was given at the back, 'for the use of tourists'. In 1842, *A Complete Guide to the Lakes, Comprising Minute Directions for the Tourist* was printed in Kendal and published both there and in London, complete with engravings of Windermere, Derwentwater, Rydal and Ullswater. Added to *Mr Wordsworth's Description of the Country, etc.* were *Three Letters on the Geology of the Lake District, by the Rev. Professor Sedgwick*. This version, the last to be prepared in Wordsworth's lifetime, went through five editions in seventeen years. SH

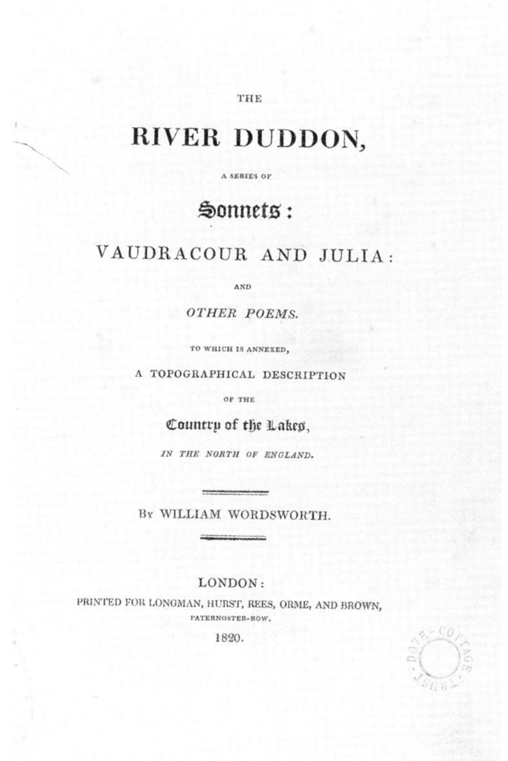

THE

RIVER DUDDON,

A SERIES OF

Sonnets:

VAUDRACOUR AND JULIA:

AND

OTHER POEMS.

TO WHICH IS ANNEXED,

A TOPOGRAPHICAL DESCRIPTION

OF THE

Country of the Lakes,

IN THE NORTH OF ENGLAND.

By WILLIAM WORDSWORTH.

LONDON:

PRINTED FOR LONGMAN, HURST, REES, ORME, AND BROWN,

PATERNOSTER-ROW.

1820.

Cat. 79

THE ARTISTS AND THE LAKES

Cecilia Powell

Note: Small Capitals signify other entries in this section of the catalogue.

John White Abbott (1763–1851)

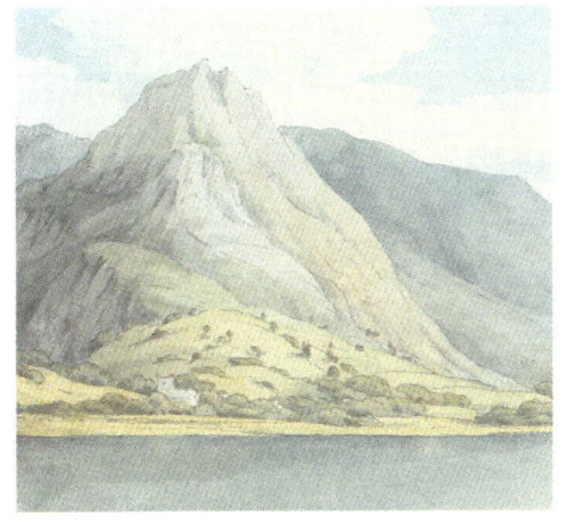

A practising surgeon and apothecary in Exeter for some twenty years, Abbott initially pursued art in his spare time, receiving tuition in watercolour as a young man from Francis Towne and exhibiting oil paintings regularly from 1793 to 1805 at the Royal Academy as an 'Honorary' exhibitor (i.e. non-professional artist). His uncle James White, an eminent Exeter barrister and non-conformist, was a close friend of Towne's and one of his companions on his Lake District tour of 1786, so it is perhaps not surprising that Abbott's only known extensive tour outside Devon was to Scotland and the Lake District. A series of eighty dated drawings, covering six weeks from 13 June (York Minster) to 28 July (Glastonbury Abbey), shows that he was in the Lakes during the second week of July 1791. He approached from the direction of Carlisle (7 July), spent two days around Ullswater, and was at Rydal on 10 July. After a couple of days in Grasmere (cat. 32) and Windermere (12 July), he sketched in Borrowdale on 13 July before turning southwards; he had reached Liverpool by 17 July.

Abbott's early exhibits at the RA received acclaim. In 1803 Towne praised his study of nature but thought he was insufficiently acquainted with works of art (Farington VI.2056) while others disliked his handling of aerial perspective and thought him self-satisfied (X.3795, 3806). By the 1810s many felt that, through remaining in Exeter and not being exposed to broader influences and outside criticism, he had failed to achieve his potential. On inheriting his uncle's property and fortune in 1825 Abbott was able to retire from his profession and devote himself exclusively to painting but he did not exhibit at the RA after 1822.

George Barret RA (1732?–84)

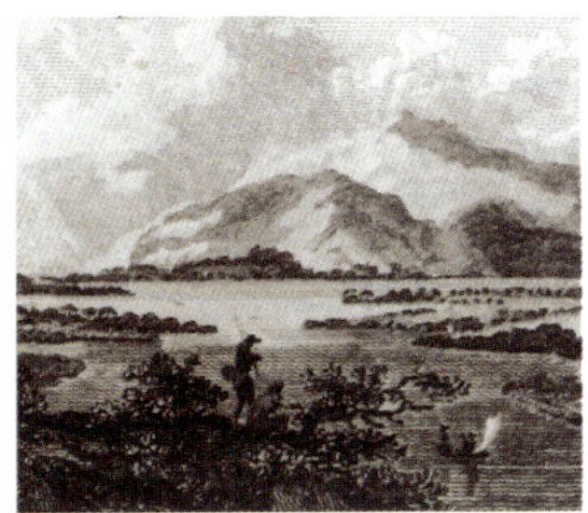

George Barret was one of the most successful and well-regarded landscape painters of his day though he was notoriously profligate and irresponsible in financial matters. He moved from his native city, Dublin, to London in 1763 and five years later became a foundation member of the Royal Academy. Throughout his career he excelled at depicting the scenery of the mountainous parts of Britain, beginning with Ireland where he had come under the influence of Edmund Burke and his *Philosophical Enquiry into the Origin of our Ideas of the Sublime and Beautiful* (1757).

Barret probably discovered the Lake District in the 1760s through his friendship with another Academician, Sawrey Gilpin, a member of a Cumberland family with whom he often collaborated and the brother of William Gilpin. He exhibited three Lakes scenes at the Academy: 1770, no. 9: *A study from Nature on the lake at Ullswater, in Cumberland* (which may correspond to cat. 26);

1772, no. 11: *A study from nature, in the mountains of Keswick, Cumberland*; 1781, no. 40: *View of Winandermere lake in Westmoreland, – the effect the sun beginning to appear in the morning, with the mists breaking and dispersing*. The title of the last work is in itself remarkable, looking forward to the long descriptive titles used by J.M.W TURNER over a decade later. However, Barret's most important work inspired by the area was not created until nearly the end of his life and occupied him for some three years; this was his decorative scheme for the Surrey home of his patron William Lock (fig. 2 on p. 6). Here (with the aid of three artists including Sawrey Gilpin) he created a continuous vision of mountains and lakes, trees, rocks and cascades that prefigured the panoramas of the early nineteenth century.

George Barret is often referred to as 'the elder' since his son George Barret 'the younger' (1767–1842) also became an artist; he is represented in the Wordsworth Trust's collection by a colourful large watercolour of Grasmere and two monochrome sketches.

SIR GEORGE BEAUMONT (1753–1827)

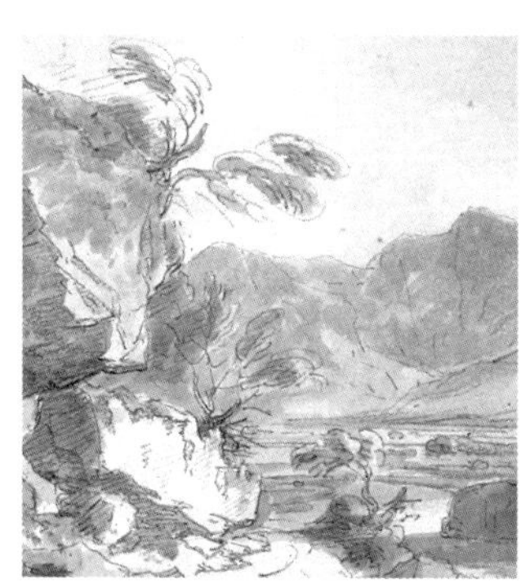

The distinguished patron and collector Sir George Beaumont had a deep love of the Lake District and visited many times following his first encounter with it in the summer of 1777. His companions that year (see cat. 15–16) were the artists THOMAS HEARNE and JOSEPH FARINGTON whom he had known since 1771 and 1773 respectively and who – together with his drawing-master at Eton Alexander Cozens, his private tutor the Rev. Charles Davy, the engraver William Woollett, and the Oxford drawing-master John Baptist Malchair – had laid the foundations for his lifelong passion for art, in particular the art of landscape. In 1778 he brought his wife Margaret to the Lodore Inn during their two-month honeymoon and the couple repeatedly returned to the Lakes, deriving great enjoyment from scenery and friendships alike (Wordsworth was to receive much generosity from the Beaumonts and he, Southey and Mrs Coleridge were all legatees on Sir George's death as was Coleridge on the death of Lady Beaumont). The Beaumonts returned in 1779, 1780 (renting Old Brathay, then known as Low Brathay, near Brathay Hall) and 1781. In 1786 they borrowed Holker Hall from Lord George Cavendish and in 1798 (the year Beaumont drew cat. 46) they spent nearly two months near Keswick after a stay at Holker, which had now passed to Lord Frederick Cavendish. Their numerous later summers in the Lakes included a return to Brathay (1799) and periods of residence at or near Greta Hall (1803, 1807, 1815, 1816, 1818) as well as several visits to Lowther Castle (1803, 1815, 1826) and to the Wordsworths at Rydal Mount (1815, 1817, 1818).

Beaumont made numerous on-the-spot sketches of the Lake District. Several of these were developed by THOMAS GIRTIN (cat. 47), about thirty of whose drawings Beaumont ultimately owned. He also depicted the area in oils, most famously perhaps in his *Peele Castle in a Storm* of 1806 (Wordsworth Trust), which the poet found deeply moving after the death at sea in 1805 of his brother John. In 1779 Beaumont exhibited *A view of Keswick, in Cumberland* at the Royal Academy as an 'Honorary' exhibitor (no. 373); this was so severely criticised that he did not exhibit there again for another fifteen years.

Ferdinand Becker (fl. 1780–1825)

There has long been uncertainty over the identity of Becker. When Farington was staying in Bath at the beginning of 1801 he called on a 'Mr Becker' who had been born in Cologne and was now working there as a drawing-master. Although the artist was not at home, he saw many specimens of his work ('much company there to see the drawings') and noted that he charged half a guinea a lesson (IV.1481, 1484). There can be no doubt that this was Ferdinand Becker who practised in Bath as a drawing-master for some thirty years, using the 'blot technique' advocated by Alexander Cozens, and died there in 1825. He is known to have lived at various addresses in the city, the list of artists in *The Original Bath Guide* published in 1811 including 'Becker, landscape painter and drawing master, Gay-street' (p. 136). He may have visited the Lakes on more than one occasion but he was certainly there in the mid 1790s, exhibiting Cumberland subjects at his own premises at Bath in 1796. Ferdinand Becker may also be identified with the artist (apparently mis-listed as 'E. Becker' rather than 'F. Becker') who exhibited two works in London in 1810, at the British Institution, giving his address as '13 Gay Street, Bath'. These works were *Applethwaite, on the Foot of Skiddaw* and *The Storm; a View of Scale,with* [*sic*; i.e. Skelwith] *Bridge Vale* (nos 302, 307).

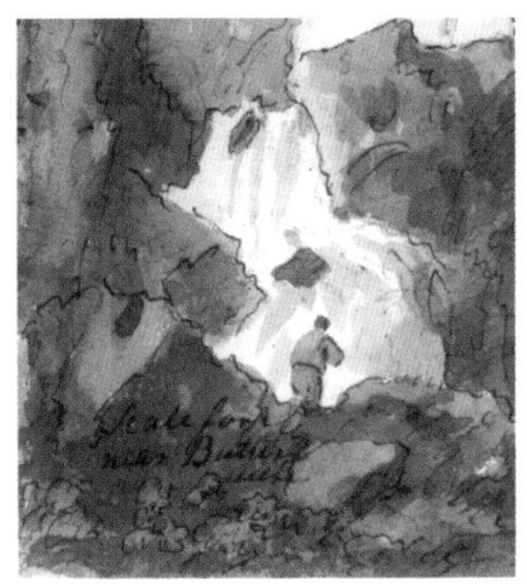

It has long been understood that an artist named 'Edmund Becker' worked in Rome in the late 1770s with Richard Cooper the younger (1740–after 1817), producing high quality monochrome drawings of ancient buildings. This artist later made several sketching tours in different parts of the British Isles including the Lake District (see cat. 37–8) and a tour of Snowdonia in 1808 that resulted in a large number of monochrome drawings (some of which are in the National Library of Wales, Aberystwyth). The main stylistic development in his work is that of increasing fluidity, the careful early Italian works evolving into the much freer Welsh and English scenes of nearly thirty years later.

Ever since Algernon Graves lumped together works by two different Beckers in his 1901 dictionary of artists who exhibited in London between 1760 and 1893, there has been confusion. (Alongside the above-mentioned 'E. Becker' works at the BI he listed those of ' – Becker, Esq', an 'Honorary' exhibitor (i.e. amateur artist) at the Royal Academy in 1793: nos 643 and 664: *A landscape in crayons, morning composition* and *A landscape in crayons, evening composition*.) In 1952 Iolo Williams was unsure whether there was a connection between 'E. Becker', described as 'a very vague figure … a minor professional' who worked from *c.*1780 onwards, and Ferdinand Becker of Bath. H.L. Mallalieu, writing in 1976, declared firmly that 'Edmund Becker' should not be confused with Ferdinand. However, the present writer believes that there was only one professional Becker at work in England during this period, namely Ferdinand, and that probably, somewhere along the way, the letters forming the signature 'Ferdinand' were misread or mistranscribed as 'Edmund'. Hence the ascription of cat. 37–8 to Ferdinand Becker.

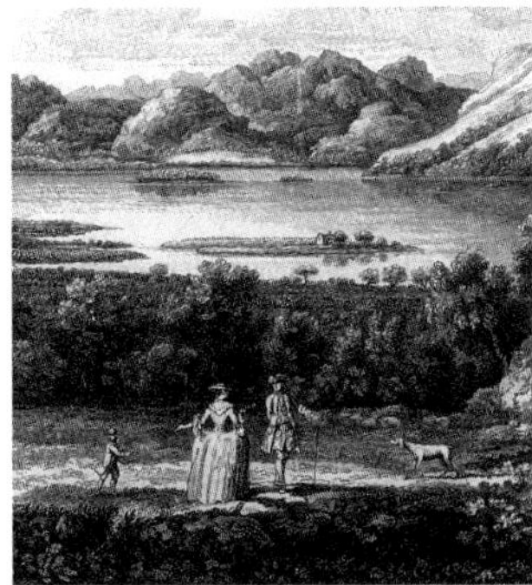

William Bellers (fl. 1734–73)

A drawing-master, print-dealer and landscape painter, Bellers was licensed to practise as an 'illuminator' within the University of Oxford in 1734; he also taught drawing and dealt in prints in both Oxford and Cambridge in the 1730s and by 1751 he was involved in garden design in Essex. He evidently visited the Lake District around this time since the engraving of one of his paintings, *A View of Derwent-Water, Towards Borrodale,* was completed by the autumn of 1752 (cat. 3). This was soon followed by five other Lakes views and a further visit may have taken place in 1758. All the prints were on display by the spring of 1754 at his house in Poppins Court, off Fleet Street. In 1763 he was listed in *The Universal Director; or the Nobleman and Gentleman's True Guide to the Masters and Professors of the Liberal and Polite Arts* as 'a very considerable Dealer in capital Prints and Drawings', with the additional comment that, 'His "Views of Lakes in the North of England" are much admired.'

Bellers exhibited regularly at the annual exhibitions of the Free Society of Artists (one of the precursors of the Royal Academy) between 1761 and 1773; these works included numerous Lake District scenes quite distinct from those that he published as engravings. The engravings themselves were also shown at the exhibition of the Free Society in 1761. He ceased exhibiting (and perhaps died) in 1773 and the following year his Lake District engravings were republished by the most important print-publisher of the day, John Boydell, and Robert Sayer (cat. 4).

James Bourne (1773–1854)

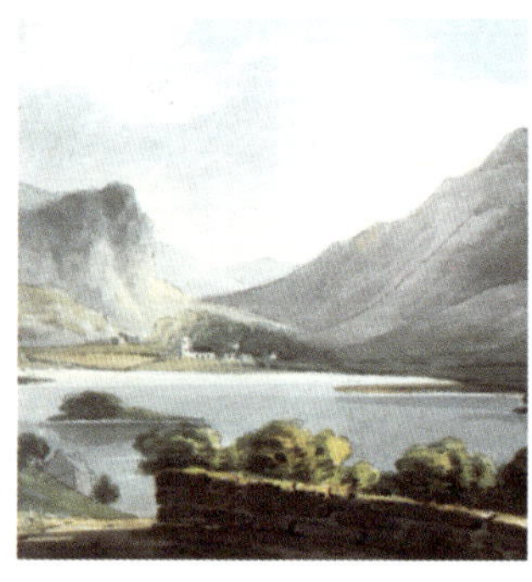

James Bourne was born in Dalby, Lincolnshire, the younger son of a country gentleman. He was educated in Louth, lived in Manchester for a time and settled in London in the late 1790s. While still in his teens he became an ardent Methodist and it was through prayer that he discovered his vocation as a draughtsman. Largely self-taught, he soon became extremely proficient. Around 1800–2 he contributed views of Dalby, Louth and other places in Lincolnshire for engraving in the *Copper-Plate Magazine*. He was introduced to the Countess of Sutherland (a talented amateur artist) and Lord Spencer and became a successful drawing-master, spending his summers with aristocratic families in the country as a kind of 'artist in residence'. He is often described as 'the Rev. James Bourne' but (unlike other early Methodists) he was not an ordained clergyman in the Church of England; his status was that of a professional artist and he supported himself and a large family by drawing. In 1838 he apparently abandoned painting for religious activities and at the end of his life was the Methodist minister at Sutton Coldfield in Warwickshire.

Bourne visited the Lake District in 1798 (the tour traced in his privately published but undated *Interesting Views of the Lakes of Cumberland, Westmoreland, and Lancashire* describes Pocklington as the 'late proprietor' of Pocklington's Island, sold in 1797, and makes no mention of any 'improvements' to the Bowder Stone and its environs, acquired by Pocklington in 1798) and he exhibited *View in the village of Coniston* at the RA in 1800 (no. 503). The sketches made on his tour enabled Bourne – or someone very closely associated with him – to make the charming small topographical watercolours that were inserted into his *Interesting Views* (see cat. 49). Bourne's later tours included ones to the West Country in 1799 and Lincolnshire in 1803 and, although he showed a dozen English and Welsh views at the RA between 1805 and 1809, none of these depicted the Lakes.

Thomas Chubbard (1738–1809)

The portrait and landscape painter Thomas Chubbard was one of the foremost Liverpool artists of his age, exhibiting initially in London in the 1760s and 1770s (with two groups that predated the foundation of the Royal Academy in 1768: the Society of Artists and the Free Society of Artists) and later in Liverpool itself. In 1769–70 he was involved in the short-lived attempt to establish a Liverpool academy in emulation of that in London. When this movement was revived in 1773–5 he was again among its active members, making a major contribution to its exhibition of 1774 (his fifteen exhibits included three views on Derwentwater); his pupils were also involved in this venture. The pattern was repeated in the 1780s when he participated in the two exhibitions of a third ephemeral body, the Society for Promoting Painting and Design in Liverpool (1784 and 1787). He appears in Liverpool directories as a 'painter' or 'portrait-painter' and at various addresses during his career. It seems likely that he made his livelihood from portraiture but his true interest lay in landscape; he also painted subject-pictures that were influenced by those of Joseph Wright of Derby who spent over two years in Liverpool in 1768–71. The Walker Art Gallery holds two small landscapes in oils by Chubbard (one of which, *Bridge over Rapids by a Mill in Mountainous Landscape* (8623), bears a distinct resemblance to Pelter Bridge at Rydal) but its holding of his miniatures was destroyed by bombing in the Second World War.

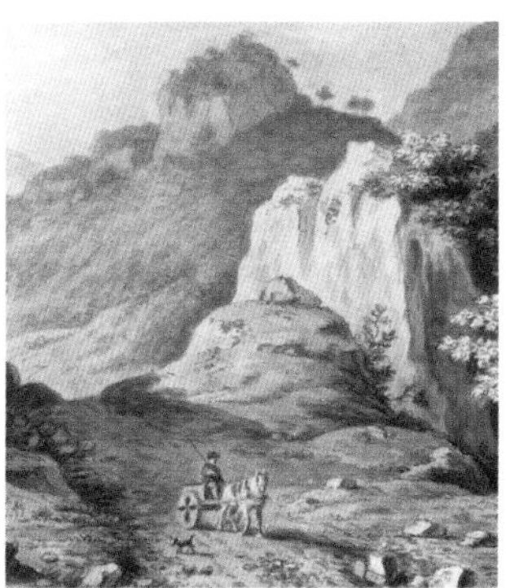

Chubbard died at his house in King Street on 30 May 1809 and was buried in St George's church. His younger brother Samuel (d. 1807), listed in directories as the proprietor of a 'Carver, Gilder and Oval Turner's Shop' and a 'Cabinet and Looking Glass Warehouse', has sometimes been associated with the development of aquatint. Modern scholars, however, believe that these experiments were actually made by Thomas, working in the early 1770s with Peter Perez Burdett, engraver, cartographer and close associate of Wright; Thomas's interest in scientific matters is mentioned in his obituary in the *Liverpool Courier* (7 June 1809).

Chubbard's small depictions of the Lakes (cat. 43–4) were made for the Liverpool collector Daniel Daulby (1745/6–98), their association of some thirty years culminating in the exceptionally interesting albums owned by the Wordsworth Trust. Daulby came from a well-known family of Liverpool brewers and, some years after his first wife Elizabeth Knowles died in childbirth in 1775, he married Margaret, the sister of another eminent Liverpudlian, the historian William Roscoe (1753–1831); she bore him seven children. Daulby's fortune from brewing enabled him to take a wide-ranging interest in the arts, forming a major collection of paintings, drawings, prints and books on art that eventually ran to some 6,000 items (he catalogued these in 1793). His particular penchant for Rembrandt led to him publishing *A Descriptive Catalogue of the Works of Rembrandt* (the most comprehensive listing at that time and the first in English) in 1796. He formed a close relationship with Wright during his stay in Liverpool and acquired several of his works, sometimes at special prices thanks to their friendship. He also bought from Henry Fuseli and in 1777 wrote to Sir Joshua Reynolds about having his portrait painted (a plan that, sadly, came to nothing, though Reynolds' reply (Ingamells, 2000, pp. 69–70) provides valuable evidence of his practice). Daulby was himself an amateur artist, contributing (alongside numerous professional artists, including Chubbard) to *The Seats of the Nobility and Gentry* engraved and published by William Watts (1779–86). He promoted the successive attempts to found an academy of art in Liverpool between 1769 and 1787, mentioned above, and exhibited with each society in turn as an amateur. Daulby visited exhibitions and artists' studios in London and was known to FARINGTON by 1793 when the latter started his diary. In 1792 his young son John made an ink and wash copy of Farington's *Nunnery near Kirk Oswald* (British Museum 1972.U.773) after a similar print published in 1789. Daulby certainly subscribed to Farington's engraved *History of the River Thames* in 1794 (I.248) and to HEARNE's *Antiquities of Great Britain*. In 1795 Farington lent him some of his own drawings for his son to copy (II.341, 346) and also seems to have been involved in some of Daulby's purchases of Old Masters.

In December 1783 Daulby took a three-year lease on Rydal Mount and became a regular visitor to the area with his growing family. He retired there in 1796 to alleviate his gout in a healthier environment than Liverpool, though his motives were sometimes misunderstood: in October 1796 Farington, on a visit to Manchester, learned that 'Mr. Daulby proposes to dispose of some of his pictures and is supposed to be gone to Ambleside for oeconomy' (III.682); 'Mr. Daulby sells his pictures but keeps his drawings & prints an Auctioneer at Liverpool, Vernon, has the disposal of the pictures' (III.683). Daulby died in March 1798 and was buried at St Thomas's church, Liverpool. On 28 October Farington recorded that Daulby's pictures had been sold in Liverpool, realising 'upwards of £1000' which was £300 more than He gave for them' (III.1077); the sale had taken place on 27 August. The works by Rembrandt and his followers were sold separately in 1799, fetching £610.

JOHN CONSTABLE RA (1776–1837)

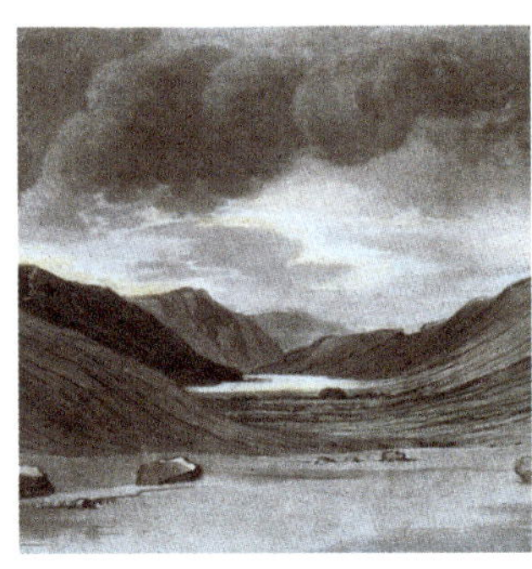

Now recognised as one of the most important figures in the history of British landscape painting, Constable had a long struggle to achieve success, first against his family's opposition to his becoming a painter and then against conservative elements in the London art world. It was only in 1829, at the age of 52, that he was elected an RA, though his exhibits at the Paris Salon of 1824 (including *Landscape: Noon*, now better known as *The Hay-Wain*) had attracted the attention of forward-looking painters such as Delacroix as well as that of French dealers. He worked out of doors in both watercolour and oils, seeking to capture the transitory effects of light and weather, and strove to maintain this feeling of naturalism and immediacy even in his six-foot canvases.

Constable's favourite subjects were the familiar views of his childhood in the Stour valley in Suffolk and he rarely made visits outside southern England. His only trip to the Lake District, in September–October 1806, lasted seven weeks and inspired nearly a hundred drawings and watercolours made on the spot and about a dozen paintings created in his studio in London; several of the latter were exhibited at the Royal Academy and British Institution in 1807–9. The visit was suggested (and financed) by Constable's wealthy maternal uncle, the former wine merchant and lifelong philanthropist David Pike Watts (1754–1816), who had recently occupied Storrs Hall on the east side of Lake Windermere; it would certainly have been encouraged by the artist's other mentors, FARINGTON and BEAUMONT, the latter encouraging him to study the works of GIRTIN for their 'great breadth and truth'. Though some details of the tour remain obscure, the broad essentials of its course may be traced through the artist's own dated sketches (such as cat. 55) and the journals of Jessy, the wife of JOHN HARDEN, who provided hospitality to Constable for two periods during his tour; it has been the focus of a Wordsworth Trust exhibition (see Hebron, Shields and Wilcox, 2006).

For much of the time Constable was accompanied by a Kendal resident, George Gardner, the barrister son of an old friend in London who had been a native of the town: the fashionable portrait painter in pastels Daniel Gardner (1750–1805). Constable approached the Lake District via Manchester (a tiny dated drawing in the Whitworth Art Gallery was made on 27 August) and his first subject was Kendal Castle (drawn on 1 September). The pair stayed briefly with one of Watts' former neighbours at Storrs, Richard Worgan, before moving, on about 8 September, to Brathay Hall where they remained with the Hardens for about a week; here Constable met Charles Lloyd of Old Brathay and, through him, Wordsworth. Although Harden and Constable went out sketching together twice, they were often kept indoors by poor weather; this led to Constable painting portraits of both his hosts; that of Jessy occupied him for five hours on a rainy Sunday, 14 September, and was finished the next day. On about 16 September the two travelling companions headed north to Keswick and thence to Borrowdale where Constable remained, sketching energetically, for around three weeks (about half of his entire visit); Gardner, bored with his role of onlooker, returned to the Hardens after ten days. Constable spent a further short period at Brathay arriving on Wednesday 15 October (another wet day, so he began a portrait of John); his last dated drawing (of Langdale) bears the date of 19 October. His return journey to London in November included a visit to Lloyd's relations in Birmingham, where he drew portraits of several members of the family including Charles's sister Priscilla who had married Wordsworth's brother Christopher in 1804.

Very few of the oil paintings of the Lakes recorded as exhibited by Constable have been traced. His *View in Westmoreland* (RA 1807, no. 52; whereabouts unknown) attracted the artist's earliest known press notice (*St James's Chronicle*, 7–9 May); a work in the National Gallery of Victoria, Melbourne, was once thought to be another of Constable's 1807 exhibits but this idea and its attribution to the artist are now regarded as dubious; in April 1809 Farington advised Constable against sending a now-unidentified five-foot Borrowdale scene to the RA, as being too sketch-like and 'wanting variety of colour & effect' (IX.3431-2).

JOSHUA CRISTALL (1768–1847)

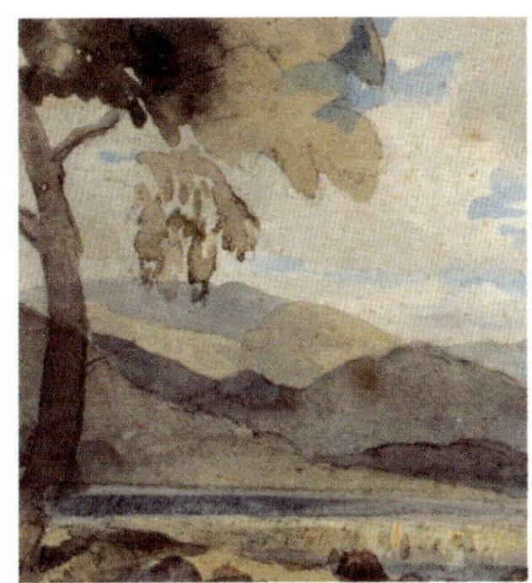

Cristall was baptised in St Botolph's, Aldgate, in the City of London on 22 April 1768. His father, a Scottish mariner, discouraged his passion for art and apprenticed him to a dealer in china and glass, so it was not until November 1792, after a period working as a travelling salesman for the Caughley porcelain factory near Ironbridge, that Joshua entered the Royal Academy Schools as a part-time student engraver. Throughout his life he struggled to make a living from his art (as his father had predicted); the risks and demands of an artistic career had also been emphasised by Mary Wollstonecraft, a friend of his sister Ann (see Todd, 2003, letters 87 and 98, both probably written in 1790). However, he received encouragement from many sources including the collector Dr Thomas Monro and artists such as John and Cornelius Varley whom he met on a tour of Wales in 1802. The following year he joined the Sketching Society, a group of young artists who met every week for drawing practice and discussion. Cristall was one of the first members of the Society of Painters in Water Colours, contributing regularly to its exhibitions from 1805 until his death with only one exception (1832) and serving three times as president (1816, 1819, 1821–31). In about 1822 he moved to Goodrich in Herefordshire for the sake of his health; the first artist of any distinction to settle in the Wye valley, he seems to have been the moving force behind two art exhibitions held at Ross-on-Wye in 1827 and 1828.

For his exhibited work Cristall specialised in figure studies, taking themes from history, literature and contemporary life, but he also had a keen eye for landscape. His only visit to the Lake District, in July 1805, was financially possible thanks to the recent sales of his work at the inaugural exhibition of the SPWC; his choice of destination was doubtless stimulated by the tour of John Glover and Robert Hills, also SPWC members, two years earlier and the success of the former with his Lakes subjects. Cristall's sketches show he was an intrepid traveller. Besides the Wordsworth Trust scenes (cat. 52–3), a sequence of dated sketches (Tate Britain) shows that he made sketches along Gatesgarthdale and reached Wasdale Head; he exhibited views of Rosthwaite at the SPWC in 1813 and 1814 and of Wasdale Head, also at the SPWC, in 1814.

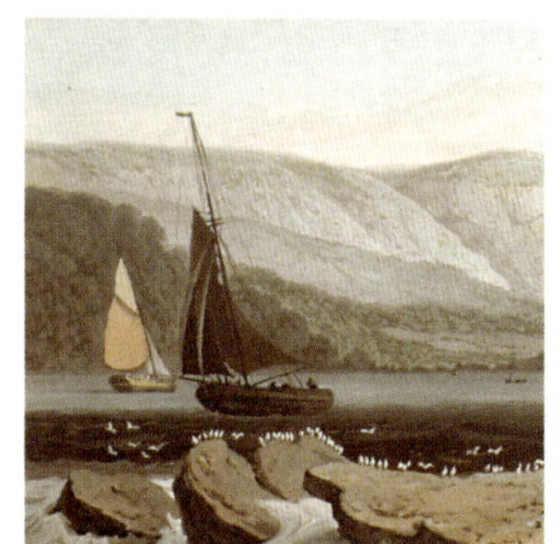

William Daniell RA (1769–1837)

William Daniell began his successful career as a topographical artist by travelling with his uncle, Thomas Daniell RA (1749–1840), and collaborating with him on his celebrated series of aquatints, *Oriental Scenery*, in 1795–1808. Later he achieved distinction in his own right for *A Voyage round Great Britain*, an ambitious project published in eight volumes in 1814-25. Its illustrations (over 300 aquatints, engraved by Daniell himself, based on his own pencil sketches) and its lengthy commentary (begun by Richard Ayton and completed by Daniell) were the fruit of a series of tours round the coast of Britain, travelling clockwise from Land's End, between 1813 and 1823. Their text was far more than a mere description or survey of coastal scenery; it covered an extraordinarily wide variety of topics, raising important issues of national – indeed universal – significance, as is shown in the caption to cat. 73.

Before the voyage of 1814 that took the travellers past the Lancashire, Westmorland and Cumberland subjects of Daniell's aquatints, he had already visited the Lake District at least once. In the summer of 1803 he made an extensive tour of Scotland and the north of England, reporting to Farington on his return that he had been especially pleased by the ride through the Newlands valley from Buttermere to Keswick, Windermere and the head of Coniston Water (VI.2114). He exhibited a work entitled *Windermere* at the British Institution in 1807 while a view of Bassenthwaite bears a date in February 1809. His wife Mary was the half-sister of William Westall.

Edward Dayes (1763–1804)

Edward Dayes, a leading topographical watercolourist, depicted British landscapes and antiquities with great skill and sometimes achieved images of remarkable grandeur (cat. 36) that were to be a formative influence on the young Turner. He was apprenticed to the miniature painter and mezzotint engraver William Pether and also attended the RA Schools. As well as producing watercolours for engraving in books and periodicals, he exhibited regularly at the RA but was never elected to membership.

Dayes visited the Lake District in 1789 if not earlier, exhibiting 'tinted drawings' of Appleby and Patterdale at the Society of Artists in 1790 (nos 59–60). At the RA exhibition of 1791 he exhibited *View on Keswick-lake, Cumberland* (no. 462), following this with another *Keswick Lake* in 1794 (no. 428) and a third in 1801 (no. 18). Two small engravings after Dayes' drawings of the area appeared in the eighteen-volume survey *The Beauties of England and Wales* published alphabetically by county in 1801–15 (and also in other editions): *Furness Abbey, Lancashire* and *Brougham Castle, Westmoreland*.

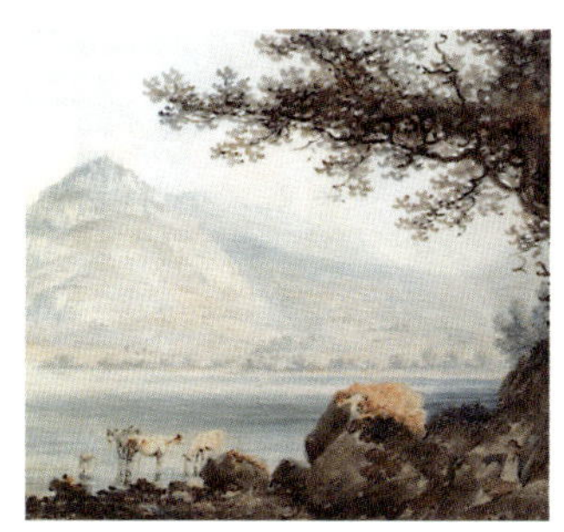

Despite the high quality, grace and charm of his best works, Dayes was frustrated by his lack of professional success in the years after 1800. Increasingly unstable mentally, he became jealous of his most famous and talented pupil, Girtin, and dismissed his drawings as 'slight' and 'the offspring of a strong imagination' in the 'Professional Sketches of Modern Artists' published a year after his suicide in *The Works of the Late Edward Dayes* (1805).

Philip James de Loutherbourg RA (1740–1812)

Philippe-Jacques de Loutherbourg was born in Strasbourg and trained in Paris. Moving to London in 1771, he anglicised his name and proceeded to show his imagination and versatility as an artist in many genres: as a scene designer and painter, working with both David Garrick and Richard Brinsley Sheridan; as the inventor of a small animated stage-set, complete with sound and light effects (the 'Eidophusikon'); and as the painter of historical subjects and contemporary naval battles.

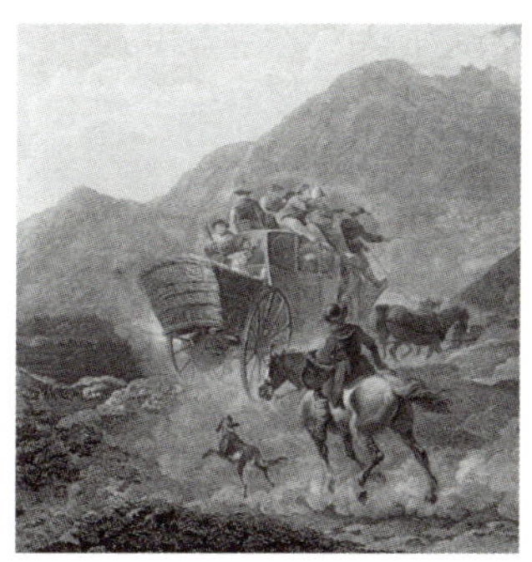

His only known visit to the Lakes took place in the summer of 1783 and stimulated a quick succession of sixteen paintings shown at the RA in 1784–7. Two depicting Windermere (1785, no. 78 and 1786, no. 204) were acquired by John Christian Curwen, and are now in Abbot Hall Art Gallery, Kendal (see fig. 26 on p. 99) while his more unusual subjects included *View of Lowswater in Cumberland* (1784, no. 212), *A slate quarry, near Rydell Water, Cumberland* (1785, no. 171) and *Brick kilns at the entrance of Keswick, with a distant view of Skiddaw and Basselthwaite* (1786, no. 139). His work became widely known through prints such as the two in this exhibition. Some were published as individual large engravings aimed at a wide international audience at a time when engravers avidly sought the right to reproduce recently exhibited works of art (cat. 25); others appeared in volumes of high quality topographical prints published during the wars against France: *Picturesque Scenery of Great Britain*, 1801, and *Romantic and Picturesque Scenery of England and Wales*, 1805 (cat. 50). It has been suggested that De Loutherbourg visited the Lake District in the company of Gainsborough but no evidence to support this has so far emerged. It seems more likely that he set off for Gainsborough's destination in a spirit of friendly competition – and he certainly benefited from the latter's break from the Royal Academy in 1784.

Anthony Devis (1729–1816)

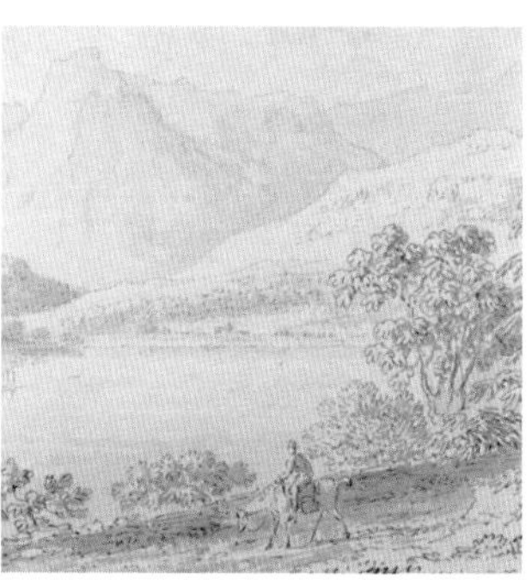

The landscape-painter and drawing-master Anthony Thomas Devis came from Preston in Lancashire and belonged to a family that included several successful artists; his older half-brother Arthur (*c*.1711–87) achieved eminence as a painter of small portraits and informal 'conversation pieces'.

Anthony was working in London by the early 1740s and exhibited there from 1761 onwards; these exhibits were usually entitled simply *A Landscape* (e.g. RA 1781, no. 148) but he is known to have had commissions from patrons with estates in Wales and the south of England. By the end of the 1750s he had begun producing Lake District views, including the oil painting now in Abbot Hall Art Gallery, Kendal, *View of Derwentwater and Skiddaw from Lord's Island*. He probably paid several visits to the Lakes, producing drawings in a lively distinctive style (cat. 10). He lived for a time in Lamb's Conduit Street, London, and in 1780 bought Albury House near Guildford in Surrey, to which he retired. Uncertainty has long surrounded his date of death, but it is clearly inscribed on his tombstone at Albury: 26 April 1816.

Joseph Farington RA (1747–1821)

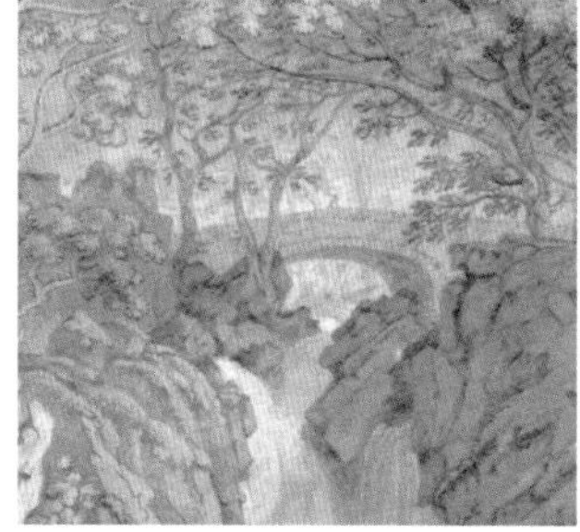

Farington, the son of a clergyman, came from an ancient Lancastrian family and was born at Leigh near Manchester. At the age of sixteen he entered the London studio of the landscape painter Richard Wilson (shortly to be a foundation member of the Royal Academy) and soon showed his talent as a careful draughtsman; in 1769 he became one of the earliest pupils to be accepted at the newly founded RA Schools. In 1775/6 he moved back to the north and devoted much of the next few years to studying and sketching the Lake District, exhibiting *A water-fall*, possibly the canvas on which he is working in cat. 15–16, at the RA in 1778 (no. 105; his address was printed as 'Creswick, Cumberland'). In the spring of 1780 he sent six depictions of the area to the RA, his address now appearing as 'Keswick'; by December of that year he was established in Upper Charlotte Street, London, where he remained until his death, but he continued to produce and exhibit northern scenes and, within a few years, to bring them to a wider public through the medium of engraving. His *Views of the Lakes, &c. in Cumberland and Westmorland* (1789; cat. 27–8) was the first of his several handsome folio volumes of topographical engravings and was highly influential. Many years later, when making drawings for the Cumberland volume of *Britannia Depicta* (the illustrated companion to Daniel and Samuel Lysons' *Magna Britannia*), he conceived the idea of a second volume of engravings after his own drawings that would be dedicated to the area of the lakes as a whole; this appeared in 1816 as *The Lakes of Lancashire, Westmorland, and Cumberland* (cat. 74–5).

Today Farington's fame rests largely on the minutely detailed diary that he kept from July 1793 to the very end of his life in December 1821 (now in the Royal Library at Windsor Castle and comprehensively published in 1978–98). This provides unique insights into the practices, politics and relationships in the art world of his day – chiefly in London (especially within the Royal Academy of which he was elected a full member in 1785) but also further afield; he paid extensive visits to many parts of Britain including the Lakes, Manchester and Liverpool. Farington's numerous friends and acquaintances included many who visited or lived in the Lake District, ranging from Beaumont and Hearne to Daulby and Harden. He received the confidences of Constable, gave advice to Turner, took an interest in Thomas Jameson, made criticisms of John 'Warwick' Smith and recorded the teaching methods of Glover. It was while staying with the Beaumonts in North Wales in 1800 that Farington produced a set of drawings designed to illustrate Thomas Gray's account of his visit to the Lakes in 1769 (now in the Yale Center for British Art, New Haven).

Thomas Gainsborough RA (1727–88)

A foundation member of the Royal Academy in 1768, despite living in Bath at the time, Gainsborough was one of the most eminent portrait painters of the eighteenth century but he also had a lifelong interest in landscape painting. He developed his own distinctive and influential style, marked by delicacy of handling and poetic sensibility; many of the elements that became known as 'picturesque' in the 1780s were already present in his landscapes of the 1750s.

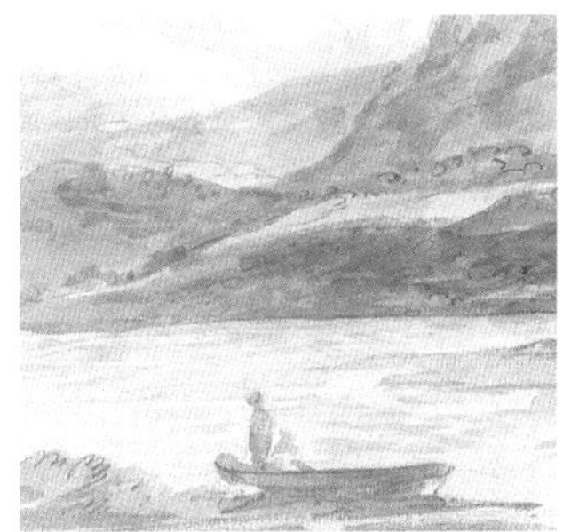

Gainsborough paid just one visit to the Lake District, in the summer of 1783; it was his sole direct experience of mountain scenery, undertaken near the end of a career spent in Suffolk, Bath and London. No details of the excursion are known, save that it was made in the company of an old friend, the Ipswich lawyer Samuel Kilderbee, and in a somewhat belligerent mood. He wrote to another friend, William Pearce, Chief Clerk of the Admiralty (and a writer of libretti for comic operas), mocking fashionable writers on the Lakes with a painterly pun and (given the fact of Brown's suicide) a rather macabre twist: 'I don't know if I told you that I'm going along with a Suffolk Friend to visit the Lakes in Cumberland & Westmoreland; and purpose when I come back to show you that your Grays and D[r]. Brownes were tawdry fan-Painters. I purpose to mount all the Lakes at the next Exhibition, in the great Stile, – and you know if the People don't like them, 'tis only jumping into one of the deepest of them from off a wooded Island, and my reputation will be fixed for ever' (Hayes, 2001, p. 153). The 'great Stile' was, for Gainsborough, the broad, intellectual and imaginative approach of the Old Masters – Claude, Nicolas Poussin, Gaspard Dughet and especially Rubens – as opposed to the slavish attention to the particularities of place displayed by many contemporary landscapists. He did not record the Lakes in on-the-spot sketches during his visit; cat. 23 was drawn from memory and imagination, probably soon after his return to the south

Sadly, this intended grand display of the fruits of his tour at the 1784 Royal Academy never came to pass, owing to a row between Gainsborough and the Hanging Committee during preparations for that show; he withdrew all his proposed exhibits and never exhibited at the RA again. From 1784 onwards he held summer displays of his work on his own premises, Schomberg House in Pall Mall, to run concurrently with those at the RA. However, the Lakes were exceptionally well represented at the 1784 RA after all – chiefly in works by De Loutherbourg who had also made a tour there, quite independently, the same summer as Gainsborough.

In 1778, a few years after his move to London, Gainsborough had painted a half-length portrait of the Rev. Sir William Lowther, first Baronet (1707–88). This failed to please Lowther's two sons, necessitating two further new portraits (see Hayes, 2001, pp. 137–8, for Gainsborough's urbane response to their criticisms). Though a trivial rebuff in Gainsborough's career, it inevitably calls to mind the difficulties encountered by Wordsworth with Sir William's kinsman Sir James Lowther.

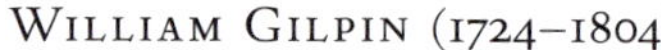

William Gilpin (1724–1804)

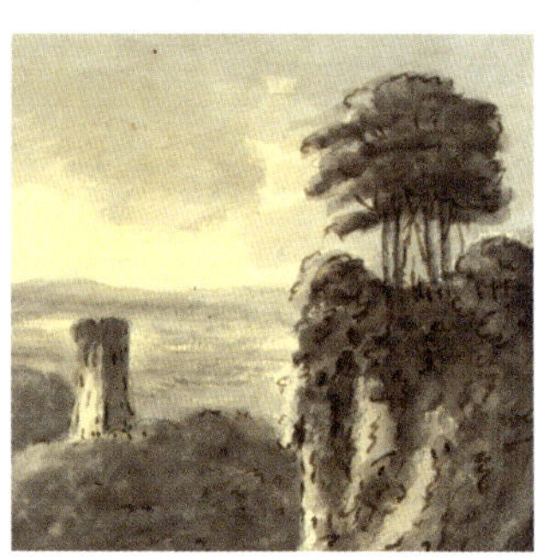

Gilpin was born at Scaleby Castle, near Carlisle, the son of an enthusiastic amateur artist Captain John Bernard Gilpin, but most of his career was spent in the south, as was that of his younger brother, the sporting and animal painter Sawrey Gilpin RA (1733–1807). Schoolmaster, parson, writer and connoisseur, William Gilpin exerted an unprecedented influence on the taste and travels of his contemporaries through his discussions of British scenery and its relationship to landscape painting. These were circulated privately in manuscript before publication in his successive volumes of *Observations, relative to Picturesque Beauty*, each dedicated to a different area, which appeared between 1782 and 1809. The two volumes that included his discussions of the Lake District (cat. 13) were published in 1786, long after the northern summer tour of 1772 during which he spent less than a week in the area, visiting Windermere, Derwentwater, Borrowdale, Buttermere and Ullswater. These volumes were embellished by oval sepia-tinted aquatints, for which he acknowledged the assistance of other artists including his brother Sawrey and John 'Warwick' Smith. Gilpin continued to make drawings for his own pleasure for the rest of his life (cat. 48).

Gilpin's pronouncements on 'picturesque beauty' stimulated intense debate not only among artists but also in the wider world and created a new occupation, 'picturesque tourism'. Within a few years of his death he was immortalised as the absent-minded and accident-prone Dr Syntax whose adventures were illustrated by Thomas Rowlandson and related in the comic verses of William Combe (cat. 58–9).

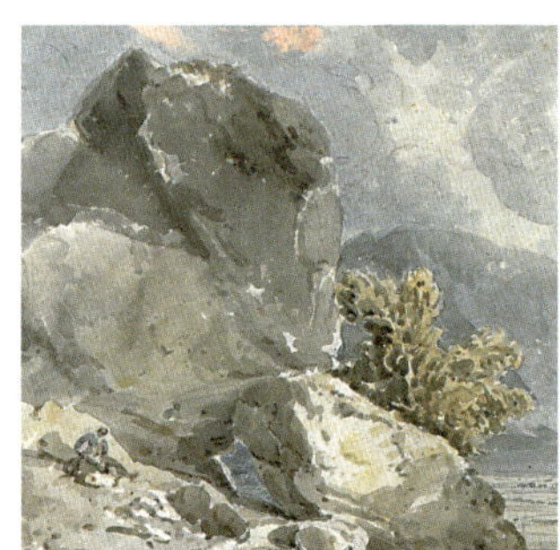

Thomas Girtin (1775–1802)

Born in Southwark, south London, Girtin was apprenticed in 1789 to Edward Dayes (cat. 36) from whom he learned the basic skills of topographical drawing but very soon, with his contemporary Turner (cat. 51), he broke away from the eighteenth-century tradition of 'tinted drawings' and transformed the art of watercolour into a medium of power and expression. Both were strongly influenced by the poetry and grandeur they found in the work of J.R. Cozens (1752–97). This they were able to study closely at the house of Dr Thomas Monro, physician to Bethlem Hospital and later to George III. Monro had care of Cozens in his final years and at the doctor's house in Adelphi Terrace Girtin and Turner spent many evenings in 1794–7 making copies of Cozens' sketches and washing in effects in return for their supper and a fee of some two or three shillings.

Although he made sketching tours of the North of England in 1796 and North Wales and Yorkshire in 1798, Girtin never visited the Lake District; all his depictions of the area are either copies or adaptations of works by other artists. Several (like some tiny watercolours in Tate Britain and elsewhere; see fig. 36 on p. 125) are copies of unidentified and untraced works he studied at

Monro's; the large number of such works in the doctor's posthumous sale in 1833 suggests he may have contemplated an engraved series in a topographical publication. Eight or nine large watercolours by Girtin, including cat. 47, are free interpretations of on-the-spot sketches (such as cat. 46) by his patron SIR GEORGE BEAUMONT whom he probably met through Monro. These were commissioned by Beaumont himself and include depictions of Grange in Borrowdale, Watendlath and Colwith Force (see Hebron, Shields and Wilcox, 2006, nos 18–23).

Girtin's promising career was cut short in his late 20s by respiratory illness, his death causing Turner to remark, 'If Girtin had lived, I should have starved.' However, the influence of his work can be seen in later artists including CONSTABLE (cat. 55, 72). Beaumont advised the latter to study the watercolours by Girtin in his own collection as examples of 'great breadth and truth' – aims that Constable was to pursue for the rest of his career.

JOHN GLOVER (1767–1849)

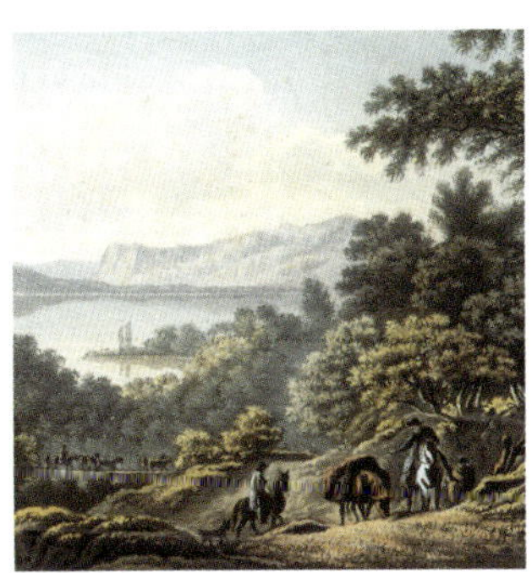

The son of a farmer, Glover was born at Houghton on the Hill, Leicestershire, and is first heard of as a writing-master or drawing-master at the Free School at Appleby, between Brough and Penrith, in the mid-1780s. By the time he met FARINGTON in December 1794 (on his fifth visit to London) he was a successful drawing-master in Lichfield and proposing to divide his year between Lichfield and London; he himself was largely self-taught, claiming to have had no more than nine drawing lessons, eight from WILLIAM PAYNE and one from JOHN 'WARWICK' SMITH (I.283-4). A decade or so later Glover had made the move to London, perfected a much-talked of method of teaching, attracted a fashionable clientele of London pupils and was enjoying considerable success with the works he exhibited (in both oils and watercolours) at the Royal Academy and at the Society of Painters in Water Colours which held its first exhibition in 1805 (he became president in 1807). His work became even more familiar to the public when it featured in popular drawing manuals aimed at amateur artists who could not afford his expensive lessons (cat. 68).

From Appleby it was easy for Glover to visit the Lake District and he must often have done so; he exhibited a watercolour *View of Ryddol, Cumberland* at the RA in 1795 (no. 591), together with a Derbyshire work and a scene near his birthplace. He had a deep love of the countryside, and of sketching from nature, later remarking (in words similar to those used by CONSTABLE), that it was 'the scenes near my native place, which helped to make me a Landscape Painter' (Roget, 1891, I.194). He continued to visit the Lake District (paying visits in 1803 and 1816) and made it the subject of many watercolours after he moved south. Exhibited in substantial quantities at the SPWC almost every year from 1806 to 1817, these brought him personal acclaim and also contributed much to the popularity of the area amongst his envious fellow-artists. About 1818 he bought a property on Ullswater: Blowick Farm on Place Fell, just north of Patterdale Common. Following a downturn of his fortunes in the 1820s he emigrated to Australia, arriving on his 64th birthday in February 1831; he named his Australian property 'Patterdale' in honour of the scenes that had been dear to him.

William Green (1760–1823)

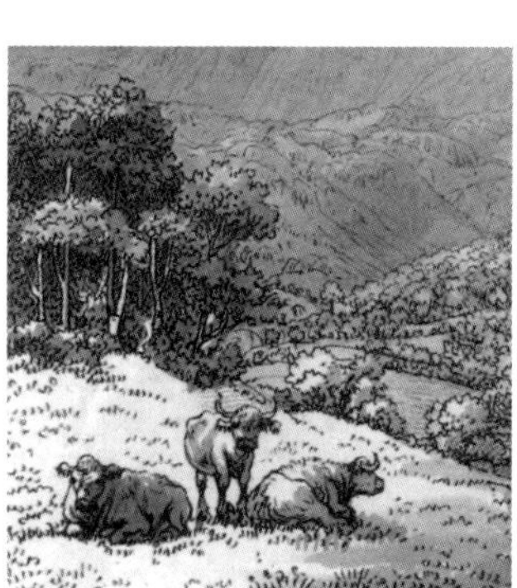

William Green was born in Manchester where he trained for a career as a surveyor. In 1778 he began acting as assistant to William Yates of Liverpool for his survey of Lancashire 'north of the sands': an occupation that provided his introduction to Lake District scenery and brought him into contact in Ulverston with Thomas West who published his *Guide to the Lakes* that very year. West encouraged Green to become an artist and when he returned to Manchester he took lessons in painting; before long he was combining the career of surveyor and cartographer with that of drawing-master. Visits to the Lakes in 1791, 1793 and 1794 provided him with material for his first aquatints and etchings of the area, published in the mid 1790s, as well as for three works exhibited at the RA after he moved to London in 1796: *Barrow-cascade* (1797, no. 500), *Silver Cove at the head of Emerdale Water* (1797, no. 651), *Derwent Water, from Castle Rigg* (1798, no. 447). His final exhibit at the RA was *View from Kirby Lonsdale church-yard, Westmoreland* in 1801 (no. 649). In 1800 he married and a few months later the couple set up home in Ambleside where they remained for the rest of the artist's life, raising a large family.

For over twenty years Green devoted himself to exploring, studying and recording his surroundings and published a stream of individual prints, books, or series of prints accompanied by letterpress, beginning with an aquatint series in 1804 and ending with *Forty Etchings from Nature* in 1822 (cat. 70–1). He thus became the first resident artist in the Lake District to make a business out of selling local views to visiting tourists. His subjects ranged from celebrated beauty spots to the meanest rustic buildings and from extensive vistas to detailed studies of wayside rocks and ferns. To promote his work he held regular exhibitions in his house in the Market Place in Ambleside (visited by John Harden who entertained Green many times at Brathay); he also hired a room in Keswick for an annual show and occasionally displayed his work in Manchester. He also supplemented his income by giving drawing lessons; in the course of time his daughters became his assistants, numbering Dora Wordsworth among their pupils. Recognising that early nineteenth-century tourists were less concerned with antiquarianism and aesthetic distinctions than the readers of West's *Guide* had been forty years earlier, he drew on his own observations and experiences to write *The Tourist's New Guide, containing a Description of the Lakes, Mountains, and Scenery, in Cumberland, Westmorland, and Lancashire*. This was published in 1819 in two volumes, complete with illustrations after his own drawings, and was available through numerous outlets both locally and nationally.

Green's tombstone in Grasmere churchyard bears an epitaph composed by Wordsworth who was a loyal patron over many years, buying numerous prints and copies of the *Tourist's New Guide*. As Wordsworth wrote, Green 'produced faithful representations of the country and lasting memorials of its more perishable features'.

John Harden (1772–1847)

A talented amateur artist and a generous and sympathetic host to artists, writers and other visitors to the Lakes for the three decades of his residence at Brathay Hall, John Harden was born in County Tipperary and was a man of private means; he is sometimes described as a lawyer but the evidence on this has been doubted and he was certainly never in practice. He spent his youth in Dublin, showing an aptitude for sketching and copying paintings, and made his earliest known visit to the Lake District in 1798. In 1800 he married but his happiness was soon cut short by the death of his wife. To recover from this blow amidst congenial company he took himself to Bath where he soon met FARINGTON; they were in almost daily contact throughout January and February 1801, Harden showing the older artist his sketchbook and talking about his future plans (IV. 1477–508 passim). They met again in London in May (IV.1545, 1550). These meetings may well have contributed to Harden's decision to revisit the Lakes in September of that year, an excursion which had a delightful outcome: on his return voyage from Holyhead to Bray in Ireland he met his future second wife, Jessy Allan of Edinburgh. They married in January 1803, spent three months in the Lakes that summer (sometimes going out sketching together) and decided to make the area their home. In April 1804 they heard they could rent Brathay and by June had taken up residence. They were to remain there – with absences in Edinburgh, Dublin and elsewhere – for the best part of 31 years, bringing up a family of children, sketching when they could (cat. 76) and having contact with many artists: both residents like IBBETSON, GREEN and Mary Dixon and summer visitors from both north (H.W. Williams) and south (CONSTABLE, HAVELL, REINAGLE and FARINGTON). The Hardens' early years at Brathay are documented in the journals sent by Jessy in 1801-11 to her sister Agnes who had accompanied her husband, a military surgeon, to India on a ten-year period of service. In 1834 the Brathay estate was sold by its owner and the Harden family moved to Field Head House, north of Hawkshead, where Jessy died in 1837.

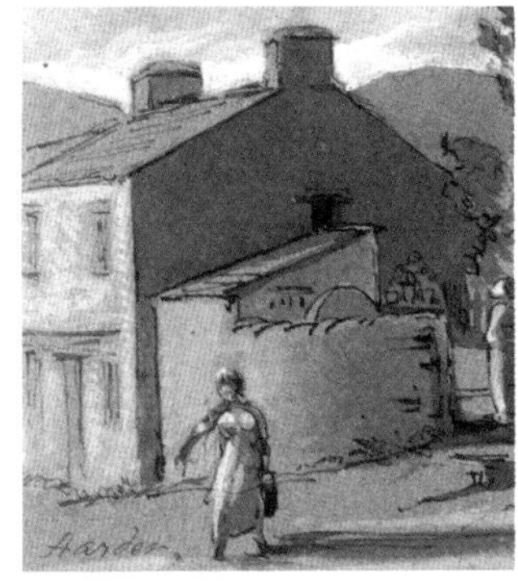

The Hardens played a full part in local society as kindly hosts and amiable, cultured guests. For a time their eldest daughter attended Miss Dowling's school in Ambleside with Dora Wordsworth, their sons were taught by Hartley Coleridge, and there was easy intercourse between the families. Farington, meeting Harden as a widower in 1801, had referred to him as a man of 'civil & decorous manners' (IV.1477); in the happier days of 1806, with Jessy and their young children, he was described to Constable as high-spirited, 'Whip Syllebub, & Spruce Beer', by his melancholic neighbour, the poet Charles Lloyd (IX.3491). In 1839 Henry Crabb Robinson referred to him as 'that good old man with the *sunny* face', attributing the phrase to Wordsworth, but perhaps the best tribute comes from Hartley Coleridge to whom Harden had once expounded on the genius and morality of Hogarth: 'he combined the brilliance of champagne, and the warmth of his compatriot poteen, with the simplicity of water. … JH was both merry and wise, but the best of the moral was himself' (*Blackwood's Magazine*, 1831).

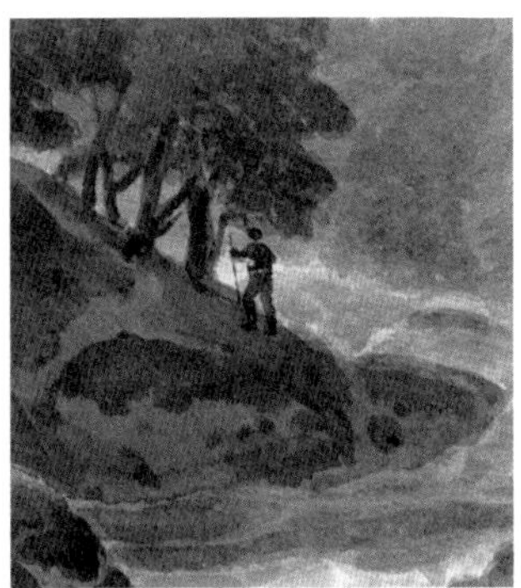

WILLIAM HAVELL (1782–1857)

The son of a drawing-master in Reading, William Havell was the most gifted of a large family of artists and engravers and worked in both oil and watercolour. When a group of artists formed the Society of Painters in Water Colours in London at the end of 1804, he was the youngest of the six other artists they invited to join the Society and participate in its first exhibition in 1805. This he did with immense critical and financial success, rivalled only by that of JOHN GLOVER. The impact of Glover's numerous Lake District scenes in the 1806 exhibition stimulated Havell and another member of the Society, Ramsay Richard Reinagle, to follow Glover's example.

It was reported to Farington in mid-August 1807 that the two artists had gone to the Lakes 'to store themselves with subjects for drawings' (VIII.3107) and in early September that 'Havil ... has taken a House near Windermere for 6 months' (VIII.3117). The house in question was one in Ambleside, where Havell intended to remain till May, and it may have been from here that he drew Stockgill Force (cat. 60). The two artists had an introduction (from the Scottish artist H.W. Williams) to John Harden and his wife Jessy at Brathay Hall and visited them on 9 August, all the party walking out to Skelwith Bridge; the following day they painted in their grounds and other meetings followed. Later, after the departure of Reinagle, Havell was joined by his sister Jane and they and the Hardens became regular companions, both Hardens borrowing Havell's drawings to copy. Harden introduced his protégé Thomas Jameson, encouraging him to study Havell's work, but Jameson later told Farington he felt he ought to be studying nature more than the works of Turner or Havell (IX.3276). Havell also met Wordsworth (who reported on his activities to Sir George Beaumont) and in March 1808 Dorothy Wordsworth wrote to her brother that she and Wordsworth's wife Mary had engaged as a new servant the young woman who had been living with the Havells and been desirous of joining the household at Grasmere.

The Lakes inspired Havell to paint richly coloured, highly detailed works of grandeur and beauty that attracted much praise from dealers but were also criticised for showing a tendency to idealise. He showed the fruits of his Lakes visit at the SPWC in 1808 and again in subsequent years as well as at the Royal Academy, British Institution and Liverpool Academy (founded in 1810). He continued to paint and exhibit the area in oil and watercolour until the mid-1850s while his images reached a wider public through engravings and aquatints, including ones published by his cousin Robert Havell.

Thomas Hearne (1744–1817)

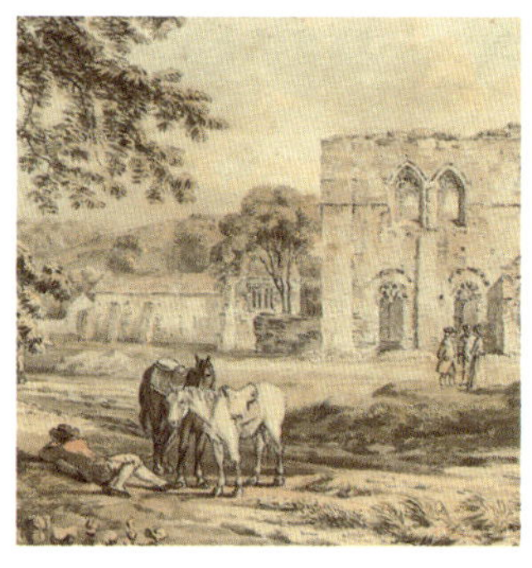

Hearne was pre-eminent among the topographical artists working in the second half of the eighteenth century when the art of watercolour consisted essentially of applying delicate tints of colour to an accurate and finely drawn outline. Having served a five-year apprenticeship to England's most outstanding landscape engraver, William Woollett, in 1765–71, he sailed for the Leeward Islands that same year as draughtsman to their Governor, Sir Ralph Payne. He returned in 1775 and, having completed his commissions for Payne, turned his keen eye and meticulous skills to very different subjects from barracks and harbours, plantations and colonial life: he produced a total of 84 drawings for engraving in his publishing project, *Antiquities of Great Britain*, issued, in parts and by subscription, from 1778 to 1786 and again from 1796 to 1806 (bound volumes were issued in 1786 and 1806). To gather material for these drawings (cat. 17) he travelled extensively round Britain, seeking out medieval ruins as opposed to the more fashionable subject for engravings, gentlemen's houses.

Hearne's travels brought him to the Lake District in 1777 and again in 1778. He enjoyed the lifelong friendship and patronage of Sir George Beaumont, having first met him when Beaumont visited Woollett's studio in 1771. In the winter of 1776–7 Beaumont proposed a joint sketching tour to the Lake District and other parts of the north of England the following year, on which they were joined by FARINGTON. This was so successful (cat. 15–16) that an even more ambitious tour followed in 1778, which lasted two months and took them through Scotland; the party on this occasion included Sir George's recent bride.

Hearne's works were greatly admired (and acquired in abundance) by another notable collector, Dr Thomas Monro, at whose London house they provided an incomparable training ground for aspiring artists including the young TURNER and GIRTIN in the 1790s. By the time of Turner's own visit to the Lakes in 1797 Hearne was far less active than hitherto, his art soon to be overshadowed by that of the rising generation. Thanks in part to Beaumont, he escaped destitution in his final years but it was Monro who took responsibility for his funeral and burial.

PETER HOLLAND (fl. 1780–1812)

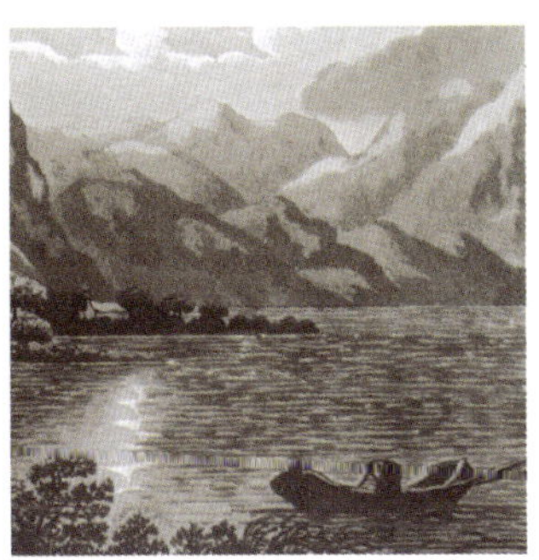

Peter Holland worked first in London and then in Liverpool where he became closely involved in successive attempts to establish an academy of art. During his London period he exhibited at the RA (1781, 1782) and contributed to the 1784 exhibition of the Liverpool Society for Promoting Painting and Design. By 1787 he was resident in Tarleton Street, Liverpool; he served as Visitor to the Society and showed four works at its exhibition of that year. When the Liverpool Academy of Art was founded in 1810 he was its first vice-president, exhibiting there until 1812.

Holland depicted the Lake District in many works. In 1792 he published his *Select Views of the Lakes in Cumberland, Westmoreland & Lancashire* (cat. 33), the first book of aquatints of the area, which he dedicated to the Liverpool 'lover of the arts' Daniel Daulby. At the RA exhibition of 1793 he showed two works with titles similar to those of the aquatints: *View of Ulswater from Gobarrow park, Cumberland* and *View of the Eagle craig, Borrowdale, Cumberland* (nos 257, 644). Further works by Holland feature among the small copies in Daulby's Lake District albums created by another Liverpool artist, THOMAS CHUBBARD.

JULIUS CAESAR IBBETSON (1759–1817)

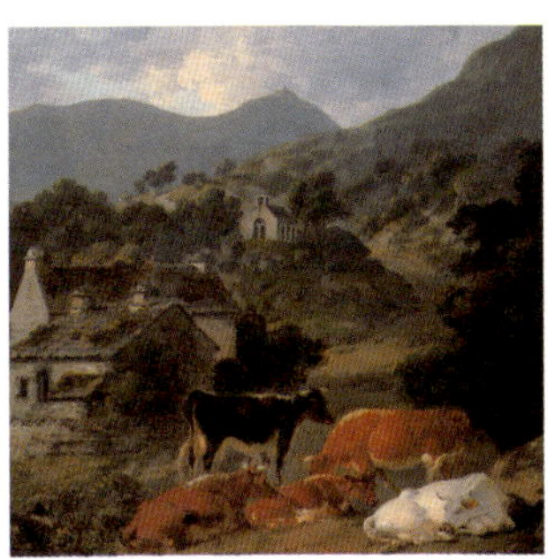

Born at Farnley Moor, near Leeds, Ibbetson had an extremely varied early career. After about ten years in London, largely working for dealers and restorers, he accompanied the Hon. Charles Cathcart's short-lived embassy to China in 1787–8 as its official draughtsman and began receiving commissions, including one from the fourth Earl of Bute (the brother of LADY MARY LOWTHER). After his first wife died, leaving him with three small children, he moved to Liverpool where he worked for the picture dealer Thomas Vernon and there was also a period working in Edinburgh. He first visited the Lake District in 1798, exhibiting three paintings of the area at the RA in 1799: no. 14, *View of Bowder stone in Borrowdale* (a topical subject: see cat. 63) and two well-established subjects, *View of Skiddaw, from the head of Derwent Water* and *View of the Lower water-fall at Sir Michael Le Fleming's, at Rydal* (nos 206, 257). That year he returned to the Lakes, taking rooms in Ambleside, and his three exhibits depicting the area in 1800 included *View of Ambleside Fair, Westmoreland, painted from Nature* (no. 291). In 1801 he married a local girl, Bella Thompson, whom he had engaged as a servant. The couple lived first at Clappersgate, in a house then known as Willy Hill, and subsequently at Crag House, Troutbeck (June 1802 to April 1805). During these years Ibbetson continued to send depictions of Lake District scenery to the RA, sometimes referring overtly to Ambleside or Troutbeck in their titles (e.g. RA 1804, nos 171–2, the first including his own home at Clappersgate).

By now, however, the painter was crippled by rheumatism and the Academy's president, Benjamin West, and FARINGTON were both shocked that his work was 'so much fallen off' (VI.2289, 2290). He later claimed that he found the Lake District unsociable (this was partly due to his own rough manners and reputation for drunkenness which resulted in the Wordsworths keeping their distance and BEAUMONT virtually adopting his eldest daughter Mary; local feelings towards the family were not improved by the conduct of his son Julius: see below). The Ibbetson family was enabled to retire to Yorkshire thanks to a generous patron, William Danby, and the artist spent the last dozen years of his life at Masham. Here he continued to paint Lake District subjects such as cat. 69, utilising his earlier sketches and drawings and revisiting favourite themes; he exhibited such works at the RA in 1806, 1811 and 1812 and at the BI in 1812.

THOMAS JAMESON (1789–1827)

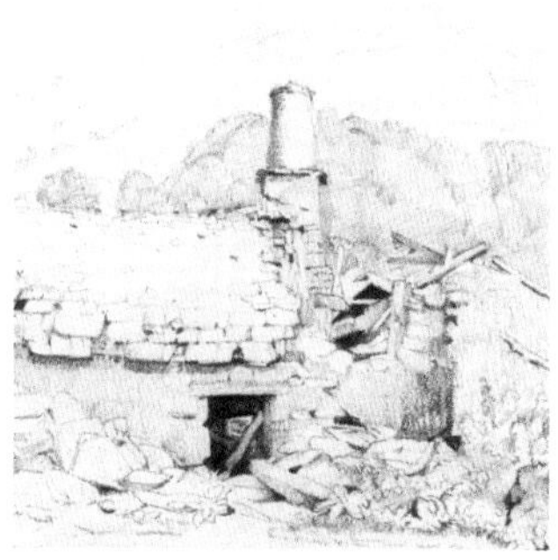

Thomas Jameson's early life in the Lake District was closely connected not only with those of several other artists in the area but also with the Wordsworths. His maternal grandfather was the Rev. Joseph Sympson (died 1807 aged 92), the rector of Wythburn for over fifty years and a highly cultivated man who inspired the character of the incumbent of a small rural chapel in *The Excursion* (VII.31–291). Dorothy's *Grasmere Journal* includes almost daily references to the Sympson and Jameson families, 'little Tommy' making a first appearance in early June 1800 when he brought gooseberries to Dove Cottage; Dorothy accompanied him for part of his walk home to High Broadrain, north of the village and facing Helm Crag. Evidently Thomas and his siblings were staying with their grandparents during the illness of their father, for three weeks later Dorothy recorded: 'Tommy's Father dead'. The Jameson children remained in Ambleside, their mother taking in paying-guests but struggling to make ends meet and within a few years falling into debt. During this period Thomas's younger brother Robert formed a close friendship with Coleridge's son Hartley, a fellow-pupil at school in Ambleside, while his aunt Elizabeth Sympson scandalised local society by falling pregnant by the son of the artist JULIUS CAESAR IBBETSON (considerably her junior). Their marriage, at the end of 1803 was followed – within the year – by the deaths of both Elizabeth and her infant daughter.

Thomas's penchant for art was clearly inherited from (and presumably fostered by) his grandfather who is known to have made engravings and excellent drawings in his spare time (*Grasmere Journal*, 22 February, 13 June 1802) but little remains of his artistic output (see cat. 64). In his teens he received encouragement from JOHN HARDEN, knew the work of WILLIAM GREEN and met WILLIAM HAVELL. In 1808 he was mentioned as talented (but overconfident) to Joseph Farington by the artist George Arnald (IX.3276) and in May 1809 Harden paid for him to go to London to gain a broader experience of art by studying works by both the Old Masters and modern painters (IX.3456, 3457). (This journey can be dated to 7 May since Dorothy Wordsworth used him to carry a letter to De Quincey.) Harden paid Jameson's mother's debts, which were preying on his mind, and settled him in lodgings, hoping he could contribute to the family income by giving drawing lessons (IX.3467–8). This plan did not succeed. By August 1810 he had decided to abandon the pursuit of art and had become a schoolmaster at Egremont (X.3705–6) where another Thomas Jameson (probably his paternal grandfather) had been rector from *c.*1743 until his death in 1776. The younger Thomas soon also entered the church, being priested at Haile (just south of Egremont) in 1813. The following year he became curate of Sherburn, Fenton and Saxton in Yorkshire and sought private pupils in order to boost his income (in this he was assisted by Wordsworth who in April 1814 recommended him to his influential Yorkshire friend Francis Wrangham); in 1822 he was appointed Master of the Free Grammar School at Sherburn. He must have been admirably suited for both these situations; as Dorothy wrote to her sister-in-law Priscilla Wordsworth in 1815, 'He is very religious and is a good Teacher, but he has not had a College Education' (Hill, 1981, p. 138). He died on 22 November 1827 at the age of 38 and is commemorated by a monument in Sherburn church.

Thomas's elder brother Joseph also entered the church, becoming a minor canon at Ripon. His sister Mary remained in contact with the Wordsworths, obtaining the position of governess at the school in Appleby run by Sara Hutchinson's friend Anna Weir, to which Dora Wordsworth was sent in 1811. His brother Robert became a barrister (and later a judge in Canada) and married Anna Murphy, daughter of the miniature-painter Dennis Brownell Murphy with whom Harden had visited the Lakes in 1798; she later achieved fame in her own right as an author after their separation.

John Laporte (1761–1839)

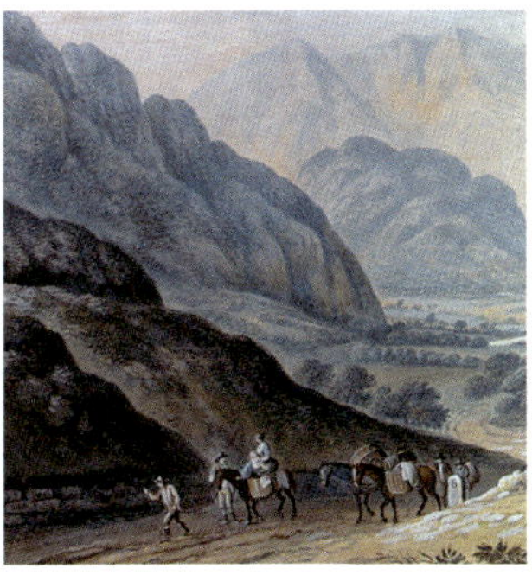

A successful landscape-painter and drawing-master, Laporte may have been born in Dublin, of French extraction, but has been identified with the John Peter Laporte who was baptised in London in March 1761. He was trained in London, probably by the Dublin-born Huguenot John Melchior Barralet, and became a highly accomplished topographical artist, working in watercolour, bodycolour and oils with equal ease. His pupils and patrons included Dr Thomas Monro whose house became an informal 'academy' for young artists including Girtin and Turner in the mid 1790s. (Around 1806 Laporte's name appears in the list of subscribers to Turner's engraving *The Shipwreck* and Turner later owned at least one of Laporte's works, now in the British Museum.) By the end of 1795 Monro appears to have outgrown his appreciation of Laporte's skills and planned to divest himself of some of his extensive collection, declaring that he 'has not enough of the great principles of the art' (Farington II.442). However, Laporte continued to be in demand as a topographer and also went on to publish a succession of books ranging from drawing manuals to a series of 72 soft-ground etchings after drawings by Gainsborough (the latter in collaboration with his friend W.F. Wells).

Laporte made many tours around Britain. He visited the Lake District in 1790 (sketches in albums in the British Museum) and in 1791 he exhibited no fewer than five Lakes scenes at the RA: two depictions of Ullswater (nos 38, 667) and one each of Coniston (486), Rydal (505) and Derwentwater (510). These were followed by further Lakes subjects in 1792, 1793, 1797 and almost yearly between 1799 and 1805. Noteworthy among them is the view of Elterwater (1797, no. 11), a lake whose modest charms led to its frequent neglect by visiting artists (see cat. 24). He also showed Lakes scenes at other exhibiting bodies: the Associated Artists in Water Colours (1810), the British Institution (1810, 1811 and 1826) and the New Water Colour Society (1833). The continuing presence of the Lake District in Laporte's exhibits suggests that he may have continued to visit the area but it is equally possible that he worked up subjects from material in his sketchbooks. He often worked on a large scale and in bodycolour, a medium that enabled his scenes to be more conspicuous in mixed exhibitions than those executed solely in watercolour, and this may have led his name to be associated with cat. 29–30.

Two engravings after Laporte's sketches appeared in John 'Warwick' Smith and John Emes' *Views of the Lakes* (1795), the series of prints intended to be bound into West's *Guide* from the fifth edition onwards; these were *Upper Cascade Rydal* and *Derwent-water from Ormathwaite*.

Lady Mary Lowther (1738–1824)

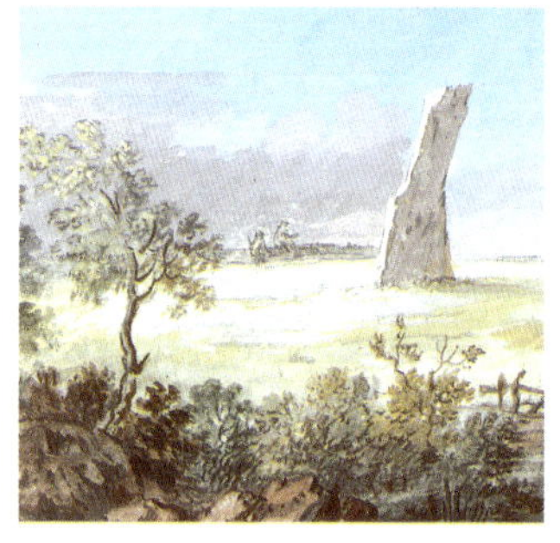

The eldest daughter of the third Earl of Bute, a distinguished patron of the arts but an unpopular secretary of state in the early 1760s, Lady Mary Stuart married Sir James Lowther (1736–1802), the richest land-owner in the north-west of England, in 1761. The marriage was unhappy and childless and before the end of the 1770s the couple had decided to live apart. However, occasional later glimpses of Lady Mary in Farington's *Diary* (as the 'Dowager Lady Lonsdale', since her husband had been created Earl of Lonsdale in 1784) show that she was on good terms with other members of the Lowther family after his death. She retired to Fulham, then a village on the edge of London, and is buried there, in All Saints' church.

As the daughter of an earl Lady Mary would have received drawing lessons from a private tutor in the family homes on the island of Bute and in London from an early age. Both her parents were painted by Sir Joshua Reynolds: her father in 1763 and her mother (the daughter of the redoubtable Lady Mary Wortley Montagu) in 1779 (both private collection; repr. in Penny, 1986, pp. 25, 145). As the wife of a baronet, virtually imprisoned in the solitude of Lowther Hall, she turned to painting as an occupation and diversion with the adaptability and fortitude that had marked the career of her grandmother. Lady Mary made excursions of the surrounding area with her sketchbooks, eventually producing over ninety finished watercolours in 1765–6, of which the Trust owns nine. Her subjects varied from Lowther Hall itself, local antiquities (cat. 7), rivers, cascades and pastoral scenes to more ambitious prospects (see Hebron 2008, pp. 21–32). All are executed with infinite pains, in the narrow range of tints that were then available. Their style suggests study of the work of Paul Sandby who painted a series of views for her father at exactly this time.

Lady Mary retained her interest in art long after she left Lowther, buying some of the sketchbooks of the Scottish architect James Playfair at his posthumous sale in January 1795 (Farington, II.290-1) and two lots at the June 1795 sale of work by William Hodges RA (IX. 3371; II.359). She gave the Playfair sketchbooks to her kinswoman, another Lady Mary Lowther (1785–1862), the daughter of William, first Earl of Lonsdale, who married Lord Frederick Cavendish-Bentinck in 1820; she, too, was assiduous in her pursuit of art, enjoying much help and encouragement from Farington as well as the acquaintance of Wordsworth who dedicated a sonnet to her.

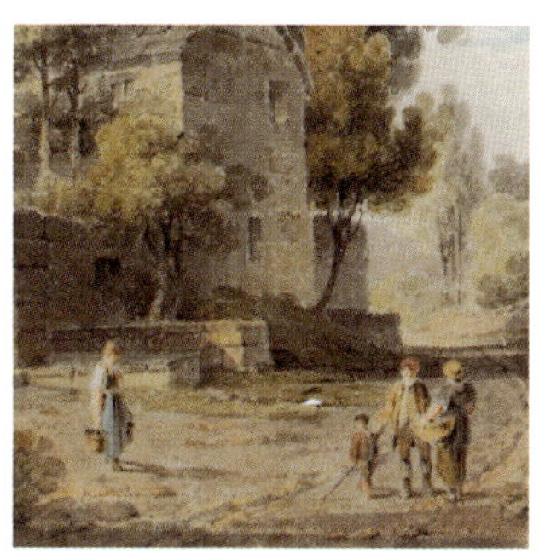

Paul Sandby Munn (1773–1845)

Paul Sandby Munn was the son of a minor landscape painter, James Munn (fl. 1764–74), and was named after one of the most versatile and inventive topographical artists of the day who is said to have been chosen as his godfather: Paul Sandby (1731–1809), a foundation member of the Royal Academy. In the 1790s he participated in two London groups frequented by bright young artists: Dr Monro's informal academy in the Adelphi and the Sketching Club founded by Girtin; he exhibited at the RA (1798–1805) and later the Society of Painters in Water Colours (1806–15). Like his fellow-artists in these circles he made tours of the parts of Britain that were in vogue, such as Derbyshire and the Lake District; he visited Wales and Yorkshire with the artist John Sell Cotman; he made drawings for engraving in topographical publications and was one of the first artists to be interested in the new art of lithography. In 1815 he retired to Hastings where he made a living as a drawing-master.

Munn first visited the Lakes in the 1790s, exhibiting six views of the area at the RA in 1799, with subjects including Windermere, Thirlmere, Patterdale, Kirkerdale and Grange (see p. 113). These were followed by a view of Derwentwater in 1800 (no. 709). Dated drawings of Rydal and Buttermere in the British Museum show that he returned in August 1804 and his three RA exhibits of 1805 included Borrowdale and Buttermere subjects as well as a depiction of Lanercost Priory, the subject he had contributed to the Cumberland volume of John Britton's *The Beauties of England and Wales* in 1803. The Lake District featured regularly in his exhibits at the SPWC between 1808 and 1815, with Ambleside, Coniston and Troutbeck (cat. 61) providing some of his favourite subjects.

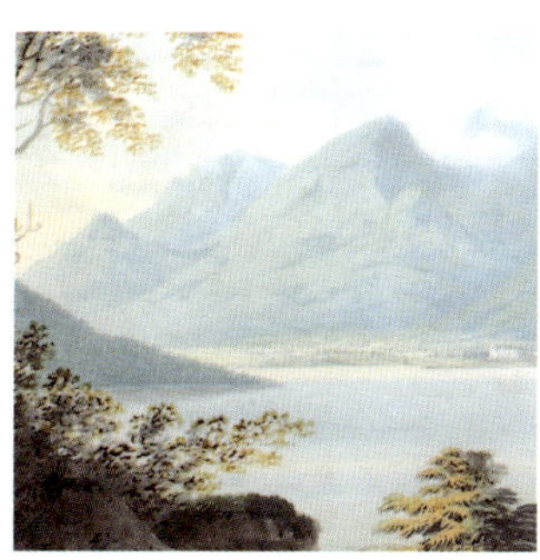

Francis Nicholson (1753–1844)

Nicholson was born and brought up in Pickering in Yorkshire and, apart from periods in London, spent most of his early career in that county, first at Whitby and then at Knaresborough and Ripon. After trying his hand at various genres he found his true métier as a landscape painter in the early 1780s thanks to a commission from Lord Mulgrave. He had an extensive clientele of northern patrons including the fourth Earl of Bute, the brother of Lady Mary Lowther, who commissioned views of the Isle of Bute in 1794–5. By 1803 Nicholson had settled permanently in London where he worked almost exclusively in watercolour and enjoyed a successful practice as a drawing-master. He was one of the oldest of the ten foundation members of the Society of Painters in Water Colours in 1804 (whose other early members included Cristall, Glover and Havell) and was briefly its president in 1812–13. Later he became interested in the developing medium of lithography:

the 1821 series of lithographs by Charles Hullmandel based on Nicholson's sketches of British scenery include the earliest published lithographs showing the Lake District.

Nicholson made two visits to the Lakes, the posthumous sale of his works in April 1844 including a total of 117 sketches of Cumberland and Westmorland drawn in 1794 and 1807 (Davies, 1931, p. 37). On the first of these tours he accompanied his Irish patrons Sir Henry and Lady Tuite whom he had met in Knaresborough and with whom he enjoyed a close relationship until *c.*1803; Sir Henry almost certainly commissioned Lakes views before his death in 1805. While staying with the Tuites in London in 1798 Nicholson was invited to make 'ten or twelve [drawings] from the Cumberland Lakes' for another Irish patron, a Mr Tighe of Arlington Street, as a possible alternative to Welsh views (Davies, 1931, p. 15). By now, however, his work had attracted the attention of a Yorkshire patron, Walter Fawkes, in whom he found a most appreciative admirer (see cat. 45).

The Lake District did not feature among Nicholson's exhibits until 1806 when he included views of Windermere and Haweswater among his works shown at the SPWCS. His repeated offering of Lake District subjects to its annual exhibitions in 1806–14 and his return to the area itself in 1807, after a long absence, were surely driven by commercial considerations at a high point in the popularity of the area.

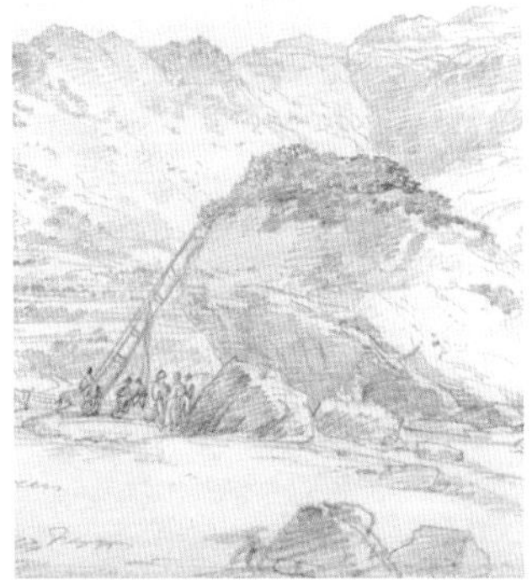

William Payne (1760–1830)

Until fairly recently the exact dates and circumstances of Payne's birth and death were veiled in mystery but these uncertainties have now been resolved. He was born in London, the son of a Westminster hop and coal merchant originally from Sussex; he died at his home in Upper Baker Street and is buried in Marylebone parish church. Nothing is recorded of his early training but he was a sufficiently good draughtsman by 1778 to be accepted by the Board of Ordnance at the Tower of London where he received instruction from the chief drawing-master. From 1783 to 1789 he was based in Plymouth where he surveyed and mapped the coastal defences of the area but he also found time to produce topographical works, which he exhibited at the Royal Academy in the late 1780s, earning the praise of its President, Sir Joshua Reynolds (himself a Plymouth man). In 1790 Payne moved back to London to pursue a highly successful career as a drawing-master – probably the most fashionable of the day – and did not need to exhibit again until 1809 when he was stimulated to do so by the arrival (and survival) on the London art scene of the Society of Painters in Water Colours (founded in 1804) and the British Institution (founded in 1805).

Payne travelled to many parts of England and Wales in search of material for his exhibits and to aid his teaching practice. He paid one visit to the Lakes in the summer of 1810, making careful dated pencil sketches (see cat. 63), and he exhibited a handful of subjects inspired by his visit, in both watercolour and oils, at the BI (1811, 1815, 1821 and 1827). He is best remembered today for his popularisation of the art of watercolour and his innovations, including 'Payne's grey' (a useful compound for foregrounds, composed of Prussian blue, lake and yellow ochre), rather than for his works themselves.

Ramsay Richard Reinagle (1775–1862)

Ramsay Richard Reinagle belonged to a family that included many artists and musicians and was descended from a Hungarian who came to Scotland with the Young Pretender in 1745. His father, Philip Reinagle RA (1748–1833), named him after his own teacher, the distinguished Scottish portrait painter Allan Ramsay (1713–84), and gave him his earliest lessons. He had his first painting accepted by the Royal Academy at the age of thirteen in 1788, spent eighteen months travelling on the continent in 1796–8, and soon became noted for his facility and speed of execution, qualities which for a time dazzled the young John Constable with whom he shared lodgings in London in 1799–1801.

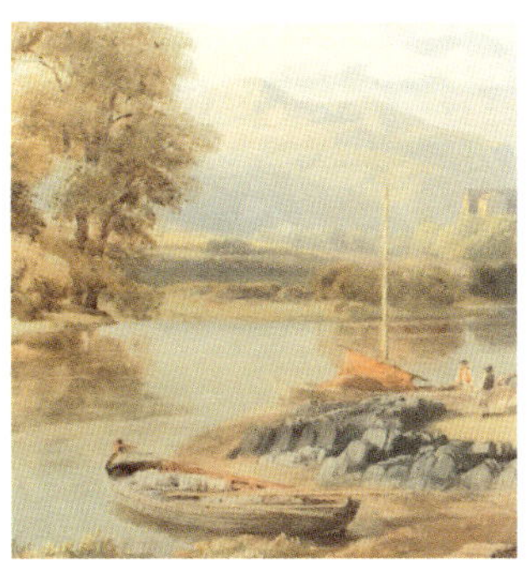

Reinagle made his first visit to the Lakes in 1807, accompanying William Havell there in August and remaining for a couple of months. Like Havell, he was keen to capitalise on the popularity of the area but, unlike Havell, he was extremely short of funds; he had lost heavily by speculating in Robert Barker's Panorama in Leicester Square. The two artists introduced themselves to John Harden at Brathay and sketched in its grounds; here Jessy Harden noted that Reinagle used oils on specially prepared paper '& made some very pretty things in a short time'. Elsewhere in the Lakes he worked at equally great speed, drawing about ten sketches a day, which, as a fellow-artist William Daniell observed, was too many by eight. Farington noted, 'Two drawings well attended to wd. have been more useful & satisfactory' (IX.3215). Reinagle's sketches around Brathay led to such works as cat. 65, showing a sight charmingly painted by Harden himself in 1813 (Foskett, 1974, pl. 1).

In 1811 Reinagle returned for a longer visit, probably stimulated by the fact that his younger brother Philip and one of his sisters had recently exhibited Lakes subjects at the RA (two of his sisters had spent six weeks at Clappersgate in August-September 1808). This time he chose the autumn for the variety of its colouring and remained until the end of November. Part of his visit he spent in or near Ambleside, but he also stayed for six or seven weeks at Portinscale near Keswick, with a Mr Spence, a friend of the caricaturist Henry Bunbury (1750–1811). Among the fruits of this tour were five works (including a view from Portinscale) shown at the SPWC in 1812 (nos 129, 233, 241, 272, 336) and two exhibited at the RA in 1816 (186, 534).

Reinagle's artistic career ended in poverty and disgrace. Elected to the SPWC in 1806, he served as its president from 1809 to 1812 when he resigned over the decision to admit oil paintings to its exhibitions. He himself then concentrated on oil painting, writing about art, and – like other members of his family – picture dealing and restoring. By 1835 he was bankrupt. Elected RA in 1823, he was later forced to resign when it was discovered that one of his 1848 exhibits was a retouched work by another artist.

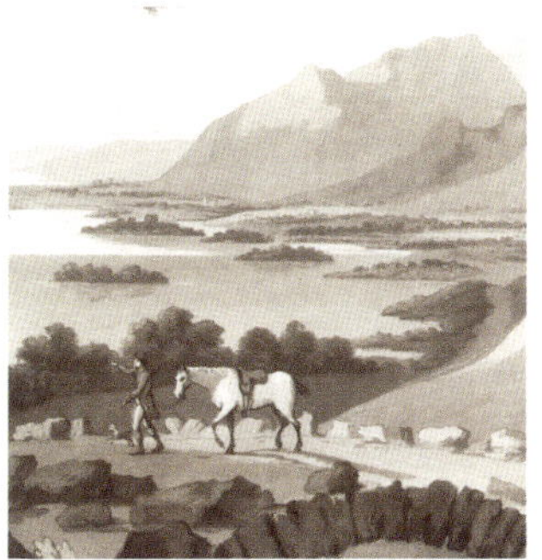

B. Rogers (fl. 1790–1803)

The landscape painter Rogers was based in Stafford where he gave lessons to Peter DeWint (1784–1849) before the latter moved to London in 1802. Rogers evidently travelled on the continent during the Peace of Amiens (1802–3), like Farington and Turner, since his exhibits included views in the Valais (RA 1803, nos 723, 728, when his address was given as 'Weeping-cross, Stafford'). In 1796 he published six large aquatints of the Lake District (cat. 42) that show an appreciation of unusual subjects and viewpoints as well as of more conventional ones. Of his handful of subsequent exhibits at the Royal Academy in 1800–3, only one depicted the Lakes: *View of Grassmere Lake, Westmoreland, by moonlight* (1800, no. 678; untraced) which is notable for having been accompanied by lines from William Lisle Bowles' 'Combe Ellen':

> The clear moon
> Emerging o'er the sable mountain, sails
> Silent, and calm, and beautiful, and sheds
> Its solemn grandeur on the shadowy scene.

An adjustment of the Academy's rules in the 1790s had enabled a return to the appending of extensive quotations (a notable feature of the earliest catalogues when there were far fewer exhibits) and many artists, including Fuseli and Turner, immediately took full advantage of this. In quoting verse to enhance his exhibit, Rogers was following the new fashion.

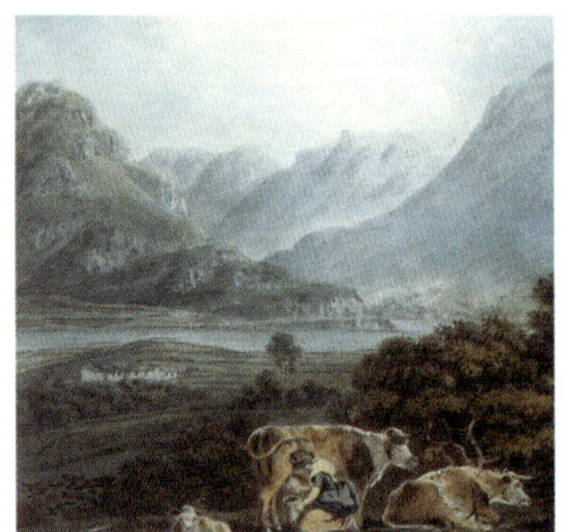

ROBERT SEATON (1785/6–1808)

This short-lived local artist does not appear in *The Artists of Cumbria* by Marshall Hall but a brief glimpse of him is provided by the *Diary* of JOSEPH FARINGTON. On his visit to the Lakes in the autumn of 1808 Farington recorded that he 'saw views of the Lakes by Seaton – a young man who died in April last aged 22 or 3 – at Kendal – a native of Cumberland – got disorder at Aberdeen & concealed it till too late. Ld. Muncaster had him there & was inclined to serve him – bad tempered – wrote to Lord M – was no longer noticed' (18 October; IX.3364). Besides cat. 54, the Wordsworth Trust also owns another large Seaton watercolour of 1805, an Arcadian and decorative view of Ullswater.

ROBERT SHERBOURNE (fl. 1775–1810)

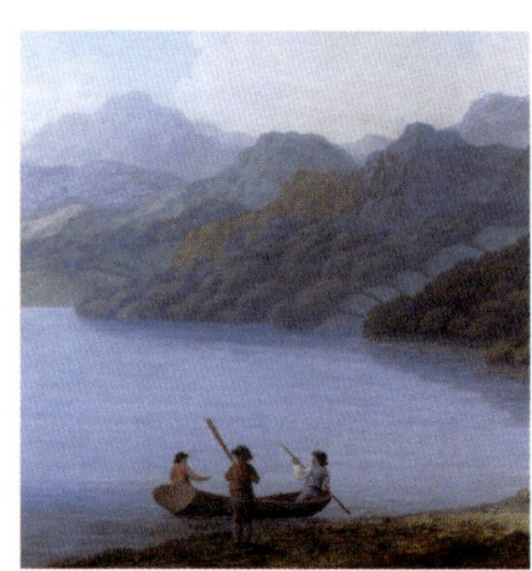

Robert Sherbourne was an illegitimate son of the Hon. Robert Digby (1732–1815) who served in the American War of Independence and retired from the Navy as Admiral of the Fleet in 1794. The Admiral's choice of a surname for his elder son appears to have been influenced by family connections: his own grandfather, the fifth Baron Digby of Geashill (1661/2–1752), had inherited the estate of Sherborne in Dorset in 1698 on the death of a kinsman. In retirement Admiral Digby and his American wife settled at Minterne near Sherborne where Robert (himself now a married man) was treated as one of the family. Both here and at Sherborne itself he came into contact with works of art; the Digbys of Sherborne owned works by Claude Lorrain and had employed 'Capability' Brown to landscape their gardens in the 1770s. By now Robert Sherbourne was already showing a talent for painting, exhibiting a miniature at the Society of Artists in 1775 and painting views at Sherborne from the 1780s onwards. He worked in both oils and bodycolour, usually on a modest scale and including an engaging figure group in the foreground (see cat. 22).

In 1792 a Robert Sherbourne was appointed manager of the British Cast Plate Glass Company operating at Ravenhead near St Helens on Merseyside. This was almost certainly the artist since the Hon. Robert Digby, his father, was named second among the original promoters of this company when Parliament was petitioned in 1773 for an Act to incorporate the business; Digby must therefore have played a major part in its establishment. Under Sherbourne's management it became highly prosperous, especially once the war had removed competition from France.

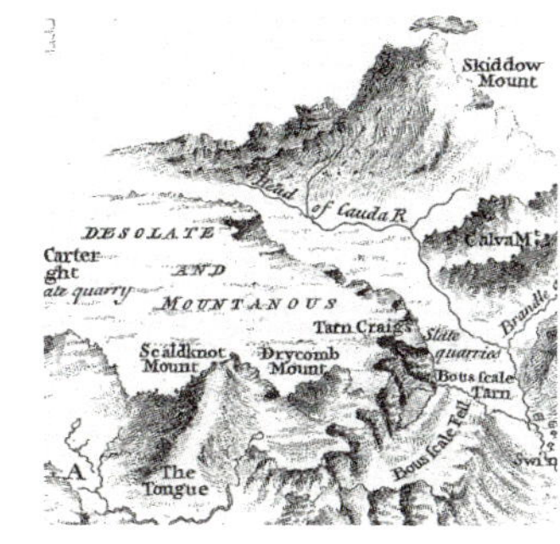

George Smith (1700–73)

George Smith was born in Scotland but moved to England where he worked for a time as a schoolmaster at Boothby near Carlisle, apparently supplementing his income by serving as a collector of excise taxes. By the 1750s he was living at Wigton where he died. Scientist, historian and antiquarian, he contributed regularly to the London magazines from 1741 onwards (see de Montluzin, 2004), a series of articles in the *Gentleman's Magazine* in 1746 consisting of his own account of Bonnie Prince Charlie's invasion of England the previous year. He himself had been arrested after the failure of the invasion but was released on showing that he had acted as a government agent, assisting in the Duke of Cumberland's recapture of Carlisle.

Many of Smith's articles were concerned with astronomy and meteorology, others with north country topography, geology and antiquities including Long Meg (see fig. 11 on p. 44). In August 1746 he surveyed the coast of Cumberland at the expense of the *Gentleman's Magazine*, publishing the results in 1748 in articles accompanied by diagrams such as fig. 6 on p. 13. Several of his articles in the magazine around this time contain not only extended descriptions of the Lake District that prefigure the later writings of philosophers, artists and travellers but also highly detailed and evocative pictorial maps – created before the invention and use of contour lines. These are among the earliest and most interesting depictions of the area north-east of Skiddaw (cat. 1) and the north-western lakes (cat. 2).

John 'Warwick' Smith (1749–1831)

John Smith was born at Irthington, a few miles east of Carlisle, the son of a gardener to a member of the Gilpin family. He received his first drawing lessons from Captain John Bernard Gilpin of nearby Scaleby Castle, an amateur artist well represented in the collection of the Wordsworth Trust (see Hebron, 2008), followed by further lessons from the captain's sons, William Gilpin (the future writer on picturesque beauty; see cat. 13 and 48) and Sawrey Gilpin RA, the animal painter and friend of George Barret. In the 1770s he was among the artists who accompanied William Gilpin on his sketching tours and who provided material for the illustrations in Gilpin's descriptive accounts and observations.

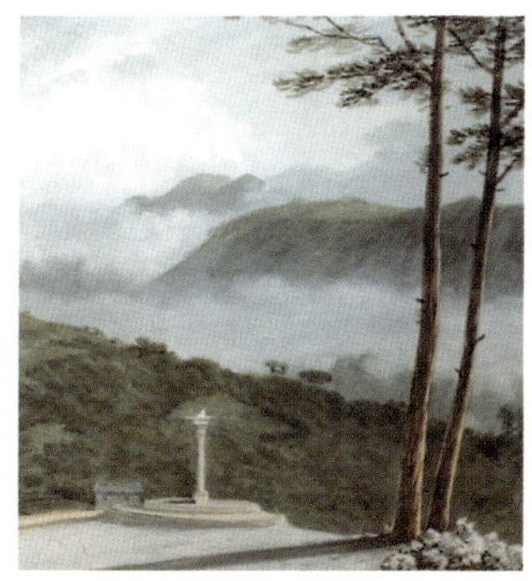

Through the Gilpins Smith was soon introduced to members of the aristocracy and his future was assured. In 1776–81 he travelled to Italy at the expense of the second Earl of Warwick, probably thus acquiring his soubriquet (though a subsequent brief residence in Warwick itself has also been suggested as its origin). His lively and colourful Italian and Swiss drawings attracted much attention, resulting in many further commissions such as that from John Christian Curwen of Workington Hall (by now the owner of Belle Isle on Windermere) for 100 watercolours of the Lake District (cat. 31).

These were executed from 1788 onwards and twenty variants on them were published as engravings in the folio volume *Views of the Lakes in Cumberland and Westmorland*, in instalments and by subscription, in 1791, 1792 and 1795 (cat 35; and see also cat. 44). In the mid 1790s Smith was also responsible, with John Emes, for providing the drawings for a more modest series of prints (sixteen small aquatints), intended to be bound in by purchasers with their copies of the latest edition of West's *Guide to the Lakes*.

Although Smith enjoyed a high reputation in his own day (somewhat modified in our own times when his originality has sometimes been disputed), his work attracted criticism from contemporary artists for widely differing reasons. FARINGTON was often distressed to discover that his watercolours were slovenly and inaccurate: both grave offences when they were commissioned for a topographical publication and had to be easily interpretable by an engraver (IX.3328, 3347; X.3692, 3756). TURNER, on the other hand, reprobated his 'mechanically, systematic process of drawing' which 'can produce nothing but manner and sameness' – both in the man himself and in admirers and pupils (IV.1303). Smith was, indeed, systematic and needed to be. In 1796 he was recorded as having enough work to last him two years: 'He enters his Commissions in a Book and finishes them in rotation' (III.703).

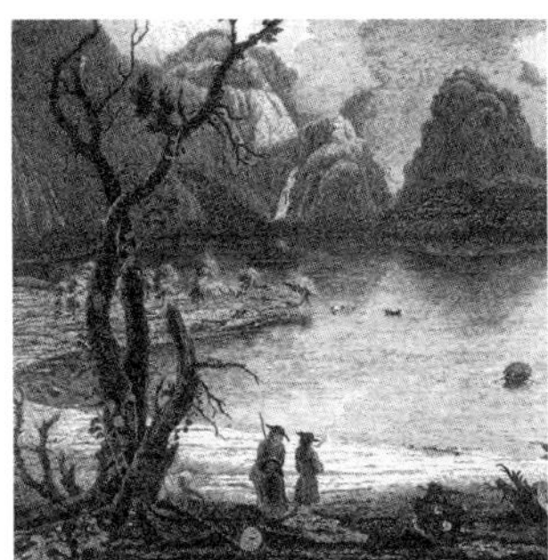

THOMAS SMITH OF DERBY (*c.*1720/4–67)

In his *Anecdotes of Painters*, published in 1808 (p. 30), Edward Edwards ARA observed that Thomas Smith was one of the first artists who 'explored and displayed the beautiful scenes of his native country'. He was born in Derby; was painting, engraving and publishing views of Derbyshire by 1743; and was first described as 'Mr Smith of Derby' in the Society of Artists' catalogue of 1761 to distinguish him from the three 'Smith of Chichester' brothers who were already well established on the scene.

Nothing is known of Thomas Smith's training so he has traditionally been described as self-taught. His penchant for dramatic and thrilling views is shown not only in paintings and engravings of the naturally wild beauties of his own county and those of Yorkshire and Staffordshire but also in depictions of man-made features: the park at Belton House, for example (with cascades, ruins and a grotto) in 1749, and a detailed view of Abraham Darby's new ironworks at Coalbrookdale in 1758 (one of the earliest representations of an industrial landscape). Following the success of WILLIAM BELLERS' depictions of the Lake District in the 1750s Smith seems to have deliberately extended his topographical range and probably visited the area in about 1759–60; he published his first three engravings of the Lakes, based on his own paintings, in 1761 (cat. 6). The copper plates for these were bought by John Boydell who republished them, together with a fourth (cat. 8), in the year of Smith's death, 1767. The scenes were reprinted later in the century in a much smaller and much inferior form, engraved by John Lodge, in publications by Alexander Hogg.

Thomas's son John Raphael Smith (1751–1812) achieved eminence in the same field as his father, specialising in portrait engravings and becoming 'Mezzotinto Engraver' to the Prince of Wales (the future George IV) in 1784 after he had engraved a portrait of the prince by GAINSBOROUGH. In 1788 the young TURNER worked in Smith's print-shop near Covent Garden, hand-colouring engravings, and may have had his first encounter with GIRTIN there.

Thomas Sunderland (1744–1823)

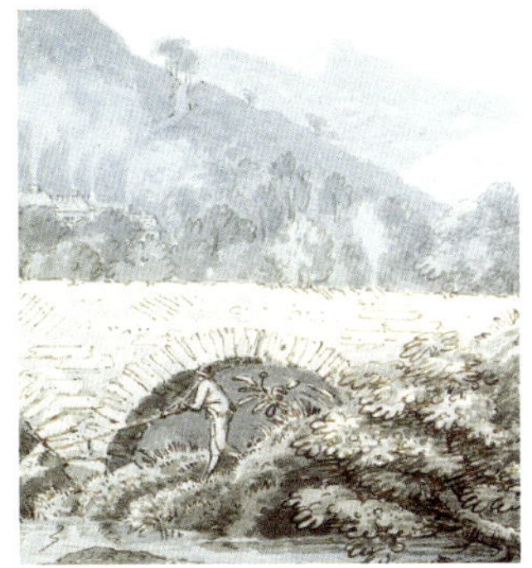

Born at Whittington Hall near Kirkby Lonsdale into a family with iron mining and smelting interests, Sunderland ran the business with great success until the early 1780s. He then retired to his large house in Ulverston, the most important town in the Furness peninsula which served as a port for fishing and trading vessels; at this date it was also the chief destination of those reaching the Lakes by foot or carriage over the sands from Lancaster at low tide. Here Sunderland devoted himself energetically to municipal affairs and his private passions for drawing and collecting. There has been much speculation about the origin of his interest in drawing and his possible teachers. One possibility, now discounted, was J.R. Cozens, another (inherently more likely) was Farington with whom he long remained in touch; it is, however, very probable that he was self-taught, making use of prints and drawings by other artists. He eventually made numerous copies of such works, often arranging them in albums to simulate the records of actual tours; this activity makes it hard to establish the extent of his own travels, let alone their chronology. He evidently had access to the collections of other art-lovers in the north of England, since there were periods when he rarely left the area. Visiting Farington in 1802 he told him it was twelve years since he was last in London (V.1797).

Living in Ulverston for some forty years, Sunderland had ample opportunities to make sketches of the Lake District and he produced many watercolours based on these, showing not only popular sights but also less frequented areas (cat. 39).

Francis Towne (1739–1816)

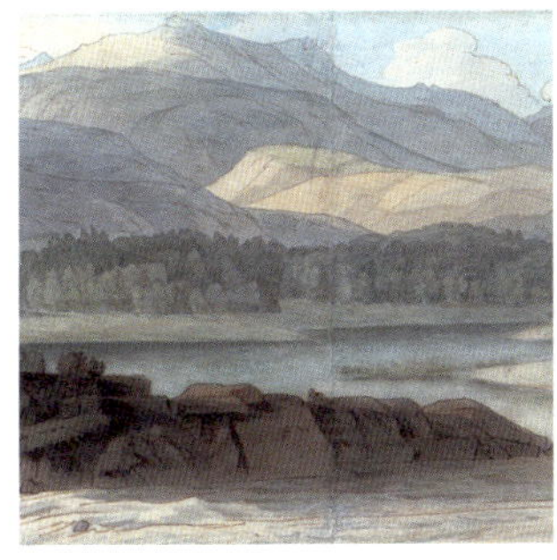

Although Towne is chiefly associated with the West Country, he was baptised in Isleworth, a Thames-side village to the west of London, and his early years as an artist were spent in that city. In 1752, at the age of thirteen, he was apprenticed to a coach painter for seven years after which he set his sights on being a landscape painter, attending the St Martin's Lane Academy and exhibiting at the Society of Artists, a regular practice prior to the foundation of the Royal Academy and its Schools in 1768. In the 1760s, however, he made his first visit to Devon, forming long-lasting and vital connections there, and for many years he divided his time between Exeter and London. His lack of commercial success with his paintings and his failure to achieve recognition at the RA (where he was repeatedly unsuccessful in his attempts to be elected an Associate) were, to some extent, balanced by his success as a teacher of drawing as a polite accomplishment to amateurs in Exeter; his numerous pupils included John White Abbott. Teaching brought Towne a respectable income, recorded by Farington as £500 a year in 1796 (III.694) and estimated by a recent scholar as £1,000, which, combined with his extreme frugality, permitted him to amass substantial savings. However, as he himself emphasised in 1803, he should not be described as 'a *provincial Drawing Master*' but as 'a *Landscape Painter*' (Wilcox, 1997, p. 163).

Towne's visit to the Lakes in August 1786 with two Exeter non-conformist friends, James White (his pupil's uncle) and John Merivale, resulted in a superb series of watercolours (see cat. 24), which he gradually worked up over a period of time from the on-the-spot drawings in his sketchbooks.

These record the principal lakes from Windermere and Coniston in the south to Buttermere, Derwentwater and Ullswater in the north and they bear dates between 7 and 23 August (Murdoch, 1984, pp. 41–2; Wilcox, 1997, pp. 106–27). A surprisingly large proportion of Towne's sketches concentrate on the southern lakes and the environs of Ambleside (the party's main base), given the contemporary preference for the wildness of Derwentwater; it seems probable that the tour was hampered by bad weather, causing the friends to reduce their time in the Lakes from five to three weeks and depriving them of further study of northerly subjects.

This tour was not, however, Towne's first exposure to mountain grandeur. In 1780 he had travelled to Rome, making the return journey through northern Italy and Switzerland the following summer with John 'Warwick' Smith. Towne's experience of the Alps, coupled with the stimulation of the younger artist's company, inspired him to create watercolours of extraordinary originality, strength and beauty (Wilcox, 1997, pp. 88–105); these have to be regarded as his greatest achievement. The lessons of the Alps were reflected five years later, on a smaller scale but with comparable quality, in his sensitive responses to the Lake District.

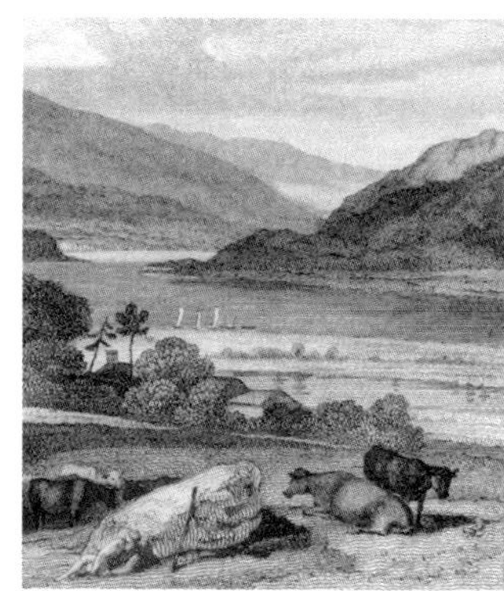

Joseph Mallord William Turner RA (1775–1851)

A barber's son from London's Covent Garden who showed a precocious talent for drawing at an early age, J.M.W. Turner became one of the most important painters of landscapes and seascapes in the history of British art. Like Girtin he transformed the practice of watercolour, elevating it from a modest and essentially descriptive medium to a vehicle of expression and emotion on a par with oil painting. However, the 'wonderful range of mind' that Constable enviously noted in Turner in 1813 resulted in a huge body of work, not only in watercolour and oils but also in bodycolour; his interest in print techniques led to his active participation in the production of his artistic manifesto, the *Liber Studiorum* (Book of Studies) in *c.*1807–19. Turner's art was based on the intensive study of nature, enriched by eclectic reading, which resulted in works that are infused with imagination and association and grow increasingly complex towards the end of his long career.

The Royal Academy, of which Turner was elected a member at the earliest eligible age (ARA 1799, RA 1802), was the chief focus and centre of his artistic and social life and he held many offices there over the years, including that of professor of perspective. He thus had frequent contact with Joseph Farington who provided guidance in his early career. However, his art was never popular with the conservative Sir George Beaumont whose criticisms included the now-famous words 'pea-green insipidity'.

Turner had an abiding passion for mountain scenery, from his earliest visits to Wales and the Lake District in the 1790s and Scotland in 1801 (when the war with France prevented travel on the continent) to his final tours of Switzerland year after year in the early 1840s. The forms of the mountains, lakes and valleys, together with atmospheric and meteorological effects and geological and historical factors, provided lifelong challenges to his aspirations as an artist. His first visit to the Lakes in 1797 inspired many impressive oil paintings and watercolours now in different museums and private collections around the world, including the comparatively straightforward watercolour commissioned in 1804 on which cat. 51 is based. Other (more vaporous and imaginative) watercolours of the Lake District were to follow in the 1830s including the Wordsworth Trust's *Ullswater* (fig. 10 on p. 20).

Thomas Walmsley (1763–1805/6)

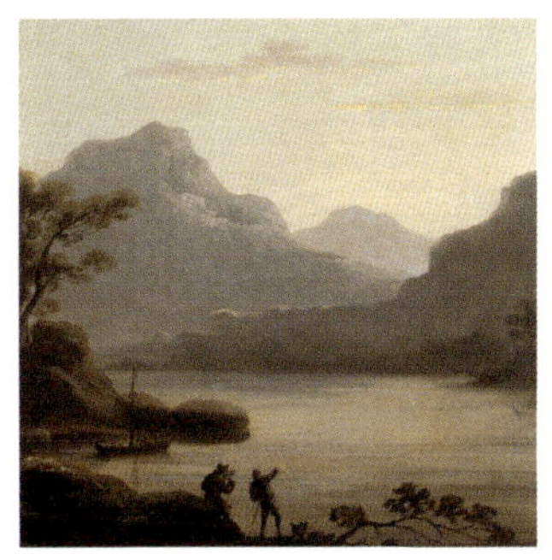

Walmsley was born in Dublin but, after quarrelling with his family, he went to London where he studied scene painting. He worked in this capacity at the Covent Garden Theatre, the King's Theatre, Haymarket, and also back in Dublin. By 1790 he was practising as a landscape painter in London and became a regular exhibitor of English, Welsh and Irish views at the Royal Academy until 1796. He probably visited the Lake District in 1790 or 1791; a bodycolour drawing of Bowness and Windermere in the Victoria & Albert Museum (of which cat. 57 is an extremely free adaptation) is dated 1791. He showed his first Lakes views at the RA in 1792 – *Ulls water from Gobray Park, morning* (no. 35) and *Ulls-Water, evening* (no. 399; see cat. 34) – following these in 1793 with *A view near Levans, Westmorland; morning* (no. 304) and *Part of Buttermere-lake, Cumberland; morning* (no. 315). As cat. 34 shows, he was producing work of great beauty and refinement before he succumbed to illness; he retired to Bath in search of a cure in the mid 1790s.

Some of Walmsley's Lake District subjects were published in highly exaggerated form shortly after 1800 and were advertised in West's *Guide* in 1802. This brought them to a wide audience before his death in his early 40s, after which they were no longer promoted in this fashion. However, such prints continued to be sold – and reprinted – for some time (see cat. 56–7).

William Westall ARA (1781–1850)

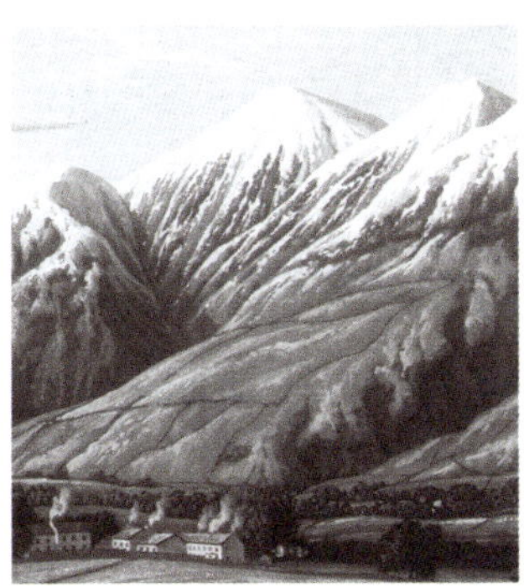

William Westall received his earliest drawing lessons from his elder half-brother Richard Westall (1765–1836) who later became a well-known painter of literary subjects. William, however, showed an aptitude for landscape and, after a period at the Royal Academy Schools, he left England as the draughtsman to Matthew Flinders on his voyage to Australia and the South Seas (a post declined by William Daniell who was about to marry Westall's half-sister Mary). Thanks to this assignment and a return voyage that took him to both China and India, Westall was abroad from July 1801 to February 1805 and for many years afterwards he concentrated mainly on creating watercolours and oil paintings relating to his voyages.

He had visited the Lake District, however, by 1811 when he exhibited *Part of Rydal Lake, from the Ambleside Road* at the RA (no. 91) and he became a frequent visitor thereafter. In the winter of 1815–16 he suffered some form of breakdown (then attributed to an illness contracted on his travels) and he spent the whole of the following summer in the Lakes. He enjoyed the support of Sir George Beaumont, who entertained him at Coleorton in Leicestershire, and the lasting friendship of Southey and Wordsworth. In a letter of 29 January 1817 Southey described him as 'a man much to my liking, who, I hope, will take up his abode in Keswick' (a desire then shared by the artist himself) while in 1818 Wordsworth composed three sonnets inspired by Westall's depictions of the Ingleton Caves, Gordale Scar and Malham Cove in Yorkshire.

A large number of Westall's watercolours were published as engravings, aquatints or lithographs, the artist possessing an exceptional interest in technical processes and an unusually wide range of skills. The first of his aquatints of the Lakes, including magnificent views of Derwentwater and Skiddaw (cat. 77), were published in 1819-21; his later commissions relating to the area included topographical illustrations to Southey's *Colloquies* (1829), a series of large aquatint panoramas (1831–9), and an uncompleted series to illustrate the poems of Wordsworth (1840).

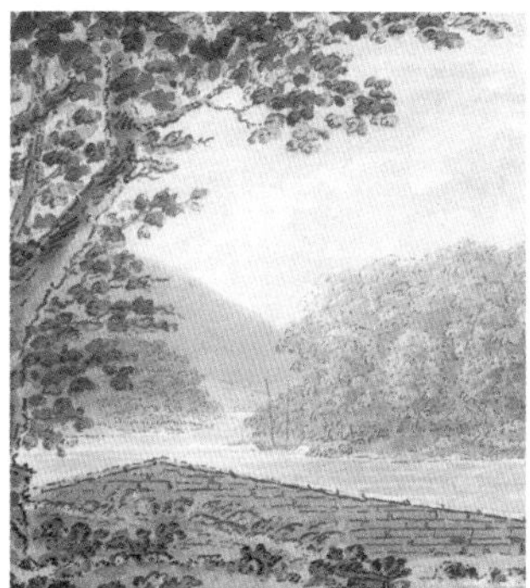

ELIZABETH WHARTON (1757–1829)

Elizabeth Wharton came from an old Durham family that distinguished itself in many fields, especially that of medicine, and fortuitously played a remarkable role in the history and discovery of the Lake District. In August 1767 her father, Dr Thomas Wharton, planned to take his Cambridge friend, the poet Thomas Gray, on a tour of the Lakes but the doctor's illness forced them back to his home, Old Park near Spennymoor, after just a few days. They made a second attempt at the end of September 1769 but once again Wharton immediately succumbed to a fit of asthma. This time Gray carried on alone, recording all his impressions and activities in small notebooks and re-using this material, within a matter of days, to compose four detailed letters to his absent friend. The twelve-year-old Elizabeth may thus have been among the first to read or hear Gray's accounts of the Lakes. These were published in 1775, four years after Gray's death, in the *Memoirs of his Life and Writings* by another close Cambridge friend, the poet William Mason, who prefixed them to a new edition of Gray's poems (cat. 12). They instantly attracted public attention through their sensitive descriptions of Lake scenery in language that is both poetical and infused with close observation; after their re-publication among the Addenda to the second edition of West's *Guide to the Lakes* in 1780 they became one of the best-known and most quoted of all writings on the area.

Born at Old Park into a family that eventually included seven children, Elizabeth grew up – and continued to live – among lovers of the Lake District. She received art instruction from a drawing-master in York recommended to her father by Gray and continued to make watercolours for much of her life, depicting both scenery and plants. The family had a long-standing friendship with the Lonsdales (distantly connected by marriage) and it was probably at Lowther Castle that Elizabeth worked on the watercolours in her Lake District album in 1811 (cat. 66). It was at Lowther, three years earlier, that FARINGTON had his first meeting with her brother Richard (MP for Durham in 1802–4 and 1806–20), Lord Lonsdale thoughtfully forewarning him that he was about to meet the son of the recipient of Gray's famous letters (IX.3370). There were further meetings in London over several years (IX.3462, 3487; XIII.4664) and in 1820 Farington enabled a 'Miss Wharton' to visit the Marquess of Stafford's collection of Old Master paintings (XVI.5510). Elizabeth's eldest brother having inherited Old Park in 1794, she lived for some time with two of her sisters in a house in the South Bailey, Durham, and is buried at the church there, St Mary the Less.

Joseph Wilkinson (1763–1831)

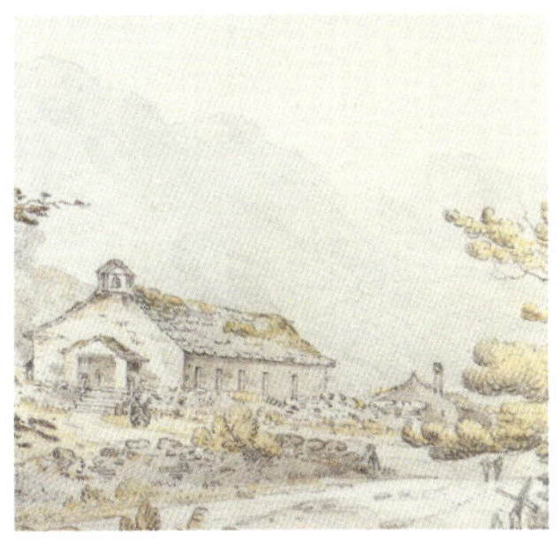

Joseph Wilkinson was born at Carlisle; is listed as a member of Queen's College, Oxford, in the subscribers' list to Hearne's *Antiquities*; and was ordained in 1790. In 1788 he married Mary Wood, daughter of Charles Wood, a Whitehaven metallurgist, and niece to one of the most distinguished scientists of the day, the chemist and physician Dr William Brownrigg. The young couple made their home with the Brownriggs at Ormathwaite Hall just north of Keswick, looking after them in their old age (Mary's aunt died in 1794, her uncle in 1800 at the age of 88). During this period Wilkinson held curacies at Irthington near Carlisle and Monkwearmouth near Sunderland as well as a living in Lincolnshire. In 1803 he was appointed to the parish of East and West Wretham, just north of Thetford in Norfolk, moving there in 1804 and remaining for the rest of his life.

Wilkinson was an enthusiastic amateur artist and during his time at Ormathwaite he made numerous sketches of the Lake District (cat. 62). After he had left the area he developed many of these into the *Select Views* published in 1810 to which Wordsworth contributed the unsigned introductory letterpress (see cat. 78). The Wilkinsons were close friends of the Southeys and Coleridges but never on intimate terms with the Wordsworths; however, Joseph's two sisters married the two brothers of Wordsworth's friend James Losh of Newcastle.

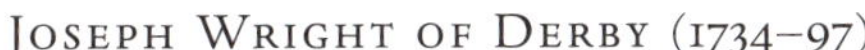

Joseph Wright of Derby (1734–97)

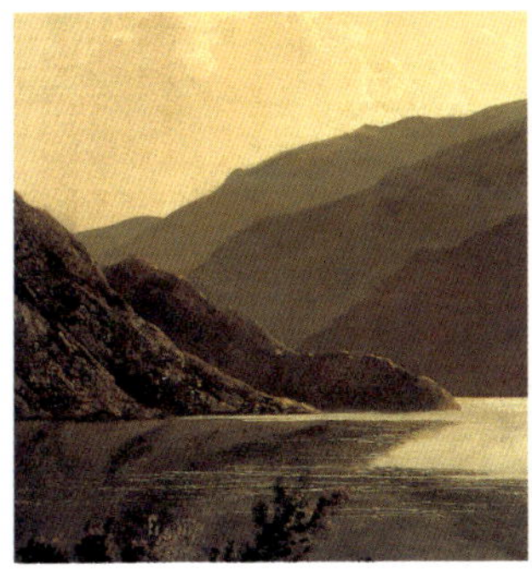

Joseph Wright enjoyed a successful career as a painter of portraits and themes from literature, making a speciality of scenes lit by lamp-light or candlelight, the latter subjects reflecting his interest in the scientific and industrial developments of his age and his contacts with eminent natural philosophers including Erasmus Darwin. His few landscapes were chiefly inspired by his native county and his long visit to Italy (1773–5). Born in Derby, he trained in London in the 1750s but returned to Derby where he remained for the rest of his life apart from just over two years in Liverpool (1768–71) and some eighteen months in Bath (1775–7). He acquired his nickname 'Wright of Derby' in the 1760s when reviewers wished to distinguish him from the now-forgotten Richard Wright of Liverpool, and he became the first important British artist to make a career outside London. He was elected ARA in 1781 but a disagreement with the Royal Academy a couple of years later led to him declining full membership and resigning his associateship.

Uncertainty has long surrounded the true number of Wright's visits to the Lake District. He paid one visit in the summer of 1793 in the course of a two-month sojourn at Bootle with several members of his family: he and Thomas Moss Tate of Liverpool took up the invitation of the Rev. Thomas Gisborne with whom they spent a week in the Lakes. In July 1794 he paid another visit to Liverpool and again accompanied Tate on a similar excursion. Both visits were later recalled by Wright's niece Hannah (a member of the 1793 party) and the artist's account book confirms that he produced a small number of Lakes paintings in the mid 1790s. These include the Wordsworth Trust's *Ullswater* (cat. 40) and a painting of the Langdale Pikes that is now known only through copies such as cat. 41 and the small watercolour made by Thomas Chubbard for Daniel Daulby (fig. 19 on p. 82).

These may not have been Wright's only visits. A letter of 7 February 1786 from Wright to Daniel Daulby shows that he planned 'to take the fashionable tour of the Lakes next Autumn' and 'your company will be a happy addition' (Bemrose, 1885, pp. 86–7); his account book includes an entry for 'A View of Borrow Dale sunset, £31.10' among the paintings of *c.*1786–8 (Nicolson, 1968, vol. 1, p. 266); a pencil and wash drawing of the late 1780s in Derby Museum (ibid., fig. 130) represents the Bowder Stone (following identification of its subject later authors assigned this to the early 1790s to accord with Wright's tours of that time). Furthermore, four drawings of the Lakes in Tate Britain – all by the same hand – bearing dates in 1787 as well as 1793 have now been attributed to Wright. These are copiously annotated in typical Wright fashion and show: a view from Heversham towards Whitbarrow Scar (12 June 1787; repr. in Wilcox, 1997, p. 21); Gowbarrow Park, Ullswater (16 June 1787), with a view of Windermere on its verso; and finally a much larger drawing of Derwentwater from between Barrow and Lodore (16 July 1793). The position is somewhat complicated by the fact that a further drawing in this group, dated 4 June 1788, depicts Llangollen. Until 1990 it was thought that Wright never went to Wales but the acceptance by scholars of an oil painting of *c.*1790–5, *Landscape near Bedgellert. North Wales*, as Wright's work has thrown doubt on that assumption (Egerton, 1990, no. 118). All in all, it seems not impossible that Wright did visit the Lake District in 1787.

Perhaps Wright may be allowed the final pronouncement in this catalogue. On returning from the Lakes in 1794 the painter spoke of his enjoyment of 'the most stupendous scenes I ever beheld', adding that 'they are to the eye, what Handels Choruses are to the ear' (quoted in Egerton, 1990, p. 213). No poet could have extolled the grandeur and nobility of the Lake District with more felicity.

SAVAGE GRANDEUR AND NOBLEST THOUGHTS IN CONTEXT

George Smith, *The Caudebec Fells* 1747 (cat. 1)

1750
Thomas Gray finishes 'Elegy Written in a Country Churchyard'

1751
The Society of Antiquaries of London granted its Royal Charter
George Smith, *Map of the Black Lead Mines &c. in Cumberland* (cat. 2)

1752
Bellers, *A View of Derwent-Water, Towards Borrodale* (cat. 3)

1753
Foundation of the British Museum (opens to the public 1759)

1754
Bellers, *A View of the Head of Ulswater toward Patterdale* (cat. 4)

1755
John Dalton, *A Descriptive Poem* (cat. 5)

1757
Edmund Burke publishes *A Philosophical Enquiry into the Origin of Our Ideas of the Sublime and Beautiful* (revised in 1759)

1760
Accession of George III
First public exhibition of art in England, at the Society of Artists in London

1761
Thomas Smith, *A View of Darwentwater &c. from Crow-Park* (cat. 6)

1766
Lowther, *Long Meg &c from the Gate* (cat. 7)

1767
Thomas Smith, *A View of Ennerdale, Broadwater, &c.* (cat. 8)
John Brown, *A Description of the Lake at Keswick* (cat. 9)

1768
Foundation of the Royal Academy of Arts, with Joshua Reynolds as its first President

1769
First exhibition of the Royal Academy, in Pall Mall
Thomas Gray visits the Lakes

1770
William Wordsworth born in Cockermouth
Barret exhibits the first named painting of the Lake District at the Royal Academy
Devis, *Winandermeer c.*1770? (cat. 10)

1771
Dorothy Wordsworth born

1772
William Gilpin visits the Lakes
Samuel Taylor Coleridge born

1774
The first provincial art exhibition in England is held in Liverpool
Thomas West publishes *The Antiquities of Furness*
William Hutchinson, *An Excursion to the Lakes* (cat. 11)

1775
Paul Sandby publishes the first series of aquatints in England: *XII Views in South-Wales*

Thomas Gray (ed. William Mason), *The Poems of Mr. Gray* (cat. 12)

1776
Richard Cumberland, *Odes* (cat. 14)

1777
Hearne, *Sketch of Sir George Beaumont and Joseph Farington painting a Waterfall* (cat. 15)
Hearne, *Sir George Beaumont and Joseph Farington painting a Waterfall* (cat. 16)
Hearne, *West Aspect of Furness Abbey* (cat. 17)

1778
Publication of the first plates in Hearne and Byrne's *Antiquities of Great Britain*
Thomas West, *A Guide to the Lakes* (cat. 18)

1779
Peter Crosthwaite opens his museum in Keswick
Death of Thomas West

1780
The Royal Academy moves to Somerset House, the Strand
Thomas West (ed. William Cockin), *A Guide to the Lakes* (cat. 19)
Cockin, *Ode to the Genius of the Lakes* (cat. 20)

1781
De Loutherbourg invents the Eidophusikon
Sherbourne, *Ullswater* (cat. 22)

1782
Gilpin publishes his *Observations* on the River Wye (delayed until 1783)

1783
Crosthwaite, *Seven Maps of the Lakes* (cat. 21)
Gainsborough, *The Langdale Pikes*, *c.*1783 (cat. 23)

1784
Publication of the first plates in Farington's *Views of the Lakes*

1785
William Cowper publishes *The Task*

1786
William Gilpin, *Observations ... Cumberland, and Westmoreland* (cat. 13)
Towne, *Elterwater* (cat. 24)

1787
De Loutherbourg, *Skiddaw in Cumberland: a Summer's sunset* (cat. 25)

1788
Barret, *Uls Water, A Lake in Cumberland* (cat. 26)

1789
The start of the French Revolution and the storming of the Bastille
Charlotte Smith publishes her novel *Ethelinde, or The Recluse of the Lake*
Farington and Cookson, *Views of the Lakes* (cat. 27)
Farington, *North View on the Road leading from Keswick to Ambleside* (cat. 28)

1790
Wordsworth visits the Alps
?Laporte, *North View on the Road leading from Keswick to Ambleside c.*1790? (cat. 29)
?Laporte, *Derwentwater, and the Vale of Keswick from Ashness c.*1790? (cat. 30)
John 'Warwick' Smith, *From Mr Parker's Gardens, Coniston Lake c.*1790 (cat. 31)

1791
Abbott, *Hill Cragg on Grasmere Lake* (cat. 32)

1792
Gilpin publishes *Three Essays* on aspects of 'picturesque beauty'
Holland, *Lodoar Waterfall* (cat. 33)
Walmsley, *Ullswater, Evening* (cat. 34)
John 'Warwick' Smith, *Entrance into Borrodale* (cat. 35)
Dayes, *Grasmere Lake, Westmorland, with Cattle watering* (cat. 36)

1793
Execution of Louis XVI. Britain and France at war
Wordsworth publishes *An Evening Walk* and *Descriptive Sketches*

1794
Turner and Girtin begin working at Dr Monro's 'Academy' in the evenings
Mrs Radcliffe visits the Lakes
Uvedale Price publishes *An Essay on the Picturesque*
Richard Payne Knight publishes *The Landscape*

1795
Becker, *Scale Force near Buttermere, c.*1795? (cat. 37)
Becker, *Barrow Cascade, Derwent Water, c.*1795? (cat. 38)
Sunderland, *Ulpha Bridge c.*1795–1800 (cat. 39)
Wright, *Ullswater* (cat. 40)
After Wright, *The Langdale Pikes c.*1795–1800 (cat. 41)

1796
Jane Austen begins writing *Pride and Prejudice* (published 1813)
Rogers, *The Lake & Vale of Keswick, with a distant view of Basinthwait Lake* (cat. 42)
Chubbard, *Haws-water, with Bampton c.*1796–8 (cat. 43)
Chubbard after John 'Warwick' Smith, *The Entrance into Borrowdale c.*1796–8 (cat. 44)

1798
Wordsworth and Coleridge publish *Lyrical Ballads*
James Plumptre publishes *The Lakers: A Comic Opera*
Nicholson, *Skiddaw from across the Lake of Derwentwater c.*1798? (cat. 45)
Beaumont, *Borrowdale* (cat. 46)

1799
Napoleon seizes power and becomes First Consul
Wordsworth and Coleridge tour the Lakes
William and Dorothy Wordsworth move into Dove Cottage

1800
Coleridge moves into Greta Hall, Keswick
Wordsworth republishes *Lyrical Ballads*, with Preface and second volume (delayed until 1801)

1801
Union with Ireland
Girtin, *Borrowdale c.*1801 (cat. 47)
Gilpin, *Landscape with a Tower* (cat. 48)

1802
Peace of Amiens (lasts fourteen months)
Marriage of William and Mary Wordsworth
?Bourne, *Grasmere from Red Bank c.*1802? (cat. 49)

1803
War resumes – invasion fears
Southey moves into Greta Hall, Keswick

1804
Coleridge leaves the Lake District and travels to Malta for his health, making only brief subsequent returns to the Lakes
Foundation of the Society of Painters in Water Colours
Napoleon crowned Emperor

1805
First Exhibition of the Society of Painters in Water Colours
Foundation of the British Institution
Battles of Trafalgar and Austerlitz
De Loutherbourg, *Lake of Wyndermere* (cat. 50)
Turner, *Patterdale* (cat. 51)
Cristall, *From Borrowdale* (cat. 52)
Cristall, *Borrowdale* (cat. 53)
Seaton, *Crummock Water* (cat. 54)

1806
First exhibition of the British Institution
Constable, *The Langdale Pikes* (cat. 55)

1807
Abolition of the Slave Trade
Wordsworth first contemplates writing *A Guide to the Lakes*
Southey publishes *Letters from England*

1808
The Wordsworth family moves to Allan Bank
Foundation of a rival watercolour society, the 'Associated Artists in Water Colours', which lasts until 1812
Walmsley, *Upper-fall at Ridal, Westmorland* *c.*1801–8 (cat. 56)
Walmsley, *Bowness on Windermere* (cat. 57)
Havell, *The Beck at Ambleside after Much Rain* (cat. 60)

1809
Munn, *At Troutbeck, Westmorland* (cat. 61)
Wilkinson, *Langdale Chapel, Vale of Langdale* *c.*1809 (cat. 62)

1810
Rowlandson, *Doctor Syntax sketching the Lake,* *c.*1810 (cat. 58)
Joseph Wilkinson, *Select Views in Cumberland, Westmoreland, and Lancashire* (cat. 78)
Payne, *Bowder Stone South* (cat. 63)
Jameson, *Derelict Cottage in Ambleside, with Wansfell in the Distance c.*1810 (cat. 64)
Reinagle, *The Slate Wharf and Village Clappersgate on the River Brathy near Windermere. Morning* *c.*1810–11 (cat. 65)

1811
George III declared insane and the Prince of Wales becomes Regent
Jane Austen publishes *Sense and Sensibility*
Wharton, *Windermere, from the Ferry Inn* (cat. 66)
Anonymous, *Windermere, from the Ferry Inn* 1811 or earlier (cat. 67)

1812
Coleridge's last visit to the Lakes
The Society of Painters in Water Colours votes to admit oil paintings at its exhibitions and becomes the 'Society of Painters in Oil and Water Colours'
William Combe and Thomas Rowlandson, *The Tour of Doctor Syntax in Search of the Picturesque* (cat. 59)

1813
Wordsworth appointed Distributor of Stamps for Westmorland
The Wordsworth family moves to Rydal Mount
Southey appointed Poet Laureate
Glover, *Windermere* (cat. 68)
Ibbetson, *Buttermere Bridge and Church, from the Fish Inn c.*1813 (cat. 69)

1814
Napoleon is defeated and exiled to Elba
Wordsworth publishes *The Excursion*
Green, *Easedale from Butterlip How* (cat. 70)
Green, *Easedale from Butterlip How* (cat. 71)
Farington, *Waterfall at Rydal* (cat. 75)

1815
Napoleon escapes but is defeated at the Battle of Waterloo
Constable, *Helvellyn* (cat. 72)

1816
Daniell, *Distant View of Whitbarrow Scar, Westmoreland* (cat. 73)
Farington and Horne, *The Lakes of Lancashire, Westmoreland and Cumberland*
Farington, *Waterfall at Rydal* (cat. 74)

1818
John Keats visits the Lakes and Scotland

1819
Harden, *Ambleside c.*1818–19 (cat. 76)

1820
Accession of George IV
John Clare publishes *Poems Descriptive of Rural Life*
Westall, *Skiddaw* (cat. 77)
Wordsworth, *The River Duddon, etc.* (cat. 79); the 'Topographical description' is republished as *A Description of the Scenery of the Lakes in the North of England* in 1822

A NOTE ON PRINT-MAKING TERMS

An ENGRAVING is a print made from a metal plate that has been scored with a very sharp tool (a 'burin' or 'graver'), which cuts a clean v-shaped groove to hold the ink, leaving slivers of metal. These are then wiped away, revealing regular lines, each tapering to a point. The process (often referred to as 'line-engraving') is repeated several times, resulting in areas of fine parallel lines and cross-hatching throughout the print. This highly skilled, labour-intensive work is carried out by professional engravers rather than artists (see cat. 25). In the period of this exhibition the metal plates would invariably have been of copper, engraving on steel plates not being introduced in Britain until the 1820s.

In an ETCHING the engraver draws with an 'etching needle' on a metal plate that has been prepared with a thin layer of a soft substance (made of waxes, gums and resins) which is impervious to acid. The drawing exposes the metal so that, when the plate is immersed in acid, these lines are bitten (or 'etched') into the plate. This process, like that of engraving, can be repeated and varied to achieve different effects, e.g. in the delicacy or thickness of the lines. The marks left by the 'etching needle' are always irregular, blunt-ended and organic in appearance, owing to the action of the acid. Since the etcher can draw on the prepared ground with as much ease as a draughtsman using pen and paper, etching has been practised by many artists. It has been regularly used to establish the overall composition of a print prior to the more mechanical and laborious work of engraving (see cat. 28). Both techniques were well established in Britain by the eighteenth century.

The process of SOFT-GROUND ETCHING is a variant of the above and enables the artist to make facsimiles of chalk or pencil drawings. The plate is prepared with a mixture that includes tallow (candle-grease) to prevent it hardening and the artist draws on a piece of soft paper placed over this ground. When the paper is lifted off, it removes the part of the ground that the artist has drawn on; the design is exposed on the plate and the action of the acid reproduces the textured and grainy effects of the artist's original drawing. Soft-ground etching reached the height of its popularity in Britain in the years covered by this exhibition (see cat. 70–1 and figs 31–2 on pp. 114–15).

AQUATINT is also a form of etching, relying on a chemical process, but, unlike those described above, it is able to produce the subtlest gradations of light and shade, from near-white to deep velvety black, together with the general effect of a watercolour wash. Here the metal plate is covered with a porous ground consisting of particles of powdered resin. When the acid bites into the plate, it creates a tiny ring round each particle; these produce the granular areas that are a characteristic feature of this medium. The first aquatints published in Britain were depictions of Wales, issued by Paul Sandby RA in the 1770s, and there was considerable interest in the technique on the part of artists visiting the Lake District (see cat. 33, 42, 77). With its power to suggest mood and atmosphere as well as the physical features of a scene, aquatint soon became an extremely popular medium for landscape prints.

MEZZOTINT was chiefly used for portraits and figure-subjects and was only occasionally employed for prints of the Lake District (cat. 72). In this process, the metal plate is roughened all over by a spiked tool known as a 'rocker', which produces an extremely rich dark effect when the plate is inked. The engraver then smoothes and burnishes the plate in order to produce highlights in particular areas; this is usually described as working 'from dark to light', the opposite of the procedure in the techniques described above, where the artist works 'from light to dark', constantly building up and intensifying the darker areas of his scene.

Several of the artists represented here later went on to produce LITHOGRAPHS but there are none in this exhibition since the earliest examples depicting the Lakes were not produced until after 1820. In this process there are no incisions or copper plates; the artist drew on a stone surface with a greasy medium such as crayon and the complex printing process is based on the simple chemical fact that grease and water repel each other.

All the above descriptions are, by necessity, extremely abbreviated. Interested readers are advised to consult the following, published by the British Museum: Antony Griffiths, *Prints and Printmaking. An Introduction to the History and Techniques* (1980 and later editions); Paul Goldman, *Looking at Prints, Drawings and Watercolours. A Guide to Technical Terms* (1988 and later editions).

BIBLIOGRAPHY

Andrews, Malcolm, *The Search for the Picturesque. Landscape Aesthetics and Tourism in Britain, 1760–1800*, Aldershot, 1989

—(ed.), *The Picturesque. Literary Sources and Documents*, 3 vols, Mountfield, 1994

Barker, Elizabeth E., Alex Kidson, *et al.*, *Joseph Wright of Derby in Liverpool*, exhibition catalogue, Walker Art Gallery, Liverpool, and Yale Center for British Art, New Haven, 2007–8

Belsey, Hugh, 'A Second Supplement to John Hayes's *The Drawings of Thomas Gainsborough*', *Master Drawings* XLIV.4, winter 2008, pp. 427–541

Bemrose, William, *The Life and Works of Joseph Wright of Derby, A.R.A., commonly called 'Wright of Derby'*, London, 1885

Bicknell, Peter, *The Picturesque Scenery of the Lake District 1752–1855. A Bibliographical Study*, Winchester, 1990

—and Jane Munro, *Gilpin to Ruskin: Drawing Masters and their Manuals, 1800–1860*, exhibition catalogue, Fitzwilliam Museum, Cambridge, and Wordsworth Museum, Grasmere, 1988

—and Robert Woof, *The Discovery of the Lake District 1750–1810. A Context for Wordsworth*, exhibition catalogue, Wordsworth Museum, Grasmere, 1982

——*The Lake District Discovered 1810–1850. The Artists, The Tourists, and Wordsworth*, exhibition catalogue, Wordsworth Museum, Grasmere, 1983

Bonehill, John, and Stephen Daniels (ed.), *Paul Sandby: Picturing Britain*, exhibition catalogue, Nottingham Castle Museum, National Gallery of Scotland, Edinburgh, and Royal Academy, London, 2009–10

Burkett, Mary, *et al.*, *The Viewfinders. An Exhibition of Lake District Landscapes*, exhibition catalogue, Abbot Hall Art Gallery, Kendal, 1980

—and V.A.J. Slowe, *Julius Caesar Ibbetson 1759–1817*, exhibition catalogue, Abbot Hall Art Gallery, Kendal, 1982

—and J.D.G. Sloss, *William Green of Ambleside. A Lake District Artist (1760–1823)*, Kendal, 1984

Clayton, Timothy, *The English Print 1688–1802*, London and New Haven, 1997

Darcy, C.P., *The Encouragement of the Fine Arts in Lancashire 1760–1860*, Manchester, 1976

Davies, Randall, 'Joshua Cristall' and 'List of Works by Joshua Cristall', *The Old Water-Colour Society's Club 1926–1927 Fourth Annual Volume*, London, 1927, pp. 1–20

—'Francis Nicholson. Some Family Letters and Papers', *The Old Water-Colour Society's Club 1930–1931 Eighth Annual Volume*, London, 1931, pp. 1–39

Dibdin, E. Rimbault, 'Liverpool Art and Artists in the Eighteenth Century', *Walpole Society* vol. 6, Oxford, 1918, pp. 59–93

Edwards, Edward, *Anecdotes of Painters who have resided or been born in England*, London, 1808

Egerton, Judy, *Wright of Derby*, exhibition catalogue, Tate Gallery, London, 1990

Fawcett, Trevor, *The Rise of English Provincial Art. Artists, Patrons, and Institutions outside London, 1800–1830*, Oxford, 1974

Foskett, Daphne, *John Harden of Brathay Hall 1772–1847*, Kendal, 1974

Gill, Stephen, 'Wordsworth and *The River Duddon*', *Essays in Criticism*, vol. 57, no. 1 (2007), pp. 22–41

Hall, Marshall, *The Artists of Cumbria*, Newcastle upon Tyne, 1979
—*The Artists of Northumbria*, Bristol, 2005
Harden, Jessy, Unpublished journals, 1801–11, typescript in Abbot Hall Art Gallery, Kendal
Hargraves, Matthew, *'Candidates for Fame': The Society of Artists of Great Britain 1760–1791*, New Haven and London, 2005
Harrison, Colin, *John Malchair of Oxford. Artist and Musician*, exhibition catalogue, Ashmolean Museum, Oxford, 1998
Hayes, John, *The Landscape Paintings of Thomas Gainsborough*, 2 vols, London, 1982
—(ed.), *The Letters of Thomas Gainsborough*, New Haven and London, 2001
Hebron, Stephen, *In the Line of Beauty. Early Views of the Lake District by Amateur Artists*, exhibition catalogue, Wordsworth Museum, Grasmere, 2008
—Conal Shields, and Timothy Wilcox, *The Solitude of Mountains: Constable and the Lake District*, exhibition catalogue, Wordsworth Museum, Grasmere, 2006
Herrmann, Luke, *British Landscape Painting of the Eighteenth Century*, London, 1973
Hill, Alan (ed.), *Letters of Dorothy Wordsworth*, Oxford, 1981
Hopkinson, Martin, 'The Print Market in Liverpool in the Late Eighteenth Century', *Print Quarterly* XXIV, 2007, 2, pp. 107–15
Ingamells, John, and John Edgcumbe (eds), *The Letters of Sir Joshua Reynolds*, New Haven and London, 2000
Joll, Evelyn, Martin Butlin, and Luke Herrmann (ed.), *The Oxford Companion to J.M.W. Turner*, Oxford, 2001
Joppien, Rüdiger, *Philippe Jacques de Loutherbourg, RA, 1740–1812*, exhibition catalogue, Kenwood, London, 1973
Lindop, Grevel, *A Literary Guide to the Lake District*, London, 1993
Liversidge, M.J.H., 'James Bourne (1773–1854)', *Connoisseur*, November 1966, 163, pp. 161–5
Long, Basil S., 'John Laporte. Landscape Painter and Etcher', *Walker's Quarterly* II (no. 8), London, 1922
—'Francis Nicholson. Painter and Lithographer', *Walker's Quarterly* IV (no. 14), London, 1924
—'John (Warwick) Smith (1749–1831)', *Walker's Quarterly* VI (no. 24), London, 1927
McCracken, David, *Wordsworth and the Lake District*, Oxford, 1984
Mallalieu, H.L., *The Dictionary of British Watercolour Artists up to 1920*, Woodbridge, 1976
Mitchell, James, *Julius Caesar Ibbetson (1759–1817). 'The Berchem of England'*, exhibition catalogue, John Mitchell & Son, London, 1999
de Montluzin, Emily Lorraine, 'George Smith of Wigton: *Gentleman's Magazine* Contributor, Unheralded Scientific Polymath, and Shaper of the Aesthetic of the Romantic Sublime', *Eighteenth-Century Life*, 28.3, Fall 2004, pp. 66–89
Murdoch, John, *The Discovery of the Lake District*, exhibition catalogue, Victoria & Albert Museum, London, 1984
Nicholson, Norman, *Portrait of the Lakes,* London, 1963
Nicolson, Benedict, *Joseph Wright of Derby. Painter of Light*, 2 vols, London and New York, 1968
Nugent, Charles, *British Watercolours in The Whitworth Art Gallery, The University of Manchester. A Summary Catalogue of Drawings and Watercolours by Artists born before 1880*, London and Manchester, 2003
Owen, Felicity, and Eric Stanford, *William Havell 1782-1857*, exhibition catalogue, Spink & Sons, London, Reading Art Gallery and Abbot Hall Art Gallery, Kendal, 1981–2
—and David Blayney Brown, *Collector of Genius. A Life of Sir George Beaumont*, New Haven and London, 1988

Owen, Hugh, *The Lowther Family. Eight Hundred Years of 'A Family of Ancient Gentry and Worship'*, Chichester, 1990

Penny, Nicholas (ed.), *Reynolds*, exhibition catalogue, Royal Academy, London, 1986

Perry, Seamus (ed.), *Coleridge's Notebooks. A Selection*, Oxford, 2002

Radcliffe, Ann, *A Journey made in the Summer of 1794, through Holland and the Western Frontier of Germany, with a Return down the Rhine: to which are added Observations during a Tour to the Lakes of Lancashire, Westmoreland, and Cumberland*, London, 1795

Redgrave, Richard and Samuel, *A Century of British Painters* (first edition 1866), Oxford, 1981

Reynolds, Graham, *The Early Paintings and Drawings of John Constable*, 2 vols, New Haven and London, 1996

Roget, John Lewis, *A History of the 'Old Water-Colour' Society*, 2 vols, London, 1891 (repr. Woodbridge, 1972)

Royal Academy of Arts, London: catalogues to the annual exhibitions, 1769–1820

Ruddick, William, and Mark G. Turner, *Joseph Farington. Watercolours and Drawings*, exhibition catalogue, Bolton Museum and Art Gallery, 1977

Smith, Alan, *The Story of the Bowder Stone*, Keswick, 2003

Smith, Greg, *et al.*, *Thomas Girtin: The Art of Watercolour*, exhibition catalogue, Tate Britain, London, 2002

Society of Painters in Water Colours: catalogues to the annual exhibitions, 1805–20, in the archive of the Royal Watercolour Society, London

Solkin, David H. (ed.), *Art on the Line. The Royal Academy Exhibitions at Somerset House 1780–1836*, London, 2001

Stephens, Richard, 'Francis Towne's Views of Rome. Time-telling and Ideology in Provincial England', *British Art Journal* X.3, 2009/10, pp. 46–55

Thomason, David, and Robert Woof, *Derwentwater: The Vale of Elysium*, exhibition catalogue, Wordsworth Museum, Grasmere, 1986

Tisdall, John, *Joshua Cristall 1768–1847. In Search of Arcadia*, Hereford, 1996

Todd, Janet (ed.), *The Collected Letters of Mary Wollstonecraft*, London, 2003

Toynbee, Paget, and Leonard Whibley (ed.), *Correspondence of Thomas Gray*, 3 vols, Oxford, 1935

Urquhart, Peter, 'Daulby's Albums', *Transactions of the Romney Society*, 13, 2008, pp. 16–23

Westall, Richard J., 'The Westall Brothers', *Turner Studies* 4.1, 1984, pp. 23–38

Whitley, William T., *Artists and their Friends in England 1700–1799*, 2 vols, London and Boston, 1928

Wilberforce, William, *Journey to the Lake District from Cambridge 1779*, a diary edited by his great-great-grandson C.E. Wrangham, Stocksfield, 1983

Wilcox, Timothy, *Francis Towne*, exhibition catalogue, Tate Gallery, London, 1997

— *The Triumph of Watercolour. The Early Years of the Royal Watercolour Society 1805–55*, exhibition catalogue, Dulwich Picture Gallery, 2005

— *Francis Towne and his Friends*, exhibition catalogue, John Spink, London, 2005

Williams, Iolo A., *Early English Watercolours*, London, 1925

Woof, Pamela (ed.), *Dorothy Wordsworth, The Grasmere and Alfoxden Journals*, Oxford, 2002

IMAGE CREDITS

Fig. 1 (p. 2) Salvator Rosa, *St John the Baptist revealing Christ to the Disciples*, Culture and Sport Glasgow (Museums).

Fig. 2 (p. 6) George Barret, *Decorative Landscape – Study for a Room at Norbury Park*, © The Samuel Courtauld Trust, The Courtauld Gallery, London.

Fig. 4 (p. 9) Claude Lorrain, *Landscape with the Marriage of Isaac and Rebecca*, © The National Gallery, London.

Fig. 12 (p. 61) Thomas Gainsborough, *Upland Landscape with Shepherd, Sheep and Cattle*, *c.*1783, Gainsborough's House, Sudbury, Suffolk.

Fig. 13 (p. 61) Thomas Gainsborough, *Landscape with Shepherd and Sheep* © bpk / Bayerische Staatsgemäldesammlungen – Alte Pinakothek München.

Fig. 18 (p. 81) Joseph Farington, Diary entry, 27 October 1796, volume 4, The Royal Collection © 2010 Her Majesty Queen Elizabeth II.

Fig. 26 (p. 99) P.J. de Loutherbourg, *Belle Isle, Windermere, in a Calm*, Abbot Hall Art Gallery.

Fig. 27 (p. 100) J.M.W. Turner, *Patterdale Old Church, looking north to the Lake*, © Tate, London 2009.

Fig. 28 (p. 100) J.M.W. Turner, *Patterdale*, private collection / © Agnew's, London, UK / The Bridgeman Art Library.

Fig. 30 (p. 113) Ramsay Richard Reinagle, *Farmstead near Ambleside*, © Birmingham Museums and Art Gallery.

Fig. 34 (p. 119) Thomas Jameson, *Ambleside*, © The Trustees of the British Museum. All Rights reserved.

Fig. 36 (p. 125) Thomas Girtin, *Scene in the Lake District, near Buttermere*, © Tate, London 2008.

Fig. 38 (p. 129) John Constable, *Leathes Water*, © V&A Images / Victoria and Albert Museum, London.

INDEX